THE BATTLE FOR MALAYA

TWENTIETH-CENTURY BATTLES

Spencer C. Tucker, editor

The Battle for Western Europe, Fall 1944: An Operational Assessment by John A. Adams
Operation Albion: The German Conquest of the Baltic Islands by Michael B. Barrett
Prelude to Blitzkrieg: The 1916 Austro-German Campaign in Romania by Michael B. Barrett
New Georgia: The Second Battle for the Solomons by Ronnie Day
The Brusilov Offensive by Timothy C. Dowling
The Siege of Kut-al-Amara: At War in Mesopotamia, 1915–1916 by Nikolas Gardner
D-Day in the Pacific: The Battle of Saipan by Harold J. Goldberg
Invasion of Norway, 1940 by Jack Greene
Balkan Breakthrough: The Battle of Dobro Pole 1918 by Richard C. Hall
The Battle of the Otranto Straits: Controlling the Gateway to the Adriatic in World War I by Paul G. Halpern
The Battle for North Africa: El Alamein and the Turning Point for World War II by Glyn Harper
Midway Inquest: Why the Japanese Lost the Battle of Midway by Dallas Woodbury Isom
China's Battle for Korea: The 1951 Spring Offensive by Xiaobing Li
The Imjin and Kapyong Battles, Korea, 1951 by S. P. MacKenzie
The Second Battle of the Marne by Michael S. Neiberg
The Dieppe Raid: The Story of the Disastrous 1942 Expedition by Robin Neillands
In Passage Perilous: Malta and the Convoy Battles of June 1942 by Vincent P. O'Hara
The Battle of Heligoland Bight by Eric W. Osborne
Battle of Dogger Bank: The First Dreadnought Engagement, January 1915 by Tobias R. Philbin
The Battle for Manchuria and the Fate of China: Siping, 1946 by Harold M. Tanner
Where Chiang Kai-shek Lost China: The Liao-Shen Campaign, 1948 by Harold M. Tanner
Battle of Surigao Strait by Anthony P. Tully
Written in Blood: The Battles for Fortress Przemyśl in WWI by Graydon A. Tunstall Jr.
The Battle of An Loc by James H. Willbanks
The Battle of Leyte Gulf: The Last Fleet Action by H. P. Willmott
The Generals' War: Operational Level Command on the Western Front in 1918 by David T. Zabecki

THE BATTLE FOR MALAYA

The Indian Army in Defeat, 1941–42

KAUSHIK ROY

INDIANA UNIVERSITY PRESS

This book is a publication of

Indiana University Press
Office of Scholarly Publishing
Herman B Wells Library 350
1320 East 10th Street
Bloomington, Indiana 47405 USA

iupress.indiana.edu

© 2019 by Kaushik Roy

All rights reserved

No part of this book may be reproduced or utilized in any form or by any means, electronic or mechanical, including photocopying and recording, or by any information storage and retrieval system, without permission in writing from the publisher. The paper used in this publication meets the minimum requirements of the American National Standard for Information Sciences—Permanence of Paper for Printed Library Materials, ANSI Z39.48-1992.

Manufactured in the United States of America

Cataloging information is available from the Library of Congress.

ISBN 978-0-253-04415-0 (hdbk.)
ISBN 978-0-253-04417-4 (pbk.)
ISBN 978-0-253-04422-8 (web PDF)

1 2 3 4 5   24 23 22 21 20 19

CONTENTS

List of Maps   vii
Preface   ix
Acknowledgments   xi
Glossary   xiii
List of Abbreviations   xv

   Introduction   1

   1. The Rise of the Singapore Naval Base   9

   2. The Allied Ground Forces in Malaya   25

   3. The Invasion   72

   4. Defeat at Slim River   113

   5. Disaster at Muar and Johore   145

   6. Endgame on Singapore Island   190

   Conclusion   235

Bibliography   243
Index   257

LIST OF MAPS

Map 1: Far East Asia   xvii

Map 2: Proposed Sites for the Naval Base   xviii

Map 3: Malaya   xix

Map 4: Japanese Advance in the Malayan Peninsula   xx

Map 5: Japanese Attack on Northern Malaya, 7/8 December 1941   xxi

Map 6: Kota Bahru, 8 December 1941   xxii

Map 7: Jitra   xxiii

Map 8: WESTFORCE Disposition in Johore, 14 January 1942   xxiv

Map 9: Northern Johore, 15 January 1942   xxv

Map 10: Johore Bahru, January 1942   xxvi

Map 11: Disposition of Troops on Singapore Island, 8 February 1942   xxvii

Map 12: Japanese Attack, Singapore, February 1942   xxviii

Map 13: The Japanese Assault and Advance and the Final Defense of the Perimeter, Singapore   xxix

PREFACE

Military history in general is not at the cutting edge of the discipline of history. And within military history, the focus is on the so-called New Military History writing, which emphasizes the social and cultural aspects of the military institutions and the effects of the armed forces on society. These aspects are certainly important, but we must note that, after all, most armies exist for fighting. So the study of the army as an institution in combat is worth pursuing. Following Carl von Clausewitz, one can say that the study of battles is like gold and silver in commercial transactions. And this is what the present volume intends to do. The objective is to study the Indian Army as an institution in the Malaya-Singapore Campaign of 1941–42. A lot of books have been written on this campaign, but the Indian Army, which constituted the biggest component of the Allied ground force in that theatre, has been left out of these studies. The present volume is a modest attempt to fill this gap. Unlike the present postmodernist slant, this work depends heavily on archival materials collected from three continents (Europe, Asia, and Australia) in order to build up the story. The battle narrative is integrated with analysis to offer a fresh insight into the Malaya-Singapore debacle. Since this book is aimed at English-speaking Western readers, Japanese names are given in the more common Western style. I sincerely hope that this book will encourage further studies in this genre.

ACKNOWLEDGMENTS

This book would not have been possible without the support of Professor Spencer C. Tucker, the editor of Indiana University Press's Twentieth-Century Battles Series, who showed interest in the subject. Credit is due to the editor Ashley Runyon for showing exceptional patience in the face of delays in the preparation of the book. Special thanks to my research assistant Jane Bryan-Brown and PhD student Moumita Chaudhury for helping me collect materials from various archives in Britain and India. I am grateful to my friends Gavin Rand and Peter Stanley for directing me to important holdings in the United Kingdom and Australia. And of course, Narender Yadav deserves praise for helping me access the Ministry of Defence Historical Section in New Delhi. My thanks to KnowTechInfo for funding some of my research trips. I am grateful to Jennifer Crane for her support while editing the manuscript. And I will not thank my wife because it would never be enough. It goes without saying that any faults in the book are mine alone.

GLOSSARY

Atta	Wheat flour
Attap	Malayan hut made of palm leaves
Blitzkrieg	Literal meaning: lightning war; this term is usually applied to explain the fast, mobile armored war practiced by the Germans in Europe and Russia between 1939 and 1942
Bushido	Way of the Japanese warrior
Dharma	Religion
Izzat	An Urdu word that stands for personal reputation
Jawan	Literal meaning: young man; the term refers to an Indian private
Kesselschlacht/ Kettelschlacht	Cauldron Battle, which involved pinning down the enemy's army frontally and enveloping its two wings and rear
Kikan	Agency/department/section
Kukri	Curved knife used by the Gurkha soldier
Luftwaffe	German Air Force during the Second World War
Mai-baap	Literal meaning: father figure; a *jawan* looked up to his commanding British officer as a *mai-baap*
Parang	A machete or cleaver used by the Malays
Raj	Literal meaning: realm; the term refers to the British government in India
Sahib	British officer of the Indian Army
Sampan	Large Chinese country boat used by the "natives" in Malaya
Sepoy	This term refers to the Indian infantry; the word is derived from the Persian word *sipahi*
Sirdar	Chieftain
Wehrmacht	German armed force during the Second World War

LIST OF ABBREVIATIONS

AA	Anti-Aircraft
ABDACOM	American, British, Dutch, and Australian Command; code name for Supreme Allied Headquarters South-West Pacific from 15 January 1942.
AIF	Australian Imperial Force
AIML	All India Muslim League
AOC	Air Officer Commanding
ARP	Air Raid Precaution
A/T	Antitank
AWM	Australian War Memorial
BAR	Browning Automatic Rifle
BL	British Library
BOR	British Other Rank
CAS	Close Air Support
C3I	Command, Control, Communications, and Intelligence
CIGS	Chief of the Imperial General Staff
CO	Commanding Officer
CoSC	Chiefs of Staff Committee
CP	Cabinet Papers
EBO	Effects Based Operation
ECIO	Emergency Commissioned Indian Officer
ECO	Emergency Commissioned Officer
FFR	Frontier Force Rifles
FOO	Forward Observation Officer
GHQ	General Headquarters
GOC	General Officer Commanding
GoI	Government of India
GR	Gurkha Rifles
GSO	General Staff Officer
ICO	Indian Commissioned Officer
IIL	Indian Independence League
IJA	Imperial Japanese Army
IJN	Imperial Japanese Navy
INA	Indian National Army
INC	Indian National Congress

IOR	India Office Records
IWM	Imperial War Museum
JAAF	Japanese Army Air Force
JNAF	Japanese Navy Air Force
KCIO	King's Commissioned Indian Officer
LMG	Light Machine Gun
LoC	Line of Communication
MODHS	Ministry of Defence Historical Section
MS	Milestone
NAI	National Archives of India
NAM	National Army Museum
NCO	Noncommissioned Officer
NMML	Nehru Memorial Museum and Library
OIOC	Oriental and India Office Collection
OR	Other Rank/Private
OTU	Officer Training Unit
PoW	Prisoner of War
PRO	Public Record Office
PWD	Public Works Department
RA	Royal Artillery
RAAF	Royal Australian Air Force
RAF	Royal Air Force
RE	Royal Engineers
RGR	Royal Garwahl/Garhwal Rifles
RN	Royal Navy
RR	Rajputana Rifles
SLoC	Sea Line of Communication
VCO	Viceroy's Commissioned Officer

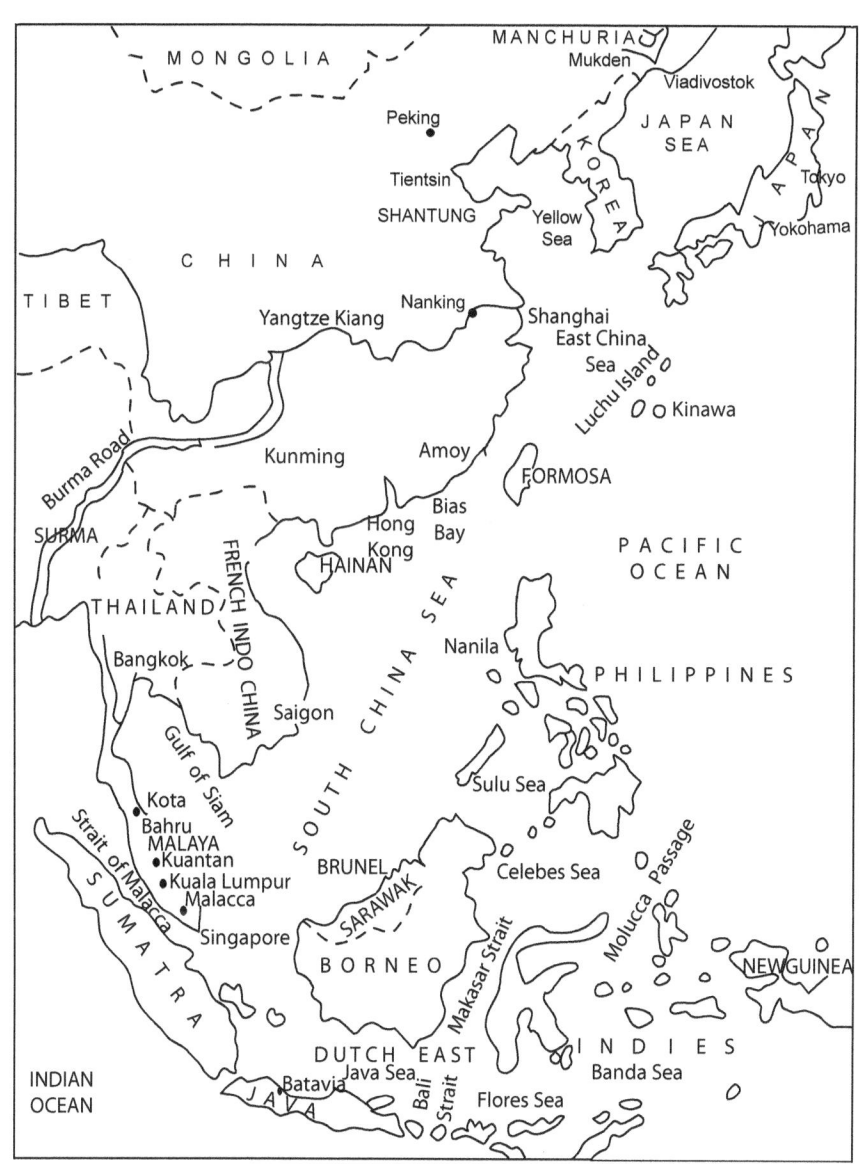

Map 1: Far East Asia

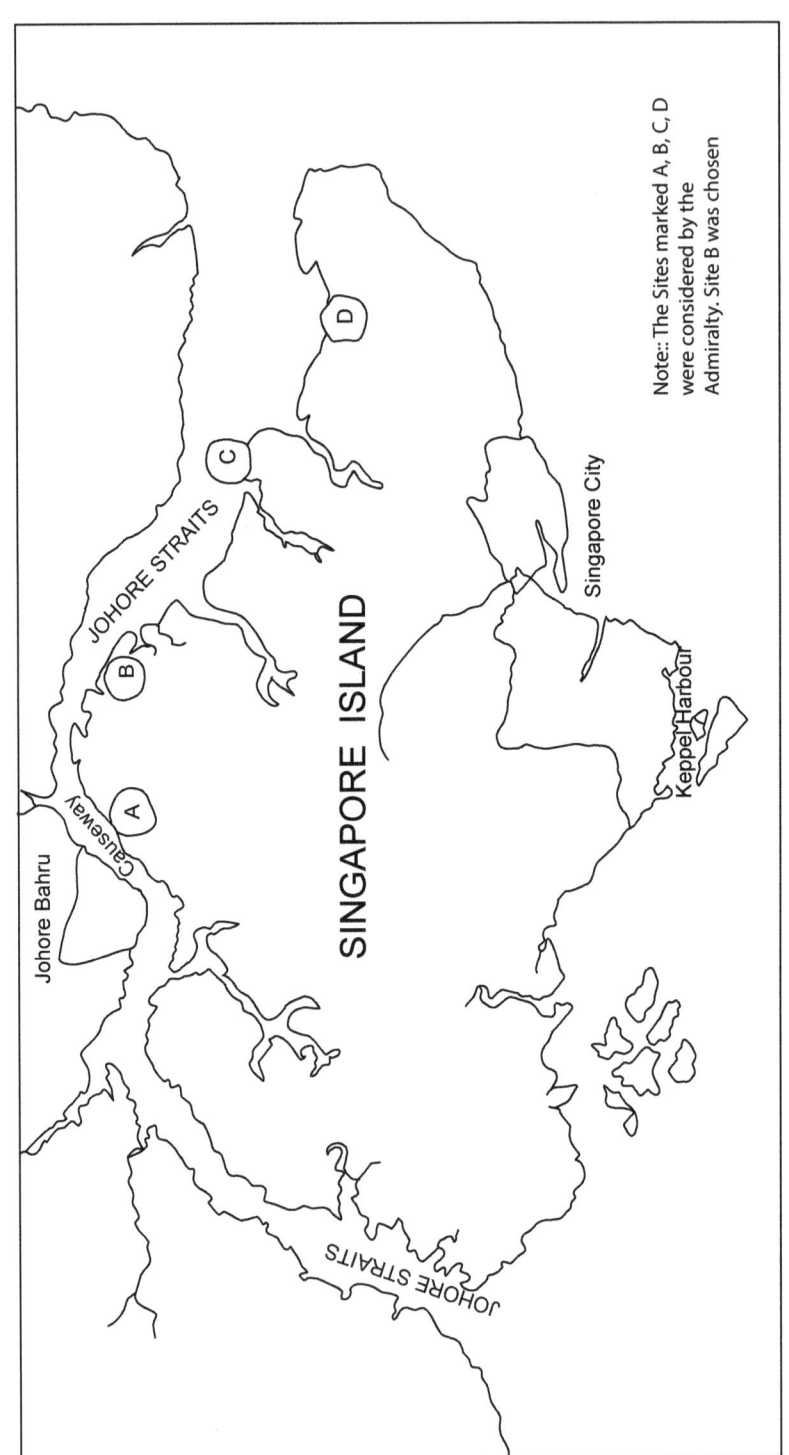

Map 2: Proposed Sites for the Naval Base

Map 3: Malaya

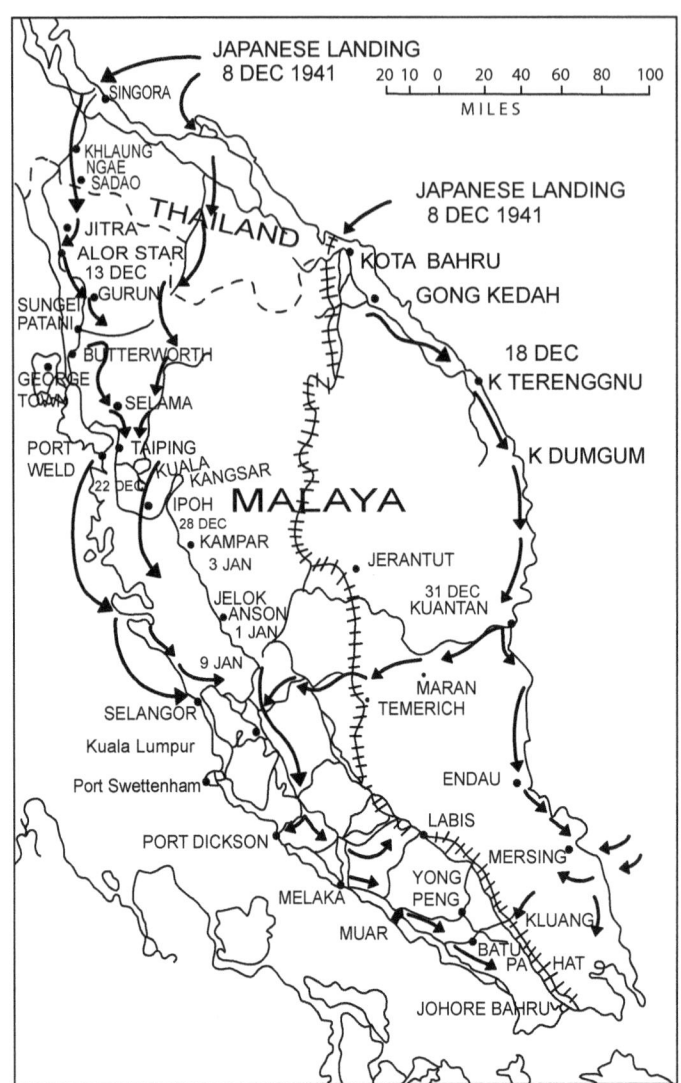

Map 4: Japanese Advance in the Malayan Peninsula

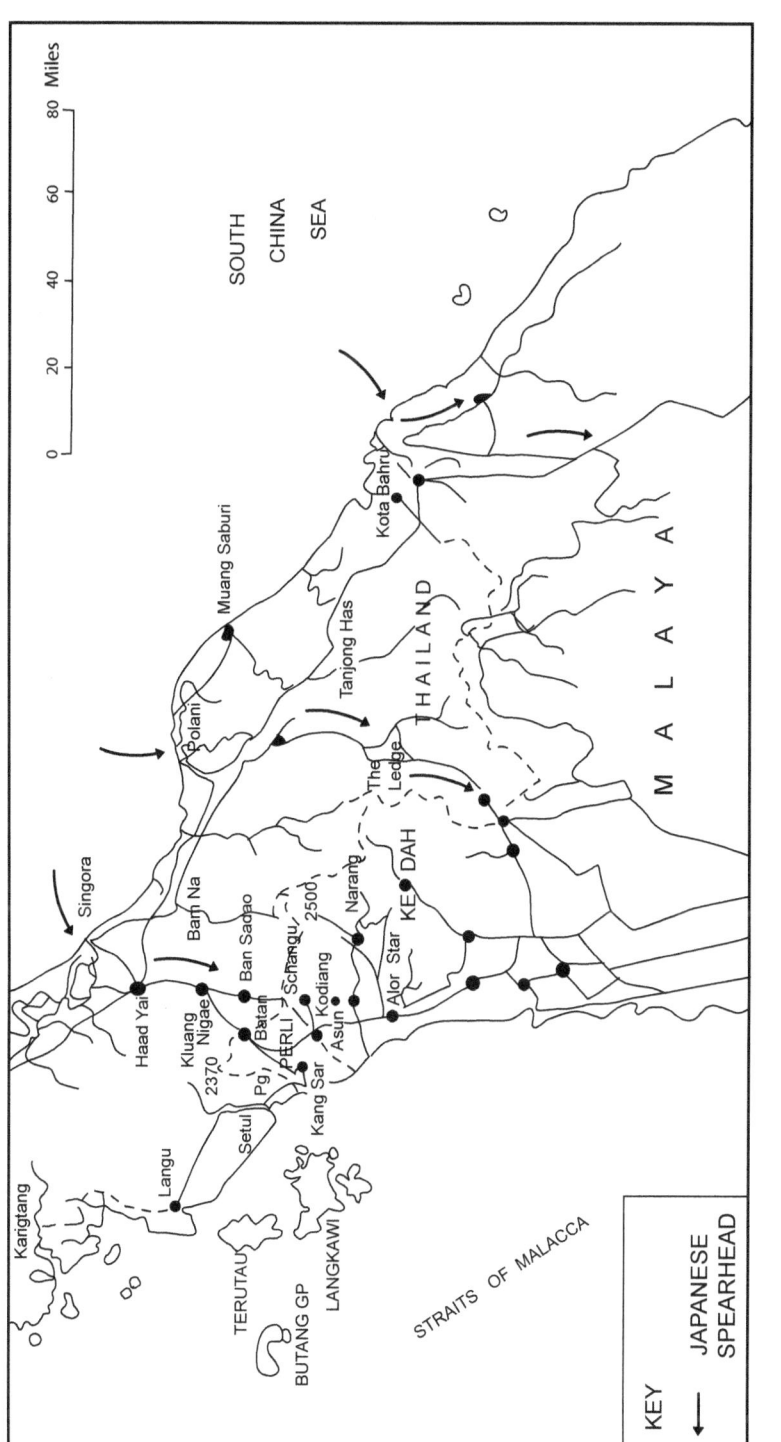

Map 5: Japanese Attack on Northern Malaya, 7/8 December 1941

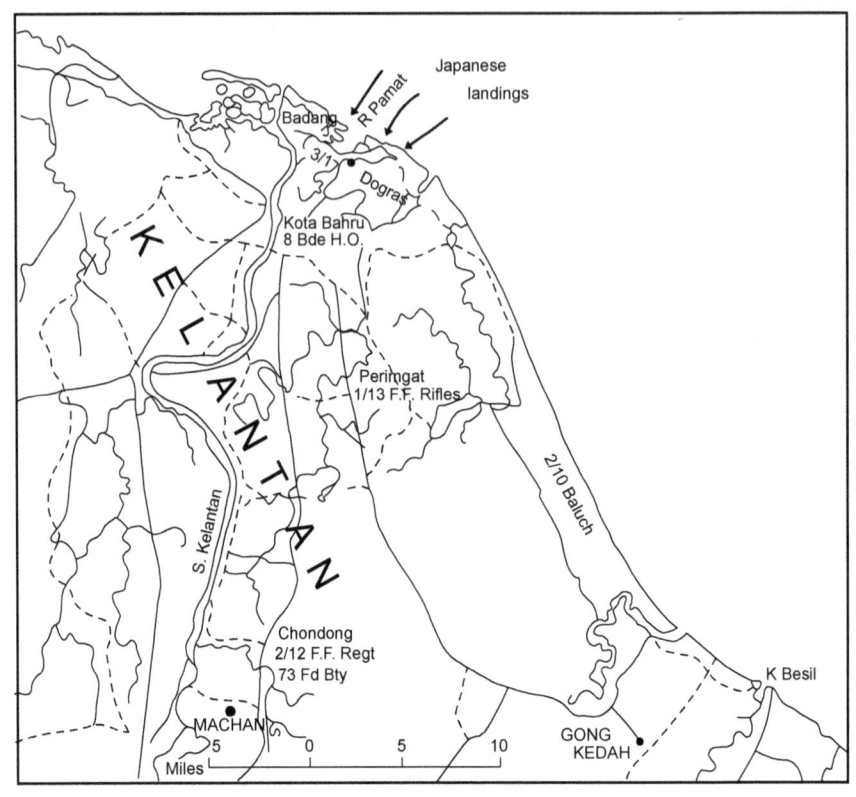

Map 6: Kota Bahru, 8 December 1941

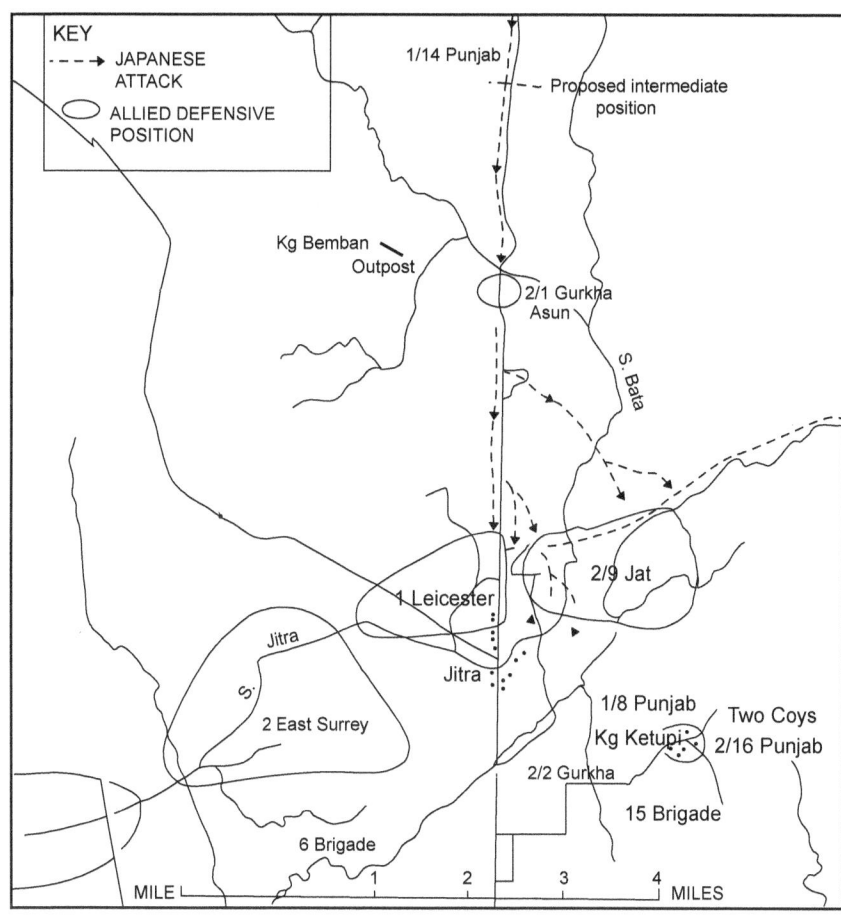

Map 7: Jitra

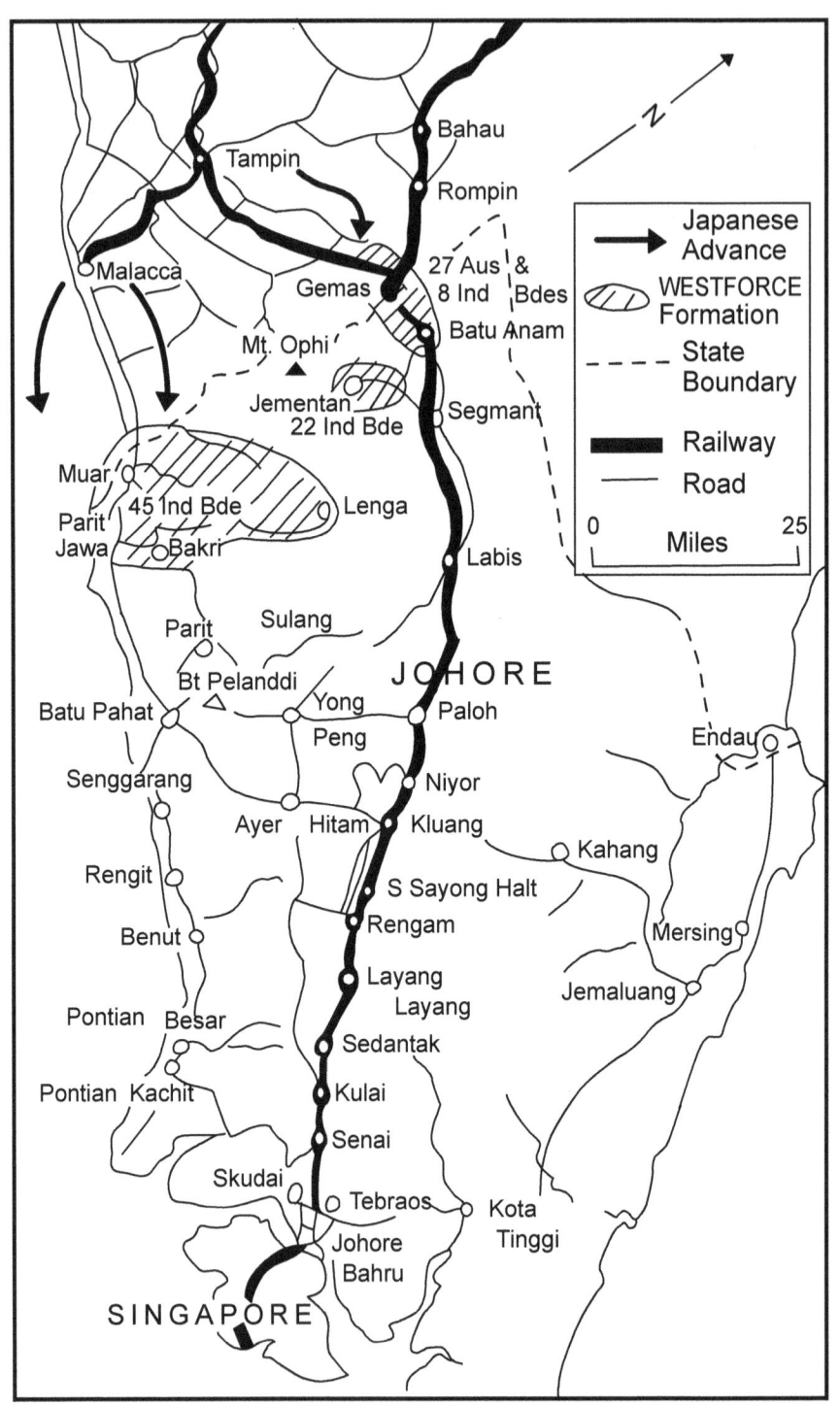

Map 8: WESTFORCE Disposition in Johore, 14 January 1942

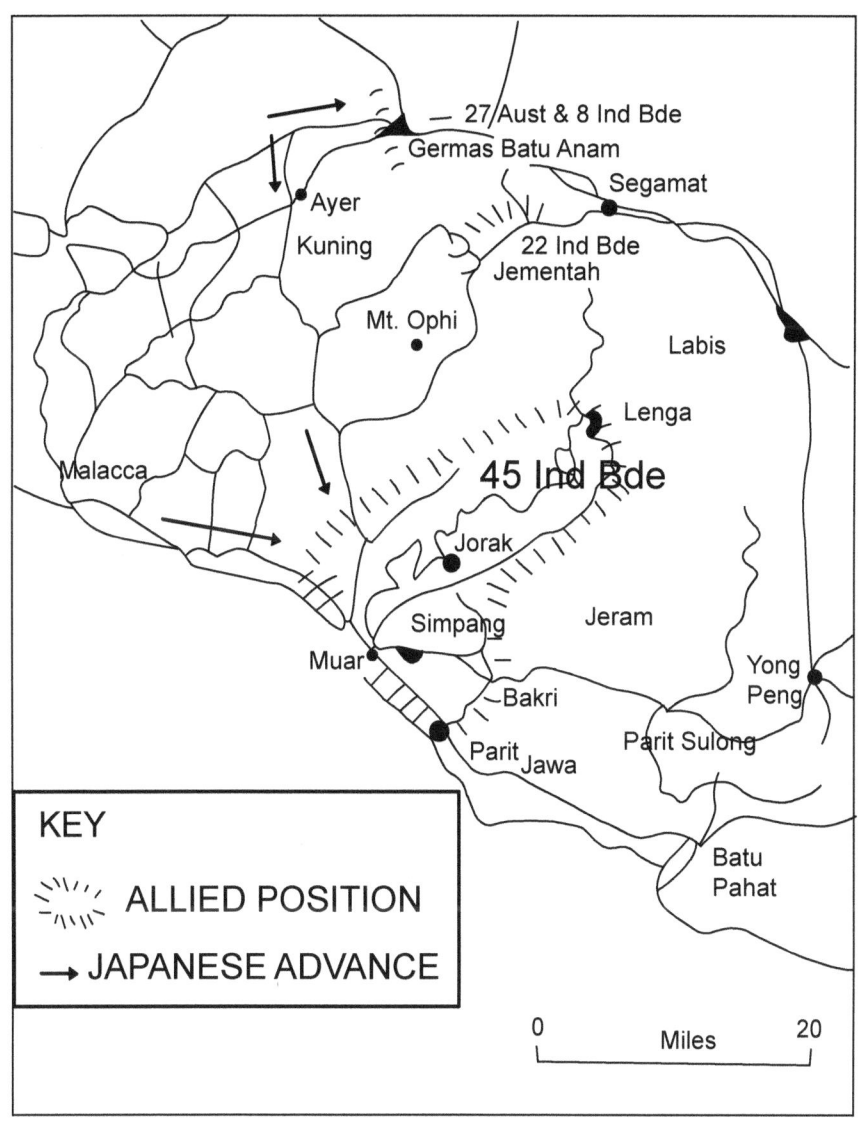

Map 9: Northern Johore, 15 January 1942

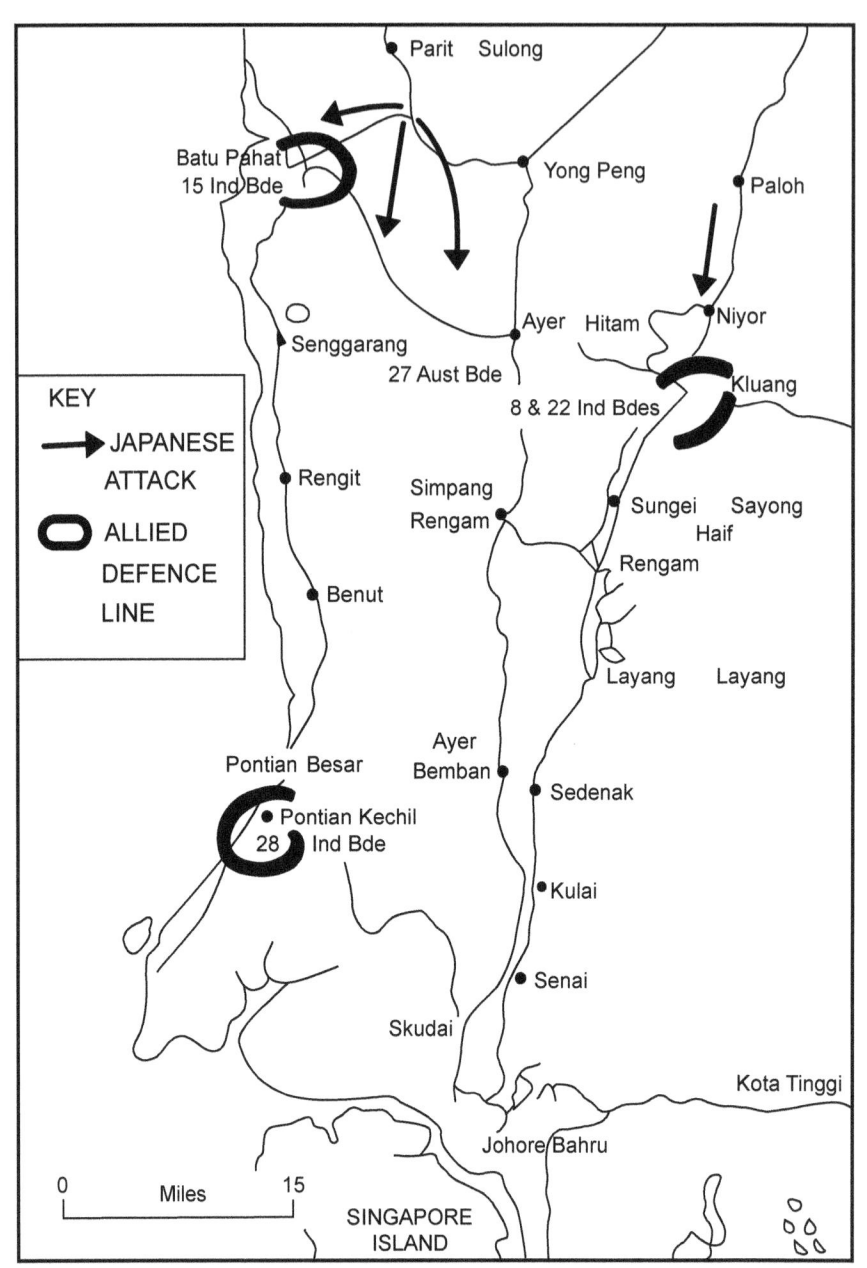

Map 10: Johore Bahru, January 1942

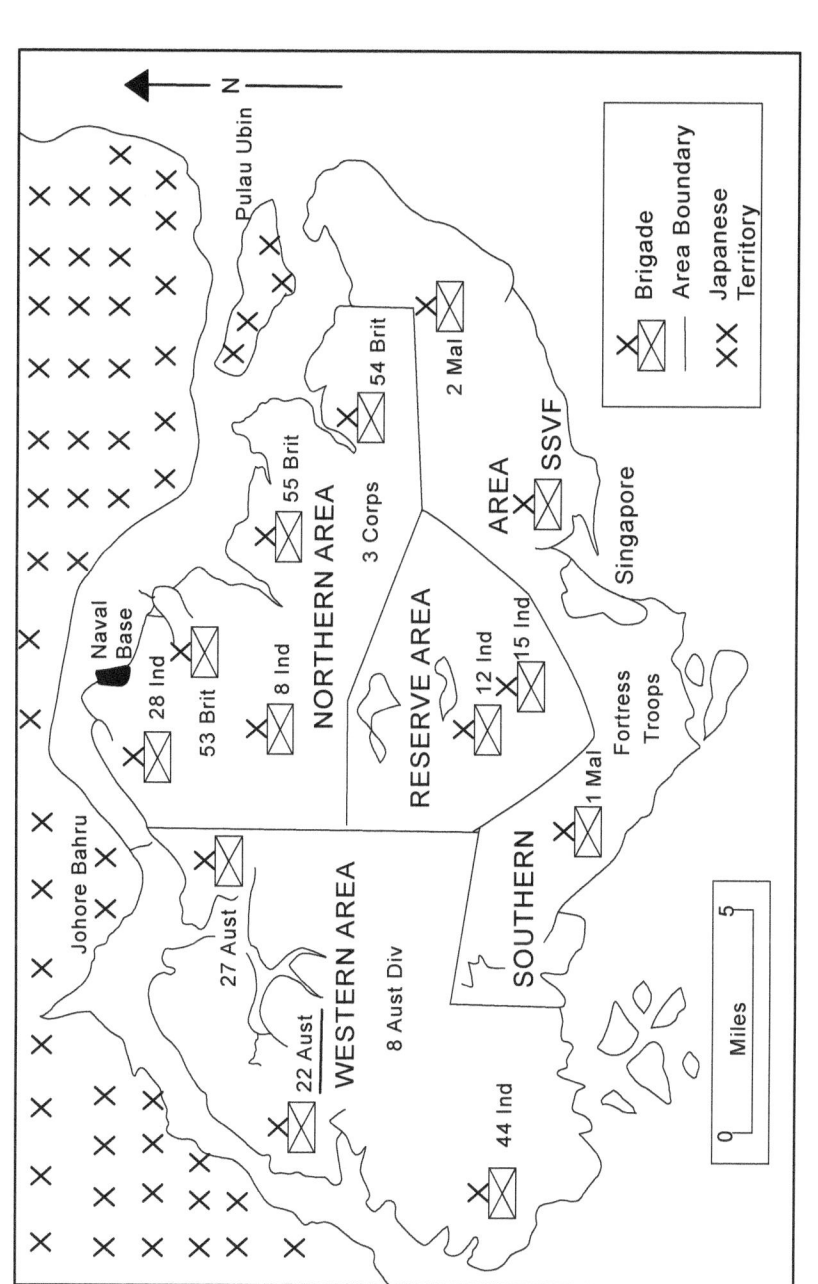

Map 11: Disposition of Troops on Singapore Island, 8 February 1942

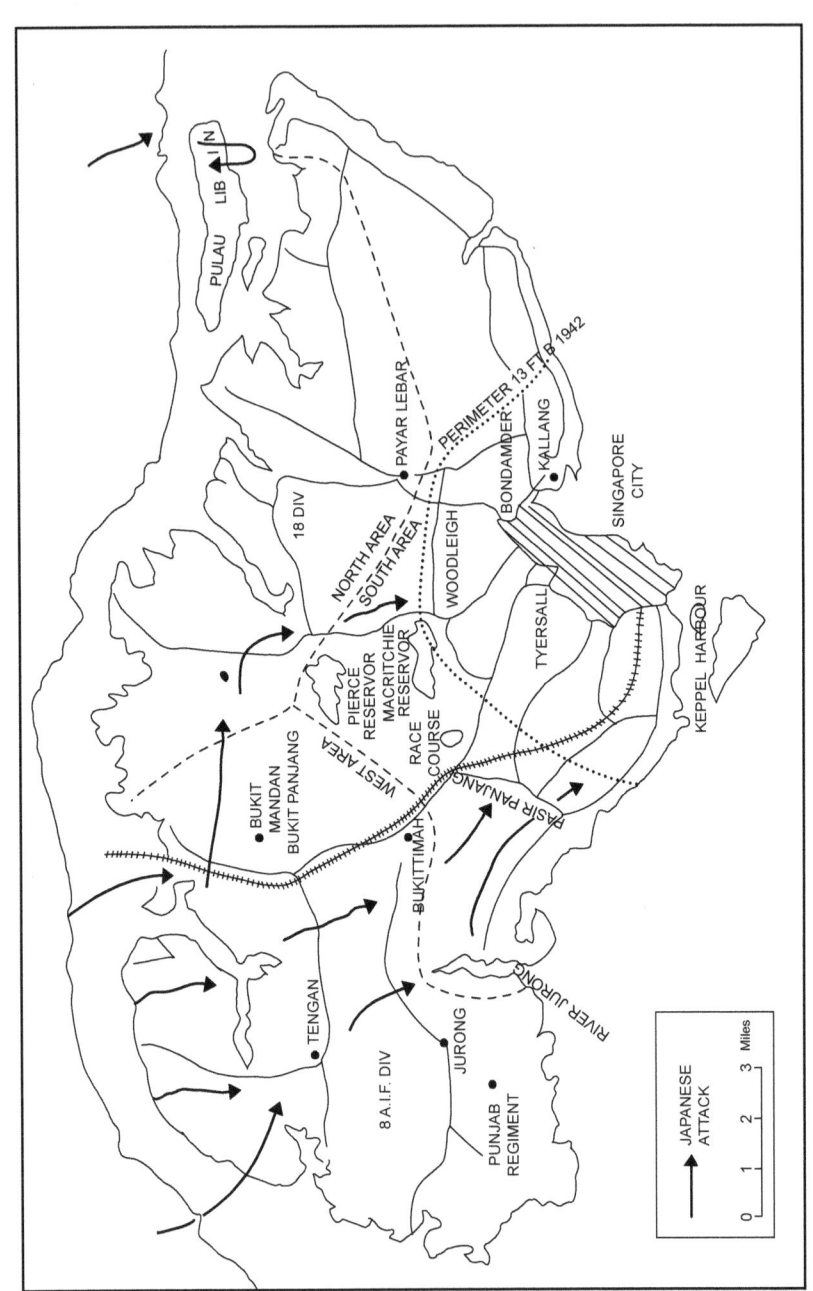

Map 12: Japanese Attack, Singapore, February 1942

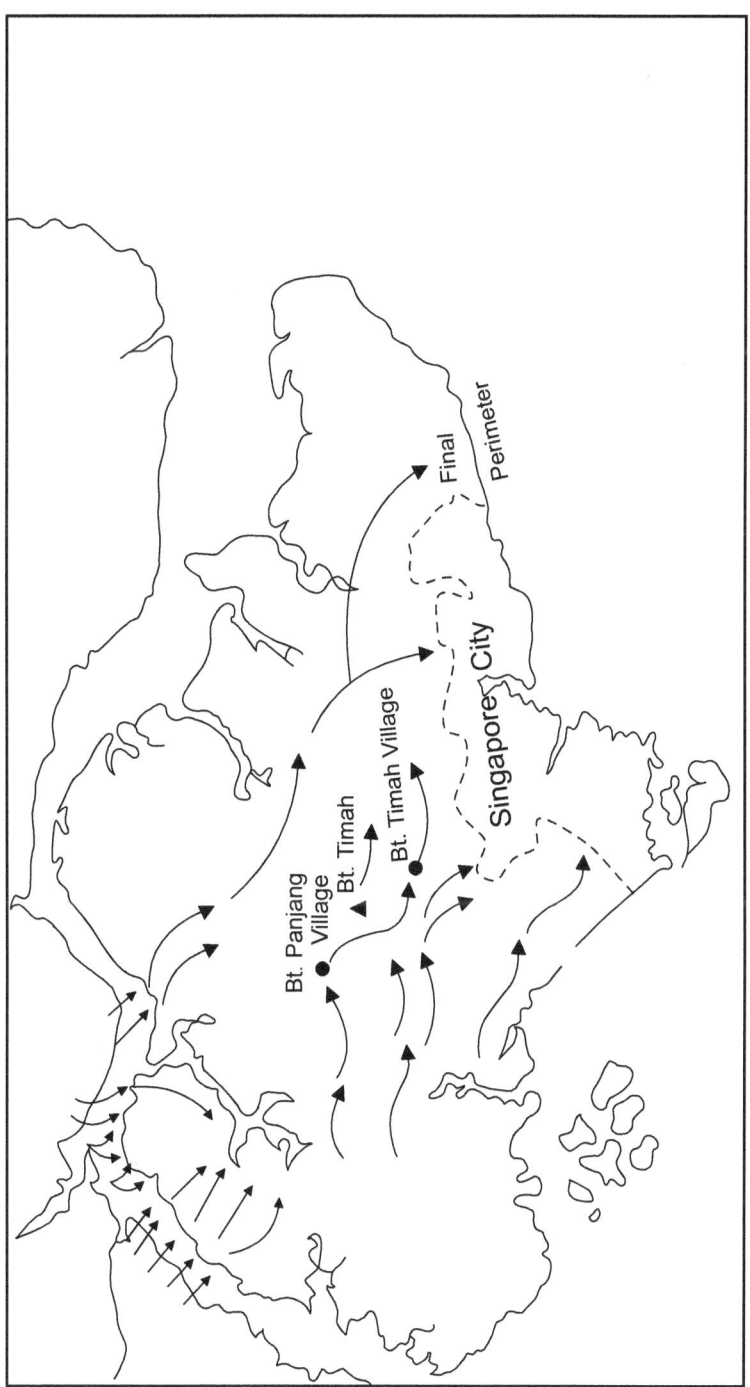

Map 13: The Japanese Assault and Advance and the Final Defense of the Perimeter, Singapore

THE BATTLE FOR MALAYA

Introduction

On 15 February 1942, Singapore surrendered to the Japanese. Numerous books have been written about the Japanese invasion of British Malaya, but most of the studies are Singapore-centric.[1] Japanese participant Colonel Masanobu Tsuji, director of planning and operation staff of the Twenty-Fifth Japanese Army of Lieutenant General Tomoyuki Yamashita, stated unequivocally that had the Commonwealth forces held out a bit longer in the Singapore Fortress, the Japanese would have been in dire straits as they were then almost out of ammunition.[2] In his study of the fall of Singapore, historian Timothy Hall agrees with Tsuji and asserts that Lieutenant General Yamashita's Twenty-Fifth Army was on its last leg, and a strong military effort by Lieutenant General A. E. Percival's (general officer commanding [GOC] Malaya) troops, especially in the streets of Singapore, would have resulted in the retreat of the Japanese.[3]

This conclusion is not valid. A stronger Allied defense might have delayed the fall of Singapore by a few days, but the course of the campaign would not have altered. The fate of Singapore had been decided much earlier. As American historian Raymond Callahan concludes, high-level decisions taken before 8 December 1941 had already sealed the fate of Singapore.[4] Andrew Gilchrist, a British civil servant stationed in Malaya, believed that Singapore was lost when Air Chief Marshal Robert Brooke-Popham, the commander in chief Far East, refused on 7 December 1941 to initiate Operation MATADOR.[5] MATADOR was the British plan to move military assets into southern Siam (Thailand) to preempt the Japanese from capturing this region's airfields. Russell Grenfell, a Royal Navy (RN) captain who later became the naval correspondent for the *Daily Telegraph*, opines that Singapore was lost when the two British capital ships *Repulse* and *Prince of Wales* were sunk by Japanese aircraft.[6]

This study asserts that the fate of Singapore was decided by the performance of the opposing ground forces in the Malayan Peninsula. Hence, only one chapter (the last chapter) of this volume focuses on the actual combat on Singapore Island. Air power played an important role as regards close air support (CAS) to the Japanese troops, but strategic bombing was absent. The Allied air force remained at the receiving end throughout this campaign. And after the sinking of two British capital ships early in the campaign, British naval power became marginal. However, even then Percival had a numerically superior imperial land force to defend Malaya. In general, the dynamics of land warfare in Malaya decided the fate of the Malayan Peninsula and Singapore.

The Malaya Campaign needs to be put in perspective. The Battle for Malaya-Singapore lasted for seventy days. Compared to the scope of carnage on the Eastern Front, Malaya was a small battle indeed. Some 35,000 combat troops of

Yamashita's 65,000 strong Twenty-Fifth Japanese Army, supported by 560 landbased aircraft (plus some sea planes), defeated 138,000 Allied troops (75,000 of whom were combat soldiers), supported by some 180 aircraft (many of which were obsolete by European standards). The Japanese suffered less than 10,000 casualties. In contrast, the USSR lost 1,200 aircraft on the first day of the German invasion. And in the Kiev encirclement during September 1941, the Germans took 665,000 Soviet prisoners.[7] Nevertheless, the Battle for Malaya is important for both political and military reasons. British military prestige was shattered. It had a trigger effect on the nascent nationalism of the Asians (especially Indians). Even after the Allied victory, the postwar world was going to be very different. Second, the Imperial Japanese Army's (IJA) tactical format as unfolded in Malaya was repeated in Burma in 1942–43. Until the Allied troops evolved adequate tactical-operational countermeasures during mid-1944 to the Japanese techniques of rapid marching, wide outflanking movements along "impossible" terrain, nocturnal attacks, and roadblocks, the soldiers of the Japanese Emperor Hirohito remained supreme in the jungle terrain.

Debate over the degree of culpability of the senior British military leaders for the disaster centers on Percival; Major General Henry Gordon Bennett, commander of the 8th Australian Imperial Force (AIF) Division; and General (later Field Marshal) Archibald Wavell, commander of the American, British, Australian, and Dutch Command (ABDACOM).[8] Rather, the focus in this volume is on the organizational analysis of the combat institution: the imperial armies. This work emphasizes the role played by the Indian Army in the Malaya-Singapore Campaign, as its soldiers comprised the greatest percentage of the Allied ground force. There have been studies of AIF and British units. However, the Indian Army is yet to record its own not-so-glorious performance in the swampy jungle terrain of Malaya.[9] Except two articles[10] and two chapters in a monograph titled *Sepoys against the Rising Sun*,[11] we do not have any book-length study of the Indian Army in Malaya. This volume attempts to fill this historiographical gap. However, the Indian Army's role is woven deftly into the overall story of Allied defeat at Malaya-Singapore.

In this volume, the Indian Army is treated as an institution. We are concerned mainly with the military/combat effectiveness of the Indian Army. Military effectiveness could be described as the capacity of a military organization to impose its will on the battlefield while engaged with hostile forces. Besides weapons, morale, and combat motivation, command is also an integral aspect of combat effectiveness. Command includes control, communications, and intelligence.[12]

The capacity to learn during battle lies at the core of combat effectiveness. This volume portrays whether the Indian Army displayed a learning curve or not in the Malaya Campaign. A learning curve involves learning new things and also unlearning a few things that are unsuitable for the new conditions of warfare. This involves both adaptation to new conditions of warfare and also adoption of certain new techniques through both learning and unlearning. The capability to learn in the midst of battle is part of the challenge-response dynamic. American scholar Williamson Murray writes that war is a contest, a complex interactive duel between two opponents. So, in order to be successful, a military organization has to adapt to the enemy's strategy, operations, and tactical approach. Adaptation has to be technological as well as conceptual. For Murray, the reasons behind successful adaptation are the necessity to identify and then learn lessons under the terrible pressures of war.[13] We will see if the Indian Army was able to adapt to the Japanese paradigm of war in Malaya by adopting required techniques, and if not, we will explore the reasons for failure.

Murray asserts that wars are won and lost at the strategic level. Mistakes in operations and tactics can be corrected but political and strategic mistakes live forever.[14] This book challenges this dictum. A military organization might have a brilliant strategy, but it might not be able to implement that strategy if it fails at the tactical-operational sphere. Similarly, a military organization with a not-so-good strategy might dominate the battlefield due to its brilliant tactical-operational repertoire. Hence, this volume will focus on the tactical-operational sphere, keeping strategy in the background. Operation is defined as the area of military activity that lies between tactics and grand strategy and aims to relate the tactical means with the strategic ends.[15] Operations involve grand tactics—that is, tactics of large formations like armies, corps, etc.[16] British Prime Minister Winston Churchill's strategy of not sending a large number of aircraft carriers and capital ships along with adequate numbers of the latest land-based aircraft might be faulty from the perspective of the Far Eastern theater, but seems proper from the Europe-centric "Beat Hitler First" strategy. Due to the commitments of global war, Britain's military assets were stretched thin. Nevertheless, the balance of ground forces in Malaya was in Percival's favor. So, Allied defeat was not inevitable. Hence, we concentrate on the tactics/combat techniques and technology of the ground battle that unfolded in Malaya and later in Singapore between December 1941 and February 1942. The focus would be at five levels: corps, division, brigade, battalion, and company. A lot of the discussion is devoted to the portrayal of small unknown actions in which platoons and companies participated. This is because the author agrees with historian John A. English's observation that small-unit tactics are the basis of every great battle.[17]

I do not intend to see the Indian Army merely through the eyes of the British commanders by focusing only on their private papers. I do consider documents that provide the "official view": government memorandums, tactical notes, Cabinet and War Office papers, and private papers of the British civilian and military officers, available at the Public Record Office [PRO] (now the National Archives [TNA]), Kew; the National Army Museum (NAM) and Imperial War Museum (IWM), London; the India Office Records [IOR] (now Asia Pacific Collections), British Library (BL), London; the Australian War Memorial (AWM), Canberra; and the National Archives of India (NAI), New Delhi. But I also highlight the Indian perspective. Files at the Ministry of Defence Historical Section (MODHS), New Delhi, which hitherto have only been used by the official historians of India, along with oral history transcripts of the commissioned Indian officers available at Nehru Memorial Museum and Library (NMML), New Delhi, are also utilized. In addition, the regimental histories (both published and unpublished) of the Indian and British armies, along with the multivolume official history, provide materials for this volume. The Indian commissioned officers (regulars and Emergency Commissioned Officers [ECOs]) have documented their experiences in their memoirs and autobiographies. Such publications are little known even within India, to say nothing of the Western world.

Quotes from the participants are included to provide insights into the psychological pressures and conditions of combat. The soldiers' views amid the heat and dust of battle open up a window about the reality of combat. But there are issues—rightly, says Murray—beyond the impressions and immediate concerns of the individuals engaged in combat.[18] History from below rejects any analytical framework for portraying the strategic and operational issues involved in the conflict. Of course, battles were messy. The units in combat rarely had a clear picture of the general events in the "fog of war." Various war diaries and memoirs of the generals who fought the battle give contradictory names of places and dates where armed encounters took place. Participants could not even agree when a particular battle started and when exactly it stopped. One encounter flows into another. Georges Duby in his book on the Battle of Bouvines (27 July 1214) criticizes the positivist historians in the following words: "They had to locate the exact position of the 'true fact' at the very spot, at once resultant and causal, lying at the juncture of the facts' ins and outs. Yet these goals are unreachable. This is so because we all know that the field of vision of all the participants in a battle, including the most prominent one, is limited; they can only see a confused melee. No one has or ever will perceive in its total reality the whirl of a thousand tangled actions."[19]

In a similar vein, John Keegan asserts that all battle history is to a great extent "myth history."[20] Taking into account all these strictures, I still believe that some amount of authorial intervention is necessary in order to create order (even if a bit artificial) out of the chaos of amorphous data for the sake of structure and analysis. Thus, due attention is given to strategic planning and operational analysis by the higher commanders. It formed the background for innumerable small-unit actions. This volume will hence be a synthesis of history from top with history from below.

The objective is not to provide a nationalist chauvinistic account of the "glorious" saga of the Indian Army[21] but rather to compare and contrast the military organization of the Indian Army with the British and the Australian armies in Malaya. At the beaches of northeast Malaya, at the Perak, Slim, and Muar Rivers, the British and Indian units and later the Australians fought side by side. So, a holistic approach of all the three armies' combat performance is necessary to understand the uniqueness (if any) of the Indian Army. And for a glimpse of the "other side of the hill,"—i.e., the IJA—translated documents in the PRO and those published by General Headquarters India (GHQ India)/India Command, are used. Chapters 3 to 6 provide a thick empirical chronological narrative of operations intertwined with analysis. The attempt is to portray whether the Indian Army experienced any tactical evolution or not in the course of their headlong retreat across the Malayan Peninsula.

Further, the aim in this study is to fuse social and cultural history with organizational/institutional (or hard military) history. For instance, the Martial Race theory that dominated the Indian Army during the interwar period was not suited for the rapid expansion of the Indian Army. And when the War Office forced GHQ India to initiate a breakneck expansion program from 1940 onward, the combat effectiveness of the Indian Army declined. And this became evident at Hong Kong, Malaya, and the First Burma Campaign. Further, due to political reasons, the Government of India (GoI) obstructed Indianization of the Indian Army's officer corps. Rapid expansion of the British Army and wartime losses created a shortage of experienced British officers among the Indian units. Moreover, cohesion of the Indian Army depended on the personal bond between the sahibs and the sepoys/*jawans*. However, wartime British officers lacked proper knowledge of Urdu (lingua franca of the Indian Army) and intricacies of the customs of the different communities like the Gurkhas, Jats, Rajputs, and Sikhs, who filled the ranks of the Indian Army. All these factors had adverse consequences in the Malayan battlefield. Then, those units that had experience of conducting "small war" along British-India's North-West Frontier in the interwar era fought well in Malaya. This was because small-unit aggressive patrols, moving across the flanks, picket duties, etc. were the bread and butter of small war in Waziristan. These techniques were partly adequate to counter the Japanese jungle warfare techniques. However, such units were few and far between. Most of them were in North Africa and in the Middle East, and the rest had been diluted due to "milking." So, to an extent, this book will try to link the Indian Army's experience of small war in North-West Frontier with jungle warfare in Malaya.

Chapter 1 traces the strategic background before the Battle for Malaya started. Recruitment, training, morale, and the combat experience of the Indian Army in particular and especially those Allied units deployed in Malaya in general, are discussed in chapter 2. An attempt is also made to compare and contrast the Indian Army with the Australian and the British armies in this chapter. The limitations of Allied training architecture vis-à-vis that of the IJA is also highlighted in this chapter. Chapter 3 details the reasons behind the fragile defense at the beaches on the east coast of northeast and northwest Malaya. Stretched thin to defend the scattered aerodromes without aircraft and tanks, the Indian and British formations without air cover retreated in confusion from Jitra toward central Malaya. Rapid bold strikes and encircling tactics of the Japanese, as chapter 4 portrays, overwhelmed the 9th and 11th Indian divisions. These two divisions got no breathing time, and their morale sagged due to continuous retreat and hostile air attacks. When one unit was attacked and retreated, the linked unit even, though not attacked, had to retreat in order to maintain a continuous front line. The Allied troops found out that positional defenses were easily bypassed by the Japanese "bicycle blitzkrieg." And the road-bound Allied units were easily cut up by Japanese roadblocks established at their rear. After the encounter at Gemas, Gordon Bennett was elated. However, his defensive position at the Muar River collapsed. And then, headlong retreat toward the Johore Causeway occurred. Bennett blamed the "raw and inexperienced" Indian units for the debacle. Not only were the Indian brigades routed, but the Australian infantry and British artillery units were also frequently ambushed by the nimble Japanese infiltrating units. And this is the theme of chapter 5. In the last chapter, the spotlight shifts from the swampy, jungle-covered creeks and rubber plantations of Malaya to Singapore Island. By the time the Japanese had landed at Singapore Island, defeat was a foregone conclusion. The question was how long the Allied units could hold out. Why the Indian units failed even in "positional warfare," which they had conducted before 1939 is analyzed. One of the limitations of the Indian Army was inadequate cooperation between artillery and infantry and poor coordination even among the infantry units. And this proved their undoing in the Malayan Peninsula and Singapore Island. Due to the importance of the Japanese-sponsored Indian National Army (INA, also known as *Azad Hind Fauj*) in India's postcolonial historiography, the evolution and legacy of this organization is discussed in the last section of chapter 6.

The conclusion analyzes the reasons behind the quick collapse of the Allied armies. However, the focus is mostly on the shortcomings of the Indian Army. The Australian officers (like Gordon Bennett) and also some British officers (like Major H. P. Thomas) accused the Indians of low morale and inherent softness, which prevented them from coping with Malaya's climate. Racial bias and climatological theories are not of much help in assessing combat effectiveness. However, Japanese and Indian agents played an important role in alienating many jawans from the Raj. This was possibly due partly to the entry of young, inexperienced British officers in the Indian units, sparse training, and the shortcomings of hardware in the hands of the Indians. Now, let us see how it all started with the rise of the Singapore Naval Base.

Notes

1. The best and the latest academic study in the field is Karl Hack and Kevin Blackburn, *Did Singapore Have to Fall? Churchill and the Impregnable Fortress* (2004; repr., Oxon, UK: Routledge, 2008). The most detailed narrative study of Singapore remains Alan Warren's *Britain's Greatest Defeat: Singapore 1942* (2002; repr., London: Hambledon Continuum, 2002). See also Brian Farrell and Sandy Hunter, eds., *Sixty Years On: The Fall of Singapore Revisited* (2002; repr., Singapore: Eastern Universities Press, 2003) and Brian P. Farrell, *The Defence and Fall of Singapore: 1940–42* (2005; repr., Stroud, UK: Tempus, 2006). *Sixty Years On* is an edited volume containing papers on grand strategy, military strategy, and tactics. An example of a quasi-popular account is Noel Barber, *A Sinister Twilight: The Fall of Singapore, 1942* (Boston: Houghton Mifflin Company, 1968). Another journalistic account is Colin Smith, *Singapore Burning: Heroism and Surrender in World War II* (2005; repr., London: Penguin, 2006). Peter Thompson's *The Battle for Singapore: The True Story of the Greatest Catastrophe of World War II* (2005; repr., London: Piatkus, 2013) and Timothy Hall's *The Fall of Singapore* (1983; repr., Oxon, UK: Routledge, 2015) stress the Australian soldiers. In all these academic and popular accounts, the Indian Army plays a cameo role. The focus remains on the British officers, the Tommies, and the Aussies.

2. Colonel Masanobu Tsuji, *Japan's Greatest Victory, Britain's Worst Defeat from the Japanese Perspective: The Capture of Singapore, 1942*, ed. H.V. Howe, trans. Margaret E. Lake (1997; repr., Gloucestershire, UK: Spellmount, 2007). See especially pages 194–95.

3. Hall, *Fall of Singapore*, 192.

4. Raymond Callahan, *The Worst Disaster: The Fall of Singapore* (1977; repr., Singapore: Cultured Lotus, 2001), 11.

5. For the strategic aspect of the Malaya Campaign, see Louis Allen, *Singapore: 1941–1942* (1977; repr., Oxon, UK: Frank Cass, 2005), Callahan, *The Worst Disaster*, and Andrew Gilchrist, *Malaya 1941: The Fall of a Fighting Empire* (London: Robert Hale, 1992). For the political aspects, see C. Bayly and Tim Harper, *Forgotten Armies: The Fall of British Asia, 1941–1945* (London: Allen Lane, 2004).

6. Letter from Russell Grenfell to Percival, June 19, 1950, Percival Papers, IWM, London.

7. David M. Glantz and Jonathan M. House, *When Titans Clashed: How the Red Army Stopped Hitler* (Lawrence, KS: University Press of Kansas, 1995), 49, 77.

8. The best biography of Wavell's generalship during World War II remains the two-volume work by John Connell. See his *Wavell: Supreme Commander*, completed and edited by Michael Roberts (London: Collins, 1969). Ronald Lewin's *The Chief: Field Marshal Lord Wavell, Commander-in-Chief and Viceroy, 1939–47* (London: Hutchinson, 1980) is empirically shallow and almost degenerates into hagiography. The best-balanced biography of the Australian commander in Malaya remains A. B. Lodge's *The Fall of General Gordon Bennett* (Sydney: Allen & Unwin, 1986). The standard biography of Percival is Clifford Kinvig's *Scapegoat: General Percival of Singapore* (London: Brassey's, 1996). Kinvig blames everybody but Percival for the debacle at Malaya-Singapore. Further, Kinvig does not deal with the issue of Percival's handling of the Indian troops.

9. This is probably because of the ideology of post-1947 Indian National Congress governments of India and the fact that there were no senior Indian officers in Malaya.

10. Alan Warren, "The Indian Army and the Fall of Singapore," in *Sixty Years On*, ed. Farrell and Hunter, 270–89; Alan Jeffreys, "The Indian Army in the Malayan Campaign, 1941–42," in *The British Indian Army: Virtue and Necessity*, ed. Rob Johnson (Newcastle: Cambridge Scholars Publishing, 2014), 177–97.

11. Kaushik Roy, *Sepoys against the Rising Sun: The Indian Army in Far East and South-East Asia, 1941–45* (Leiden: Brill, 2016). See chapters 3 and 4. However, there is scope for further study.

12. According to the current manual of the British Army, command includes leadership, decision making, and control. Mungo Melvin and Stuart Peach, "Reaching for the End of the Rainbow: Command and the Revolution in Military Affairs," in *The Challenges of High Command: The British Experience*, ed. Gary Sheffield and Geoffrey Till (Hampshire, UK: Palgrave Macmillan, 2003), 201.

13. Williamson Murray, *Military Adaptation in War: With Fear of Change* (Cambridge: Cambridge University Press, 2011), 1–2, 311.

14. Murray, *Military Adaptation in War*, 30. The argument that strategy is the ultimate arbiter of combat effectiveness is also pushed in the three edited volumes titled *Military Effectiveness* by Allan R. Millett and Williamson Murray (1988; repr., Cambridge: Cambridge University Press, 2010).

15. Brian Holden Reid, "Introduction," *Journal of Strategic Studies* 19, no. 4 (1996): 2.

16. Stephen Hart, "Montgomery, Morale, Casualty Conservation and 'Colossal Cracks': 21st Army Group's Operational Technique in North-West Europe, 1944–45," *Journal of Strategic Studies* 19, no. 4 (1996): 133.

17. John A. English, *On Infantry* (1981; repr., New York: Praeger, 1984): xx.

18. Williamson Murray, *War, Strategy, and Military Effectiveness* (Cambridge: Cambridge University Press, 2011), 46–47.

19. Georges Duby, *The Legend of Bouvines: War, Religion and Culture in the Middle Ages,* trans. Catherine Tihanyi (Cambridge: Polity, 1990), 5.

20. John Keegan, *The Face of Battle: A Study of Agincourt, Waterloo and the Somme* (1976; repr., Harmondsworth, UK: Penguin, 1978), 35.

21. One example is Lieutenant General S. L. Menezes, *Fidelity and Honour: The Indian Army from the Seventeenth to the Twenty-First Century* (New Delhi: Viking, 1993).

1 | The Rise of the Singapore Naval Base

Singapore, the Cape of Good Hope, Alexandria, Gibraltar, and Dover, in the opinion of Lord Fisher (Admiral John Fisher, First Sea Lord, 1904–10), constituted the five "keys" of the world that gave the United Kingdom command over the Indian Ocean and the Mediterranean. Control over the Cape of Good Hope, Aden, and Singapore made the Indian Ocean almost a "British Lake."[1] This chapter portrays the gradual development of the Singapore Naval Base and the shifting threat to it during the interwar period. The failure of the British high command to come up with a coherent defensive strategy is highlighted. This chapter is divided into two parts. The first part deals with the evolution of defense policy regarding Singapore during the 1920s and the mid-1930s. The second half charts the complications that resulted in the defense of Singapore Naval Base, due to an increase in the range of aircraft and the rise of the Japanese threat in the Far East from the late 1930s until the beginning of the Pacific War.

Evolution of Singapore's Defense in the Interwar Era

Singapore was acquired from the Sultan of Johore in 1819 by Thomas Stamford Raffles on behalf of the East India Company and had been transformed by the end of the First World War from an uninhabited island to one of the greatest transit ports in the world.[2] For the first 140 years of British occupation, Singapore was a drain on the East India Company's budget. In 1818, Raffles was appointed as the governor of Bencoolen (in Indonesia) on the southwest coast of Sumatra. The British plan at that time was to expand the China trade. The route from British India to China had to pass through Southeast Asia. Since the late seventeenth century, Britain's commercial rival Holland had dominated Southeast Asia's sea lanes. Holland had succeeded in closing all the British trading posts in this region except Bencoolen. Raffles thought that the British could attract Malay trade to Singapore. Singapore (traditional name Singapura) was in fact an old Malay trading port that had declined, and Raffles wanted to rejuvenate it. The British merchant community in India also enthusiastically supported the acquisition of Singapore. Initially, Raffles was afraid of a Dutch attack against Singapore. In 1824, in accordance with the Treaty of London, the British agreed to evacuate Bencoolen, and in return the Dutch accepted British primacy in the Malayan Peninsula and in Singapore. After that, no European power posed any threat to Singapore, at least until the end of the First World War.[3]

Meanwhile, British power in the Malayan Peninsula was also increasing. British acquisitions in Malaya could be divided into three categories. First, there was the colony of the Straits Settlements of Penang with Province Wellesley, Malacca, and Singapore. This was a British territory governed as a Crown colony by a governor, acting through a legislative council and an executive council. The second group consisted of the Federated Malay States of Perak, Selangor, Negri Sembilan, and Pahang, a British-protected and British-administered Malay territory. The governor of the Straits Settlements also acted as the high commissioner of the Malay States. In the Federated Malay States, the British exercised direct administration and complete control except in matters of Malay customs and Islamic religion. The third category comprised the five Unfederated Malay States of Johore, Kedah, Perlis, Kelantan, and Trengganu. These states were governed by their own sultans, who were assisted by British advisors. The four northern states of Perlis, Kedah, Kelantan, and Trengganu were under Siamese suzerainty until 1909, when an agreement was made between the British and Siamese governments, as a result of which all these four polities came under the protection of the British Crown. After 1914, Johore concluded a similar treaty with the British. Among these five Unfederated Malay States, Johore enjoyed the greatest autonomy. All these states were incorporated within the British Empire through separate treaties. In these treaties, Britain accepted the obligation to defend these states against external aggression. Overall, regarding civil affairs the Malay states were under the high commissioner, who reported to the Colonial Office and in matters of defense came under the British GOC in Malaya, who reported to the War Office in London.[4]

In August 1919, Admiral of the Fleet Lord John Jellicoe, who had commanded the British Grand Fleet between 1914 and 1916 and was then First Sea Lord, considered Japan to be the "Germany of the Far East." Japan's commercial penetration into India was disadvantageous to Britain. He predicted that Japanese and British interests were bound to clash.[5] In 1919, he toured the Pacific and recommended the construction of a naval base at Singapore.[6] The RN put forward the War Memorandum (Eastern), which was a plan for a possible Anglo-Japanese War in 1920. The aim was to redeploy the RN from Europe to Asia in order to obtain a decisive victory over the Imperial Japanese Navy (IJN). This plan in turn provided a rationale for making Singapore a naval base to support the fleet operation. Further, this plan also required the use of Hong Kong as an advance base for blockading Japan. However, Churchill at that time questioned the wisdom of this plan. He argued that a long and costly war against Japan was hardly viable or worthwhile. In December 1919, Britain maintained one aircraft carrier, one destroyer, one sub tender, one minesweeper, one submarine, one heavy cruiser, and three light cruisers at the China Station.[7] Historian Christopher M. Bell asserts that until the 1920s and the early 1930s, the Singapore Naval Base was intended to provide the docking and repair facilities for a British fleet operating in the Far Eastern waters, but it was not expected to serve as the principal base from which to launch operations against Japan. This role was ideally to have been fulfilled by Hong Kong. At that time, defense of Hong Kong was considered difficult but not impossible.[8]

Actually, as early as 1919, the British cabinet's Standing Defence Sub-Committee had proposed abandoning Hong Kong as a main fleet base and concentrating on Singapore.[9] Hong Kong in the 1920s was the greatest imperial port outside the British Isles. It was the "door to the Far Eastern markets." However, Hong Kong was sidelined for several reasons. Britain could not afford to maintain a garrison of forty thousand troops, considered necessary to secure this island against a Japanese invasion. Also, Hong Kong is 1,600 miles from Japan, while Singapore is 2,900 miles from Japan. Though the Japanese could easily mount an invasion of Hong Kong from the Chinese mainland, this was not possible in the case of Singapore. Singapore was chosen because it was considered the gateway to the Pacific, on the shortest possible route from the Indian Ocean to the Pacific Ocean, and an ideal base for a fleet seeking to guard against probable Japanese attack on the trade of the Indian Ocean, particularly the trade route from India to Australia, and to hold open the line of advance toward Japan through the Malay Barrier.[10]

Japan was Britain's chief commercial rival in the Far East, and during the First World War, it pushed its trade forward at Britain's expense.[11] As early as December 1920, the Admiralty pointed out that an aggressive move by Japan in the Far East that coincided with a threat to British security in Europe posed an insoluble problem.[12] The Anglo-Japanese Treaty of 1902 lapsed in 1921.[13] The Anglo-Japanese alliance was based on the fact that Czarist Russia was the principal enemy of Britain in the Far East. In accordance with this alliance, if Russia moved against British India from Central Asia, Japan would aid Britain. Also, if Russia moved against Japan in Manchuria, then Britain would aid Tokyo. Japan defeated Russia during the 1904–5 Russo-Japanese War, and the reduction of Russian strength enabled Britain to shift some naval assets in 1911 from the China Squadron to the North Sea in order to meet the rising challenge of the German High Sea Fleet. However, after the end of the First World War, the decline of Russian strength in the Far East and the rise of Japan as the third naval power in the world changed the strategic calculus for Britain. Further, Britain was unwilling to continue its alliance with Japan because the United States considered Tokyo a threat and a competitor.[14] On 2 May 1921, the Standing Defence Sub-Committee of the cabinet, chaired by Arthur James Balfour (prime minister of Britain from 1902 to 1905 and foreign secretary from 1916 to 1919), considered the Admiralty and War Office papers of October 1919 and March 1920. He concluded that Hong Kong was practically indefensible and agreed to develop Singapore as Britain's principal Far Eastern naval base in view of its strategic importance and lesser vulnerability. Balfour suggested that the Overseas Defence Committee discuss the argument not only against Hong Kong but also against Sydney as the probable Eastern British naval base. Sydney did not satisfy the offensive criterion due to distance, as a fleet based there could not operate in Japanese waters, nor could it prevent the intrusion of Japanese naval units in the Indian Ocean through the Malay Barrier and the consequent severing of its own line of communication (LoC) through Singapore, Colombo to Aden.[15]

On 16 June 1921, the British government decided to construct a naval base at Seletar on the northern shore of Singapore Island to protect the British Far

Eastern possessions against a rising Japan. The naval base was to be located on the estuary of Sembawang River. Singapore Naval Base was to be used as a fueling and repair base for the main British fleet in case of war with Japan. It was approached by the eastern arm of the Johore Straits and was within the hand-held arms (rifles and machine guns) range of the mainland of the Malayan peninsula.[16]

Singapore had no significant agricultural production. Food supplies were imported from the Malayan hinterland and Thailand.[17] Malaya was vital not only for providing protection to the British naval base in Singapore but also because it produced 40 percent of the rubber and over half of the world's tin.[18] Britain obtained 70 percent of its rubber and 57 percent of its tin from Malaya.[19] However, at that time, the range of land-based aircraft was limited. For attacking Singapore, the Japanese had to have airfields near Mersing on the east coast of Malaya. In the 1920s, of course, Japanese forces were not occupying either south China or French Indochina. The British therefore concluded that the RN's control of the sea approaches to Singapore would be sufficient to protect the naval base there. If a threat by sea arose, major naval reinforcements could reach Singapore from Britain within six weeks. The British thus concluded that, in the absence of any major threat by land, only a small garrison of ground forces would be necessary at Singapore.[20] In 1921, the British strategic managers believed that Singapore might be threatened by a squadron of armored cruisers and a raiding force of about two thousand men. In 1922, the Admiralty assumed that the Japanese could send six battleships against Singapore. The Washington Conference (November 1921) agreed to limit naval armaments on a 5:5:3 basis for the United States, Great Britain, and Japan. The Washington Treaty was signed by Britain, France, Italy, Japan, and the United States in 1922. The signatories agreed to maintain the status quo in Asia and to limit warship construction. In the Washington Naval Treaty of 1922, Britain formally surrendered its long tradition of maritime supremacy.[21]

The Admiralty's 1924 Eastern War Memorandum prescribed that if Singapore was lost, the fleet would be immobilized for want of fuel and would be incapable of relieving the pressure on Hong Kong in time to save it from falling into the hands of the Japanese. But as long as Singapore was held, the British could maintain a presence in the region even if Hong Kong was occupied. So the safety of Singapore became the keynote of British Far Eastern strategy.[22] In line with this thinking, at the beginning of the Far Eastern War, British grand strategy gave more importance to Singapore as compared to Hong Kong. The Singapore Sub-Committee Report of 1925 stated that due to difficult terrain, the approach of a hostile force through the State of Johore would be attended with numerous difficulties, and the scenario would favor the defenders. The consensus was that the overland threat through the Malayan Peninsula to Singapore was not serious, and the main threat was perceived to come from the sea and landings on Singapore Island itself. The jungle north of Singapore Island was considered impassable for hostile infantry.[23]

In 1928, the Royal Air Force (RAF) came to Singapore,[24] but the limited range of military aircraft at that time still enabled the fleet to control the Sea Line of Communication (SLoC).[25] While the RN wanted to defend the naval base with fixed heavy batteries, the RAF wanted torpedo bombers escorted by fighters and reconnaissance aircraft for defense.[26] In May 1932, the Sub-Committee of the Committee of Imperial Defence emphasized the importance of shore-based guns as a deterrent against a hostile naval threat and identified the RAF as the secondary weapon of defense for Singapore.[27]

By the 1930s, the increase in the range of land-based aircraft and the potential threat posed by Japanese carrier-based aircraft led to a reassessment of strategy.[28] In April 1933, Japan withdrew from the League of Nations.[29] Japan renounced the Washington naval limitations in 1934.[30] At that time, the only RAF airfield was at Seletar in Singapore. Construction of two further airfields at Singapore Island was immediately started. It was decided to build aerodromes on the east coast with the objective of bombing hostile troopships in case they approached the east coast of Malaya to make landfall. Due to the limited range of aircraft and the difficulties of flying over the mountain range in central Malaya, especially during bad weather, the RAF insisted on building airports on the east rather than along the west coast of Malaya.[31] In 1935, new airfields were planned at Kahang in Johore, Kuantan, and Kota Bahru/Bharu in Malaya to cover the approaches from the South China Sea.[32] The construction of these aerodromes increased the responsibility of the army to protect them.

Britain's breach with Italy posed a potential danger to British interests in the Mediterranean (the link between Europe and Britain's Asian possessions) and the Middle East (Britain's source of oil). This development further exacerbated the issue of defense of the Far East.[33] Besides the worsening scenario in Europe, Japan became more aggressive in Asia in the 1930s. In the London Naval Conference of 1930, Britain and the United States had proposed a 5:5:3 ratio for cruisers of the United States, Britain, and Japan. However, Japan had demanded a 10:10:7 cruiser ratio. In the end, the Japanese had accepted the Western powers' proposed ratio for building cruisers, but on 15 January 1936, Japan walked out of the London Naval Conference.[34] The Washington Naval Treaty expired in 1936.[35] Bell asserts that the rise of a single European challenger need not have prevented the transfer of a British fleet to the Far East. During the 1920s, Britain possessed a substantial margin of naval superiority over its rivals, and London might have maintained a large fleet in the Far East and still dominated European waters. This possibility was undermined by the rise of a triple threat from Germany, Italy, and Japan in the mid-1930s. In that period, the problem facing the British planners was not whether they could send a fleet to the Far East but whether they could dispatch enough ships for an offensive strategy or only those adequate for a defensive one. British naval strength was still sufficient to allow for a vigorous defensive stance in both regions simultaneously. As long as Britain had a reliable ally (France) in Europe, London was in a position to assume the offensive in one of these theaters.[36] Until 1936, defenses were constructed to meet an attack on

Singapore from the sea. But from 1937 onward, Malaya Command believed more and more that a hostile attack would come from the north.[37]

Singapore and the Strategic Context before the Far Eastern War

According to Lieutenant General Lewis Heath, commanding officer (CO) of the III Indian Corps during 1941–42, an enemy intent on capturing Singapore would not attack across the eastern shore of the island, due to the presence of the coastal guns, but would make a landfall on the eastern coast of Malaya. The army, for Heath, was supposed to play a minor role in the defense of Singapore. The RN was to play the premier role, but after 1934, the probability of a fleet being dispatched to the Far East started declining. Then, writes Heath, the RAF took over the duty of protecting Singapore. Arthur Ernest Percival disagrees and asserts that it was only in 1940 when it became evident that a fleet could not be sent to Singapore and the RAF took over the principal duty of protecting the naval base.[38]

In 1937, defense policy was based on the assumption that the British main fleet would arrive from northwestern Europe within 70 days, and the army's job was to hold out on the island for that period.[39] In 1921, London had estimated that the main fleet would arrive in Singapore in the case of war in the Far East within 42 days; in 1937, however, due to the deteriorating strategic situation as a result of the rise of the Italian-German threat in Europe, the period of relief had increased by another 28 days. In late 1937, Colonel Percival, then chief staff officer of Major General William Dobbie (GOC Malaya since 1935), in a report confirmed that north Malaya might become the battleground; the Japanese might capture the east-coast landing sites in Siam (Thailand) and Malaya to acquire the aerodromes and gain local air superiority.[40] Percival noted that the territory of southern Siam might be used by the Japanese to invade Malaya with the ultimate aim of capturing Singapore. Japanese occupation of southern Siam would enable them to cut off Singapore's food supply. Further, as Percival correctly noted, it would allow the Japanese to establish airfields from where Japanese aircraft could threaten British aerial superiority over Malaya. Therefore, Britain should be prepared to use diplomatic force. And if necessary, Britain should be ready to use naval and aerial force to prevent the Japanese from occupying southern Siam. Hence, to protect Singapore, Johore and northern Malaya needed to be defended. Percival continued that at the time the defense of northern Malaya had been entrusted to the Malay States Volunteer Force, assisted by certain units of the Straits Settlement and of the Unfederated Malay States, and the defense of Johore was in the hands of the Johore military and Johore Volunteer Engineers. Percival considered these forces to be weak. He wanted regular infantry assisted by Royal Engineers (RE) and Royal Artillery (RA) for the defense of Penang and southern Malaya. Percival for the time being was not underrating the Japanese military machine. He pointed out that the amphibious expeditions launched by the Japanese along the coast of China were worth examining. He lauded such Japanese expeditions as combined operations including air force, infantry, and navy. In the near future, he feared, the Japanese might land infantry and tanks with special landing crafts along Changi and Singapore City. Percival was worried that the Japanese might conduct nocturnal landing operations. To counter such a threat, Percival demanded two infantry battalions for Singapore Island.[41]

On 14 February 1938, the naval base in the northeast corner of Singapore Island was opened.[42] The dry dock was completed but construction work continued until the outbreak of the Far Eastern War in 1941.[43] In May 1938, Dobbie also proposed that an attack from the north toward Singapore posed a great danger.[44] Interestingly, Dobbie pointed out that the Japanese could land during the northeast monsoon, and the jungle of Malaya in most cases was not impassable. He was in favor of establishing a defensive line along the Johore River, Kota Tinggi, Kulai, and Pulai River.[45] This defense line was considered to be adequately far away from Singapore to prevent the Japanese artillery from shelling the island. For protecting this line, he demanded fifteen tanks and sixteen (at that time he had four) armored cars.[46] In August 1939, Dobbie was succeeded by Major General Lionel V. Bond.[47]

Historian Malcolm H. Murfett rightly says that the bulk of the RN could not afford to sit more than eight thousand nautical miles away from its home bases for months at a time when there was a real threat to the security of the British Isles posed by Nazi Germany.[48] After rejecting the cruiser limitations at the 1930 London Naval Conference, the Italian and German navies had expanded, and they in turn became a serious threat to the RN. By 1940, the Italian Navy had six battleships, seven heavy cruisers, twelve light cruisers, sixty-one fleet destroyers, and 105 submarines.[49] In January 1938, the War Office noted the fact that the Japanese, being heavily engaged in China, must be taken into consideration while assessing the threat to Singapore. Further, the British main fleet would sail for Singapore regardless of the situation in the European waters.[50] However, the strategic situation was changing quickly. In March 1939, Churchill, in a lengthy memorandum to British Prime Minister Neville Chamberlain, noted that the Mediterranean was more important than the Far East as far as deployment of the RN was concerned.[51] Later, as prime minister, Churchill would hold on to this aspect of strategy. On 5 April 1939, Vice Admiral Andrew Cunningham, the deputy chief of Naval Staff of Britain reported that naval strength was at rock bottom, with only ten out of the fifteen capital ships being available for immediate operation.[52] However, British naval strength, though declining in the Far East, was not negligible. In June 1939, the RN maintained one aircraft carrier, one sub tender, two destroyers, three heavy cruisers, one light cruiser, and four submarines in the China Station. In addition, there were thirteen long-range submarines either in Hong Kong or in Singapore, which could threaten Japanese shipping around the home islands.[53] This naval detachment could not be totally brushed aside by the IJN. But with the beginning of the European War in September 1939, British naval strength in the Far East was considerably reduced. Further, in 1939, the American policy makers gave more attention to European affairs than to the Far East.[54]

In June 1939, there were forty British aircraft in Singapore, all of them obsolete.[55] At that time, the Admiralty considered that at best only two British capital ships could be sent to the Far East without weakening the defense of home waters and the Mediterranean.[56] In December 1941, this strategy would be put into effect. In July 1939, it was postulated that the main fleet would arrive within 90 days after the outbreak of hostilities in the Far East, and three months later the period was extended to 180 days.[57] In February 1942 the Japanese would arrive at Singapore in a campaign lasting 55 days.

The Chiefs of Staff Committee (CoSC) did not follow any long-term coherent plan for strengthening the air defense of Singapore. Rather, their policy wavered with time. On 18 March 1940, the CoSC assessed that the chance of war breaking out with Japan had decreased. So the CoSC ordered that the two Blenheim medium bomber squadrons that had been transferred from India to Singapore should be shifted to Iraq or Egypt.[58] In June, one of these squadrons was sent to Egypt and another to Aden.[59]

In April 1940, Major General Bond (GOC Malaya), unlike Dobbie, believed that the defense of the whole of Malaya was necessary in order to protect Singapore. For this task, he demanded between thirty-nine and forty-two infantry battalions. Bond noted that the Japanese could establish their bases in south Indochina. So northern Malaya needed to be defended against a substantial hostile force, which in turn would require at least forty battalions and two tank regiments. However, noted Bond, if the RAF could assure a vigorous offensive against the enemy force, then twenty-five battalions with three antitank (A/T) batteries would suffice. And he had only nine regular infantry battalions in his possession. He was against the opinion that the RAF should take over the primary responsibility for defense of Malaya as in Iraq. But the RAF, in Bond's view, was made responsible for the destruction of the Japanese expedition before it landed. And if this task proved impossible for the RAF, then at least by repeated bombardment, the air force should ensure that no base could be maintained by the Japanese within striking distance of British aerodromes. Being a realist, Bond understood that he would not get much help from the RN as the main fleet might not be sent from Britain to Malaya-Singapore in time.[60] For the first time, the army was coming in a big way for the defense of Singapore Island. But the relationship between Bond and Air Officer Commanding (AOC) Air Vice Marshal J. T. Babington was sour,[61] which in turn prevented intimate joint planning between the RAF and the army for the defense of Malaya-Singapore.

On 10 May 1940, Churchill became the British prime minister, the same day that the Battle of France and the Low Countries began. The campaign started badly for the Allies. It seemed the Germans might also invade Britain after the collapse of France. The secretary of state for Dominion Affairs admitted that as things stood now, there seemed to be no prospect of sending a fleet to Singapore.[62] On 25 June 1940, the CoSC, comprising Air Chief Marshal C. L. N. Newall, General (later Field Marshal) John Dill (chief of the Imperial General Staff/CIGS), and Admiral T. S. V. Phillips (vice chief of Naval Staff), noted that in those circumstances, a fleet could not be spared for the Far East. The only option was to strengthen the land and air defense in Malaya. In the worst possible scenario, the objective was to retain a foothold in that area. Supply of troops from the United Kingdom would prejudice the defense of Britain, and troops could not be spared from the Middle East. The only possible sources of troops were India and Australia. India, it was estimated, could make one brigade available immediately and one division in September. These troops, who were originally earmarked for service in Iraq and Iran, were to be diverted to Malaya. Australia promised to send five thousand men in July, another thirty-four thousand in August, and two squadrons of aircraft. At this stage the CoSC emphasized the retention of the garrison at Hong Kong. The three members of the Chiefs of Staff ended their report by noting: "We recommend that authority be accorded now to the Governor of Malaya to institute the necessary measures to bring the Malayan defenses up to a state of readiness, which will enable them to be fully effective within five days of warning."[63]

On 27 July 1940, the CoSC warned that since Britain was heavily engaged in Europe and in the Middle East, all possible steps must be taken to avoid an open clash with Japan. The committee advised considerable concessions to Japan, such as the closure of the Burma Road, as part of the general settlement. And due to a shortage of resources, occupation of Indochina by Japan could not be regarded as a casus belli; war should be started only in case of a direct Japanese attack to any British possessions.[64] The CoSC accepted that in the absence of a fleet, the defense of Malaya-Singapore had to depend primarily on air power. It was accepted that for the defense of the naval base, it was no longer sufficient merely to concentrate upon the defense of Singapore Island, but it was necessary to hold the whole of Malaya. The objective was to replace the 88 obsolete aircraft with 336 modern first-line aircraft by the end of 1941. This contingent did not include the aircraft necessary for the defense of Burma, and any augmentation of aircraft for Hong Kong was also turned down.[65] Interestingly, the CoSC in their report neglected the crucial issue of where these new aircraft were to come from.

As early as 1936, French attention was concentrated on Europe, and defense of the Far East was considered an unaffordable luxury.[66] On 27 September 1940, Japan signed the Tripartite Pact with Germany and Italy.[67] In September 1940, Japan secured bases in northern French Indochina (especially Tonkin).[68] The 5th Japanese Division under Lieutenant General Akihito Nakamura from south China invaded Vietnam and seized the railroads. After 25 September, the Japanese controlled all of northern Vietnam south of the Chinese border to Hanoi.[69] This not only allowed them to cut the lifeline of the KMT (Kuomintang) from Haiphong to Chungking but also to move their forces within striking distance of Thailand and Malaya.[70] The Japanese move into Indochina, and especially southern Indochina, put the Philippines within the orbit of long-range Japanese bombers. And this move triggered US economic sanctions against Japan, which later led to the Japanese attack on Pearl Harbor.

On the basis of CoSC's appreciation of July 1940, the three British military branches—the army, navy, and RAF—of Malaya generated a tactical appreciation that became the agenda of a conference held at Singapore in October 1940, attended by representatives of all commands in the Far East. The conference recommended that instead of 336 aircraft, 582 aircraft were required. The CoSC responded that 582 aircraft was the ideal figure, but taking into consideration the strategic position in Great Britain, Malta, and the Middle East, the 336 figure should be considered.[71]

Air Chief Marshal Robert Brooke-Popham, who had retired from the RAF in 1937 and had been appointed as the governor of Kenya, was made commander in chief Far East on 18 November 1940. His Far Eastern Command included the aerial and land forces in Burma, Malaya, Borneo, and Hong Kong.[72] In 1936, the headquarters of the naval commander and the army headquarters at Fort Canning were in Singapore city. However, the RAF headquarters was at Seletar on the north side of the island. Until November 1940, the three services worked independently, and the commanders of the army and air force were responsible directly to their own ministries. The senior naval officer at Singapore was responsible for the naval defense of Singapore Island and local defense of the surrounding waters. Later, as rear admiral Malaya, he became responsible for the security of the Malayan coastline. From July 1940 onwards, the naval commander in chief China Station flew his flag on Singapore and assumed responsibility for all waters off the coast of Malaya, except the responsibility for local defense of Singapore, which remained with the rear admiral Malaya. Brooke-Popham was responsible to the Chiefs of Staff for operational control in Malaya, Burma, and Hong Kong and for coordination of plans for the defense of these territories. However, GOC Malaya was to correspond with the War Office on all matters that he had hitherto dealt with. The commander in chief Far East had no control over the naval forces, nor did he have any administrative control. The various commands continued to deal with their respective ministries. The commander in chief Far East had only a small operational staff and no administrative staff.[73] Further, the Combined Intelligence Bureau on which the three services relied for information of Japanese intentions and troop movements remained under the control of the RN and not under Brooke-Popham. And the RN displayed reluctance in sharing all the information with the other two sister services.[74] Thus, unified command in the true sense of the term did not apply in the case of Brooke-Popham's command. Despite his title, Brooke-Popham's power was limited. Lack of unity of command hampered the defensive preparations.

The Far East Combined Bureau (Intelligence) under the commander in chief China was located at the naval base. The commander in chief Far East was dependent on this bureau for intelligence, so he established his headquarters at the naval base with the aim of moving to the Sime Road area in case of war breaking out. Just before the outbreak of the Second World War in the Far East (the Pacific War), the RAF's new headquarters was completed at Sime Road near the golf club in the center of the island. Thus, when the war started, army headquarters, RAF headquarters, and the civilian government were grouped in one area, while those of the two commanders in chief and of the rear admiral Malaya were in another area some ten miles away. No unified command headquarter was ever created.[75]

Brooke-Popham was told by London that the requirements of Britain's defense, the Battle of the Atlantic, the Middle East, Russia, and Iraq and Iran took precedence over the Far East. Brooke-Popham accepted that his principal task was to protect the naval base and to a lesser degree Malaya for its rubber and tin production. The hostile aircraft had to be kept away from bombing the Singapore Naval Base. This, he reasoned, required extending the defensive line right up to the northern end of Malaya. He demanded a minimum of 336 aircraft.[76] Brooke-Popham's scheme of defense for Singapore included construction of modern airfields in the northeast coast of Malaya and Borneo.[77] The protection of these airfields was the duty of the army, but the army was not taken into confidence in the scheme involving selection and construction of the aerodromes. Heath asserts that the airfields on the east coast of Malaya were ill chosen from the army's point of view.[78] In fact during 1936–37, AOC Far East Air Commodore S. W. Smith decided to construct a string of airfields in eastern Malaya.[79] The RAF argued that airfields at Gong Kedah and Machang were necessary for making reconnaissance over Indochina. Constant cloud cover over the central mountain range in Malaya handicapped flight from the west coast of Malaya toward the east coast and the South China Sea. Reconnaissance over the South China Sea was very important because it was from this direction that the threat to Malaya by sea was greatest. Hence, a number of airfields along the east coast of Malaya were absolutely necessary.[80] Only from northeast Malaya could British aircraft reach southwest Indochina. The short range of available aircraft, especially the Vildebeeste, also forced the RAF to establish airfields on the not-so-defensible northeast Malaya.[81] The War Office counterargued that the army lacked the necessary manpower to garrison these airfields.[82] Heath goes on to say that the airfields on the east coast of Malaya were vulnerable to amphibious assault. The airfields were neither dispersed nor concealed, and they were not constructed among the paddy fields in the interior, to avoid the hassle or expense of the acquisition of the land.[83] British military officer turned historian Louis Allen agrees with Heath's criticism.[84] Heath notes that there was a lack of cooperation between the RAF and the army in preparing the defensive scheme.[85]

When Brooke-Popham was appointed to his high-sounding post, there were only eighty-eight RAF aircraft in the Malaya-Singapore theater. Of them, twenty-four were Blenheim bombers, twenty-four Hudsons, and twenty-four obsolete Vildebeeste torpedo bombers. In addition there were twelve Wirraways and four flying boats.[86] In December 1940, Robert Menzies, the Australian prime minister, unsuccessfully tried to persuade Churchill to transfer three or four vessels from the Mediterranean Fleet to Singapore.[87] On 10 January 1941, the Chiefs of Staff estimated that though 582 aircraft was the ideal number for holding Malaya, 336 aircraft could be delivered before the end of 1941.[88] On 24 April 1941, Air Vice Marshal C. W. Pulford became AOC RAF Far East Command. He held his command till 11 February 1942, and two days later he left Singapore. By midsummer 1941, the Far East Command RAF included Hong Kong, Borneo, Malaya, Ceylon/Sri Lanka, and Burma, with headquarters at Singapore. The command stretched across the Indian Ocean to Durban and Mombasa. The principal functions of this command were to protect the naval base at Singapore and to cooperate with the RN to ensure security of the SLoC in the Indian Ocean and South China Sea.[89] In the autumn of 1941, more than one hundred

RAF squadrons, twenty-five divisions, and half the RN battle fleet were guarding Britain.[90] During the first half of 1941, Middle East Command received 1,300 aircraft (724 fighters, 421 light bombers, and 108 heavy bombers).[91] Even in the autumn of 1941, GHQ concluded that the RAF would be able to destroy 40 percent of the hostile landing force in Malaya before it could be landed. When the Japanese attack started, the RAF had only 158 machines in Malaya.[92] Historian John R. Ferris asserts that the presence of 300 Spitfires and Hurricanes in Singapore would have deterred the Japanese.[93] Such an assertion is questionable, but one thing is certain: the presence of a substantial number of Hurricanes and Spitfires in Malaya-Singapore during 1941 would surely have prevented the Japanese from gaining air superiority so easily, and this would have significantly changed the course of the land campaign.

On 16 May 1941, Percival became GOC Malaya in place of Bond. He had served as chief of staff Malaya Command (General Staff Officer/GSO 1st) in 1936–37. On 10 July 1941, Group Captain E. B. Rice became the fighter defence commander of Singapore and coordinator of air defences of Malaya.[94] And the commander in chief China Station was Vice Admiral Geoffrey Layton. Rear Admiral Malaya was Vice Admiral Ernest John Spooner.[95] On 23 July, the Vichy authorities bowed to Japanese demands for the use of ports and airfields in southern Indochina.[96] On 18 October 1941, Hideki Tojo became the prime minister of Japan.[97]

Major General B. W. Key, CO of the 8th Indian Brigade, asserts that without five infantry divisions, 350 aerial machines, and naval support, Malaya was indefensible.[98] Just before the outbreak of war in the Far East, the RAF had the necessary infrastructure (airfields, repair stations, etc.) but lacked the adequate number of aircraft.[99] It is to be noted that the Japanese enjoyed aerial and naval superiority in the Malaya-Singapore theater, but the Allied forces had numerical superiority as far as ground force was concerned. So the issue of why the Allied land forces in Malaya were not able to translate their numerical superiority into military power is worth examining.

Conclusion

Until the end of the First World War, there was no strategic threat to the British-dominated Malaya-Singapore region. The rise of Japan as a potential enemy after 1919 resulted in the British decision to develop a naval base in the Singapore Island. The British government lacked a long-term consistent policy for defending Malaya-Singapore. The British strategic managers could not decide on the nature (aerial or amphibious, etc.) and direction (to the island or north Malaya) of the Japanese threat to Singapore. In the late 1930s, as the Japanese threat grew in the Far East, simultaneous with the resurgence of Italy and especially Germany in Europe, Britain's overall strategic scenario deteriorated. And absence of a unified command in the Malaya-Singapore theater further obstructed military effectiveness of the Allied air-land-sea forces deployed in this region. When all was said and done, the Japanese did not enjoy any numerical superiority in land forces, and the British imperial armies fought badly in Malaya and Singapore. Why did the Allied land force fold up so easily and quickly? Let us focus on the organization of the Allied ground force, especially its biggest component, the Indian Army. This is the subject of our next chapter.

Notes

1. James Neidpath, *The Singapore Naval Base and the Defence of Britain's Eastern Empire, 1919-1941* (Oxford: Clarendon, 1981), 2, 9.
2. Neidpath, *Singapore Naval Base*, 13.
3. Malcolm H. Murfett et al., *Between Two Oceans: A Military History of Singapore from 1275 to 1971* (1999; repr., Singapore: Marshall Cavendish, 2011), 36-61.
4. Nadzan Haron, "Colonial Defence and British Approach to the Problems in Malaya: 1874-1918," *Modern Asian Studies* 24, no. 2 (1990): 279-80.
5. Ong Chit Chung, *Operation Matador: World War II, Britain's Attempt to Foil the Japanese Invasion of Malaya and Singapore* (1997; repr., Singapore: Marshall Cavendish, 2003), 5.
6. Louis Allen, *Singapore: 1941-1942* (1977; repr., Oxon: Frank Cass, 2005), 38.
7. Kwong Chi Man and Tsoi Yiu Lun, *Eastern Fortress: A Military History of Hong Kong, 1840-1970* (Hong Kong: Hong Kong University Press, 2014), 73, 75.
8. Christopher M. Bell, "'Our Most Exposed Outpost': Hong Kong and British Far Eastern Strategy, 1921-1941," *Journal of Military History* 60 (1996): 61.
9. Martin Thomas, "Disaster Foreseen? France and the Fall of Singapore," in *Sixty Years On: The Fall of Singapore Revisited*, ed. Brian Farrell and Sandy Hunter (2002; repr., Singapore: Eastern Universities Press, 2003), 70.
10. Neidpath, *Singapore Naval Base*, 13, 36, 47, 51.
11. Neidpath, *Singapore Naval Base*, 38.
12. Raymond Callahan, *The Worst Disaster: The Fall of Singapore* (1977; repr., Singapore: Cultured Lotus, 2001), 23.
13. Karl Hack and Kevin Blackburn, *Did Singapore Have to Fall? Churchill and the Impregnable Fortress* (2004; repr., Oxon, UK: Routledge, 2008), 30.
14. Chung, *Operation Matador*, 11; Allen, *Singapore*, 37; Antony Best, *British Intelligence and the Japanese Challenge in Asia, 1914-1941* (Basingstoke, UK: Palgrave Macmillan, 2002), 14-15.
15. Neidpath, *Singapore Naval Base*, 42, 51.
16. Note on the Malayan Campaign by LMH, LMH 5, P 441, Lewis Heath Papers, IWM, London, 1; Hack and Blackburn, *Did Singapore*, 31; Chung, *Operation Matador*, 13, 29.
17. Chung, *Operation Matador*, 49.
18. Hack and Blackburn, *Did Singapore*, 14.
19. Neidpath, *Singapore Naval Base*, 47.
20. Lieutenant General A. E. Percival, "Operations of Malaya Command from 8 December 1941 to 15 February 1942," *Second Supplement to the London Gazette*, February 26, 1948 (London: HMSO, 1948), 1249; Neidpath, *Singapore Naval Base*, 51.
21. Callahan, *Worst Disaster*, 22-23; Allen, *Singapore*, 38; Man and Lun, *Eastern Fortress*, 74.
22. Bell, "'Our Most Exposed Outpost,'" 66.
23. Chung, *Operation Matador*, 36, 39.
24. Henry Probert, *The Forgotten Air Force: The Royal Air Force in the War against Japan, 1941-45* (London: Brassey's, 1995), 1.

25. Notes by Lieutenant General A. E. Percival on the Brief Outline Narrative of the Mainland Operations in Malaya 8 Dec. 1941 to 31 Jan. 1942, Prepared by the Combined Inter-Services Historical Section (India), June 1947, Percival Papers, IWM, 1.
26. Probert, *Forgotten Air Force*, 2–3.
27. Percival, "Operations," 1249.
28. Percival, "Operations," 1249.
29. Peter Thompson, *The Battle for Singapore: The True Story of the Greatest Catastrophe of World War II* (2005; repr., London: Piatkus, 2013), 37.
30. Hack and Blackburn, *Did Singapore*, 31.
31. Percival, "Operations," 1249.
32. Allen, *Singapore*, 41.
33. Callahan, *Worst Disaster*, 24.
34. Saki Dockrill, "Britain's Grand Strategy and Anglo-American Leadership in the War against Japan," in *British and Japanese Military Leadership in the Far Eastern War, 1941–1945*, ed. Brian Bond and Kyoichi Tachikawa (London: Frank Cass, 2004), 10; Dan Van Der Vat, *Standard of Power: The Royal Navy in the Twentieth Century* (2000; repr., London: Pimlico, 2001), 154–55.
35. Bill Yenne, *The Imperial Japanese Army: The Invincible Years 1941–42* (Oxford: Osprey, 2014), 79.
36. Christopher M. Bell, "The 'Singapore Strategy' and the Deterrence of Japan: Winston Churchill, the Admiralty and the Dispatch of Force Z," *English Historical Review* 116, no. 467 (2001): 607.
37. Letter from Lieutenant General A. E. Percival to Major D. N. Kann, War Office, London, January 16, 1949, Percival Papers.
38. Comments made by Percival on the Notes on the Malayan Campaign by LMH, LMH 5, P 441, Lewis Heath Papers.
39. Percival, "Operations," 1249.
40. Hack and Blackburn, *Did Singapore*, 39.
41. A. E. Percival, Deductions from Japanese Appreciation of the Attack on the Fortress of Singapore, 1937, Percival Papers.
42. Thompson, *Battle for Singapore*, 7.
43. Chung, *Operation Matador*, 6.
44. Hack and Blackburn, *Did Singapore*, 40.
45. Percival, "Operations," 1250.
46. Murfett et al., *Between Two Oceans*, 170.
47. Thompson, *Battle for Singapore*, 49.
48. Malcolm H. Murfett, "Reflections on an Enduring Theme: The 'Singapore Strategy' at Sixty," in Farrell and Hunter, *Sixty Years On*, 16.
49. Ong Chit Chung, "Major-General William Dobbie and the Defence of Malaya, 1935–38," *Journal of Southeast Asian Studies* 17, no. 2 (1986): 285.
50. Allen, *Singapore*, 45.
51. Raymond Callahan, "Churchill and Singapore," in Farrell and Hunter, *Sixty Years On*, 158.
52. Chung, "Major-General William Dobbie," 286.
53. Man and Lun, *Eastern Fortress*, 75–76.
54. Greg Kennedy, "Symbol of Imperial Defence: The Role of Singapore in British and American Far Eastern Strategic Relations, 1933–1941," in Farrell and Hunter, *Sixty Years On*, 61.

55. John R. Ferris, "Student and Master: The United Kingdom, Japan, Airpower, and the Fall of Singapore, 1920–1941," in Farrell and Hunter, *Sixty Years On*, 114.
56. Callahan, *Worst Disaster*, 26.
57. Allen, *Singapore*, 48; Callahan, *Worst Disaster*, 26.
58. Memorandum by the Chiefs of Staff Committee, March 18, 1940, WP(40)102, Cabinet Papers (hereafter CP), NMML, New Delhi.
59. Reports for the Month of May 1940 for the Dominions, India, Burma and the Colonies, Protectorates and Mandated Territories, Report by the Secy. of State for India, Para 26, June 6, 1940, WP*(40), 164, CP, NMML.
60. Notes by Lieutenant General A. E. Percival on Captain Russell Grenfell's Draft, July 1950, Percival Papers; Percival, "Operations," 1250; Murfett et al., *Between Two Oceans*, 173–74.
61. Colin Smith, *Singapore Burning: Heroism and Surrender in World War II* (2005; repr., London: Penguin, 2006), 29–30.
62. Murfett et al., *Between Two Oceans*, 173.
63. Report by the Chiefs of Staff Committee, War Cabinet, Immediate Measures Required in the Far East, 25 June 1940, WP(40)222, CAB/66/9/2, PRO, Kew, London, 2.
64. Report by the Chiefs of Staff, Far Eastern Policy, War Cabinet, WP(40)289, CAB 66/10/20, PRO, Kew, 1.
65. Air Vice Marshal Paul Maltby, "Report on the Air Operations during the Campaigns in Malaya and Netherland East Indies from 8 December 1941 to 12 March 1942," *Third Supplement to the London Gazette*, February 26, 1948 (London: HMSO, 1948), 1349.
66. Thomas, "Disaster Foreseen?," 69.
67. Ken Kotani, "Pearl Harbor: Japanese Planning and Command Structure," in *The Pacific War: From Pearl Harbor to Hiroshima*, ed. Daniel Marston (2005; repr., Oxford: Osprey, 2010), 33.
68. Hack and Blackburn, *Did Singapore*, 39.
69. Yenne, *Imperial Japanese Army*, 70.
70. Thompson, *Battle for Singapore*, 55.
71. Maltby, "Report," 1349.
72. Ian Morrison, *Malayan Postscript* (London: Faber and Faber, 1942), 12–13.
73. Percival, "Operations," 1247.
74. Timothy Hall, *The Fall of Singapore* (1983, repr., Oxon: Routledge, 2015), 14.
75. Percival, "Operations," 1248.
76. Despatch on the Far East by Air Chief Marshal Robert Brooke-Popham, Commander-in-Chief Far East (17 Oct. 1940–27 Dec. 1941), September 8, 1942, CAB/66/28/33, PRO, 5–6, 8.
77. Note on the Malayan Campaign by LMH, Heath Papers, 2; Thompson, *Battle for Singapore*, 56.
78. Note on the Malayan Campaign by LMH, Heath Papers, 3.
79. Callahan, *Worst Disaster*, 27–28.
80. Maltby, "Report," 1350.
81. Note on the Malayan Campaign by LMH, Part 1, Heath Papers, 4; Comments by Air Chief Marshal R. Brooke-Popham on Major-General Percival's Despatch "Operations of Malaya Command," July 28, 1946, Percival Papers, 1.
82. Thompson, *Battle for Singapore*, 38.
83. Note on the Malayan Campaign by LMH, Heath Papers, 4a–4b.

84. Allen, *Singapore*, 41.
85. Note on the Malayan Campaign by LMH, Part 1, 6.
86. Thompson, *Battle for Singapore*, 59.
87. Bell, "The 'Singapore Strategy' and the Deterrence of Japan: Winston Churchill, the Admiralty and the Dispatch of Force Z," 619.
88. Allen, *Singapore*, 50.
89. Maltby, "Report," 1347–48.
90. Brian P. Farrell, "1941: An Overview," in Farrell and Hunter, *Sixty Years On*, 176.
91. Callahan, *Worst Disaster*, 95.
92. Allen, *Singapore*, 51.
93. Ferris, "Student and Master," 13–14.
94. Maltby, "Report," 1347.
95. Percival, "Operations," 1247–48.
96. Callahan, *Worst Disaster*, 97.
97. Yenne, *Imperial Japanese Army*, 73.
98. Major General B. W. Key, 11th Indian Division, p. 456, IWM, 4.
99. Probert, *Forgotten Air Force*, 12.

2 | The Allied Ground Forces in Malaya

In 1941, the bulk of the Allied ground force in Malaya and Singapore comprised Indian soldiers. This chapter focuses on the social composition and organization of the Indian Army in particular and the Allied formations deployed in Malaya in general. Recruitment and combat experience of the Indian Army along with the state of command, doctrine, training, equipment, discipline, and morale of the Allied units deployed in Malaya have been placed under the scanner. The IJA's organizational format is also contrasted with that of the Allied land force. An attempt is made to assess how far Percival's ground force was prepared organizationally and conceptually to meet the special type of warfare which developed in the unique terrain of Malaya-Singapore.

The Allied Armies: Structure and Functions

This section discusses the structure and functions of the Indian Army especially and the Australian plus British forces in general in comparison with the IJA. The population of Japan was about 100 million.[1] The population of India was 400 million.[2] During the Second World War, India raised 2.5 million troops. Australia, from a smaller population pool (7 million), raised an army that was smaller than that of India. In March 1939, the part-time militia numbered to 70,000 men. It was poorly trained and lacked tanks and modern artillery. And the regular army had only 4,000 personnel.[3] In 1940, the Australian Army numbered 191,802 persons, and in 1945, it had 377,598 personnel.[4] In 1939, the IJA (including regulars and reservists) numbered 1,196,000. And in 1945, it had 5,950,000 personnel.[5] Despite having a greater population base compared to Japan, the expansion of the Indian Army was not as impressive as that of IJA. This was because of several factors. First, the United Kingdom government did not want a mass Indian Army at least until 1942. Second, lack of weapons hampered the expansion program of the Indian Army. Third, the recruitment ideology and ethnic structure of the Indian Army also slowed down the pace of expansion.

Expansion of the Indian Army was dependent on the import of weapons and ammunition from Britain. The Indian Army was short of guns and howitzers.[6] The six ordnance factories in India were underdeveloped, and their productive capacity was limited. They manufactured guns and ammunition that were becoming obsolete in the United Kingdom. And there was no civil armament industry in India. Unlike India, in United Kingdom, the ordnance factories relied on the civil industry for many of the accessories essential for armament production.

Machine and machine tools remained the most serious bottleneck for expansion of production. Shortages of technicians and craftsmen further hampered the production of military goods. Even for the expansion of small arms ammunition production, technicians from Royal Ordnance Factories of United Kingdom were required. And after September 1939, due to the United Kingdom's own needs and shipping difficulties, flow of supplies in significant quantities and technicians in large numbers were not possible.[7] In August 1940, the GoI informed the secretary of state for India that India even lacked mountain artillery for equipping the new units that were being raised, to say nothing of heavy artillery.[8] On 19 September 1940, the CoSC comprising C. L. N. Newall, J. G. Dill, and Admiral of the Fleet Alfred Dudley Pound accepted, with reservation, the grim scenario in India as regards equipment hampering expansion in the following words: "We consider, therefore, that the minimum equipment necessary for training should be sent out to India as soon as the immediate needs of the Middle East and certain other overseas garrisons have been met."[9] In October 1940, Major General T. J. Hutton (he would later fight in Burma against the IJA), deputy chief of the General Staff of India, was sent to United Kingdom to request arms, equipment, and British officers for the units that were being raised.[10] All these factors in combination somewhat slowed the pace of expansion.

In August 1939, the 12th Indian Brigade under Brigadier A. C. M. Paris arrived in Malaya from India.[11] During September 1939, 34,000 men joined the Indian Army, and of them 19,000 came from Punjab. The premier of Punjab, Sikander Hyat Khan, was more than willing to help in the recruitment process.[12] In October 1939, the secretary of state for India, Lord Zetland, informed Viceroy Lord Linlithgow that there was no need at that time to go for a large expansion of the Indian Army. Zetland emphasized that the strategic scenario did not warrant it, and also the issue of financing a large army was a problematic one.[13] Within India, though there was tremendous enthusiasm for joining the army in Punjab, due to the activities of the Indian National Congress (INC), the response in Central Province (now Madhya Pradesh) and in the United Provinces (present-day Uttar Pradesh) was somewhat muted.[14] In September 1939, the Indian Army had 237,000 men (including British troops and noncombatants). Of them, 4,000 were serving overseas. On 1 April 1940, about 23,581 men of the Indian Army were serving overseas. In May 1940, the Indian Army numbered 250,000 men.[15] During the quarter ending 30 June 1940, 23,367 recruits for the various arms were enrolled. The number for the corresponding period of the previous year was 2,945.[16] Between 20 June and 15 November 1940, thirty-five infantry battalions were raised.[17] During July 1941, personnel for one heavy antiaircraft (AA) regiment were sent from India to Singapore.[18] On 26 September 1940, GoI offered to send one division to Malaya in May 1941.[19]

From May 1940 to September 1941, 5,200 officers (of them 1,400 Indians) were recruited along with 550,000 Indians as rank and file. On an average, monthly recruitment was 50,000 and 9,000 in the technical branches. On 1 October 1941, the strength of the Indian Army came to about 820,000. Of them, 264,000 officers and men were serving overseas. The breakdown was 91,000 in Iraq, 56,000 in

Malaya, 20,000 in Burma, and another 20,000 in the Middle East. The rest were serving in Aden, Ceylon, East Africa, North Africa, Seychelles, etc.[20] In January 1942, the 45th Indian Infantry Brigade of the 17th Indian Division sailed from India to Malaya.[21] During the above-mentioned period, most of the units raised by India had been sent to the Middle East rather than to the Far East.

Who joined the Indian Army and why? Noted fiction writer Amitav Ghosh in his *The Glass Palace* (2000) poses the question of why the Indians joined the army and then fought, got wounded, and even died for the British. While Rajkumar, a boatman from India who had migrated to Burma, claims that the sepoys were mindless tools in the hands of their British masters, another character named Saya John (an orphan who was brought up by the Christian missionaries) asserts that the Indian soldiers were pure and simple mercenaries.[22] We will see later (especially in the context of the rise of the INA), the sepoys/jawans had a mind of their own. And the category "mercenary" does not really explain totally the complex motivation of either the colonial or metropolitan soldiers.

People join the military service due to a combination of precombat and in-combat motivations. Precombat motivation refers to the factors that led one to join the army. And in-combat motivation refers to the reasons that enable a soldier to encounter the dangerous fire-filled battlefield. The British in India for political reasons never resorted to conscription. Military service in British India remained voluntary. They were attracted to military service due to pay, pension, and gratuity in the context of colonial underdevelopment.[23] The Indians were quasi mercenaries. But this was not unique to the Indian Army. Tim Carew, a British officer in the Gurkha Battalion who had fought in Burma, observed this about the motivation for recruits joining the British Army: "The British soldier between the wars enlisted in the Army for economic, alcoholic, amatory but rarely patriotic reasons. He joined at a time when there was no Welfare State and no overtime . . . he enlisted, in fact, because he was out of work and the problem of the next square meal was becoming increasingly pressing."[24] The 2nd Argylls, which fought in Malaya and Singapore, comprised men from Scotland's industrial belt between the Forth and the Clyde (Falkirk, Stirling, Edinburgh, and Glasgow port) and also from Newcastle and County Durham. Some came from rural areas and from lochside towns like Dunoon, Lochgilphead, and Sandbank. Most of the recruits joined due to poverty, and many were from broken or deprived homes. About 40 percent of the personnel were orphans or were not in touch with their real parents.[25]

It would be wrong to argue that all the social groups of India joined the army for pay only. For instance, the Tiwanas (Rajput landlords) from Shahpur District in Punjab and Garewal Jats from Ludhiana District of Punjab joined the army because military service was considered honorable in their communities.[26] Most of the Indian soldiers were long-service volunteers. In contrast to the Indian Army, the IJA was based on conscription.[27] In December 1926, a conscription law was passed in the Diet that made all Japanese males over twenty years old eligible to undergo three years' service in the navy or two years in the army, with a further four to five years in the reserves and ten more years' subreserve training.[28]

Service in the armed forces was considered honorable in Japan and in colonial India. Draft dodging was never a problem in wartime Japan.[29] One can argue that the metropolitan armies depended on nationalism in order to stiffen the morale of the troops in the battlefield. There could not be any question of the presence of nationalism in the British-officered Indian Army. The Axis powers did not threaten the livelihood and the homeland of the Indians. However, in recent times, the role of nationalism in strengthening the morale of the personnel of even nation-state armies is questioned.

The German troops relied on the racist ideology of National Socialism in order to strengthen their resolve to encounter the ugly "face of battle."[30] Historian Dennis Showalter asserts that the American troops had no ideological motivation to fall back upon. Their homeland was not under attack. Their worldview was to complete the "job" quickly and efficiently.[31] Both the British and Indian armies encouraged regimental esprit de corps. Take for instance the case of the Argylls. The men fought not for their commanding officer or king and country but for the regiment.[32] The British, with the aid of "martial race" ideology, fused territorial, ethnic, tribal, and clan ties with religious sentiments in order to create regiments in the Indian Army. The Indian troops also did not have any ideological motivation. As far as their in-combat motivation was concerned, the regimental spirit and bonding with the British officers who led by personal example kept the jawans going. One commissioned Indian officer who fought in Malaya noted that the Indian Army's mainstay was the esprit de corps and tribal traditions.[33] The Germans followed the practice of recruiting and reinforcing divisions from the same region.[34] The German Army's units were formed of men from the same province or city, and replacement of casualties came from the same places, and the hospitals returned the wounded back to the units from where they came originally.[35] This was done to ensure territorial loyalty among the personnel of a division. Thanks to the martial race ideology, which we will discuss below, the Indian regiments recruited selected communities from particular localities. The Indian Army, with the aid of caste, clan, and territorial links, built up primary group solidarity within the units. Primary groups could be defined as a group characterized by intimate face-to-face association and cooperation. It resulted in sympathy and mutual identification among the members of the group.[36]

According to the martial race ideology, only some communities hailing from particular regions were martial in nature due to biological and climatic reasons. The ideologues of martial race theory claimed that cold, hilly frontier regions gave birth to martial people. Further, due to the Aryan conquest of India at the dawn of history, asserted the martial race ideologues, only the Aryan communities had martial skill. The rest of the Indians were unmartial. The martial races for the British officers were Pathans, Punjabi Muslims, Sikhs, Garwahlis/Garhwalis, Kumaunis/Kumaonis, Gurkhas, Dogras, Jats, Rajputs, and Marathas.[37] The Pathans were recruited from the North-West Frontier Province; Punjabi Muslims from west Punjab (especially the Salt Range); Sikhs from central Punjab; Dogras, Garwahlis, and Kumaunis from Himachal Pradesh (east

Table 2.1. Comparative Figures of Some of the "Martial" Communities Recruited during 1939–40

Communities	Quarter ending 30 June 1939	Quarter ending 30 June 1940
Punjabi Muslims	749	5,951
Sikhs	463	3,022
Madrassis	90	2,164
Dogras	196	1,726
Jats	241	1,469
Marathas	155	1,278
Pathans	182	1,259
Rajputs	218	1,060
Garwahlis	31	949
Kumaunis	122	718
Ahirs	28	425
Gurkhas	23	18
Total	2,498	20,039

Note: During the first quarter ending 30 June 1939, only about four hundred recruits belonged to the so-called nonmartial classes. And three thousand recruits for the quarter ending on 30 June 1940 belonged to the "nonmartial" communities.

Source: L/WS/1/136, Appendix 19, OIOC, BL, London.

Punjab); Gurkhas from central Nepal; Jats from United Provinces; and Rajputs from United Provinces and Rajputana.[38] While discussing recruitment, Vegetius in the fourth century CE noted that fishermen, fowlers, and weavers were not to be recruited into the army.[39] The martial race theorists believed that only peasants should be recruited into the army. The small peasants joined the Indian Army mainly due to economic inducements.[40] The martial race theorists were not eager to recruit men from the urban centers. Interestingly, the IJA also assumed that city boys from the streets of cities like Tokyo and Osaka had low morale, lax discipline, and lackadaisical attitudes, and they made poor soldiers.[41] Table 2.1 gives an idea about the volume of recruitment of the martial races during 1939–40.

The Indian Army was a multireligious, polyethnic force. In January 1932, the Indian Army had 52,863 Muslims (including 41,720 from Punjab and 6,847 from North-West Frontier Province), 66,011 Hindus (including 18,703 Gurkhas), and 22,828 Sikhs.[42] In January 1941, there were 117,490 Muslims (of them 82,893 were Punjabi Muslims) in the Indian Army, and their numbers rose to 176,000 (100,004 Punjabi Muslims) during July of the same year.[43] On that date, 48 percent of the military manpower was from Punjab; 15.5 percent from north, west, and central India (Bombay, Central Provinces, United Provinces, and Bihar combined); and 11 percent from Nepal.[44] On 1 February 1942, of the 690,000 men in the Indian Army, there were 341,000 Hindus (including 57,000 Gurkhas), 239,000 Muslims, 72,000 Sikhs, and 38,000 belonging to the other communities.[45]

The Allied Ground Forces in Malaya 29

In July 1943, Lieutenant General G. N. Molesworth (deputy chief of the General Staff India) an advocate of martial race theory who was in charge of recruitment, noted:

> Some census figures (1941) are however of interest if we rely merely on statistics. The all India total is given as 388,000,000. I then deduct 60 per cent of the total, which I think is a low figure, for women, incapacitated children, males above and below recruitable age, etc., which leaves us 165,320,000. We can thus safely, allowing for the 60 per cent cut above, deduct the 'unrecruitable areas' . . . i.e. Bengal, Assam, Bihar, Orissa, Sind, 1/2 Central Province, Berar. This leaves us 88,200,000. Certain further deductions are I think justifiable, i.e. States and Agencies . . . which leaves us a final figure . . . 29,088,000 recruitable bodies all over India, who might join the army if they wanted to. I think from this figure we have to make large deductions, for labor generally. . . . I have always believed myself that the true recruitable figure is somewhere in the neighbourhood of 10,000,000—that is including classes not recruited pre Great War II. If, under the voluntary system, we have recruited 2,000,000 of a possible 10,000,000, I do not think we have done too badly. . . . Annual intake roughly of 650,000.[46]

Besides combat troops, Molesworth was also against recruiting nonmilitary labor from the so-called nonmartial races. Annually five to six million Indians died due to disease. Malnourishment and disease due to general poverty actually made many Indians unsuited for military service.[47] The low standard of physique due to malnutrition as a result of poor agrarian economy was another obstruction as regards mass recruitment.[48] But the martial race theory's spokesmen explained it through the lens of racial degeneration and climactic factors.

The martial race theory was modified a bit as a result of the increasing demands for recruits during the Second World War. Between 1 November 1941 and 25 September 1942, many new communities hitherto classified as nonmartial were recruited. Due to rising demand during the Second World War, the Madrassis were categorized as a martial race. The other new communities recruited included Deccani Muslims, Brahmins, Mahars, Meos, and Indian Christians. Their percentage came to about 49.3 of the total numbers recruited in the above-mentioned period. However, most of the "nonmartial" classes went to the technical branches. Combatant units were, raised from the Madrassis, but the problem was acquiring trained and experienced Madrassi VCOs (viceroy's commissioned officers like jemadar, subedar/resaldar, and subedar-major/resaldar-major) and NCOs (noncommissioned officers like naik/lance-dufadar, havildar/kot-dufadar, and havildar-major/dufadar-major) for these units.[49] Historian William Arthur rightly notes that the martial race theory taken in its own time represented the most modern military thinking of the day. Race-based recruiting was not seen at that time as antithetical to modernity. Rather, race-based recruitment was the most modern model that had been devised gradually in order to ensure the operational effectiveness of the army.[50]

John Keegan writes that men fight due to the concept of male honor as judged by their immediate comrades, because of inducements, or because of coercion.[51] Ethnic pride, clan, class, and territorial ties motivated the men within the Indian units. Because most of the jawans were illiterate or semiliterate, they have left us with little written material about their military experiences. However, some of the letters written by the Indian soldiers from France during the First World War have survived. In these letters, while the Sikhs emphasized their martial religious ethos, the Rajputs harped on their tradition of being a fighting caste. For the Rajputs, their *Kshatriya* bearings demanded that they sacrifice their lives on the battlefield. *Kshatradharma* (religion of the *Kshatriyas*) lays down that fighting and dying in the battlefield is honorable and ensures a straight road to paradise. Garwahlis noted the reputation of their families, which had provided soldiers for three generations. Jat combat prowess stemmed from their concept of *namakhalali* (loyalty to the salt giver). Since they had eaten the salt of the *sarkar* (GoI), they were supposed to remain loyal to the British. The Dogras on somewhat similar lines believed that *dharma* required remaining loyal to their salt giver (employer—i.e., GoI) and if one dies in the battlefield, then one goes straight to heaven. For the Pathans, fighting prowess was related to the pride of their clans. The Punjabi Muslims stressed their *izzat* (personal honor). Historian David Omissi writes that *izzat* refers to honor, reputation, credit, and prestige. Fame was linked with *izzat*. If a man performed valorous deeds that raised his *izzat*, he might be spoken of and remembered even after his death. The soldiers were also aware that they should fight well to uphold the prestige of their battalions.[52] The IJA also emphasized individual honor. The Field Service Regulations of 1941 enjoined the Japanese soldiers to avoid the disgrace of being taken prisoner.[53] The British built upon sentiments of individual honor and religious pride and created ethnic units. For motivating the troops, the British absorbed the traditional war cries of the various ethnic groups. The war cry of the Pathans was "*bal, bal bal.*" And the war cry of the Sikhs was "*Fateh Guru or Wa Guru.*" The war cry of the Punjabi Muslims was "*Allah, Allah.*"[54]

What about combat motivation of the Japanese soldiers? Some (especially sons of the veterans) fought to uphold family honor, others merely to survive another day, and most due to "buddy feelings"—that is, to support their comrades. Historian Edward J. Drea writes that vertical solidarity between junior leaders (sergeants and lieutenants) and the conscripts played an important role in combat motivation. In addition, tough training (an aspect that we will study later), army indoctrination (absent in the Indian Army), and small-unit leadership raised the cohesiveness of the Japanese units.[55] The Japanese armed forces did not award medals or other citations to its personnel for performing heroic deeds.[56] Japanese soldiers were fanatical. In general, they never surrendered. This was because captivity was regarded as the ultimate disgrace, and they would be social outcasts if they ever returned home.[57] The "will to war" of the Japanese soldiers was partly the product of training. The IJA inculcated devotion to the emperor. Constant ceremonies highlighted loyalty to the emperor.[58] Training was indeed harsh in the Japanese armed forces. Saburo Sakai, who joined as a seaman at the age of sixteen in the Sasebo Naval Base in 1933, noted that life was of monstrously harsh discipline and severity beyond his wildest nightmare. Such harsh discipline was beyond the imagination of the Westerners. For small breaches of discipline, beatings by the officers were common. Their aim was to terrorize the recruits.[59] Sakai writes: "We were automatons who obeyed without thinking."[60] Further, violence in the barracks (beating of privates by the officers for the slightest indiscipline) was institutionalized.[61]

The British, being an alien ruling power, could not use the national sentiment of the Indians. So they had to utilize the hereditary fighting traditions of a caste or a tribe to sustain the morale of the Indian soldiers. The Indian Army thus encouraged tribal prejudices and caste exclusiveness. The British officers' technique of motivating the Indian soldiers was to pamper their parochial vanity and respect the peculiarities of different communities.[62] Nirad C. Chaudhuri, a Bengali scholar, asserts that the caste system within the Indian Army was more rigid than that which operated in Indian society. The different ethnic groups were distributed in various units in such a way that they retained local communal and tribal loyalties.[63] Stephen Peter Rosen, an American political scientist, writes that the British separated the Indian Army from Indian society by constructing regiments from a number of self-contained, inward-looking military communities with their own languages and habits. These self-contained units were separated from each other linguistically, sociologically, and geographically. An army so divided cannot conduct a coordinated campaign against an external enemy.[64] We will analyze the construction of Indian units in some detail below.

The Indian infantry battalions were organized as class units and as class company units. A class battalion comprised a particular ethnic group from a particular region. The Gurkha Rifles were class units. A class company unit comprised two to four ethnic communities organized into different companies. The 2nd/35th Sikhs was a class company battalion. It had two Sikh companies and two Jat companies. Another class company battalion was the 2nd/72nd Punjabis which had two Sikh companies, one Pathan company, and one Punjabi Muslim company.[65] The different ethnic groups were not mixed within a company. Each ethnic community in a particular company was officered by VCOs drawn from that particular community. The VCO functioned as a link between the junior British commissioned officers and the jawans. The VCOs led platoons and sections and also managed the interior economy of the units. Class units were more cohesive and combat effective. However, the British maintained class company units as part of their *divide et impera* policy. As Molesworth puts it, "absence of homogeneity in India as regards race, religion, language . . . militates against mixing of classes indiscriminately. Northerners are foreigners in the south and vice versa."[66] Organization of the different communities within a battalion prevented the emergence of any potential anti-British feeling within the different Indian communities. And the British continuously encouraged competition among the different communities within a battalion. Commanding a class company unit was a problem, as the British officers had to be fluent in the different vernaculars of the men. Still, the British maintained them as part of political security. So the British made a compromise between political security and military efficiency. Expanding the class community battalions was time consuming. The recruits could not be simply inducted wholesale into the units. Different communities had to be integrated into the different companies, and VCOs of a particular community were required to be their officers.

Again, the policy of GoI was that men from a particular locality should be serving in a particular unit. The aim was to allow friends and relatives to serve in the same battalion. One assumption was that a jawan would think twice before displaying cowardice for the fear that it would be reported by his peer group back in his village where he would then lose face. Soldiers who had behaved dishonorably on the battlefield might also feel shame when they returned home. Omissi writes that shame was infectious and could be passed from the soldier to his immediate family. The people of his village would be disgusted by his shameful behavior.[67] The second assumption was that men who knew each other would develop a better cohesion and would fight well. Sociologist Anne Hoiberg writes that group cohesion was strong when individuals knew each other and had similar background experiences.[68] The ancient Chinese theoretician Wei Liao-Tzu, around 200 BCE, noted: "Ensure that the members of the squads of five and ten are like relatives, the members of the companies and their officers like friends."[69] The British regiments, like the Indian ones, had the characteristics of being an extended family. Family connections existed among many members of a particular regiment. Many men followed their grandfathers, fathers, and brothers into the regiments.[70]

In May 1940 it was decided that to obtain the maximum efficiency in the new units as quickly as possible, the existing units were to be "milked" of trained personnel.[71] It was accepted that this would result in the existing units being in a fluid state for some time.[72] Officers, NCOs, and privates needed to stay together long enough to create a feeling of belonging and pride and to establish a relationship of trust, which is an essential component of combat effectiveness.[73] But milking increased personnel turbulence, which in turn reduced combat effectiveness. Milking was not unique to the Indian Army. When Napoleon Bonaparte created new units, the freshly created units had to be provided with a kernel of veterans. So some seasoned soldiers were mixed with the draftees.[74] This process of milking was going on in the Indian Army on a large scale when the Japanese struck in Malaya in December 1941.

The most important duty of the Indian Army before the Second World War was to launch repeated punitive expeditions along the North-West Frontier against the frontier tribes for protecting the Raj. Infantry and pack mules dominated frontier warfare. Close cooperation between the infantry and mountain artillery characterized such operations.[75] The Gurkhas excelled in mountain craft.[76] Light infantry drills, in accordance with which all movements were executed with extreme speed and a minimum of orders, characterized training of the battalions.[77] During the 1919–20 Waziristan Campaign, the Indian troops became proficient in digging trenches, the use of hand grenades, Stokes Mortars and were efficient with bayonets. They were excellent rifle shots and knew the use of terrain.[78] However, in Malaya where such combat techniques would have been useful, battles were fought not by the troops who were proficient in North-West Frontier warfare but by raw, untrained soldiers.

The biggest operational experience of the Indian Army during the interwar period was the 1936–37 Waziristan Campaign. In total fifty-two infantry battalions were used. About seven thousand Wazir tribesmen supported by five thousand Afghans who had crossed India's borders took part in the anti-Raj uprising. The tribesmen put up roadblocks, ambushed the road-bound convoys, mined the roads, and often constructed booby traps with grenades.[79] The tribesmen's tactics involved sniping from the heights. The Waziristan Campaign involved some amount of crude infantry-air cooperation. Two infantry brigades, light tanks, and armored cars along with aircraft constituted the KHAICOL (the brigade-size assault column). KHAICOL, provided with close air support (CAS), advanced through the Khaisora Valley. Six RAF squadrons participated, and they conducted reconnaissance, aerial photography, supplying and reinforcing of the isolated garrisons, etc. This was also possible because the RAF faced no aerial opposition. However, in Malaya no attempt was made to initiate training for cooperation between the RAF and the Allied battalions. TOCOL comprised two infantry battalions and a cavalry squadron. It was supported by bombings carried out by the RAF as it moved over uneven terrain to join hands with RAZCOL (an assault column comprising several battalions), which had four battalions and three mountain batteries. Brigadier (later Major General) B. W. Key was in the TOCOL.[80] He would later command the Indian troops in Malaya. In the Waziristan Campaign, the Argylls did not perform well. In one encounter they lost nine men and left the dead bodies of their comrades behind. In North-West Frontier warfare, the soldiers always brought back the dead bodies of their comrades to prevent their mutilation and give them a proper burial.[81] The Argylls later fought in Malaya. Of the 61,000 troops plus the RAF units and the mechanized tank companies deployed for military operations and in road building in Waziristan, the Indian Army had 245 killed and 684 wounded, and another 73 died from diseases.[82] The Waziristan Campaign proved that in the rugged terrain, the role of heavy artillery and armored cars was limited. But the twelve Vickers-Berthier and eight Vickers machine guns carried by each Indian battalion proved useful.[83] Sniping, booby traps, and establishment of roadblocks as practiced by the Wazirs were techniques used by the Japanese in Malaya. But most of the Indian soldiers deployed in Malaya-Singapore were newly recruited rookies, not experts of North-West Frontier warfare.

Unlike the Indian Army, the IJA had experience conducting large-scale conventional warfare in China and Russia. The battles in which the IJA engaged in these two countries had been bloody. In 1937, there were 200,000 Japanese troops in north China. In total, there were some 600,000 Japanese soldiers in China.[84] In late March 1938, the IJA sent forces to Taierchwang in China. In April of the same year, the 60,000 strong Japanese forces suffered some 40,000 casualties.[85] By mid-1940, the IJA had 850,000 troops in China.[86] The command system and doctrine of the Indian Army to a great extent mirrored those of the British Army and are the subjects of the next section.

Command and Doctrine

A coherent and realistic doctrine is a must for waging war successfully. Doctrine shapes command and training. It integrates and institutionalizes the tactical methods.[87] The British doctrine and command were designed for waging attrition warfare. Attritionalism means attempts to achieve victory by harnessing the weight of metal. It rests on deliberate formalized decision-making cycles.[88] The Allied command system involved giving direct orders in great detail, instead of the subordinates sizing up the tactical scenario and operating in accordance with their initiative.[89] Attrition requires the enemy to be willing or obliged to fight on the same terms.

The Japanese, by changing the rules of the game, fought on different terms. The Japanese conducted maneuver warfare. Maneuver war means concentrating force to achieve surprise, psychological shock, physical momentum and moral dominance over the enemy. The aim is to unhinge the enemy's plan and to shatter the cohesion and will to fight. It involves doing the unexpected by using initiative, creativity, and a ruthless determination to succeed. Maneuver war aims to defeat the enemy by destroying his will and desire to continue fighting through seizing the initiative and applying constant and unacceptable pressure at times and places where the enemy least expects.[90] The Japanese tactical doctrine was based on offensive action implemented with determination coupled with the speed of maneuver to disrupt the hostile forces. Surprise, thorough reconnaissance, infiltration, and envelopment, were principal features of their attack.[91]

Historian Martin Samuels writes that German military philosophy viewed combat as inherently chaotic, and the road to success lay in the ability to operate effectively in this uncertain environment. In contrast, British combat philosophy emphasized structure. The British military philosophy assumed that combat is inherently structured, and effectiveness could be achieved through the maintenance of order.[92] Human beings conduct warfare in the real world, where actions reflect chance and nonlinear factors. The behavior of a military system in combat is unpredictable and chaotic. A stable military system with regular, simple, and predictable dynamics is an exception to the rule. Human affairs, especially during combat, involve innumerable independent variables. So reductionist solutions are useless. The objective should be to bring order out of chaos.[93] And this is what German philosophy for maneuver warfare attempted to achieve.

Maneuver war on the part of the Germans involved sudden and violent action geared to dislocate one part of the enemy's structure in the first stage. Dislocation means displacement and disarrangement of parts causing disorder. The second stage involved the enemy's reaction to his early dislocation. The third stage involved a second violent attack at another point. And the enemy, having committed his reserves, cannot react effectively to this new threat. The final stage involved further actions to maintain the pressure and to prevent the enemy from gaining composure.[94] The German doctrine concentrated on exploitation, speed, leadership from the front, and a combined-arms approach. It focused on an offensive mind-set and decentralization of authority; officers, including the NCOs, were required to show judgment and initiative.[95]

The random and fluid nature of maneuver warfare creates a wide variety of opportunities that appear and disappear suddenly. To utilize these opportunities, a decentralized command system that can ensure rapid movement and small-unit initiative is necessary. Only then can these fleeting advantages be converted into battlefield success. However, a command system that is centralized and is based on rigid schedules for achieving objectives cannot utilize such fleeting opportunities. The requirement to exploit the fleeting opportunities was an essential part of the German philosophy of combat.[96]

On the other hand, in accordance with the British philosophy of combat, the focus was on centralized planning. The seizure of fleeting opportunities would disrupt this process, and hence it was rejected. The British command was unsuitable to maintain a high tempo, which is a must for waging maneuver war.[97] Tempo means rate or rhythm of activity relative to the enemy. Tempo at the tactical level is the rate of activity relative to the enemy within engagements and at the operational level is the rate of activity relative to the enemy between the engagements. High tempo is achieved by a fast decision-action cycle (the so called Observe-Orientate-Decide-Act [OODA] Loop or Boyd's Loop).[98] Victory would go to the side that acted through the loop first. So basically tempo means making fast decisions and maintenance of pressure on the enemy, giving the latter no time to react comprehensively so that the enemy is unable to recover his balance.[99]

Maintenance of tempo, a sine qua non for waging maneuver warfare, requires decentralized command. Decentralization of decision making is required to speed up response, while referral of decisions to higher authority is always a time-consuming process. While the German command system was based on directive/mission-oriented command, the British command system was based on restrictive control and umpiring. The directive control command system is based on decentralized decision making. Commanders at every level are assigned general tasks and then allowed to complete their tasks by means of their own initiative within the context of the whole. Commanders act on their own initiatives and are guided rather than driven by their superiors. The principal characteristics are flexibility, independence, and initiative. Conversely, the restrictive command system is based on centralized decision making. The commanders are assigned detailed missions that they are to carry out exactly as prescribed. The principal characteristics are rigidity, conformity, and reliance on exact orders.[100]

Operating a decentralized command system requires a high level of training of both the individuals and the units. Successful tactics for maneuver war emphasize adaptability to circumstances and rapidity of response. In contrast, a centralized command system emphasizes the development of rigid obedience, and tactics are characterized by standard solutions and detailed advance planning.[101] The basic Japanese tactic involved extreme decentralization. A small unit or even an individual soldier was given an objective.[102] Orders were issued orally for attacking specific objectives.[103] The Japanese were reluctant to make a frontal push but attempted to gain their objective from the flanks.[104] The Japanese laid great stress on offensive actions, surprise, and rapidity of movement, with all commanders and staff operating well forward in order to keep themselves constantly informed of the changing situation. Japanese training emphasized seizure and retention of the initiative, bold and independent action by the subordinate commanders, and prompt and energetic leadership. The Japanese commanders issued fragmentary operational orders to initiate deployment of the troops. Japanese combat regulations warned the commanders against waiting for detailed orders before attacking. Orders were brief and to the point. The divisional commander, instead of making detailed plans, decentralized control to his subordinates, and the latter were encouraged to display their initiatives in attacking the enemy.[105] The Japanese were probably influenced by the German command and tactical system. The Army War College at Minato in Tokyo was founded in 1882 and was modeled on the Prussian War Academy. Lieutenant General Yamashita, who led the invasion of Malaya, had attended this college.[106]

Lieutenant General Heath, CO of the III Indian Corps, points out the shortcomings of the British officers in the following words: "Most Pre War trained officers were imbued with Pre War Text Book procedure for the conduct of withdrawal. Where they failed was not in lack of knowledge of the accepted procedure but in their failure to make an appreciation of the situation taking into full consideration every factor; and the situation in Malaya introduced factors to which their Pre War training had been foreign."[107] Similarly, Field Marshal Alanbrooke, CIGS of Britain, during September 1941 noted in his diary: "Training is far too stereotyped to fit in with varying conditions of possible operations."[108] In a mission-oriented command system, the subordinates are to adapt to the local situations, exploiting each and every opportunity to the maximum, always aiming to further the overall intent to the best of their ability and allowing their own initiative full play rather than merely implementing orders from above.[109] This characteristic was missing among the British officers in Malaya. On the other hand, German combat leadership was superior because the officers of the Wehrmacht were capable of displaying great capacity for independent action, avoidance of a fixed pattern of action, and the ability to make complete, clear, and unambiguous decisions.[110] And we have seen that the IJA also encouraged a somewhat similar decentralized command system. *Auftragstaktik* (mission-oriented command) encouraged the lower-echelon commanders to exploit local opportunities. In line with this approach, training of the officers emphasized initiative, a risk-taking attitude, and leading from the front at all levels.[111]

After the First World War, the United Kingdom allowed the entry of ten Indian cadets annually to the Royal Military Academy Sandhurst. After 1928, twenty Indians were allowed entry to Sandhurst annually.[112] From 1932 onward, Indian officers were trained at the Indian Military Academy (IMA) at Dehra Dun. They spent thirty months at IMA, with the course mirroring Sandhurst except in length. Probably, the training at IMA was better compared to Sandhurst, especially in the inculcation of tactical skills. Even at Sandhurst competition was fierce for entering the Indian Army, as only the top 60 officers who passed out of Sandhurst could apply for the Indian Army. Thus, the Indian Army was no backwater. By 1939, 60 Indian officers and 120 British officers were commissioned annually into the Indian Army.[113] In 1939, the Indian Army's officer corps comprised 1,912 British and 344 Indian officers.[114] The problem about the Indian units in Malaya was that due to the raising of new units, most of the battalions had lost the bulk of the prewar trained officers. Patrick Rose asserts that in the interwar period, the Indian Army during its campaigns in the North-West Frontier encouraged initiative and flexibility among the junior commanders. The junior officers were trained to act at least one level above their rank. However, employment of ad hoc higher tactical organizations and geographically defined administrative regional headquarters to control major operations proved to be a weakness. The absence of formal executive command structures to institutionalize the trend toward decentralized command culture was a grave failure on the part of the Indian Army.[115] At least, leading from the front was part of the command culture of the Indian Army. And when the British officers and VCOs displayed heroic command, the jawans fought well. However, a point of caution is necessary. Captain Mohan Singh of the 1st/14th Punjab notes in his memoirs that not all the British officers took the profession of soldiering seriously. Most of them spent their time in drinking and dancing.[116]

Major General Gordon Bennett, CO of the 8th AIF Division, noted that the British tactical doctrine was based on the First World War template of demolishing the enemy with massive artillery fire and then advancing the infantry under artillery cover.[117] In addition, British military doctrine held the infantry in low esteem. The success of heavy artillery in smashing the German lines on the Western Front during the First World War and the success of German armor in the initial period of the Second World War blinded the British military establishment to the importance of infantry. The British military failed to realize that in German doctrine infantry remained the principal arm, and all the other arms supported it.[118] And this resulted in a combined arms maneuver. Especially in jungle warfare, as we will see, the infantry remained the queen in the battlefield. The next section focuses on training.

Training

Training is the life blood of an army. Soldiers obey orders due to the conditioning process that is inculcated through training. Training leads to habituation and helps the soldiers to overcome fear. It emphasizes repetition. Through training, the soldiers practice their individual duties repeatedly until they have been learnt so well that the soldiers can perform them by rote under the most frightful and distracting circumstances.[119] Hew Strachan writes that training creates unit cohesion. The value of sending into action a group of men who have trained together and who are commanded by officers who have been responsible for this process is remarkable. Training functions as a force multiplier. A clear-cut suitable doctrine is essential for laying down an efficient and coherent training regime. And a doctrine is implemented through training. Training allows soldiers to assimilate new tactical thinking to the point where it becomes instinctive in its application.[120]

This section argues that the Allied troops were not prepared for jungle warfare. Jungle warfare in this volume broadly includes combat in dense, thick jungle, scrub, bush, mangrove swamps, and rubber plantations. Jungle warfare required both unique tactical methods and certain principles derived from warfare in general. Monsoon rain, mostly falling in torrential downpours, results in dense evergreen rainforest.[121] Over 72 percent of the terrain of the Malayan Peninsula was covered with jungle.[122] Malaya Command never issued a doctrine that emphasized jungle warfare. A few units autonomously conducted some jungle training exercises.[123] Brigadier W. Carpendale, CO of the 28th Indian Brigade, noted that the Malaya Command did not bring out a training manual that discussed minor tactics for jungle warfare. Rather, each formation was expected to come up with some idea.[124] And most of the unit commanders accepted the Malaya Command's dictum that the jungle was impassable.[125] We will see that not only were the Allied units badly trained, but worse, they were trained for the wrong war.

Just before the Second World War, Western ignorance and contempt resulted in serious underestimation of the IJA. John Ferris, a historian, writes that the British observers judged the IJA by its ability to fight in Europe, and not in Asia. He continues: "By 1941, they measured Japanese and British quality by the standard of western Europe rather than eastern Asia; and assumed that this standard and these rankings would prevail in a third environment, that of south-eastern Asia."[126] Between 1937 and 1941, the IJA's tactical standard improved, and it fought well against the Chinese. But, due to mixture of racism and ethnocentrism, the British military observers concluded that the IJA's successes in China were due to the inferior fighting capability of the Chinese armies.[127] The Japanese soldiers were regarded as slow witted with poor eyesight, poor marksmen, and almost blind at night.[128] The 11th Indian Division assessed the IJA as between the Italian and the Afghan armies in terms of military effectiveness.[129] This sort of attitude seeped in among the British officers in Malaya. Harbakhsh Singh, a burly Sikh (in independent India he would rise to the position of lieutenant general) who was company commander of 5th/11th Sikhs deployed in Malaya, notes in his autobiography: "Many British and Commonwealth generals visited us, and gave talks in which they mostly derided the Japanese soldiers as bandy-legged and with poor eye sight who daren't attack the British."[130] Gordon Bennett believed that the Japanese would be untrained.[131] Such an attitude probably resulted in the absence of rigorous realistic training of the Allied soldiers in Malaya. However, they were in for a rude shock when the Japanese capability of fighting in the swampy and forested terrain became evident as the Malaya Campaign unfolded.

Combat, especially in jungle conditions, required a high level of endurance. High heat and high humidity quickly enervated and exhausted physically unfit men.[132] Both Gordon Bennett and Major H. P. Thomas, who commanded the Mixed Reinforcement Camp at Singapore, noted that the Japanese in contrast to the Allied troops displayed a higher level of endurance. Thomas goes on to argue that because the British were from a society with higher living standards, they failed to exhibit the same toughness which the Japanese, coming from a society with poor living standards, were able to display. The Japanese were able to live frugally on rice and fish. Thomas goes on to say that though both the Japanese and the Indians were being drawn from a poorer society with low material consumption, the Japanese proved to be tougher than the Indians. Bennett and Thomas conclude that due to racial reasons, the Indians were softer than the Japanese.[133] Actually, the issue has nothing to do with economic conditions of the society from which the soldiers were drawn or with racial reasons. The Germans, despite being drawn from a society with high material standards, displayed toughness on the Eastern Front. Training imparted toughness and hardiness among the soldiers. The real problem was lack of general training, and especially specialized jungle training, of the Allied troops. The Japanese were superior because they possessed general training and also specialized training as individual jungle fighters.

The Japanese tactical doctrine, which was geared for conducting combat in North Asia, had certain general principles that were also applied by them while fighting in tropical conditions. The field service regulations emphasized the inherent superiority of offense and noted that even when a commander had to be on the defensive due to enemy action, he should strive for gaining the initiative by launching offensive action. Envelopment was the preferred Japanese offensive maneuver. This was accompanied by a determined frontal pressure while the main force attacked the flank. Depending on conditions, the Japanese carried out both single and even double envelopment. Even when suffering from numerical inferiority, utilizing speed and surprise, the Japanese carried out double envelopment. The attacking units did not try to retain a rigid alignment but pressed ahead at all costs. The Japanese had a penchant for carrying out nocturnal attacks. Finally, the combat and training manuals emphasized attacking through the terrain generally considered impassable in adverse weather conditions, to achieve surprise in the direction and time of attack.[134]

In addition, the IJA also took certain steps to inculcate specialized training for tropical conditions. Colonel Masanobu Tsuji, the aggressive, obstinate, bald-headed officer who had served in Manchuko and China, was the director of Planning and Operations Staff under Lieutenant General Yamashita, CO of the Twenty-Fifth Japanese Army during the Malaya Campaign. He emphasizes that only in September 1941 did the IJA start preparing for the "big push" to the south.[135] In his memoirs, Tsuji writes: "Prior to the outbreak of war in the Pacific, I was a staff officer of Imperial General Headquarters, and at the end of 1940 was assigned to prepare plans for operations in Malaya. Just before the actual commencement of hostilities there, we carried out maneuvers in tropical warfare in southern Indochina."[136] At Taipei (capital of Taiwan), on New Year's Day in 1941, the Taiwan Army Number 82 Unit (Taiwan Army Research Section) was established. Under the direction of General Itagaki, chief of staff to the commander in chief of Japanese forces in China, Tsuji was appointed as the officer in charge of the Research Department of the Taiwan Army.[137]

Tsuji notes that the Japanese soldiers had experience in conducting war in the cold regions of Manchuria but not in the hot and humid jungle areas. The Doro

Nawa Unit (also known as the Taiwan Army Research Department) first collected data about the tropical areas. In addition, Tsuji had to deal with the organization of army corps, equipment, sanitation, supply, military strategy, tactics, and geography. Tsuji's area of responsibility included, besides Malaya, the Philippines, Indonesia, and also Burma. Tsuji had six months to complete his job. Only 20,000 yen was accorded to the research unit.[138] He brought in professors from the Japanese university in Taiwan, who briefed his team on tropical diseases and hygiene.[139] The Doro Nawa Unit with thirty people on its staff came out with an instruction book on tropical warfare for Japanese soldiers. Tsuji writes that the maps of Malaya available with the Japanese were inaccurate, small-scale publications. However, Tsuji and his men concentrated on the geographical details of the theater intensely while preparing the campaign plan.[140] For conducting jungle warfare in the tropics, the Japanese put great emphasis on reconnaissance through aerial photography, employment of agents, fifth columnists, and reconnaissance patrols.[141] Tsuji himself flew from Saigon on two aerial reconnaissance missions over the Malayan Peninsula in late October 1940.[142]

Malaya was thickly covered with vegetation. The dense forest in some regions was difficult to penetrate, but in other parts heavy timber was penetrated by men and animals. Rice was grown in the north of the Malayan Peninsula and also along the west coast. In addition, there were regions covered with coconut plantations. A large area was covered with rubber plantations. In the center and in parts of the north, there were tin-mining areas. The climate was humid and enervating.[143] Jungle war in Malaya included combat in the swampy coastal creeks covered with sparse vegetation, grass-covered areas, rubber plantations, and the outskirts of tropical forest. The British introduced rubber trees into Malaya. The plantation managers were mostly British and Australians. The employees were all Tamils and Ceylonese. The road within the rubber estates traversed the plantations in a crisscross pattern. The jungle started from the edges of the plantation. There were several fast-flowing rivers in Malaya, and thick mangrove forests grew on their banks.[144] The Allied troops were not allowed to train along the rubber plantations because of the objection of the governor and the London government.[145]

Gordon Bennett describes the jungle-covered landscape in Malaya in the following words:

> It is everywhere dark, damp and steamy, with tangling vines and undergrowth tying together the giant trees which stretch themselves upward reaching for the light of heaven. To the newcomer, the jungle is fearsome, frightening. Its deathly silence is broken by the soft drip-drip from the hanging foliage, or by the crack of a twig as some strange wild animal sneaks about in search of prey.... Now and then a heavy tropical rainstorm darkens the already dark twilight, and streams of water pour down the tree-trunks, making the ground more marshy than ever, and the deep leafy mould which covers it soggy and steamy, filling the air with a pungent odour of decay.[146]

Malaya receives about two hundred inches of rainfall per year. And the campaign unfolded during the monsoon season.[147] There were innumerable roads and tracks through the jungles and rubber plantations.[148] And the fact that the Japanese could approach the Allied defensive positions through them was neglected by the British and Australian commanders and their troops due to unimaginative training.

In the interwar period, the training of the British Army's regular cadre was defective, especially as regards combined arms maneuver. Imperial commitments like policing duties in India in the 1920s and early 1930s prevented large-scale formation exercises. The focus was on fighting insurgencies rather than high-intensity conventional war. Further, most of the exercises held by the British Army were stage managed. The exercises focused on staff work and administrative duties rather than the practice of actual frontline combat. The umpires failed to impose tactical realism, encourage excellence, and discourage incompetence. The attacks during the exercises tended to be set piece affairs, and mopping up (hand-to-hand combat) was neglected.[149] In addition, rapid expansion of the British Army between 1939 and 1941 resulted in dilution of its trained prewar cadre, which seriously reduced the military effectiveness of the British Army.[150] The second principle also holds true for the Indian Army, which underwent rapid expansion between 1940 and 1942.

Historian Timothy Harrison Place asserts that during the Second World War, most of the recruits in the British Army were townsmen with little of the instinct in fieldcraft that was present in the men raised in the countryside and used to stalking wild animals. Further, the influx of socially less well-connected officers from a lower social background and unversed in field sports exacerbated the problems of inadequate fieldcraft instinct. In general, the privates and the noncommissioned officers did not receive adequate training in minor tactics (single-arm tactics) and in fieldcraft. Overall, infantry-tank cooperation in the British Army remained substandard. And like the American infantry, the British infantry was unwilling to fight unless supported by a high volume of firepower. Further, like the Indian soldiers, the British troops were unwilling to fight when their officers became casualties. In actual combat, artillery fire and support from aircraft and medium machine guns could only neutralize but not destroy well-dug-in enemy troops. The latter's destruction required close-quarter combat by the infantry.[151]

Gordon Bennett accuses the obsolete British training system, which the Australians also followed. He writes that such training was suited for combat in the open desert with few natural obstacles and clear fields of fire rather than in the closed jungle country with lots of natural obstacles that resulted in limited visibility and fields of fire. Bennett asserts in his memoirs that from the very first, he realized that in the unique landscape of Malaya, a different sort of training for the troops was required. He had written that the manuals, clothing, and equipment of the troops were suited for a war in the European theater. The tactical methods were mostly shaped by combat in the desert of North Africa. But, concluded Bennett, jungle fighting required different tactical techniques.[152]

Jungle fighting required a lot of marching rather than motor transport. The British infantry battalions, unlike the IJA infantry, were not trained for long-term physical endurance exercises.[153] In September 1941, Alanbrooke admitted that the tails of British formations were far too large.[154] And this would cause a serious problem for the British in Malaya during 1941–42. The Allied troops, trained for deployment in Libya, Iraq, and Persia, were overburdened with motor transport. These troops had gone through an intensive course of motorization.[155] Motorization saved time and toil and won battles in the flat desert terrain but not in the jungle-clad swampy terrain. One journalist noted that the Allied troops had lost the art of marching. They expected transport to carry them from one place to another and also during retreat. The Allied infantry failed to develop light infantry techniques to get behind the hostile formations and conduct infiltration tactics.[156] Brigadier W. St. J. Carpendale, CO of the 28th Indian Brigade, noted that it was impossible to get the vehicles and carriers off the road into the rubber plantations on either side. The roads on either side had water-filled ditches. Again, in some regions the roads were surrounded with paddy fields, where the vehicles also could not operate. Carpendale realized that the troops had to get used to cutting their way through the thick jungles that existed on the high ground at some distance from the roads and beyond the rubber plantations and paddy fields.[157] But, in general, Allied troops in Malaya were not trained for such actions.

Fully supplied with ammunition and rations, a Japanese soldier carried a load of about sixty pounds.[158] Japanese soldiers were famous for making long marches. Their training emphasized marching. To give an example, the 2nd Company of the 7th Japanese Infantry Regiment at Kanazawa during 1934–35 would often march for fifty-six miles from five in the morning until ten in the morning of the next day.[159] Individual Japanese soldiers were trained hard in range practice, bayonet practice, and physical training.[160] Physical training, in comparison with the British army, seemed to be a bit better for the Australian troops. About them, one report stated: "Equipped with rifle, ammunition, bayonet, small haversack, water bottle and steel helmet, run at jog trot one mile, march two miles, run one mile, rest 15 minutes, run two miles, walk one mile, run one mile with sprint at this end and bayonet practice for five minutes. The majority finish the course which is a pretty severe test."[161] The American army, like the British and Indian armies, was not trained to march hard and fight hard. Colonel Milton A. Hill of the American army accepts this contrast with the Japanese in the following words: "Our pre-war training in marching and endurance, I think lacked reality most of all. The way to train troops for the rigors they are bound to meet sooner or later in war is to give them some actual practice, not only in making thirty or forty miles on foot, but in doing it hungry."[162] The Japanese training also emphasized outpost duty and patrol works.[163]

Lewis Heath noted after the Malaya campaign: "The superiority displayed by the picked and salted Japanese troops in close country fighting. . . . Whereas our own troops had no practical experience in fighting of any kind and had been sadly milked of officers, NCOs and peace trained men, the bulk of Japanese troops had been well bloodied in close country conditions in the China War. Furthermore, experience gained in China had been turned to good and practical account . . . its proper adaptation to the special needs of jungle warfare."[164] The Imperial

Guards Division under Lieutenant General Takumo Nishimura had men with good physical standards. However, this division had not seen any active service after the Russo-Japanese War.[165] The 5th and 18th Japanese divisions had combat experience in Russia and China.[166] The Japanese infantry was trained to conduct deep penetration and outflanking movements.[167] Tactically, the Japanese soldiers were trained to take great risks.[168] Heath accepted that the Japanese infantry displayed a marked superiority in fighting within the jungle and close country. Unlike the road-bound Australian, British, and Indian troops, the Japanese infantry was proficient in acquiring mobility by utilizing the numerous country bicycles in the almost roadless terrain of the Malayan Peninsula.[169]

It would be wrong to assume that the Japanese soldiers were specially trained in conducting jungle warfare for a long period. The Japanese infantry were just veteran, combat-experienced troops who, being well trained, were able to adapt to the jungle conditions of Malaya and Burma quickly and efficiently. The Japanese were trained in infiltration and outflanking the hostile positions. They were able to move through the enemy line in small parties and coalesce into larger groups behind the rigid and inflexible enemy line, thus threatening the hostile formations' rear communications.[170] The Japanese also improvised in jungle conditions. They became experts in climbing treetops and using them for sniping and reconnaissance of enemy positions.[171] Again, for deception purposes while moving through jungle country, the Japanese soldiers were brilliantly camouflaged. Their uniforms were dyed green to melt with the greenery in Malaya, and they had strips of metal sewn on for the purpose of inserting bushes. The soldiers' tin hats were also covered with greenery to make them as invisible as possible in closed country where visibility was low.[172]

The Japanese also used noise as a weapon to upset the morale of the enemy. It was aimed at disrupting the psychological balance of the defending soldiers. Their tactics were geared to create jitters/anxiety among the Allied troops (known as a jitter attack). They let off firecrackers and fired indiscriminately from unexpected directions and also at times shouted and howled. Before attacking they shouted and yelled a lot. Both in Malaya and in the Philippines, the Japanese used a sort of time bomb thrown from the mortar. On striking the ground, the bomb burst open and set off a fuse that fired intermittent explosives that sounded like machine-gun fire or a pack of firecrackers. All these had an unnerving effect on the raw and unseasoned Allied infantry. It required training on the part of the Allied soldiers to ignore eerie and uncanny noises made by the Japanese during the night. Again, the Japanese aerial tactic was to blanket an area by dropping twenty to thirty bombs simultaneously. The noise was very loud, and on the physically drained troops, the psychological effect was enormous. Allied soldiers who were under mortar and artillery fire became extremely uneasy after such aerial bombings.[173]

The techniques of aggressive patrolling and infiltration were taught in the Indian Army before the beginning of the Second World War.[174] However, such skills were diluted due to the rapid expansion of the Indian Army and subsequent entry of a large number of raw recruits between 1939 and 1941. For instance, between September 1939 and December 1942, the total number recruited in the Indian Army came to 1,348,000.[175]

Although Indian Army units deployed in Malaya underwent additional training on arrival in Malaya, it proved inadequate for the task at hand. The 8th Bareilly/Indian Brigade arrived in Malaya in October 1940. It was under Brigadier B. W. Key. This brigade was destined for North Africa and was going to Jhansi for training when it was ordered to proceed to Malaya. At Malaya, the 8th Indian Brigade was deployed in the beach area, and behind the beach were paddy fields and then jungle. In some areas, the jungle stretched up to the beach. Key's battalions lost 250 trained men, NCOs, and VCOs who went to India to act as a nucleus for new battalions that were then being raised. Their positions were filled by novice recruits who had fired barely fifty rounds. Communication between the British officers and the jawans was necessary for commanding and controlling the latter in the heat of battle. However, most of the young British officers had no knowledge of Hindustani, which was spoken by the jawans in this brigade.[176] The 9th Indian Division, which comprised the 8th and 22nd Indian brigades, had many jawans whose mother tongue was not Urdu. Verbal communication not only between the British officers and the Indian soldiers but even among different ethnic groups of Indian soldiers were a problem.[177] One aspect of command is leadership, and its function is to inspire and motivate the men to fight and die.[178] Inspirational leaders raise and sustain morale.[179] The jawans were willing to follow their officers to death if the latter won their trust.[180] The newly commissioned, inexperienced British officers, without any means of communicating with the Indian troops, and the new VCOs and NCOs (who in several cases failed to communicate even among themselves) failed to win the trust of the men they commanded and to inspire and motivate them in the battlefield. Key admits that he focused on beach defense but not on training for jungle warfare.[181] When the Japanese broke through the thin crust of the linear defensive line along the beach, the troops retreated and were lost in the jungle. Had they received jungle training, they could have harried the Japanese on the beach from the jungle. Since most of the personnel of the 8th Indian Brigade lacked regular/general training, they could not adopt specialized training and adapt to jungle warfare.

The 2nd/10th Baluch, which belonged to the 8th Indian Brigade, arrived at Singapore on 11 November 1940. Its camp under the rubber trees was dark, and it was continuously raining. The men were depressed. The battalion was given Bren Gun Carriers, and forty jawans were detailed for a six-week carrier course. About fifty VCOs and NCOs went back to India for raising new battalions. In December 1940, the battalion was moved into a camp that consisted of *attap* huts with wooden walls, concrete floors, and palm leaf roofs. This battalion trained in the use of two-inch and three-inch mortars, Bren Guns, and eighteen-pounders. But continuous loss of drafts to India for raising new units weakened the cohesion of the battalion.[182] And the new draftees had to be retrained again. When the officers conversed with the men in the latter's language, the soldiers responded with warmth.[183] But few British officers were able to speak their language. The linguistic difficulty of the new British officers badly affected the combat effectiveness of the 2nd/10th Baluch.[184]

The 5th/11th Sikh Regiment of the 22nd Indian Brigade had fought on the North-West Frontier. The men were physically fit. This battalion left Quetta in April 1939. All the officers commanding the companies were Indians. Harbakhsh Singh commanded the Manjha Sikh Company. The personnel of the 5th/11th were not jungle savvy. They were afraid of snakes.[185] The marshes in Malaya were filled with leeches and mosquitoes. And huge snakes hung on the undergrowth and slithered on the ground. Cobras, pythons, and kraits were common. In addition, there were hornets and scorpions.[186] Jungle fear was not unique among the 5th/11th Sikhs. While moving through the jungle, the personnel of 4th/19th Hyderabad (12th Indian Brigade) were horrified to find themselves covered with brown and black shiny leeches. They learned, however, to remove them by sprinkling them with salt or touching them with the end of lighted cigarettes or *bidis* (tobacco wrapped in a leaf).[187] The Australians were also afraid of giant frogs (8.5 inches at full size), scorpions, centipedes, huge huntsman spiders, and jumping spiders.[188] Before the departure of 5th/11th Sikh for Malaya in April 1941, this unit was milked thoroughly for new raisings, and 450 recruits with six new British officers who had no knowledge of Urdu, essential for communicating with the jawans, had joined. In October, this battalion lost another large bunch of officers—NCOs and jawans who left for India to raise a machine-gun battalion.[189]

The 28th Indian Brigade (2nd/1st, 2nd/2nd and 2nd/9th Gurkhas) was raised in April 1941 in Secunderabad as part of the 6th Indian Division. This division trained for duty in the Middle East. By early August, the units had completed platoon and battalion training and motor transport exercises.[190] As the troops were settling down at Ipoh, they were visited by staff officers of the III Indian Corps. Brigadier Carpendale notes: "I asked if unit representatives could be sent to a Jungle Warfare School. Was informed that such a School did not exist, and that it was not proposed to start one."[191] Let us evaluate the state of the component battalions of this brigade.

On 30 July 1941, the 2nd/1st Gurkha Rifles (GR) received six three-inch mortars and twenty-three Bren Guns. On 5 August, this battalion practiced defense of a part of the perimeter of the brigade "harbor." The men had improved the defense by digging their positions. Next day, this unit made a march of ten miles across the country. On 11 and 12 August, the men practiced firing the Bren and Tommy guns. The men also practiced with Thompson submachine guns. Compared to the other Indian battalions, the 2nd/1st GR was in a better state. The vehicles of this battalion were painted in dark and light green in order to merge with the jungle background. This was an exception because the vehicles of the other Indian battalions were not painted in jungle color for camouflage. However, the problem with this battalion was that it remained overdependent on trucks (fourteen 30 cwt Chevrolet lorries and fifty-four 15 cwt Ford trucks). And lorries would prove a burden in the roadless jungle terrain of Malaya. On the night of 24/25 August, this battalion with a strength of fifteen British officers, twenty-two VCOs, and 864 privates left Bombay for Malaya.[192]

The 2nd/9th GR arrived at Port Swettenham on the Straits of Malacca on 3 September 1941 with 750 jawans. Then, it moved to Taiping. The personnel were told that the jungle was impassable, and attempts to maneuver in the undergrowth would result in loss of control. Centralized top-down command culture of the British Army required tight control over the men by their officers during battle. It was further stated that the paddy swamps and mangrove forests would slow down any advancing troops.[193] And such a mode of tactical thinking along with the absence of antitank (A/T) rifles would prove detrimental during the actual campaign.

At least one battalion was partially prepared for jungle war. After their not-so-good experience in Waziristan, the 2nd Argylls came to Singapore in 1939 and became part of the 12th Indian Brigade. Many of the personnel were mature, unmarried soldiers aged twenty-five years with several years of service behind them. This battalion was blessed with the presence of senior NCOs. Untrained men quickly became exhausted in the hot and humid climate. Once lost in the jungle, they got mentally depressed. So Ian Stewart, the CO, took certain steps. Unlike the Gordons, the 2nd Argylls practiced long marching under sunlight. During one exercise, they covered 116 miles in eight days. While marching, the men were given hot sweet tea five times per day in order to give them an energy boost. The men were tasked to move at least one thousand yards every hour through the jungle. Again, the platoons were tasked with cutting their way through with machetes while moving through the jungle. In the jungle, the visibility was about thirty to forty yards, and there were few landmarks for navigation except the rivers and the tracks. The personnel learned to move through the jungle and rubber plantations with the aid of a compass and trained to travel through the jungle in single file. The front man cut the way with his *parang*, the second widened the path, and the third man checked the route with his compass. The men of the 2nd Argyll Battalion learned not to fear the jungle wildlife.[194] All this training would pay them good dividends during the Japanese invasion.

Belatedly, Malaya Command took some *ad hoc* steps to initiate brigade-level training. At Sungei Patani and Tanjong Pau, the 15th and 6th Indian brigades along with representatives of the 28th Indian Brigade were sent for training. They got some lessons in digging. Early in September 1941, the 28th Indian Brigade was visited by Percival. He lectured that any sea-borne invasion of Malaya was impossible and the Japanese would not be able to bring their troopships into the South China Sea because of Allied air and naval bases at the Philippines, Borneo, Java, Sumatra, and Malaya itself. Again, due to the monsoon, commented Percival, any landing along the east coast of Malaya would be impossible.[195] He could not have been more wrong.

Between mid-September and early November 1941, Carpendale, on his own initiative, tried to introduce platoon training aimed at moving confidently through close country with limited visibility. Both during day and night, the troops were trained to move through the jungle with the aid of a compass. The men tended to bunch together in semidarkness within the rubber plantations and in the jungle. It was drilled into their minds that the enemy could attack them from all sides at close quarters. So it was necessary to disperse. Some forms of training to overcome roadblocks were also initiated. Platoons and sections were informed of the necessity of carrying out envelopment and encircling movement in such cases. Flank protection was emphasized. The soldiers were warned of ambushes they might encounter in actual combat conditions. However, training in motor transport movement was also continued. Interestingly, the troops were trained to retreat with the aid of lorries supported by Bren Carriers. And Carpendale noted that armored cars were invaluable.[196] The British officers were unable to conceptualize the necessity of fighting and moving without motor transport. During actual fighting in the rubber country and in the jungles, the armored cars and Bren Carriers were just sitting ducks for the nimble Japanese infantry armed with mortars and grenades. Lack of VCOs and NCOs prevented thorough training of the 28th Indian Brigade. Erroneous assumptions regarding impenetrability of the jungles reduced the effectiveness of tactical training on the ground. When in the course of an exercise, the 2nd/9th GR slipped along an unguarded plantation track and lodged in the rear of the defending brigade, the umpires pronounced this move unreal.[197]

Whatever little training the III Indian Corps Headquarters conducted was unrealistic. In early November 1941, one such exercise was held in which the 12th and 28th Indian brigades participated. Carpendale was appointed as the chief umpire. The 12th Indian Brigade was designated as the Japanese force, which had landed at the beaches and was intent on moving inland. The troops were brought to the training areas in lorries instead of ordering them to march. And when there was rainfall, the exercise was stopped. When it was time for providing hot food to the troops, the exercise was stopped again. Again, the exercise was stopped at night so that the troops could get some sound sleep. In actual combat conditions, there might be rainfall and there might not be any opportunity to provide hot food regularly to the troops. The troops were supposed to carry two to three days' rations during such exercises. And the Japanese were proficient in launching nocturnal attacks. So resting during the night was out of question. Only in 1942, did the British Army in North Africa conduct training that continued during the night and also in adverse weather conditions. Again, the III Indian Corps' exercise focused on holding positions along the road when the center of attention should have been the surrounding countryside through which the Japanese would actually advance and attack. While holding road junctions and bridges, a system of in-depth defense was not created. The battalions were scattered in penny packets of platoons and sections. Lastly, infantry–artillery cooperation remained poor. The infantry either in attack or in defense failed to make use of field artillery, which remained at the rear.[198]

Like several Indian battalions, the 8th AIF had conducted some preliminary training in Australia in preparation for waging combat in the Middle East. In the densely vegetated region of Malaya, the effectiveness of long-range weapons and mechanical transport was nullified. Later in Malaya, training focused on proficiency with their personal weapons. During the exercise, Bennett realized that maintenance of communication and speedy transmission of information remained problematic.[199] This problem was not solved during the actual campaign. Timothy Hall writes that at the beginning of the Asia-Pacific War, most of the personnel of the Australian Military Force were neither disciplined nor trained.[200] This assertion applies to a great extent to Gordon Bennett's force also.

By November 1941, it dawned on at least certain British officers that the troops might be required to fight in jungle conditions. They would have to cross numerous streams and rivers by themselves. It was stressed that infantry might have to cross the water obstacles without the assistance of engineers. The infantry was taught to construct rafts with bamboos and ropes. Ropes were to be made from the creepers. Officers and men were taught to cut only the branches and not the trees in order to make a narrow passage for moving through the jungle. They were ordered to carry only rice for rations and learned to light fire without matches. This course was run at Grik. Before all the battalions could be instructed to go through this training, the war intervened.[201] The inadequate number of staff officers responsible for training was another handicap. Those who were present were themselves poorly trained and overburdened with other duties.[202]

On 25 April 1941, Percival asked the War Office and commander in chief, India, for an Indian Employment Platoon in order to train the Malayan recruits.[203] Due to rapid expansion of the Indian Army, the training establishments of India were incapable of training the Indian recruits properly. And the Indian Army, itself being unready, was not in a position to train the Malay recruits. The GOC Malaya's request was like a case of "the blind leading the blind."

The Allied units unnecessarily spent time in preparing for chemical warfare. As early as March 1941, Percival stressed to the War Office and commander in chief, India, that the troops must be prepared to counter chemical warfare, which might be practiced by the Japanese. Percival asked India to send some chemical warfare experts.[204] Like Percival, the 9th Indian Division also overreacted as regards the possibility of the Japanese conducting chemical warfare in Malaya. On 21 April 1941, the 9th Indian Division issued the following instructions: "Some units regard anti-gas training as a dull business and a regrettable nuisance. Such units may one day learn to their cost that their negligence has resulted in disaster to their own men. A thorough understanding by every individual of the measures necessary for personal decontamination and a high standard of anti-gas discipline are essential if casualties are to be avoided. Commanders of all grades must realize their personal responsibility in this matter and see that training is carried out on a systematic basis."[205] The 9th Indian Division warned its men that the IJA had practiced chemical warfare in China in 1937 and might use mustard gas in Malaya.[206] Overall, we see that the individual and collective training were inadequate. India Command had trained the troops for desert warfare, and Malaya Command wasted time in preparing for chemical warfare.

The last word goes to Field Marshal Archibald Wavell (commander in chief, India, and later Commander of ABDACOM), who noted:

> As regards troops of the 9th and 11th Indian divisions, any faults in their training and experience for the type of fighting to be anticipated must be laid at the door of

the Malayan Command rather than on India. Of the five infantry brigades in these two divisions, two had been in Malaya for 14 months before the outbreak of the Japanese war, one for thirteen months, one for nine months and one for 8 months; while the HQ of the 9th Division had been nine months in Malaya, and of the 11th Division 14 months. The 12th Indian Infantry Brigade had been in Malaya for over two years before the Japanese attack. Practically all the battalions in this brigade were pre-war battalions. It is true that these battalions had been subject to the process of "milking," to provide a nucleus of trained officers and men for the formation of fresh units; but the "milking" had been no more severe than, for instance, in the 4th and 5th Indian divisions, which succeeded in maintaining their standard of efficiency in the Middle East theater of war.[207]

Wavell was right in arguing that the Malaya Command was responsible for failing to impart the right kind of training to the Indian units. Proper training of the 4th and 5th Indian divisions had been able to ward off the negative effect of milking. But erroneous training plus the negative effect of milking generated a dangerous situation in the 9th and 11th Indian divisions. The next section of this chapter focuses on the arms with which the units were equipped.

Weapons

As regards equipment, Bennett notes in his account that jungle warfare demanded close quarter combat, and this in turn required short-range weapons like the Thompson submachine gun and mortars.[208] The Japanese infantry traveled lightly equipped with light automatic weapons and light mortars.[209] Their automatic light machine gun (LMG) was lighter than the British Bren Gun.[210] The Japanese Nambu LMG was a gas-operated, air-cooled, hopper-fed gun with a bipod support fixed near the muzzle. This gun could also be mounted on a tripod support for use against low-flying aircraft. And it weighted merely 22.4 pounds. The Japanese also had heavy machine guns that were air cooled. These weighted about 61.6 pounds.[211] The Japanese rifle, unlike the .303 of the British and Indian soldiers, had no recoil. This allowed the Japanese soldiers to use their rifles easily while lying down in the dense undergrowth of the Malayan terrain. Further, the Japanese were equipped with magnetic A/T grenades. Their A/T gun was like the British two-pounder but because of the shorter barrel was lighter.[212] The Japanese infantry was well trained to use mortars after their experience in China.[213] Their 90 mm mortar had a maximum range of 4,155 yards and threw a bomb weighing eleven pounds and ten ounces. The total weight of the weapon came to about 350 pounds and eight ounces. Further, for close infantry support, the Japanese had a light infantry battalion gun. The gun and its mount weighed 101 and 77 pounds respectively. The overall length of this weapon was five feet and the effective range was 1,500 yards. It fired ten rounds per minute.[214] This gun was handy and effective compared to the heavier British RA guns, which could not be moved easily across the jungle terrain of Malaya. The Japanese were liberally supplied with hand and discharger grenades. The Japanese marksmanship was not great. Rather, the Japanese fired blindly toward the enemy target. And the effect on "raw" Allied troops was devastating.²¹⁵ Overall, the Japanese made more use of machine guns, submachine guns, mortars, and grenades and not much use of artillery.²¹⁶ And in the relatively roadless jungle and swamp-covered terrain of Malaya, their relative lack of field artillery did not prove to be a disadvantage.

Against the Japanese light infantry armed with handy weapons, Percival had slow-moving infantry equipped with firepower-heavy weapons. Percival demanded eighteen-pounder guns for static beach defense of northeast Malaya and mobile A/T units. He was told that captured Italian Breda A/T guns would be sent to him from Egypt.²¹⁷ There was a shortage of rifles, pistols, and other equipment for the Indian troops in Malaya. On 1 June 1941, the commander in chief, India, informed Percival that India could provide rifles and pistols but not motorcycles for liaison purpose.²¹⁸ The Malaya Command was not improvising. Instead of motorcycles, the liaison officers could have used the country bicycles that were used later with great effectiveness by the Japanese soldiers during their invasion of Malaya. In fact, the Germans during their invasion of Norway had used bicycles for moving inland.²¹⁹

Let us move on to the state of weaponry of the Allied units. In July 1940, the CoSC had warned that the troops from India were on a lower scale of equipment compared to the standard level. The danger was that such troops might get involved in serious fighting. India could not provide mortars and A/T rifles to the newly raised units. And due to Britain's own needs and shipping difficulties, the War Cabinet was unable to equip these newly raised units fully.²²⁰ On 29 June 1940, the secretary of state for India warned the Indian contingents that these forces, though considerable, were extremely weak in artillery and in automatic weapons.²²¹

The 5th/11th Sikh Regiment was not issued any A/T mines. The Vickers-Berthier, which replaced the Lewis Gun and Sten Browning guns along with three-inch and two-inch mortars plus antipersonnel mines, were issued to this unit just before the Japanese invasion.²²² So one can presume that the men did not have much chance to train with their new "toys." Proper use of three-inch mortars could have been devastating to the Japanese, especially in close-quarter combat.²²³ Again adequate numbers of Bren Guns were not available. So, many Indian infantry units continued to use the Lewis Gun mounted in twins on a tripod for AA purpose. However, these guns proved worthless as they stopped firing after the first burst.²²⁴

The 28th Indian Brigade had some training in firing two-inch and three-inch mortars and Bren guns but not in using A/T rifles. In early September 1941, this brigade concentrated at Ipoh. Carpendale then requested ammunition to enable the troops to practice firing their weapons, but the ammunition for mortars and Bren Guns was received only in late October 1941. However, no tracer ammunition was supplied. So the brigade was not able to carry on AA practice firing.²²⁵ Only in early November, each company in this brigade received two two-inch mortars and the full complement of Bren Guns. Carpendale grimly noted: "It is considered that the majority of the men had to go into action having fired only the minimum amount of rounds from their weapons. Under such conditions can they have had the confidence in their weapons that they should have had?"²²⁶

As early as April 1941, the 9th Indian Division noted that a large number of personnel, especially those concerned with guarding the headquarters of various formations, were equipped with pistols. It was duly noted that pistols were almost useless and what was required instead were .303 rifles. But rifles as well as ammunition were in short supply in this division. It was estimated that between 1 April 1941 and 31 March 1942, the three infantry brigades (one of the brigades was later transferred to the 11th Indian Division) would be given seventy-five thousand rifles, another forty thousand for the divisional troops, and ten thousand pieces as reserve.[227] But the Japanese attacked before the allotment could be completed.

Let us analyze the weaponry carried by a British battalion. There were three platoons in a rifle company and four rifle companies in a battalion. In May 1940, a platoon comprised thirty-six men. By 1939, the Lewis Gun was replaced by the lighter Bren Gun in the platoon. Each platoon had three sections, each with one Bren Gun. Further, two-inch mortars were issued to the platoons. It fired smoke and high explosive rounds to a range of 470 yards. Each platoon had one such mortar in the platoon headquarters. The latter also had one Boys 0.55-inch A/T Rifle introduced in 1937. Each section (eight to ten men) was commanded by a corporal. The section commander carried a submachine gun, two men worked the Bren Gun, and the rest carried rifles. Each battalion had two three-inch mortars, which proved useful in jungle fighting.[228] But the 2nd Argylls lacked two-inch mortars in Malaya.[229]

Each British battalion had thirteen carriers armed with Bren Guns in a designated armored carrier platoon whose function was to provide the battalion with a mobile firepower reserve. Carriers were not combat vehicles, and the men were supposed to fire the Bren Gun dismounted except in an emergency. The carrier's armor was proof against normal small arms fire and not against armor-piercing projectiles. However, the carriers were also used for reconnaissance, transporting stores to the front, and carrying reinforcements to neutralize an enemy strongpoint.[230] In the roadless, swampy, jungle terrain of South-East Asia, Bren carriers as we will see, proved almost useless.

The Allied forces had no tanks in Malaya.[231] But the Japanese made excellent use of their light and medium tanks in supporting their infantry's rapid advance.[232] Tanks emerged during the latter part of the First World War to break the impasse of trench warfare. The demand was for a machine with a caterpillar track that could cross the trench covered with armor to protect the crew of the vehicle from enemy bullets. Two types of tanks emerged: infantry support vehicles and light tanks for reconnaissance and exploitation.[233] The tank was a weapon system designed to transform positional warfare into maneuver warfare by providing speed, surprise, and mobility and unnerving raw, untrained hostile troops.

The tactical doctrine of the IJA emphasized the decisive role of the infantry both in offence and in defense.[234] Tanks were used by the Japanese independently or in direct support of the infantry. Sometimes tanks were sent for distant raids.[235] The IJA had independent tank groups, each with 2,500 personnel and comprising three tank regiments. The IJA also had some independent tank regiments. Each tank regiment had three companies. The strength of an independent tank regiment varied from 500 to 800 men. Each company had five medium tanks and four light tanks.[236] The light Japanese tank Type 95 was armed with a 37 mm gun and Nambu Machine-Gun. A 3/4-inch armor belt protected the four-man crew. The tank could cover fifteen miles per hour.[237] The weight came to about 10 tons (loaded), length was about 14 feet 4 inches, width was about 6 feet 9 inches, and height was about 7 feet.[238] In Malaya, the Japanese used Type 95 tanks. They had proved useful in infantry support duties in Manchuria and China.[239] Another type of light Japanese tank weighed sixteen tons and carried a 57 mm gun and two 7.7 mm machine-guns. A third weighed eight tons and had a 32 mm gun and one 7.7 mm machine gun.[240] The oldest model of the Japanese medium tank was 89A of 1929 model. It had a 57 mm low-velocity gun with a 360-degree traverse in the turret. Its weight came to about 13 tons, length 19 feet 3 inches, width 7 feet 1 inch, and height 8 feet 6 inches. It had a four-man crew with a speed of fifteen miles per hour and a range of one hundred miles. This tank was able to clear a trench 8 feet 3 inches deep.[241] The tank columns were in the forefront of rushing Allied defensive positions, outflanking and outmaneuvering the British and Indian troops. There were motorable roads inside the rubber plantations through which the tanks were driven with ease.[242]

As early as 1937, Major General Dobbie, GOC Malaya Command, had requested tanks, and his successor Lionel Bond also repeated this request. On 10 January 1941, the Chiefs of Staff informed the commander in chief Far East that tanks could not be supplied nor was A/T artillery available, but A/T mines would be sent.[243] On 2 August 1941, Percival asked for one hundred tanks. Even in the first half of 1941, the British Army suffered from a shortage of two-pounder A/T guns. Toward the end of November 1941, the British Army's skill in antitank shooting was below average.[244] However, even an adequate amount of A/T mines were not available for the 9th Indian Division.[245] In total, the Japanese used about two hundred tanks during the Malaya Campaign. Only at Singapore was Percival able to deploy one squadron of obsolete light tanks, and only half of them were operational.[246]

Percival's army, however, possessed armored cars and Bren Carriers. The Bren Gun Carrier was armed with a Bren Gun, a .303 Vickers Machine Gun, and a .45 Thompson Machine Gun. There were two types of armored cars. The Lanchester Armored Car had two Vickers Machine Guns and a .5 A/T machine gun. The Marmon Armored Car had a Vickers Machine Gun and a .55 Boys A/T Rifle. It was a heavy, long-barreled rifle with a five-round, top-mounted magazine and fierce recoil.[247] About 175 Marmons were delivered to Malaya.[248] The armored cars' and Bren Carriers' armor was easily pierced by the armor-piercing bullets used by the Japanese riflemen.[249] Rather, a large number of wheeled vehicles that were unsuited for the Malayan terrain proved to be a burden for the Allied formations.[250] The Japanese had the Model 92 Osaka Armored Car armed with two light machine guns. Its speed was about thirty-seven miles per hour, and range of action was about 150 miles. It weighed about 6.4 tons, was about 16 feet 5 inches in length, 6 feet wide, and 8 feet 8 inches in height. It had a crew of four to five men and had an armor varying between 8 and 11 mm.[251]

Communication set up within the units was also bad. Key's 8th Indian Brigade's battalions lacked radios. Only the brigade headquarters had wireless but not the battalions.[252] Bennett, in his autobiography, notes that on 17 July 1941, Major General A. E. Barstow, CO of the 9th Indian Division, dined with him. This division was given the task of garrisoning Kota Bahru and Kuantan. However, Barstow lacked A/T and AA guns. Bennett wrote that defending some forty miles of front with a couple of battalions was a hopeless task for Barstow. Bennett made a prophecy that the situation would turn out to be like another Crete.[253]

During their invasion, the Japanese completely dominated the skies over Malaya. The Japanese air force was well trained both in providing CAS to the IJA and in conducting the counter-air campaign. Before the war, the British believed that the Japanese aircraft were obsolete and their pilots were unskilled.[254] However, the reality was different. The British had Brewster Buffalo fighters and Vildebeestes/Wildebeestes torpedo bombers. The Brewster Buffalo introduced in 1939 was inferior to the Japanese Mitsubishi A6M2 Zero/Zeke (Japanese Type O/Navy O fighter). With a maximum speed of three hundred miles per hour, it was twenty miles per hour slower than the Zero. Further, its rate of climb of 2,400 feet per second was poor compared to the Zero's 3,100 feet per second. And the Buffalo's range of 960 miles was less than that of the Zero. The Buffalo was armed with four .50-caliber machine-guns or two 30 mm guns and two 50 mm cannons.[255] The Brewster Buffalo was heavy and underpowered with a slow rate of climb. It lacked Very High Frequency (VHF) radio. The maximum range of RT/WT was nine miles, being frequently less when atmospherics were bad. Intercommunication between aircraft was unreliable.[256] The Zero was as fast as the Spitfire and the Messerschmitt-109 and more maneuverable than both. The Zero had a tight turning circle and was armed with two 20 mm cannons and two 7.7 mm machine guns. It first flew in China in 1940. The Zero's range was remarkable. With drop tanks on its wings, the Zero could fly for one thousand miles.[257] The Hurricanes arrived in insufficient number and too late during the campaign to turn the aerial balance in favor of the Allies.[258] The RAF's Bristol Blenheim bombers (introduced in 1937) and the Lockheed Hudson (introduced in 1939) were inferior compared to the Japanese Navy Air Force's (JNAF) twin-engine Mitsubishi G3M Nell and G4M Betty bombers and the Japanese Army Air Force's (JAAF) heavier KI-21 Sally bombers. In general, the range of the Japanese bombers was twice that of the British bombers.[259]

The Germans, during the interwar era, developed the concept of CAS. The objective was to shatter the enemy's morale by launching repeated aerial attacks in close formation at a decisive point. Alanbrooke realized that the single-seater fighter, by strafing, and heavy fighter-bomber aircraft with its cannon firing could seriously disorganize hostile ground formations.[260] In other words, Alanbrooke was a votary of the effectiveness of CAS. Nevertheless, the RAF disdained CAS and focused on strategic bombing. The dominant perception was that CAS by fixed-wing aircraft was costly, and this obstructed development of this technique in the RAF until 1944.[261] Historian Henry Probert asserts that the inferior RAF officers were sent to the Far East.[262] There was no training between the Allied ground force and the RAF to provide aerial reconnaissance during the battle.[263] The British pilots also lacked collective training, which was necessary to build up unit spirit.[264] Milking adversely affected not only the Indian infantry battalions but also the crews of the Allied air units. In spring 1941, selected pilots were withdrawn from several Blenheim squadrons to assist in the formation of the first two fighter squadrons in Malaya. Number 1 and 8 Royal Australian Air Force (RAAF) squadrons lost the fully trained aircrews for further expansion of the RAAF in Australia. They were replaced by untrained crews. Further, from May 1940 until the spring of 1941, there had been severe flying restrictions imposed on the Blenheim squadrons due to lack of spares. During this period, flying hours were restricted to five hours monthly per aircraft.[265] Again, due to inadequate supply of munitions, British fighter pilots could not practice air gunnery with bullets. Beer bottles were dropped to simulate bombs.[266]

In contrast, training and cooperation between the Japanese air force and the IJA was remarkable.[267] Percival admitted after the war: "There is no doubt that our Air Force Intelligence greatly underestimated the value of Japanese Air Force. I remember being told many times in Staff College lectures that, for some curious reason, the Japanese could never become good airmen. This theory was, of course, quite untrue, but it prevailed even until war experience disproved it. Our airmen were undoubtedly surprised by the efficiency of the Japanese pilots and machines over Malaya."[268] Japanese bombing skills were remarkable, and the Japanese aircraft during the Malaya Campaign, through constant dive bombing and machine gunning, demoralized the Allied ground troops. The Allied ground troops were not trained in passive air defense skills. Enjoying complete air superiority, the Japanese aircraft bombed from a height of only one thousand feet, and the adverse effect on the inexperienced troops was marked.[269]

Morale

Morale is a group-based concept that expresses the combat willingness of the unit. Tactical effectiveness requires a sound morale.[270] Napoleon used to say that morale vis-à-vis the physical is three to one, and Harbakhsh asserted that it was five to one.[271] Major General Bennett noted that the Eastern races were less able to withstand the strain of modern war.[272] Such a racial assumption is invalid. Morale depended on good leadership, firm discipline, effective and realistic training, physical fitness, proper man management, and sound logistical support.[273] We have seen previously that the British officers were not always able to provide good leadership, and training was neither realistic nor effective. Again, morale depended on the men in the units getting to know their comrades in order to build up a relationship of trust.[274] Milking of the Indian battalions for raising new units resulted in the entry of a lot of new men in the battalions, which somewhat obstructed the creation of bonding among the personnel.

Carl von Clausewitz, the Prussian military philosopher of the nineteenth century, has written that the true spirit of war lies in mobilizing the energies of every individual in the army to the greatest possible extent and in infusing him with bellicose feeling so that the fire of war spreads to all elements in the army.[275] Due to several reasons, the "fire of war" was not kindled adequately among many Allied commissioned officers and privates.

The Indian officers were angry due to the obstructions placed in the path of Indian cadets to enter the commissioned officer ranks in the Indian Army. While one group of historians (who could be categorized as Imperialists) argue that the British were following a grand plan in slowly Indianizing the officer corps of the Indian Army, the other group of scholars (who could be labeled as Nationalists[276]) assert that for controlling India, the British always wanted to keep the commissioned officer corps in the Indian Army a "white preserve." The Raj was afraid, continue the Nationalist historians, that opening up of the commissioned ranks to the Indians would result in the loss of British control over the principal coercive apparatus. The Nationalist historians opine that only under the pressure of the Second World War and lobbying by the nationalist politicians, were the Indian Army's officer corps Indianized. Between the First and Second World Wars, the GoI and the United Kingdom jointly set up various committees to study the issue of Indianization of the Indian Army's officer corps. In 1925, the Skeen Committee (under the chairmanship of Andrew Skeen) assumed that only in 1952 would 50 percent of the officer corps be Indianized. The Simon Commission in 1930 argued that the martial races, being uneducated, would not be able to furnish commissioned officers, and if Indian officers were recruited from the educated urban Indian middle class, then the martial races would not obey their commands. Between 1919 and early 1939, only 250 Indian officers were commissioned. Again, the British prevented subordination of the British officers to the Indian officers by separating the units earmarked for Indianization. Also, the Indian officers were discriminated against as regards command of squadrons and companies. Once the Second World War erupted, the Indian Army started expanding, which raised the demand for officers. Not only were the British cadets inducted into the expanding British Army to replace officer casualties due to the ongoing war, but also British officers from the Indian Army were taken away to fill the officer slots in the British Army. Then, the floodgates opened for the Indians to join the commissioned ranks. Besides recruiting regular Indian officers, many middle-class Indians were also granted emergency commissions. Emergency commissions were also granted to British civilians from the Dominions in order to check the volume of entry of the Indians. In October 1939, there were 396 Indians in the officer corps. In January 1940, their numbers increased to 415, and in January 1942, the figure stood at 596.[277]

In 1941, the Indian Army was slowly Indianizing its commissioned officer corps, and the commissioned Indian officers, being educated, were politically conscious. Compared to the King's Commissioned Indian Officers (KCIO), the Emergency Commissioned Indian Officers (ECIO) was more vulnerable to wider political opinion. The morale of the Indian commissioned officers was somewhat seriously dampened by the racial discrimination of the British. There was a strict color bar between the white men and the Asians in Malaya. Harbakhsh Singh writes: "Everything for the white man was exclusive-clubs, swimming pools, buses, railway carriages, and even sheds against rain."[278] Like Harbakhsh, Mohammad Zaman Kiani of the 1st/14th Punjab Regiment also noted the issue of racial discrimination. Kiani was GSO III in the 11th Indian Division's Headquarters at Sungei Patani. He mentions that there was a European club in Ipoh that Asians were not allowed to enter.[279] After the Battle of Jitra, many Indian officers and jawans from Kiani's unit would join the Japanese-sponsored INA (also known as *Azad Hind Fauj*). When the 5th/11th Sikhs was deployed in Malaya, the Raja of Perak invited only the British officers for a dinner party. And the CO of the battalion, Lieutenant Colonel John Parkin, went with the British officers for the dinner. This act somewhat embittered the Indian officers of the unit.[280]

Also, the issue of higher pay for the European soldiers disheartened the Indian personnel.[281] While a jawan received Rs 25 per month, a British private got Rs 75 monthly. While an Indian lieutenant got Rs 400 (inclusive of all allowances) monthly, a British lieutenant was paid Rs 600 per month plus allowances.[282] In fact, the ECIO was paid less than the KCIO.[283] Occasionally, the British officers (especially the British Emergency Commissioned Officers [ECOs]) misbehaved with the VCOs.[284] There were cases of friction between the British officers and commissioned Indian officers. The British officers behaved rudely with the Indian commissioned officers senior to them, and the British soldiers did not salute the Indian officers.[285] In Malaya, the junior British officers superseded senior Indian commissioned officers.[286]

Captain Mohan Singh, a commissioned Indian officer of 1st/14th Punjab, rightly noted that patriotism had nothing to do with combat motivation of the Indian Army. Its efficiency was based on discipline and tradition.[287] Mohan Singh described his feelings at the beginning of the Second World War in the following words:

> Our brave soldiers, who were going to be committed in various battlefields, in the East or the West were to fight as mercenaries, were not even supposed to know why the war was on.... We had not forgotten the bitter experience of World War I.... The British victory achieved through the untold sufferings of the Indian soldiers, further strengthened the chains of our bondage.... The fact was that Britain was not as strong in 1939 as it was in 1914, on the other hand, India had gone stronger many folds in the wake of World War I. We seemed to be in a better position to demand our rights. By this war, I thought, India was bound to gain, whatever the outcome.[288]

Kiani opines that most of the Indian commissioned officers were driven by pride in their profession rather than patriotism. Their sympathy lay with the Germans. The officers hated to serve in an inferior position as subjects of the British. They understood that they were not fighting for their own selves but for the British cause. And vaguely they believed that with the defeat of the British, things would change for the better in India. After the British surrender at Singapore, Kiani joined the INA and rose to the position of major general. The unfavorable conditions of the poor Indians compared to the laboring classes of Malaya further embittered the Indian commissioned officer corps. Kiani in his memoirs writes that the unskilled labor in Malaya earned eight times more than their counterpart in India. And the conditions of the lower middle class in Malaya were much better than those of India.[289]

Back in India, despite the rising tide of nationalism, Viceroy Lord Linlithgow was against any devolution of power to the Indians. On 21 January 1942, Linlithgow in a telegram informed the Secretary of State for India: "I take very seriously, too, in reaching my conclusions . . . that further transfer of power would give marked encouragement to Quisling activity. Recent report from military authorities in Eastern India is to the effect that there is a large and dangerous potential fifth column in Bengal, Assam and Bihar and Orissa, and that, indeed, potentiality of pro-enemy sympathy and activity in Eastern India is enormous. Sarat Bose has been a lesson. . . . But Cabinet will, I think, agree with me that India . . . have no natural association with Empire."[290] Sarat Bose was ex-INC leader Subhas Bose's brother, and the latter would later join the Axis powers. Linlithgow continued that India was in the British Empire because it was conquered by force and in the case of a British defeat the Indian political leaders might be willing to make terms with the victor.

Even though most of the jawans were illiterate and semiliterate rustics, they were still somewhat influenced by the wider political currents in India. One of the dominant "martial" groups of the Indian Army was the Sikh community. The Sikhs were somewhat disturbed by the All India Muslim League's (AIML) Pakistan Resolution of 1940, which was issued with the encouragement of Linlithgow. The Sikhs were concerned about their future due to AIML's demand that Punjab be incorporated within the separate Muslim homeland of Pakistan. The Sikhs doubted the Raj's support in securing their interest.[291] And the personnel of the 1st/14th Punjab were not keen for overseas service. They believed that this war was not India's war. India was not threatened at this time either by the Japanese or the Germans or the Italians. Moreover, the Indian leaders were not consulted before the viceroy declared war on behalf of India against the Axis powers. The jawans and their Indian officers believed that they were being exploited by the British.[292] And this battalion would be one of the first to defect to the Japanese after the disastrous Battle of Jitra.

The Japanese added fuel to the fire. Japanese agents were active in Singapore. They spread propaganda regarding the bad treatment of the Indian troops by the British officers. Their attempt to subvert the loyalty of the Indian troops had some effect. The 4th/19th Hyderabad had sailed from India in August 1939 as part of Force EMU (12th Indian Brigade). Lieutenant Muhammad Zahiruddin of this battalion displayed anti-British activities. His assumption, like that of Mohan Singh, was that the Second World War would last long enough to exhaust the British Empire, which in turn would enable the Indians to turn the British out of India. He was sent back to India. On 7–8 May 1940, there was trouble in the A (Ahir) Company, and it spread to B (Jat) Company. The Ahir soldiers shouted slogans for Zahiruddin's reinstatement, and the Ahir Company was disarmed. Finally, Major K. S. Thimayya (who in post-1947 India would become the chief of army staff), commander of D Company, handled the situation well and restored normalcy in this battalion.[293]

In January 1941, there were reports of disaffection among the Sikh troops and also the Sikh community in Hong Kong.[294] As early as 19 June 1941, the GOC Hong Kong warned the War Office and commander in chief, India: "Subversive activities from Japanese and other sources against Indian troops continue unabated and most important that these should be watched and countered."[295]

In October 1941, Major Fujiwara Iwaichi arrived in Thailand following a report sent by the military attaché in Bangkok named Colonel Tamura Hiroshi to Tokyo on the possibility and advantages of supporting rising Indian nationalism in Thailand and Malaya.[296] Fujiwara's order was to control and support the members of the Indian independence movement. The Indian Independence League (IIL) had its headquarters in Bangkok and had branches in Shanghai and Hong Kong. In June 1941, the IIL approached the Japanese military attaché in Bangkok to obtain help from the Japanese government against the British and to develop Indo-Japanese collaboration.[297] The Japanese were in touch with those revolutionary Indians like Satyanand Puri, *Sirdar* Giani Pritam Singh, and others who had established a base at Bangkok.[298] Fujiwara *Kikan*'s (Section) orders were to give shape to the Tamura-Pritam Singh agreement and to send out liaison officers with each column (during the Japanese invasion of Malaya) to secure proper treatment of the Indian PoWs and Indian civilians in the areas occupied. The aim was to prevent friction between the IJA and the Indians in Malaya.[299] There were many Indians in Malaya. The Tamils worked as laborers in the rubber plantations and in the railways, and the Punjabis served as watchmen and money lenders.[300] The Malays probably hated the Indian immigrants who had taken up jobs in their country. And the Malays for this reason probably displayed racial contempt toward the Indian immigrants. Amitav Ghosh, in his fictional account dealing with wartime Burma, portrays that the Indians were called by the derogatory term of *kala aadmi* (blacks).[301] This was probably the situation in Malaya also. Fujiwara established contact with Pritam Singh.[302] It was decided that the IIL would advance with the IJA into southern Siam and later into Malaya, where the IIL would be expanded and engage in encouraging anti-British feelings and activities. The IIL was to undertake a vigorous propaganda campaign both in the occupied areas and in India proper. Fujiwara pointed out that at present, the IIL was dominated by the Sikhs. Pritam Singh agreed with him that other Indian communities should also be brought within its fold. Pritam Singh also suggested that the IIL was to organize a voluntary army that would fight for Indian independence. This army, later known as the INA, was to be staffed by Indian Army officers and men and also local Indian volunteers. By October 1941, at least two Indian commissioned officers, Captain Mohan Singh of 1st/14th Punjab and Lieutenant Colonel N. S. Gill of 4th/19th Hyderabad, were in touch with Fujiwara *Kikan*.[303]

On 5 December 1941, Pritam Singh made the following appeal from Bangkok:

> Dear Indian soldiers in Malaya and Burma.... The programme for you is that you should never obey the orders of your English commanders when they would order

to attack Thailand. Thailand is connected with India through religion of Lord Buddha, culture and Sanskrit literature. Therefore Thailand is a brother country to India. So you should not fight this in any case. And you should never fight Japan, Germany or any country who is enemy of British, because all such countries are our indirect friends. If English lose this war there would be an ample chance for India's freedom. Some deceiving English propagandists would cheat you and the writer has heard that English dogs bark before the innocent Indians to show that they (English) are saving India from Germany, Japan or some other enemy countries of England who want to govern India.[304]

Pritam Singh and his company not only targeted the Indian military personnel but also the Indian diaspora in Southeast Asia. On 9 December 1941, on the occasion of the opening of the IIL in Bangkok, Singh asked the Indians to refrain from helping the British in their war effort. He emphasized: "The whole of Japanese nation unanimously in a single voice has taken a pledge to stake her fate for the fulfillment of her incomprehensible spiritual aim of liberating the whole of Asia from British yoke. We welcome this God-given opportunity that Indians have been waiting for since 1904. . . . Thus the Asiatics would no more be the black coolies of the white Anglo-Saxon."[305]

The morale of the British soldiers deployed in the Far East remained low. Most of the British personnel considered the war against Japan of secondary importance. They were more interested in events in Europe. The British soldiers were disenchanted with the lack of publicity regarding war in the Far East compared to the war in western Europe. They hated the hot and humid climate and diseases that were prevalent in Southeast Asia.[306] American, Australian, and British troops suffered from depression in the jungles of the southwest Pacific and Malaya. Due to the absence of sunlight and daylong twilight, an atmosphere of melancholy pervaded the men. Peter Schrijvers writes that when the Caucasoid soldiers came face to face with the tangled mass of vegetation in the tropics, their feeling of ecological estrangement became acute. The Western armed forces personnel deployed in the Far East believed that the tropical jungle possessed the most dangerous animals, such as flies, mosquitoes, crocodiles, and snakes. The Allied troops were not confident of moving and fighting in the darkness of the night.[307] They demanded aerial and artillery superiority as well as numerical superiority before colliding with the hostile ground forces.[308] The first would not be available in the forthcoming Malayan Campaign. The Japanese infantry's fluid tactics in close jungle country would negate the possibility of using mass artillery fire against them. As we will see, these two factors in combination would nullify the Allied numerical superiority as regards ground troops.

Conclusion

The prewar Indian Army was a tactically proficient force with a forward-looking command structure. However, the wartime expansion of the British and Indian armies reduced their cohesiveness and caused organizational turmoil. The state of training and equipment of the rapidly expanding Allied force was poor. It could have been partly rectified if the Malaya Command had followed the right policies. Ironically, the Allied forces had more time than the IJA to prepare for war in the jungle conditions. But this time was not judiciously used. The units deployed in Malaya for several months were not trained for jungle war (especially utilization of the terrain) and the newly arrived partially trained units were given erroneous training. The Allied soldiers were deficient both in individual and collective training. Their training was neither realistic nor tough. All the failures of the Allied armies could not be blamed on the absence of tanks or shortages of aircraft. Tanks were an essential element in the defeat of the Allied forces detailed to hold Malaya. It must be noted that unlike the Allied infantry in Malaya, the well-trained German infantry in Russia in 1941 repeatedly knocked out heavy Soviet tanks by applying creative techniques. And the German infantry from mid-1943 onward put up a stout defense despite the Luftwaffe losing aerial superiority to the Allied and Red Air Force. The Allied philosophy for conducting warfare was defective. Combat effectiveness of the troops deployed in a particular terrain was partly dependent on the fine tuning between the physical environment and proper training plus equipment of the force. And this fact was neglected by the Allied commanders in Malaya. Historian T. R. Moreman notes that the IJA's equipment and light infantry doctrine was easily adaptable to jungle warfare.[309] In addition to weapons and training, how a soldier will actually perform during the firefight depends on his "will to combat." David French rightly says that morale is fluid and often changes with the changing battle scenario.[310] In other words, what was happening in the fire-swept field shaped the morale of the combat units. The low state of morale and weak training of the Allied units might not hold if the situation went awry.

Notes

1. Lieutenant Colonel Paul W. Thompson, "Behind the Fog of War: A Glance at the History and Organization of the Jap Army," in *How the Jap Army Fights*, ed. Lieutenant Colonel Paul W. Thompson, Lieutenant Colonel Harold Doud, and Lieutenant John Scofield (1942; repr., New York: Penguin, 1943), 10.

2. S. C. Aggarwal, *History of the Supply Department: 1939–46* (New Delhi: Manager of Publications, 1947), 145.

3. David Horner, "Australia in 1942: A Pivotal Year," in *Australia 1942: In the Shadow of War*, ed. Peter J. Dean (Melbourne: Cambridge University Press, 2013), 14–5.

4. Jeffrey Grey, *A Military History of Australia* (Cambridge: Cambridge University Press, 1990), 71.

5. Edward J. Drea, *Japan's Imperial Army: Its Rise and Fall, 1853–1945* (Lawrence, KS: University Press of Kansas, 2009), 235.

6. Sri Nandan Prasad, *Expansion of the Armed Forces and Defence Organization 1939–45* (Calcutta: Saraswaty, 1956), 58.

7. Aggarwal, *History*, 159–63.

8. Telegram from GoI, Defence Department to Secy. of State for India, August 9, 1940, 2177K, CP, NMML, New Delhi.

9. Memorandum by the Chiefs of Staff Committee, September 19, 1940, WP(40)380, CP, NMML.

10. Prasad, *Expansion*, 61.

11. Peter Thompson, *The Battle for Singapore: The True Story of the Greatest Catastrophe of World War II* (2005; repr., London: Piatkus, 2013), 42.

12. Extract from a Private Letter from Linlithgow to Zetland, September 25, 1939, L/WS/1/136, OIOC, BL, London.

13. Extract from a Private Letter from Zetland to Linlithgow, October 2, 1939, L/WS/1/136.

14. Enclosure to the Private Secy. to the Viceroy, Letter no. 5178, September 16, 1939; From the Secy. District Soldiers Board, Etawa to the Assistant Recruiting Officer, Lucknow, no. 418/SB, September 21, 1939, L/WS/1/136.

15. Prasad, *Expansion*, 53–54, 56.

16. Recruitment in India, Appendix 19, L/WS/1/136.

17. Prasad, *Expansion*, 60.

18. Reports for the Month of July 1941 for the Dominions, India, Burma and the Colonies and Mandated Territories, Report by the Secy. of State for India, Para 21, WP*(41)53, CP, NMML.

19. Prasad, *Expansion*, 61.

20. Memorandum by the Secy. of State for India, January 30, 1942, WP(42)54, CP, NMML.

21. Reports for the Month of December 1941 for the Dominions, India, Burma and the Colonies and Mandated Territories, Report by the Secy. of State for India, January 24, 1942, WP(R)(42)5, Cabinet Papers, NMML.

22. Amitav Ghosh, *The Glass Palace* (New Delhi: Ravi Dayal, 2000), 29–30.

23. Prasad, *Expansion*, xxviii–xxix.

24. Tim Carew, *The Longest Retreat: The Burma Campaign 1942* (1969; repr., Dehra Dun: Natraj, 1989), 17.

25. Jonathan Moffatt and Audrey Holmes McCormick, *Moon over Malaya: The 2nd Argylls and Plymouth Argyll Royal Marines in Malaya and Singapore* (Gloucestershire: History Press, 2014), 15.

26. David Omissi, *The Sepoy and the Raj: The Indian Army, 1860–1940* (London: Macmillan, 1994), 77.

27. Thompson, "Behind the Fog," 8.

28. Saki Dockrill, "Hirohito, the Emperor's Army and Pearl Harbor," *Review of International Studies* 18, no. 4 (1992): 322.

29. Alvin D. Coox, "The Effectiveness of the Japanese Military Establishment in the Second World War," in *Military Effectiveness*, vol. 3, *The Second World War*, ed. Allan R. Millett and Williamson Murray (1988; repr., Cambridge: Cambridge University Press, 2010), 8.

30. Jurgen Forster, "From 'Blitzkrieg' to 'Total War,'" in *A World at Total War: Global Conflict and the Politics of Destruction, 1937–1945*, ed. Roger Chickering, Stig Forster, and Bernd Greiner (Cambridge: Cambridge University Press and German Historical Institute, Washington, DC, 2005), 106–7.

31. Dennis Showalter, "Global Yet not Total: The US War Effort and its Consequences," in *A World at Total War*, ed. Chickering, Forster, and Greiner, 119, 127.

32. Moffatt and McCormick, *Moon over Malaya*, 32.

33. *India's Freedom Struggle and the Great INA, Memoirs of Major-General Mohammad Zaman Kiani* (New Delhi: Reliance, 1994), 24.

34. Showalter, "Global Yet not Total," 112.

35. John Keegan, *Six Armies in Normandy: From D-Day to the Liberation of Paris* (1982; repr., London: Pimlico, 1992), 320.

36. Edward A. Shils and Morris Janowitz, "Cohesion and Disintegration in the Wehrmacht in World War II," *Public Opinion Quarterly* 12, no. 2 (1948): 283.

37. Note by General Molesworth on Indian Army Recruitment, July 21, 1943, L/WS/1/136.

38. Nirad C. Chaudhuri, "The Martial Races of India," Part 1, *Modern Review*, 48, no. 1 (1930): 43–44.

39. Martin Van Creveld, *The Art of War: War and Military Thought* (London: Cassell, 2000), 51.

40. Nirad C. Chaudhuri, "The Martial Races of India," Part 3, *Modern Review* 49, no. 1 (1931): 79.

41. Drea, *Japan's Imperial Army*, 160.

42. Extract from the Official Report of the Council of State Debates, March 6, 1933, L/WS/1/456, OIOC, BL.

43. Annual Return showing Class Composition of the Indian Army, Indian States Force, Frontier Corps and Levies, Military Police, Assam Rifles, Burma Frontier Force and Hong Kong Singapore Royal Artillery on 1 Jan. 1941, L/WS/1/456.

44. Communal Strengths of the Combatant Groups on 1 Jan. 1941, L/WS/1/456.

45. Communal Strengths of the Combatant Groups on 1 Feb. 1942, L/WS/1/456.

46. Note by Molesworth.

47. Chaudhuri, "The Martial Races of India," Part 4, *Modern Review* 49, no. 2 (1931): 221.

48. Note by Molesworth.

49. Note by Molesworth.

50. William Arthur, "The Martial Episteme: Re-thinking Theories of Martial Race and the Modernization of the British Indian Army during the Second World War," in *The British Indian Army: Virtue and Necessity*, ed. Rob Johnson (Newcastle: Cambridge Scholars, 2014), 163–64.

51. Keegan, *Six Armies*, xiii.

52. Omissi, *Sepoy and the Raj*, 79; David Omissi, ed., *Indian Voices of the Great War: Soldiers' Letters, 1914–18* (Basingstoke, UK: Macmillan, 1999), 31, 41–42, 50, 53–54, 57–58, 126, 142, 157–58, 191, 236, 268–69, 294, 319.

53. Edward Drea, "The Imperial Japanese Army (1868–1945): Origins, Evolution, Legacy," in *War in the Modern World since 1815*, ed. Jeremy Black (London: Routledge, 2003), 111.

54. Chaudhuri, "Martial Races of India," Part 3, 79.

55. Drea, *Japan's Imperial Army*, 258.

56. Saburo Sakai with Martin Caidin and Fred Saito, *Samurai!* (1957; repr., Annapolis MD: Naval Institute Press, 1991), 6.

57. Peter Schrijvers, *Bloody Pacific: American Soldiers at War with Japan* (2002; repr., Houndmills: Palgrave Macmillan, 2010), 165.

58. R. E. S. Tanner and D. A. Tanner, *Burma 1942: Memories of a Retreat, The Diary of Ralph Tanner, 2nd Battalion the King's Own Yorkshire Light Infantry* (Gloucestershire: The History Press, 2009), 50.

59. Sakai, *Samurai!*, 20–21.

60. Sakai, *Samurai!*, 21.

61. Drea, "Imperial Japanese Army," 103.

62. Chaudhuri, "Martial Races of India," Part 4, 218.

63. Chaudhuri, "Martial Races of India," Part 1, 45.

64. Stephen Peter Rosen, *Societies and Military Power: India and Its Armies* (New Delhi: Oxford University Press, 1996), 195.

65. Army Despatch from GoI, January 11, 1918, L/WS/1/456.

66. Note by Molesworth.

67. Omissi, *Sepoy and the Raj*, 83.

68. Anne Hoiberg, "Military Staying Power," in *Combat Effectiveness: Cohesion, Stress, and the Volunteer Military*, ed. Sam C. Sarkesian (Beverly Hills: SAGE, 1980), 232.

69. *The Seven Military Classics of Ancient China*, trans. Ralph D. Sawyer with Mei-chun Sawyer (Boulder: Westview, 1993), 248.

70. Tanner and Tanner, *Burma 1942*, 53.

71. The term "milked" or "milking" refers to when trained jawans, NCOs, and VCOs were transferred from one unit to new unit that was being raised. The transferred personnel provided stiffening and experience to the newly raised unit. The vacancies in the original unit were filled with novices. Replacement of trained personnel with the novices somewhat reduced the combat effectiveness of the original formation. However, milking was essential when an army was expanding.

72. Prasad, *Expansion*, 58.

73. Guenter Lewy, "The American Experience in Vietnam," in *Combat Effectiveness*, ed. Sarkesian, 103.

74. David Gates, *The Napoleonic Wars: 1803–1815* (London: Arnold, 1997), 208.

75. T. R. Moreman, "'Small Wars' and 'Imperial Policing': The British Army and the Theory and Practice of Colonial Warfare in the British Empire, 1919–1939," *Journal of Strategic Studies* 19, no. 4 (1996): 115–16.

76. Ronald Lewin, *Slim, The Standardbearer: A Biography of Field-Marshal the Viscount Slim* (1976; repr., London: Pan, 1978), 22.

77. John Masters, *Bugles and a Tiger: My Life in the Gurkhas* (1956; repr., London: Cassell, 2002), 25.

78. Operations in Malaya and Singapore, E. E. Bridges, report drawn up by Major H. P. Thomas, July 27, 1942, WP(42)314, CAB/66/26/44, PRO, Kew, London, 14.

79. Robert Johnson, "Small Wars and Internal Security: The Army in India, 1936–1946," in *The Indian Army, 1939–47: Experience and Development*, ed. Alan Jeffreys and Patrick Rose (Surrey: Ashgate, 2012), 222; Elisabeth Mariko Leake, "British India versus the British Empire: The Indian Army and an Impasse in Imperial Defence, circa 1919–39," *Modern Asian Studies* 48, no. 1 (2014): 309; Simon Coningham, "Air-Ground Cooperation between the RAF and the Indian Army in Waziristan, 1936–7," in *The British Indian Army*, ed. Johnson, 130.

80. Major General B. W. Key, 11th Indian Division, P 456, Key Papers, IWM, London, 44–45; Coningham, "Air-Ground Cooperation," 130–31.

81. Key, 11th Indian Division, 46–47.

82. Johnson, "Small Wars," 223; Leake, "British India," 309.

83. Alan Warren, "'Bullocks Treading Down Wasps'? The British Indian Army in Waziristan in the 1930s," *South Asia* 19, no. 2 (1996): 48–49.

84. Meirion and Susie Harries, *Soldiers of the Sun: The Rise and Fall of the Imperial Japanese Army* (New York: Random House, 1991), 210; Drea, *Japan's Imperial Army*, 197.

85. Lieutenant Colonel Paul W. Thompson, "The Jap Army in Action: Campaigns in the China Incident," in *How the Jap Army Fights*, ed. Thompson, Doud, and Scofield, 50–51.

86. Drea, *Japan's Imperial Army*, 209.

87. Wayne P. Hughes Jr., "The Strategy-Tactics Relationship," in *Seapower and Strategy*, ed. Colin S. Gray and Roger W. Barnett (London: Tri-Service, 1989), 55.

88. Andrew Gordon, "Ratcatchers and Regulators at the Battle of Jutland," in *The Challenges of High Command: The British Experience*, ed. Gary Sheffield and Geoffrey Till (Hampshire, UK: Palgrave Macmillan, 2003), 32.

89. General Mike Jackson, "The Realities of Multi-national Command: An Informal Commentary," in *The Challenges of High Command*, ed. Sheffield and Till, 141.

90. Robert Lyman, "The Art of Maneuver at the Operational Level of War: Lieutenant-General W.J. Slim and Fourteenth Army, 1944–45," in *The Challenges of High Command*, ed. Sheffield and Till, 89, 95.

91. US War Department, *Handbook on Japanese Military Forces*, with an Introduction by David Isby and an afterword by Jeffrey Ethell (1944; reprint, Baton Rouge: Louisiana State University Press, 1991), 85.

92. Martin Samuels, *Command or Control? Command, Training and Tactics in the British and German Armies, 1888–1918* (London: Frank Cass, 1995), 5.

93. Williamson Murray, "Innovation: Past and Future," in *Military Innovation in the Interwar Period*, ed. Williamson Murray and Allan R. Millett (Cambridge: Cambridge University Press, 1996), 302–3.

94. Samuels, *Command or Control?*, 4.

95. Williamson Murray, "Armored Warfare: The British, French and German Experiences," in *Military Innovation in the Interwar Period*, ed. Murray and Millett, 37–39.

96. Samuels, *Command or Control?*, 5.

97. Samuels, *Command or Control?*, 5.

98. For tempo and OODA loop, see John Kiszely, "The British Army and Approaches to Warfare since 1945," and Alistair Irwin, "The Buffalo Thorn: The Nature of the Future Battlefield," *Journal of Strategic Studies* 19, no. 4 (1996): 180, 250.

99. Samuels, *Command or Control?*, 4.

100. Samuels, *Command or Control?*, 5, 10, 14.

101. Samuels, *Command or Control?*, 5–6.

102. Thompson, "Jap Army in Action," 71.

103. Military Intelligence Division, *Notes on Japanese Warfare on the Malayan Front*, Information Bulletin No. 6 (Washington, DC: War Department, 1942), 1.

104. Thompson, "Jap Army in Action," 71.

105. US War Department, *Handbook on Japanese Military Forces*, 85–87, 89, 90, 121.

106. Francis Pike, *Hirohito's War: The Pacific War, 1941–1945* (London: Bloomsbury, 2015), 216.

107. Note on the Malayan Campaign by LMH, Part 3, LMH 5, P 441, Lewis Heath Papers, IWM, 17.

108. Lord Alan Alanbrooke, *War Diaries 1939–1945*, ed. Alex Danchev and Daniel Todman (London: Weidenfeld & Nicolson, 2001), 185.

109. Samuels, *Command or Control?*, 18.

110. Lieutenant General John H. Cushman, "Challenge and Response at the Operational and Tactical Levels, 1914–45," in *Military Effectiveness*, vol. 3, ed. Millett and Murray, 330.

111. Barry Watts and Williamson Murray, "Military Innovation in Peacetime," in *Military Innovation in the Interwar Period*, ed. Murray and Millett, 373.

112. Lieutenant Colonel Gautam Sharma, *Nationalisation of the Indian Army: 1885–1947* (New Delhi: Allied, 1996), 63–64, 150.

113. Alan Jeffreys, "Training the Indian Army, 1939–1945," in *The Indian Army*, ed. Jeffreys and Rose, 73–74.

114. David Omissi, "A Dismal Story? Britain, the Gurkhas and the Partition of India, 1945–1948," in *The Indian Army*, ed. Jeffreys and Rose, 198.

115. Patrick Rose, "Indian Army Command Culture and the North West Frontier, 1919–1939," in *The Indian Army*, ed. Jeffreys and Rose, 54–55.

116. Mohan Singh, *Soldiers' Contribution to Indian Independence* (New Delhi: Army Educational Stores, 1974), 36.

117. From CGS Australia to War Office, April 3, 1942, L/WS/1/952, OIOC, BL.

118. Timothy Harrison Place, *Military Training in the British Army, 1940–1944* (London: Frank Cass, 2000), 42.

119. William L. Hauser, "The Will to Fight," in *Combat Effectiveness*, ed. Sarkesian, 188–89.

120. T. R. Moreman, *The Jungle, the Japanese and the British Commonwealth Armies at War, 1941–45: Fighting Methods, Doctrine and Training for Jungle Warfare* (London: Frank Cass, 2005), 7; Hew Strachan, "Training, Morale and Modern War," *Journal of Contemporary History* 41, no. 2 (2006): 216.

121. Timothy Hall, *The Fall of Singapore* (1983; repr., Oxon, UK: Routledge, 2015), 7.

122. Ian Morrison, *Malayan Postscript* (London: Faber and Faber, 1942), 23.

123. Operations in Malaya and Singapore, Bridges, 14.

124. Brigadier W. Carpendale, CO 28th Indian Brigade, Report on Operations of 11 Indian Division in Kedah and Perak, L/WS/1/952, OIOC, BL, 1.

125. Moreman, *The Jungle*, 17.

126. Quoted from John Ferris, "'Worthy of Some Better Enemy?': The British Estimate of the Imperial Japanese Army, 1919–41, and the Fall of Singapore," *Canadian Journal of History* 28, (Aug. 1993): 231.

127. Ferris, "'Worthy of Some Better Enemy?,'" 237.

128. Coox, "The Effectiveness of the Japanese Military Establishment in the Second World War," in *Military Effectiveness*, vol. 3, ed. Millett and Murray, 2.

129. Moreman, *The Jungle*, 22.

130. Lieutenant General Harbakhsh Singh, *In the Line of Duty: A Soldier Remembers* (New Delhi: Lancer, 2000), 93–94.

131. A. B. Lodge, *The Fall of General Gordon Bennett* (Sydney: Allen & Unwin, 1986), 50.

132. Moreman, *The Jungle*, 13.

133. Operations in Malaya and Singapore, Bridges, 11.

134. US War Department, *Handbook on Japanese Military Forces*, 86, 88, 91–92.

135. Colonel Masanobu Tsuji, *Japan's Greatest Victory / Britain's Worst Defeat from the Japanese Perspective: The Capture of Singapore, 1942*, ed. H. V. Howe, trans. Margaret E. Lake (1952; repr., Gloucestershire, UK: Spellmount, 2007), 18.

136. Tsuji, *Japan's Greatest Victory*, xvii.

137. Tsuji, *Japan's Greatest Victory*, 2.

138. Tsuji, *Japan's Greatest Victory*, 3.

139. Bill Yenne, *The Imperial Japanese Army: The Invincible Years 1941–42* (Oxford: Osprey, 2014), 25.

140. Tsuji, *Japan's Greatest Victory*, 9, 24–5.

141. US War Department, *Handbook on Japanese Military Forces*, 121.

142. Yenne, *Imperial Japanese Army*, 87–88.

143. Lieutenant General A. E. Percival, "Operations of Malaya Command, from 8 December 1941 to 15 February 1942," *Second Supplement to the London Gazette*, February 26, 1948 (London: HMSO, 1948), 1246.

144. H. Gordon Bennett, *The Fall of Singapore* (1944; repr., New Delhi: Natraj, 1990), 7–8.

145. A Statement by Ms H. Dane, L/WS/1/952, 72.
146. Bennett, *Fall of Singapore*, 6–7.
147. Thompson, "Jap Army in Action," 63.
148. Note on the Malayan Campaign by LMH, Part 2, LMH 5, P 441, Heath Papers, 5.
149. Place, *Military Training*, 31, 38.
150. David French, "Big Wars and Small Wars between the Wars, 1919–39," in *Big Wars and Small Wars: The British Army and the Lessons of War in the 20th Century*, ed. Hew Strachan (2006; repr., London: Routledge, 2008), 36, 42.
151. Place, *Military Training*, 1, 37–38, 45, 48.
152. Bennett, *Fall of Singapore*, 9, 11.
153. Tanner and Tanner, *Burma 1942: Memories of a Retreat*, 51.
154. Alanbrooke, *War Diaries*, 183.
155. Operations in Malaya and Singapore, Bridges, 13.
156. G. W. Seabridge, Report on the Fall of Singapore, April 25, 1942, WP(42)177, CAB/66/24/7, PRO, Kew, 3.
157. Carpendale, Report on Operations of 11 Indian Division, 2.
158. Lieutenant John Scofield, "The Japanese Soldier's Arms and Weapons," in *How the Jap Army Fights*, ed. Thompson, Doud, and Scofield, 25.
159. Lieutenant Colonel Harold Doud, "Peace-Time Preparation: Six Months with the Japanese Infantry," in *How the Jap Army Fights*, ed. Thompson, Doud, and Scofield, 41.
160. Singapore Island and Johore, 12–22 Aug. Impressions and Facts, P 23, F 47, Percival Papers, IWM, 6.
161. Quoted from Singapore Island and Johore, 12–22 Aug. Impressions and Facts, P 23, F 47, Percival Papers, 6.
162. Colonel Milton A. Hill, "Lessons of Bataan," in *How the Jap Army Fights*, ed. Thompson, Doud, and Scofield, 92.
163. Doud, "Peace-Time Preparation," 41.
164. Note on the Malayan Campaign by LMH, Part 2, Heath Papers, 8.
165. Tsuji, *Japan's Greatest Victory*, 23–24.
166. Colin Smith, *Singapore Burning: Heroism and Surrender in World War II* (2005; repr., London: Penguin, 2006), 107.
167. Note on the Malayan Campaign by LMH, Part 2, Heath Papers, 14.
168. Thompson, "Jap Army in Action," 47.
169. Note on the Malayan Campaign by LMH, Part 3, LMH 5, P 441, Heath Papers, 10–11.
170. War Cabinet, The Malayan Campaign, April 4, 1942, WP(42)145, CAB/66/23/25, PRO, Kew, 2.
171. Operations in Malaya and Singapore, Bridges, 13.
172. Singapore Island and Johore, 12–22 Aug. Impressions and Facts, P 23, F 47, Percival Papers, 7.
173. Operations in Malaya and Singapore, Bridges, 12; General Headquarters, India Military Intelligence Directorate, War Information Circular Foreign Armies Non-Operational Intelligence, No. G 15, February 1, 1943, L/MIL/17/5/284, OIOC, BL, 2–3.
174. Jeffreys, "Training the Indian Army," 72.
175. Ashley Jackson, "The Evolution and Use of British Imperial Military Formations," in *The Indian Army*, ed. Jeffreys and Rose, 28.
176. Key, 11th Indian Division, 1, 3.
177. War Diary of 9th Indian Division, G Branch, Training Instruction of 1941, April 21, 553/5/22, AWM, Canberra, 7.

178. Gary Sheffield, "The Challenges of High Command in the Twentieth Century," in *The Challenges of High Command*, ed. Sheffield and Till, 3.

179. Mungo Melvin and Stuart Peach, "Reaching for the End of the Rainbow: Command and the Revolution in Military Affairs," in *The Challenges of High Command*, ed. Sheffield and Till, 201.

180. Lewin, *Slim*, 138.

181. Key, 11th Indian Division, 3.

182. Lieutenant Colonel J. Frith, History of the 2/10 Baluch in the Malayan Campaign, 1973-06-121, NAM, London, 2.

183. Lewin, *Slim*, 137.

184. Frith, History of the 2/10 Baluch.

185. Singh, *In the Line of Duty*, 85–86, 89.

186. Bennett, *Fall of Singapore*, 7.

187. Brigadier Jasbir Singh, *Escape from Singapore* (New Delhi: Lancer, 2010), 20.

188. Hall, *Fall of Singapore*, 24.

189. Major General Prem K. Khanna and Pushpindar Singh Chopra, *Portrait of Courage: Century of the 5th Battalion, The Sikh Regiment* (New Delhi: Military Studies Convention, 2001), 157.

190. Carpendale, Report on Operations of 11 Indian Division, 1.

191. Carpendale, Report on Operations of 11 Indian Division, 1.

192. War Diary of 2/1 Gurkha Rifles, July-August 1941, WO 172/136, PRO, Kew.

193. *9 Gurkha Rifles: A Regimental History (1817–1947)* (New Delhi: Vision Books, 1984), 157, 159.

194. Moffatt and McCormick, *Moon over Malaya*, 11, 14–15, 18, 24, 33–35.

195. Carpendale, Report on Operations of 11 Indian Division, 1.

196. Carpendale, Report on Operations of 11 Indian Division, 2–3.

197. *9 Gurkha Rifles*, 159.

198. Carpendale, Report on Operations of 11 Indian Division, 4–5; Strachan, "Training, Morale," 223.

199. Lodge, *Fall of General Gordon Bennett*, 50.

200. Timothy Hall, *New Guinea: 1942–44* (1981; repr., London: Routledge, 2015), 63–64.

201. Carpendale, Report on Operations of 11 Indian Division, 5.

202. Moreman, *The Jungle*, 16.

203. From GOC Malaya to War Office and Commander-in-Chief India, April 25, 1941, L/WS/1/645, OIOC, BL.

204. Telegram, From GOC Malaya to the War Office and Commander-in-Chief India, March 1, 1941, From Commander-in-Chief India to GOC Malaya and War Office, March 8, 1941, L/WS/1/645.

205. Quoted from War Diary of 9th Indian Division, G Branch, Training Instruction of 1941, April 21.

206. War Diary of 9th Indian Division, G Branch, Training Instruction of 1941, April 21.

207. Summary of Comments by Lord Wavell on General Percival's despatch on Operations of Malaya Command, Appendix B, Percival Papers, 1.

208. Bennett, *Fall of Singapore*, 11.

209. War Cabinet, The Malayan Campaign, April 4, 1942, 3.

210. Singapore Island and Johore, 12–22 Aug. Impressions and Facts, P 23, F 47, Percival Papers, 6.

211. Military Intelligence Division, *Notes on Japanese Warfare*, 4–5.

212. Singapore Island and Johore, 12–22 Aug. Impressions and Facts, P 23, F 47, Percival Papers, 6.
213. Note on the Malayan Campaign by LMH, Part 2, 3.
214. Military Intelligence Division, *Notes on Japanese Warfare*, 6, 8.
215. War Information Circular Foreign Armies Non-Operational Intelligence, No. G 15, February 1, 1943, 2.
216. Military Intelligence Division, *Notes on Japanese Warfare*, 1.
217. Telegram, From GOC Malaya to the War Office and Commander-in-Chief India, February 28, 1941, L/WS/1/645.
218. Telegram from Commander-in-Chief India to GOC Malaya, June 1, 1941, L/WS/1/645.
219. Carpendale, Report on Operations of 11 Indian Division, 3.
220. Memorandum by the Chiefs of Staff Committee, July 25, 1940, WP(40)291, CP, NMML.
221. Memorandum by the Secy. of State for India, June 29, 1940, COS(40)504, CP, NMML.
222. Singh, *In the Line of Duty*, 91.
223. War Information Circular Foreign Armies Non-Operational Intelligence, No. G 15, February 1, 1943, 2.
224. Singh, *In the Line of Duty*, 91.
225. Carpendale, Report on Operations of 11 Indian Division, 1.
226. Quoted from Carpendale, Report on Operations of 11 Indian Division, 6.
227. War Diary of 9th Indian Division, G Branch, Training Instruction of 1941, April 21, 4.
228. Place, *Military Training*, 41.
229. Moffatt and McCormick, *Moon over Malaya*, 27.
230. Place, *Military Training*, 10.
231. Louis Allen, *Singapore: 1941–1942* (1977; repr., Oxon, UK: Frank Cass, 2005), 3.
232. Military Intelligence Service, *Japanese Tanks and Tank Tactics* (Washington, DC: Military Intelligence Service, War Department, 1944), vii.
233. Ian Hogg, *Tank Killing: Anti-Tank Warfare by Men and Machines* (London: Sidgwick and Jackson, 1996), 1, 6.
234. Military Intelligence Service, *Japanese Tanks and Tank Tactics*, 1.
235. US War Department, *Handbook on Japanese Military Forces*, 86–87.
236. Military Intelligence Service, *Japanese Tanks and Tank Tactics*, 3, 6.
237. Scofield, "Japanese Soldier's Arms," 31.
238. Military Intelligence Service, *Japanese Tanks and Tank Tactics*, 40.
239. Yenne, *Imperial Japanese Army*, 87.
240. Lionel Wigmore, *The Japanese Thrust*, vol. 4, *Australia in the War of 1939–45*, Series One, *Army* (Canberra: Australian War Memorial, 1957), 133.
241. Military Intelligence Service, *Japanese Tanks and Tank Tactics*, 54–55.
242. Note on the Malayan Campaign by LMH, Part 3, LMH 5, P 441, Heath Papers, 7.
243. Allen, *Singapore*, 45–46, 50–51.
244. Alanbrooke, *War Diaries*, 155, 197.
245. War Diary of 9th Indian Division, G Branch, Training Instruction of 1941, April 21, 6.
246. Note on the Malayan Campaign by LMH, Part 2, 2.
247. Thompson, *Battle for Singapore*, 45; Moffatt and McCormick, *Moon over Malaya*, 41.

248. Moffatt and McCormick, *Moon over Malaya*, 40.
249. Note on the Malayan Campaign by LMH, Part 2.
250. War Cabinet, The Malayan Campaign, April 4, 1942, 2.
251. Military Intelligence Service, *Japanese Tanks and Tank Tactics*, 75.
252. Key, 11th Indian Division, 3.
253. Bennett, *Fall of Singapore*, 5.
254. Henry Probert, *The Forgotten Air Force: The Royal Air Force in the War against Japan, 1941-45* (London: Brassey's, 1995), 44, 65.
255. Smith, *Singapore Burning*, 44; Pike, *Hirohito's War*, 219.
256. Air Vice Marshal Paul Maltby, "Report on the Air Operations during the Campaigns in Malaya and Netherland East Indies from 8 December 1941 to 12 March 1942," *Third Supplement to the London Gazette*, February 26, 1948 (London: HMSO, 1948), 1356.
257. Smith, *Singapore Burning*, 45–6; Daniel Marston, ed., *The Pacific War: From Pearl Harbor to Hiroshima* (2005; repr., Oxford: Osprey, 2010), 250.
258. Operations in Malaya and Singapore, Bridges, 7.
259. Pike, *Hirohito's War*, 221.
260. Alanbrooke, *War Diaries*, 192–93.
261. Richard R. Muller, "Close Air Support: The German, British and American Experiences, 1918–41," in *Military Innovation in the Interwar Period*, ed. Murray and Millett, 148, 152.
262. Probert, *Forgotten Air Force*, 63.
263. Note on the Malayan Campaign by LMH, Part 2, Heath Papers.
264. Probert, *Forgotten Air Force*, 76.
265. Maltby, Report on the Air Operations during the Campaigns in Malaya and Netherland East Indies from 8 December 1941 to 12 March 1942, 1356.
266. Pike, *Hirohito's War*, 221.
267. Tsuji, *Japan's Greatest Victory*, 41.
268. Notes by Lieutenant General A. E. Percival on Captain Russell Grenfell's Draft, July 1950, Percival Papers.
269. Operations in Malaya and Singapore, Bridges, 7, 12.
270. David Englander, "Mutinies and Military Morale," in *The Oxford Illustrated History of the First World War*, ed. Hew Strachan. (Oxford: Oxford University Press, 1998), 191.
271. Singh, *In the Line of Duty*, 82; Hauser, "'Will to Fight," 187.
272. War Cabinet, The Malayan Campaign, April 4, 1942, 1.
273. Stephen Hart, "Montgomery, Morale, Casualty Conservation and 'Colossal Cracks': 21st Army Group's Operational Technique in North-West Europe," *Journal of Strategic Studies* 19, no. 4 (1996): 136.
274. David French, "'Tommy Is No Soldier': The Morale of the Second British Army in Normandy, June–August 1944," *Journal of Strategic Studies* 19, no. 4 (1996): 156.
275. Azar Gat, *The Origins of Military Thought from the Enlightenment to Clausewitz* (Oxford: Oxford University Press, 1989), 184.
276. See for instance Sharma, *Nationalisation of the Indian Army*.
277. Sharma, *Nationalisation of the Indian Army*, 79–81, 105, 107–8, 154–55, 165, 177, 184.
278. Singh, *In the Line of Duty*, 91.
279. *India's Freedom Struggle and the Great INA*, 14–15.
280. Singh, *In the Line of Duty*, 92–93.

281. Seabridge, Report on the Fall of Singapore, 5.
282. Chandar S. Sundaram, "Soldier Disaffection and the Creation of the Indian National Army," *Indo-British Review* 18, no. 1 (1990): 157.
283. Srinath Raghavan, *India's War: The Making of Modern South Asia, 1939–1945* (New Delhi: Penguin, 2016), 284.
284. *India's Freedom Struggle and the Great INA*, 43; Raghavan, *India's War*, 286.
285. *India's Freedom Struggle and the Great INA*, 42–43; Sharma, *Nationalisation of the Indian Army*, 195.
286. Raghavan, *India's War*, 285.
287. Singh, *Soldiers' Contribution*, 41.
288. Quoted from Singh, *Soldiers' Contribution*, 42–43.
289. *India's Freedom Struggle and the Great INA*, 1, 13, 15–16.
290. Telegram from Viceroy to the Secy. of State for India, January 21, 1942, WP(42)43, NMML.
291. Raghavan, *India's War*, 183.
292. Singh, *Soldiers' Contribution*, 45–46.
293. K. C. Praval, *Valour Triumphs: A History of the Kumaon Regiment* (Faridabad: Thomson, 1976), 102–3; Sundaram, "Soldier Disaffection," 155–56.
294. Reports for the Month of January 1941 for the Dominions, India, Burma and the Colonies, Protectorates and Mandated Territories, Report by the Secy. of State for India, Para 34, February 17, 1941, WP(R)(41)13, CP, NMML.
295. From GOC Hong Kong to War Office, Commander-in-Chief India, June 19, 1941, L/WS/1/645.
296. Sibylla Jane Flower, "Allied Prisoners of War: The Malayan Campaign, 1941–42," in *Sixty Years On: The Fall of Singapore Revisited*, ed. Brian Farrell and Sandy Hunter (2002: repr., Singapore: Eastern Universities Press, 2003), 209.
297. T. R. Sareen, ed., *Select Documents on Indian National Army* (Delhi: Agam Prakashan, 1988), 11.
298. *India's Freedom Struggle and the Great INA*, 39–40.
299. Sareen, *Select Documents*, 15.
300. Major General Gurkbakhsh Singh, *Indelible Reminiscences: Memoirs of Major-General Gurbakhsh Singh* (New Delhi: Lancer, 2013), 29–30.
301. Ghosh, *Glass Palace*, 7.
302. Raghavan, *India's War*, 282.
303. Sareen, *Select Documents*, 14–15, 26.
304. Quoted from Sareen, *Select Documents*, 1.
305. Quoted from Sareen, *Select Documents*, 2–3.
306. Report on the Morale of British, Indian and Colonial Troops of Allied Land Forces South-East Asia for the Months of November and December 1944 and January 1945, Part 2, British Troops, General, Para 7, L/WS/2/71, OIOC, BL, London.
307. Schrijvers, *Bloody Pacific*, 119–20, 126, 129, 163.
308. Allan R. Millett, "The United States Armed Forces in the Second World War," in *Military Effectiveness*, vol. 3, ed. Millett and Murray, 61.
309. Moreman, *The Jungle*, 25.
310. French, "'Tommy Is No Soldier,'" 155.

3 | The Invasion

On Monday, 8 December (7 December across the international dateline at Pearl Harbor) 1941, Japan declared war on the United States and British Empire. The declarations followed its attacks on the United States in Hawaii and on the British in Hong Kong and Malaya. The Japanese landing along the coastal areas of Malaya and intrusion through southern Thailand occurred on the same date. Soon all Allied resistance across northeast and northwest Malaya collapsed, and the Japanese surged in the southern direction. This chapter details the reasons behind the rapid collapse of the British and Indian units against the Japanese thrust along both the northeast coast and northwest Malaya. The first section portrays the architecture of opposing forces, and the second section narrates the breakdown of Allied defense along the east coast of northeast Malaya. The third section analyzes the disintegration of the British-Indian defense along northwest Malaya.

Deployment of the Allied Units in Malaya

> I found on arrival in the Far East that there was considerable ignorance of modern war conditions, both in the Army and the Air force. This could not, of course be made good entirely by documents; personal experience was essential.
>
> Robert Brooke-Popham[1]

Robert Brooke-Popham lacked combat experience under modern conditions, as before coming to Singapore, he was the governor in Kenya. Before assessing the limitations of his command capabilities, let us first discuss the linkages between the physical topography and the disposition of Allied forces in Malaya, just before the Japanese invasion. From the border of Thailand to the southeastern tip of the Malayan Peninsula is about 450 miles. At its narrowest point, the peninsula is 100 miles wide, and its widest point is some 200 miles. Malaya is bounded on all sides by the sea except in the north. The length of the main road and the west-coast railway from Singapore to the Malaya-Thailand frontier is roughly 600 miles. An extensive mountain range forms the backbone of the Malayan Peninsula, and the communication between east and west coasts then was underdeveloped. Several rivers and streams rising in the mountain range traverse the coastal areas before reaching the sea. The largest of them is Perak River in the northern part of the west-coast area. The west coast was more developed and thickly populated than the east coast. There were some good beaches on the west coast, but most of the coastline was covered with mangrove swamps. Through the west coast ran the main road and rail communications that linked Singapore with the north. There was a coastal road and a number of lateral roads especially in the central region and branch railway lines that linked the main line with the coastal centers. The east-coast railway branched from the main line at Gemas and ran east of the mountain range, striking the coast in Kelantan in northeast Malaya, and then ran parallel to the coast and rejoined the main line at Haad-yai in Thailand. There were a few roads in the east-coast area, and the important ones were those constructed to connect the ports of Mersing, Endau, and Kuantan with the interior and the road system in Kelantan.[2] It seems that the physical geography of Malaya was good for defensive purposes against a road-bound, mechanized army. However, a skilled infantry with as little artillery as the IJA could operate with deadly force in this terrain.

Percival, who was appointed as GOC Malaya on 16 May 1941, had just 205 days to prepare his heterogeneous army for combat with the IJA.[3] Aged fifty-five years, he had two Indian divisions—the 9th and 11th—and the 8th AIF Division to defend Malaya. He would receive some more reinforcements (including a British division) in the course of the campaign. Percival had fought in the First World War, was a highly decorated officer, and had served in Malaya as chief of staff during 1936–37 before becoming GOC Malaya. Personally, he was a brave officer. He won the Military Cross at Somme and displayed bravery at Ypres and Passchendaele. Percival had the experience of commanding a brigade in combat in 1918. He had skipped the levels of division and corps command and was directly promoted to command an army. This was partly because he was a protégé of the CIGS, John Dill. The tall Percival, with his protruding front teeth, was a brilliant staff officer but was yet to show his mettle in commanding large formations in combat.[4] In the event, he would prove deficient in displaying imagination, drive, and ruthlessness.

Overall, Percival had 85,000 troops, and of them 15,000 were noncombatants.[5] In addition, Percival had 30,000 volunteers (5,000 British, 5,000 Chinese, 4,000 Indians, and 16,000 Malays). The officers and staff of the volunteer forces were British civilians of Malaya. These were not frontline units but mainly protected the LoC and thus released the regulars for battle.[6] The Japanese estimated that Percival had 80,000 troops (30,000 British, 30,000 Indian, and 20,000 Australian) supported by 20,000 Malay volunteers.[7] Thus, the Japanese estimate about the strength of Percival's ground force was more or less accurate. The 9th Indian Division under Major General A. E. Barstow and the 11th Indian Division under Major General D. M. Murray-Lyon comprised the III Indian Corps under Lieutenant General Lewis "Piggy" Heath. Heath came to Malaya in November 1940 and set up headquarters at Kuala Lumpur. Before coming to Malaya, he had commanded the 5th Indian Division in East Africa. His performance against the Italians could not be categorized as sterling but was not incompetent either. In September 1940, the 11th Indian Division comprised 12,000 personnel.[8] In Malaya, while the 9th Division under Murray-Lyon covered the east coast, the 11th Division covered the west coast. And each of these divisions had two brigades.[9]

Overall, the 11th Indian Division was badly trained (individual training was below average, and the men did not carry out combined training with all their

The Invasion 73

arms), and the officers (both at the brigade and battalion levels) were inexperienced.[10] The division was not trained in off-road navigation and in launching counterattacks along the heavily forested terrain.[11] Percival and Heath were not on the best of terms. And Percival found that Heath was not very forthcoming when he inquired about the state of training of the III Indian Corps. Percival unfortunately lacked the forceful personality to force a showdown with Heath.[12] The 11th Indian Division in Kedah State was geared to prevent an attack from Singora. It comprised the 6th Indian Brigade (1st East Surreys, 1st/8thPunjab, and 2nd/16th Punjab) and the 15th Indian Brigade (1st Leicestershire, 2nd/9th Jat, and 1st/14thPunjab). The artillery consisted of the 155th Field Regiment Royal Artillery (RA), 22nd Mountain Regiment, and 80th A/T Regiment. All these units were heavily milked of senior and experienced personnel for raising further units in India. The 28th Indian Brigade was placed under III Indian Corps reserve but was attached to the 9th Indian Division for training and to the 11th Indian Division for operation.[13] It was at best a cumbersome command arrangement. On 1 December 1941, the troops were brought to the second degree of readiness. They were to be ready to implement MATADOR or the alternative plan of occupying Jitra. However, the MATADOR plan was more popular with the 11th Indian Division.[14]

The MATADOR plan evolved from Operation ETONIAN. According to the latter plan, one brigade of the 11th Indian Division from Tanjong-Pau and another brigade from the same division from Sungei Patani were to advance into Thailand and capture Patani and Singora. Heath was against this plan. He believed that it was difficult to advance into Thailand with two brigades, and the attempt to preempt the Japanese was almost impossible. General Headquarters Far East, however, supported the plan. They believed that Thailand would declare war on the side of the Allies, and the British would be invited to advance into the country from Malaya. ETONIAN gradually evolved into MATADOR, which involved capturing the beaches of Singora before the Japanese could get there. Heath opposed MATADOR tooth and nail and assumed that, at the most, instead of advancing into Patani, the forward elements of the 11th Indian Division would be able to move to the Ledge position, which was thirty miles inside Thailand along the Patani Road. He was rightly convinced that the Thais would never invite the British into their country, and the plan for advance into Thailand could only be activated and implemented after the Japanese had violated Thai neutrality. But by that time, it would be too late.[15]

The 9th Indian Division's 8th Indian Brigade was in the neighborhood of Kota Bahru, guarding the beach areas and three aerodromes. And its other brigade (the 22nd) protected Kuantan. The 8th AIF Division—under the flamboyant ginger-haired, cantankerous, and egomaniacal (somewhat like General Douglas MacArthur)[16] Gordon Bennett—with two brigades (22nd and 27th) was guarding Endau, Mersing, and Johore State. Endau gave access to the aerodromes in north Johore, and the Endau River was navigable. Mersing gave access to the main road to Singapore and across the country to Kluang. Occupation of Endau and Mersing by the Japanese would have cut off the Allied troops in north Malaya. Percival feared that the Japanese might land at Mersing and then advance to Kota Tinggi and then down the river to Changi.[17] Robert Lyman, the British military historian, writes that Bennett was a militia officer and lacked the command capabilities of professional staff-trained officers of the regular Australian Army. The 22nd AIF Brigade (including 2nd/18th, 2nd/19th, and 2nd/20th) was under Brigadier H. B. Taylor, and the 27th Brigade (including 2nd/26th, 2nd/29th, and 2nd/30th) was under Brigadier D. S. Maxwell. Including signalers, technicians, and clerks, Bennett had fifteen thousand men under his command. Bennett's headquarters was at Johore Bahru. The Singapore Fortress Division, with two brigades, was defending the southern shore of the island. The Malaya Command, with headquarters at Singapore, had only the 12th Indian Brigade as reserve. This brigade was stationed at the Port Dickson area on the west coast of Malaya.[18]

Historian Francis Pike asserts that since Malaya was not provided with an adequate number of aircraft, Percival's attempt to protect the airfields was a perverse decision.[19] Percival actually had no choice. He had to protect the largely empty airfields that the British had constructed to prevent them from being captured by the IJA and being utilized by the Japanese aircraft. Percival admitted that his troops were scattered over a wide area due to the necessity of protecting the airfields in north Malaya and to prevent the Japanese from establishing any airfields in this region.[20] However, Percival had dispersed his strength throughout Malaya and Singapore without keeping a substantial mobile reserve intact. Thus, his troops were present everywhere and strong nowhere.[21] And he lacked the reserves to contain the Japanese attack at the latter's point of choosing. Let us look into the disposition of the 9th Indian Division in greater detail and the theory of defense that this division implemented.

As regards the defense of northeast Malaya, there were several schools of thought. One school argued that there were insufficient numbers of troops available to effectively defend any length of the beach. Hence, the enemy would be able to land outside the defended portion, thus outflanking the defenders and possibly cutting them off. So the troops should be prepared to fight from prepared positions in the rear where the roads leading to the interior could be defended. This school argued that attempts to hold the beaches would result in a purely linear defense with insufficient troops for launching a counterattack. However, the view of General Headquarters Far East was that it was essential to hold the beaches because it was during the period of landing that the hostile forces would be most vulnerable. If the beaches were given up voluntarily, then the enemy would be able to consolidate its position and intrude inland with greater strength. Again, if the Japanese were attacked when they were landing, then effective cooperation between the Allied forces' army, navy, and air forces would be most effective. This school argued that the problems of linear defense could be overcome by adjusting the forces retained in reserve and those detailed for holding the beaches themselves. Another view was all-round defense. It was difficult with the available forces to position units in a group of perimeter posts and at the same time to protect an adequate length of beach. Further, in such a scheme the defenders should be prepared to hold on for a period of weeks even if surrounded by the enemy and cut off. This scheme of defense was not possible because adequate reserves were not available in the rear to attack the enemy and restore the situation by linking up with the besieged perimeter posts. The 22nd AIF Brigade in Mersing established perimeter defense for units mutually supporting each other and primarily defending the beaches. But in this case, the 27th AIF Brigade was available in Johore for launching a large-scale counterattack. Such large amounts of reserve, noted Brooke-Popham, were not available in Kuantan and Kota Bahru. So Brooke-Popham finally supported the linear scheme of beach defense.[22]

Interestingly, a somewhat similar debate occurred among the German officers in France during early 1944, just before the Normandy invasion. One group of generals, led by General Heinz Guderian and supported by Major General E. Feuchtinger and Field Marshal Gerd von Rundstedt, wanted the armor to be stationed deep inland. And once the zone of Allied invasion became clear, then the armor was to be used in a concentrated punch. In contrast, Field Marshal Erwin Rommel and his lobby argued that the Allies would be most vulnerable when they were landing in the beaches. So the panzers, if needed, should be scattered along the beaches in penny packets or at least should be stationed very close to the potential landing grounds on the beaches. Rommel further pointed out rightly that the panzers would not be able to advance from the inland areas and deploy along the beaches after the completion of Allied landings due to intervention by superior Allied air power.[23] Fortunately for the Allied armor, Rundstedt won out.

Timothy Hall writes that the linear defense of the beach could have been effective if RAF cooperated with the Allied ground units. But, in the absence of RAF's CAS to the Allied ground troops, it was a mistake on the part of Brooke-Popham to cling to this sort of defense.[24] This author asserts that defense of the interior centered on road junctions would also not have worked for the Allies. Due to Japanese air superiority and inadequate training of the Allied units, the Allied battalions would have been unable to advance toward the beaches from inland to attack the Japanese after the latter had consolidated their positions along the beaches. Rather, the Japanese would have infiltrated (as they did later along the Malayan Peninsula) across the countryside and would have bypassed or outflanked the road-bound defense scheme centered on the interior. In hindsight, one could infer that if the 9th Indian Division had put 50 percent of its troops in reserve and the rest along well-defended posts on the beaches, then there was a better chance of stopping the Japanese invasion. But this was not the way in which the two brigades of the 9th Indian Division were deployed just before the Japanese invasion.

The coastal area of northeast Malaya was intersected with creeks and streams, and there were extensive swamps and stretches of jungle.[25] The 8th Indian Brigade (2nd/10th Baluch, 1st/13th Frontier Force Rifles [FFR], and 3rd/17thDogras) under Brigadier (later Major General) B. W. "Billy" Key (who had experience of fighting during the Third Anglo-Afghan War of 1919 and in the North-West Frontier in the late 1930s) with one mountain battery were responsible for a front of fifteen miles from Kelantan to Kuantan. The 9th Indian Division's other brigade (the 22nd) guarded seventeen miles of sea front. The force-space ratio was huge. Generally, in the First World War on the Western Front, a division held four to five miles of front. There was no proper road along the sea side. Key's task was to prevent the three aerodromes in his area from falling into the hands of the invaders. Key could not defend this vast area by building defensive structures all along them, nor could he patrol this region in strength. He focused on selected defensive localities and spread his troops very thinly throughout the area. For building beach defense, Key could not depend on the civilian labor as the latter were concerned essentially about running the civilian economy.[26] In fact, it was stressed upon the British and Indian troops that rubber constituted the lifeblood of the country. Hence, they were not allowed to damage or cut the rubber trees.[27] So felling of rubber trees for conducting training or to establish clear fields of fire was not allowed. Besides rubber and tin, Malaya was second only to Nigeria in the production of palm oil required for the manufacture of candles, soaps, and lubricating grease.[28] Malaya was, after all, the dollar arsenal of the British Empire. Malaya's dollar earnings rose from $98 million during 1938–39 to $135 million in 1940–41.[29]

Key's northernmost battalion was the 3rd/17th Dogras, which held the front between Kemassin to Kelantan River.[30] The Dogras occupied concrete pill boxes a hundred yards apart, and between them were L-shaped firing dugouts and behind them were nests for Bren Guns. Each pillbox had twelve men with two to three Bren Guns, fifteen thousand rounds of .303 ammunition, and a hundred grenades. The defensive posts were well stocked with food, water, and medical kits. This sort of elaborate static beach defense would be unable to stop the swarming Japanese infantry. This was because such defensive structures did not cover all the beaches but only patches of them. And the Japanese infantry was able to infiltrate between the patches of beach defense and also concentrated on a particular patch of beach defense and overwhelmed them. The mouth of the Kelantan River created a deltaic area with lagoons, creeks, and low islands that were submerged due to monsoon rainfall.[31] And this region remained undefended. The British commanders wrongly believed that the Japanese infantry would be unable to operate in this difficult terrain. This region was an Achilles Heel for the Allied defense.

The 2nd/10th Baluch was allotted the coastal sector from Besut River to Kemassin River. The central sector (Telong area) under this battalion was wooded and considered impassable. So this portion was left unguarded. It was an erroneous assumption on the part of the battalion commander. Nothing was impassable or impenetrable for the Japanese infantry. The 2nd/10th Baluch and the 3rd/17th Dogras had two eighteen-pounder guns each.[32] The beach defense constructed by the 2nd/10th Baluch was impressive. First shrapnel mines were laid, and then there was the fence. Shrapnel mines were connected by tripwires to the fences. And then there were pillboxes and dug down posts. Behind them came the eighteen-pounder guns and the A/T minefield. And behind it was the company headquarters. The pillboxes and the forward dugouts were connected by telephone with the company headquarters. The battalion headquarters was at Pasir Puteh village. The 2nd/10th Baluch besides the beach also had to protect the Gong Kedah aerodrome. The latter was guarded by two companies of the Mysore Infantry and one platoon of the Hyderabad State Infantry.[33]

The 22nd Indian Brigade (5th/11th Sikhs, 2nd/12th FFR, and 2nd/18th Royal Garwahl Rifles [RGR]) under Brigadier G. W. A. Painter was located at Kuantan protecting the airport there and the road to Kuala Lumpur, which was the only road north of Mersing connecting the east coast with the west coast.[34] The 2nd/18th RGR was ordered to defend ten miles of beach frontage extending from the mouth of Kuantan River to the south of Balok River in the north. To defend this region, widely scattered pill boxes were constructed, and A/T mines were laid along with wire obstacles. As a point of comparison, before the First World War, in the Western Front, an infantry company occupied a battle frontage of two hundred meters, and a battalion with four companies was expected to defend a frontage of eight hundred meters with a firing, support, and reserve line. The 5th/11th Sikh Regiment was tasked to hold the Soi River, including the ferry and the road approaches to Pekan. This battalion was ordered to guard the aerodrome and also to prepare against potential enemy airborne landings or probings on the LoC from Pahang River in the south to jungle tracks in the north.[35] Let us see the disposition of the 5th/11th Sikh in detail. The B Company (comprising Punjabi Muslims) with mortars and machine guns held the Balat Bridge, the junction of the Belat and Kuantan Rivers, and the Pekan Road. The B Company's position at the beaches went under water during the high tide. The C Company with machine guns defended the east bank of Belat River. A Company with machine guns and two eighteen-pounder guns defended the airport. The Headquarters Company was near the rubber plantation, and the D Company was in reserve.[36]

Overall, on the east coast, an elaborate system of beach defense was prepared especially in the Kota Bahru and Kuantan area. But the 8th and 22nd Indian brigades lacked the manpower to man the pillboxes and provide adequate reserves for launching a counterattack. Moreover, the deployment of the brigades was faulty. The bulk of the troops was deployed in a scattered fashion among the different small strongpoints along the front line with little backup reserves. The widespread dispersion of the troops hampered their collective training. It was further assumed that the RAF would intervene decisively to break up the Japanese landing parties.[37] If the RAF failed to intervene decisively (as happened on 8 December), the wobbly ground defense would not hold. Bennett rightly concluded that the beach defense was faulty. The long, thin line of posts was without depth, and vulnerable flanks were susceptible to Japanese tactics of infiltration and outflanking. Rather, flexible perimeter defense with shorter flanks would have been more effective.[38]

Brooke-Popham noted the nature of beach defense constructed and the deleterious effect of the construction of beach defense on the training of the Indian soldiers in the following words:

> I found it necessary in the case of Malaya to issue orders that the first line of defense was to be the beaches. Previously, except on Singapore Island and Penang,

beaches were going to be occupied only by watching posts, and the first lines of defense were sited inland. This change involved a considerable amount of work and preparation of obstacles and defense posts at Mersing, Kuantan and Kota Bahru. It was found at one period that the work of preparing positions and putting up obstacles was taking up so much time that the training of the troops was being hampered; and in addition, the wire generally required renewing after about six months. Also, I was always on guard against too much reliance upon wire obstacles, barbed wire and pill-boxes, in case this should lead to a Maginot Line complex to the detriment of the offensive spirit. Consequently, a division of available hours was drawn up, allowing a proportion for training, a proportion for renewals, and the balance for new work. As far as practicable, troops constructed the actual defenses in which they would normally fight. New works carried out included not only defensive preparations, but facilities for making counter-attack, e.g., preparation of hidden paths for Bren Carriers.[39]

Percival's opponent, the unusually tall (at six feet two inches) Japanese commander "Tiger" Tomoyuki Yamashita had combat experience in north China. He had commanded a brigade in 1936 in northern China and the 4th Japanese Division at Manchuko during 1938 and 1940.[40] During late 1940 and early 1941, he had been in Italy and Germany as part of the Japanese Military Mission and had met Adolf Hitler. Probably, Yamashita was influenced by the German Blitzkrieg. For the invasion of Malaya, his Twenty-Fifth Japanese Army (which came under Southern Army/Southern Expeditionary Army Group of General [later Field Marshal] Hisaichi Terauchi) had the 13,000 strong Imperial Guards Division (3rd, 4th, and 5th Konoye regiments) under Lieutenant General Takumo Nishimura, 5th Japanese Division (9th Brigade with 11th and 41st regiments and 21st Brigade with 21st and 42nd regiments) with 16,000 personnel under Lieutenant General Takuro Matsui and the 18th Japanese Division (23rd Brigade with 55th and 56th regiments and 35th Brigade with 114th and 124th regiments) with 13,000 men (mostly coal miners from northern Kyushu) under Lieutenant General Renya Mutaguchi (who would later fight the Imphal-Kohima Campaign). The 5th Japanese Division had combat experience from China and had clashed with General Georgy Zhukov's mechanized Soviet forces at Nomonhan. This division had trained in combined arms and amphibious operations. In total there were about 60,000 men supported by four hundred guns (including trench mortars). In addition, the 56th Japanese Division under Lieutenant General Masao Watanabe was at standby in Japan as reserve.[41] As we will see later, Yamashita would not require this division for the Malaya-Singapore Campaign.

The III Japanese Army Air Corps and the 22nd Naval Air Flotilla/Fleet had 600 operational aircraft.[42] As a point of comparison, 350 Japanese aircraft participated in the Pearl Harbor attack.[43] The Japanese overestimated the number of planes that the British and Australians disposed in Malaya-Singapore. Before the war, the Japanese Southern Army assumed that the British had 330 aircraft (108 bombers, 108 fighters, 48 reconnaissance planes and the rest torpedo bombers and seaplanes) in the Singapore-Malaya theater.[44] On 7 December 1941, Allied air strength in Malaya and Singapore was 181 serviceable aircraft.[45] Of them, 158 were operational on the day of invasion. The breakdown was as follows: 60 Brewster Buffalo fighters, 35 Blenheim bombers, 12 Blenheim fighters, 24 Hudson, 24 torpedo bombers, and 3 flying boats.[46]

Besides obsolete aircraft, the infrastructure of the Allied air force establishment was problematic. While constructing the airfields in north and central Malaya, the principles of dispersal and camouflage were not taken into account. Both Alor Star and Kota Bahru were old civil grounds with little room for dispersal. The buildings at Alor Star were constructed on the old RAF peacetime layout and were congested and very close to the runway. Most of the aerodromes had no form of camouflage. The ground was first deforested, and, strangely, while the aerodromes were constructed, no attempt was made to utilize the natural surroundings or irregular outlines to obtain concealment. This was probably due to sheer negligence and utter contempt of Japanese air power. The airfields stood out stark and bare against the surrounding country. Further, financial considerations prevented the acquisition of sufficient land for effective dispersal of the aircraft. Except the airfields at Kota Bahru and Kuantan, the other airfields suffered from lack of an adequate number of AA guns for protection. Moreover, most of the airfields were guarded by Indian State Troops, whose level of training was below average.[47] Hence, these airfields were vulnerable to Japanese bombing and capture by infiltration of the Japanese infantry.

The Allied commanders had seriously underestimated Japanese aviation. The Japanese were regarded as a poor sort of people who fought with swords and could not fly airplanes properly. They were considered slit eyed, so they couldn't see in the dark. Brooke-Popham added that the Japanese were neither air minded nor were properly trained.[48] Air Vice Marshal Paul Maltby, Assistant AOC RAF Far East Command (12 January–10 February 1942), accepted that "training and assessment of operational readiness had, however, been based on an underestimation of the enemy. The tactics thus taught and practiced proved unsuitable and costly against Japanese Navy 'O' fighter, which was greatly superior to the Buffalo in performance. Moreover, advanced training had suffered because, prior to the formation of an OTU in September 1941, all pilots had joined their squadrons without having received individual operational training."[49] The Allied air establishment was further plagued by a serious shortage of reserve aircraft and reserve pilots.[50]

The III Japanese Army Air Corps under Lieutenant General Michiyo Sugawara played the principal role in the Japanese air campaign against the Allied troops in Malaya. It was placed under Headquarter Southern Army in Indochina, as besides supporting Yamashita's troops in Malaya-Singapore, this air group was also in charge of supporting the 15th Japanese Army in Burma and the 16th Japanese Army in Sumatra. The III Japanese Army Air Corps had under it the 3rd Air Group, 7th Air Group, 12th Air Group, 15th Independent Air Fleet, and 81st Air Fleet. The 3rd Air Group had the 27th Air Fleet (light bombers), 59th Air Fleet (fighters), 75th Air Fleet, and 90th Air Fleet. The 7th Air Group had the 12th Air Fleet (heavy bombers), 60th Air Fleet (heavy bombers), 64th Air Fleet (fighters), and 98th Air Fleet (heavy bombers). The 12th Air Group had the 1st Air

Fleet (fighters) and the 11th Air Fleet (fighters). The 15th Independent and the 81st Air Fleets had reconnaissance aircrafts.[51] Besides Zero fighters, the Japanese Army Air Corps used the Nakajima KI 27 (Nate), which had a range of 390 miles, and also the KI 43, which had a range of 740 miles.[52] In general, the Japanese aircraft had greater range than the British ones.

In addition to enjoying air superiority, Yamashita had two hundred light and medium tanks.[53] And Percival had no tanks at all. Due to the presence of a large number of small bridges in Malaya, the Allied commanders believed that heavy infantry tanks could not be deployed in this theater. So they asked for fourteen-ton light tanks. But none were supplied. Thus, the Japanese enjoyed substantial aerial and armored superiority over the Allied forces in Malaya. However, besides numerical superiority in ground troops, Percival enjoyed substantial superiority over Yamashita's force as regards field artillery.[54]

Japanese knowledge about the climate and topographical features of the Malayan Peninsula was excellent, thanks to the reconnaissance raids by Tsuji and his company and also due to the information supplied by the resident Japanese of Malaya. They owned iron mines and rubber estates and operated freighters along the east coast of Malaya and Singapore up to Japan. They not only had an intimate knowledge of the coastline but also kept a watch on the Allied defensive activities and military movements. Japanese sales representatives moved about freely just before the onset of the Pacific War, and many of them were professional photographers. All of them passed information back to Tokyo.[55]

Major Kunitake was the author of the Japanese invasion plan of Malaya. Planning for the conquest of Malaya was set in motion in the Operations Section Headquarters of the General Staff in August 1940, and the plan was formulated by the end of October 1941.[56] The Japanese plan was that, with the aid of naval force and under an aerial umbrella, the principal elements of the Twenty-Fifth Japanese Army were to be embarked near the frontier of Thailand and Malaya. The aim was to avoid any fighting with Thailand's force, but if the latter interfered with Japanese operations, then they should be crushed. The Japanese ground force was to advance to Sungei Perak on Malaya's west coast within fifteen days. Then, there should be an advance to the southern end of the Malayan Peninsula opposite Singapore Island. Landings might occur in the southeast of the Malayan Peninsula in the Kuantan-Mersing area by the 56th Japanese Division if necessary to assist the overland drive. The 5th Japanese Division was to land at Singora (on the east coast of Kra Isthmus) and Patani in Thailand near Malaya. Its order was to advance from the Sadao and Betong area to the Perak River and to capture the vital points and the airfields. Then, it was to advance along the west coast of Malaya and capture Kuala Lumpur. The 9th Japanese Brigade was to advance along the Singora-Alor Star Road, and the 42nd Japanese Regiment of the 21st Japanese Brigade was to advance along Patani-Kroh Road. After capturing Kuala Lumpur, the troops would move toward Johore Strait and capture the Johore Bridge if possible. The 56th Japanese Infantry Regiment of the 18th Japanese Division was to land at Kota Bahru and then advance south along the east coast of Malaya. The rest of the 18th Japanese Division was to land at Singora and Patani in January 1942 and move into northern Malaya and Penang. While the initial landings were to be made by the 5th and 18th Japanese divisions, the Imperial Guards Division was to move overland from Bangkok. The Imperial Guards Division was to follow the advance of the 5th Japanese Division. It was assumed that Singapore could be captured by early March 1942.[57] Actually, the Japanese would advance ahead of their timetable and would be able to capture Singapore before that date. Yamashita, somewhat like Field Marshal Erwin Rommel, decided to gamble with his supply lines and aimed to push his force to the extreme in order to seize the initiative and drive back the enemy without pause, never giving the latter a chance to regroup and dig in. Yamashita called it *Kirimomi Sakusen* (driving charge).[58] Thus, at the tactical-operational realms, the Japanese plan was to carry out bold maneuvers against numerically superior Allied forces, and it ultimately paid them dividends.[59]

Hisayuki Yokoyama asserts that the Japanese aviation aimed to gain control of the air by aerial extermination action (offensive counter-air operation that involved destruction of the enemy aircraft in the air and on the ground) and considered CAS as secondary.[60] This author believes that the Japanese aerial plan considered providing CAS to the Twenty-Fifth Japanese Army to be as important as the counter-air operation against the Allied air force. Yamashita established a rapport with the air commanders and held a conference at Saigon on 15 November 1941 to discuss the issue of interservice cooperation.[61] The Japanese Army Air Force (JAAF) units were expected to gain control of the air by preemptive attack on Allied airfields jointly with the Japanese Navy Air Force (JNAF) units.[62] Japanese concentration of the air units for the Malayan Campaign occurred in two phases. The first phase involved concentration and deployment of the air units in northern Indo-China. This phase was undertaken between 15 November and 1 December 1941. And the second phase involved concentration and deployment in southern Indochina. The second phase was completed by 6 December 1941. The 3rd and the 10th Japanese Air Brigades were to annihilate hostile aerial units in the Kota Bahru area, and the 27th Air Regiment was to support the advance of the Japanese ground forces from Singora. The 7th Air Brigade was ordered to annihilate the hostile aerial units in the Kedah area. The 12th Air Brigade was charged with the air defense of Indochina.[63] To sum up, the Japanese had a clear-cut invasion plan ready to be implemented by salted troops supported by an experienced and numerically superior air force. In contrast, Percival's not-so-well-trained troops suffered from doctrinal confusion about the best way of defending themselves.

Retreat from the Beaches

On 6 December 1941, the slow Japanese troop transports were sailing west toward northeast Malaya along the south Indochina coast. The troopships had fighter cover. On the same day, despite tropical rainfall, the reconnaissance mission was flown from Kota Bahru. A Hudson of Number 1 Royal Australian Air Force (RAAF) Squadron under Flight Lieutenant J. C. Ramshaw located two approaching convoys at noon. One convoy comprised of a motorboat, a minelayer, and a minesweeper about 185 miles from Kota Bahru. Another convoy comprising a battleship, five cruisers, and seven destroyers was spotted about 265 miles from Kota Bahru. At 1300 hours another Hudson from the same squadron observed another convoy comprising two cruisers, ten destroyers, and ten merchant vessels roughly 260 miles from Kota Bahru. By 1517 hours, another message came that the third convoy had twenty-one merchant vessels. One of the Hudsons was chased by a Japanese aircraft. So the Japanese knew that they were being watched. In fact, the Japanese feared that the British would launch a massive aerial attack on the Japanese bases along south Indochina. Had such an attack been launched, the Japanese plan for conquering Malaya-Singapore would have been seriously jeopardized.[64] From 5 December onward, the 11th Indian Division had been on a half hour's notice for MATADOR, which at this stage was designed for an advance into Singora only and not to Patani.[65] On 6 December, despite the authority given to Brooke-Popham from London, the latter decided not to initiate MATADOR.[66] On 7 December 1941, the commander in chief, China Station, informed Brooke-Popham and Percival that aircraft reconnaissance over the southern part of the Gulf of Siam was handicapped by bad visibility. However, scattered Japanese surface units had been sighted, but there was no definite indication of their intentions.[67] The Japanese were surprised that even twenty-four hours after their invasion force was sighted, the British did not bomb the airfields in south Indochina.[68]

Andrew Gilchrist opines that Churchill was against initiating MATADOR.[69] The plan envisaged the 11th Indian Division advancing from north Kedah to deny Japanese landing near Singora. In the absence of MATADOR going off, the 9th Japanese Brigade landed at Singora and the 42nd Japanese Regiment with a section of field artillery regiment at Patani in south Thailand. Landings also occurred in Kota Bahru in the northeast of Kelantan.[70] Rough sea hampered Japanese landing operations at Singora and Patani, and many landing craft overturned and also sank and ran aground. Initially, 13,500 troops landed at Singora and 7,550 at Patani. Yamashita himself landed with the first wave at Singora. The total number of troops landed at these places and at Kota Bahru was about 26,640, and of them 17,230 were combat soldiers. The rest were service and air base support troops.[71] The Allied high command in Malaya before the war estimated that the RAF would be able to destroy 45 percent of the invasion fleet. In reality, only two or three empty transport vessels were sunk.[72]

On 8 December, Japanese aircraft bombed Gong Kedah aerodrome.[73] The Japanese air force also targeted Singapore Island. At 0415 hours, the Japanese aircraft dropped bombs at random on the civilians and Tengah airfield. The Air Raid Precaution (ARP) was not manned, and the lights in the town were on. There was no blackout. Nobody in the Malaya Command expected a Japanese air raid. The assumption was that the Japanese aircraft at Indochina were too far away to launch a raid on Singapore.[74] The Allied commanders should have remembered that in August 1937 the Japanese used Mitsubishi twin-engine bombers to attack Chinese cities from bases seven hundred miles away in Taiwan and Kyushu.[75] The ARP people in Singapore had joked that the ARP stations need not be manned in the night because the Japanese pilots were myopic and could not fly in the dark.[76] The raid resulted in sixty-one fatal casualties, and 193 injured persons (most of them were Chinese and some Indians) were taken to the hospital. When Governor of Singapore Island Shenton Thomas (who was previously a schoolmaster) received the news that the Japanese were landing at Kota Bahru, he immediately issued instructions for the internment of all the Japanese and seizure of the fishing vessels in Singapore. He further assured the secretary of state for Colonies that despite the "terror" bombing, the behavior of the civilians was exemplary.[77] It must be said that while attacking Singapore Island, the Japanese aerial plan was not to terrorize the civilians but to concentrate on bombing the airfields, military factories, water works, power plants, fuel storage, military areas, army headquarters, and administrative organizations. The JNAF units were to concentrate on the naval installations and ships.[78]

The Japanese attack at Kota Bahru in Malaya started well before Pearl Harbor. The Japanese naval aircraft started their attack on the American naval base at 0755 hours, Hawaiian time, on 7 December (8 December Far Eastern Time).[79] The Japanese ships had neared Kota Bahru at 2220 on 7 December (local time). Many landing craft were capsized due to the turbulent sea. The Takumi Detached Force (5,300 troops) started landing at Kota Bahru at 0130 on 8 December (7 December at Hawaii) 1941.[80] Major General Hiroshi Takumi's force included the 56th Japanese Regiment of the 18th Japanese Division, one battery of mountain guns, two quick-firing guns, one battery of AA guns, one company of engineers, one section of signalers, one section of medical and sanitation personnel, and a field hospital.[81] By 0330, 8 December, the landings were well under way. Despite heavy rain, turbulent sea, and heavy fire from the defenders, the Japanese converged on the beach defense.[82] If the Allied aircraft and the Force Z (whose fate we will discuss later) had made a joint attack either on 7 or 8 December on the Japanese troopships, the contours of the Malaya-Singapore Campaign would have been different.[83] The Allied defeat in Malaya-Singapore was not inevitable. The day of 7–8 December 1941 was a probable turning point. It came and went without Percival and Brooke-Popham taking advantage of this window of opportunity.

Kota Bahru was five miles up the Kelantan River from the coast of northeast Malaya.[84] There were pillboxes on the beaches of Kota Bahru at every one thousand yards. Only at Kota Bahru was beach defense somewhat successful. The initial Japanese beachhead was only three thousand yards wide, and they gradually expanded it. Moving over the Japanese corpses, the Japanese wire cutters cut the barbed wire of the Indians' defensive posts. Behind them, the Japanese infantry soldiers piled up the sand in front of them with their steel helmets and crept forward like moles. At Kota Bahru, the Japanese lost some 1,500 men, but they relentlessly pushed on.[85] The Allied soldiers were good in defending static defensive positions, and this was proved in the case of Kota Bahru. Strong Indian defense at Kota Bahru created anxiety in the mind of the top echelons of the Japanese high command. Admiral Matome Ugaki, commander of the 8th Heavy Cruiser Division and later chief of staff of the Combined Fleet under Admiral

Isoroku Yamamoto, in his diary made the following entry on 8 December 1941: "In the Malaya area, our forces reportedly succeeded in landing at 1330 (Tokyo time), but it's quite dubious whether the landing at Kota Bahru, which is more important was a success or not. I understand that after the first landing the rest apparently withdrew. I am very worried about this issue."[86] The losses that the Japanese suffered at Kota Bahru had no effect on their subsequent rapid exploitation. Moreover, the Japanese captured twenty-seven field guns, seventy-three machine guns, 157 vehicles, and thirty-three railway trucks at Kota Bahru.[87] Some twenty-eight Japanese light bombers escorted by eleven fighters carried out operations in the Kota Bahru area. In the ensuing aerial combat, the British lost ten fighters, and five Japanese aircraft were seriously damaged.[88]

The campaign did not start well for the Indian troops. At 0630 hours, in Machang a Japanese aircraft dropped smoke bombs on one company of the Mysore Infantry. The jawans panicked, believing that they were being gassed. Next, the Japanese aircraft dropped high-explosive bombs, which caused thirty-five casualties.[89] Not all the beaches could be guarded by the British and Indian troops. And sections of the beach that were held by penny packets of Indian troops were overwhelmed by the enemy, who concentrated troops at their point of choosing, and some defensive posts were bypassed and then outflanked from behind. The Japanese infiltrated between the Dogra's defensive position and the Kota Bahru airfield. Key ordered the gap to be pinched off. The 1st/13th FFR of the 8th Indian Brigade and the 2nd/12th FFR of the 22nd Indian Brigade ordered for this purpose failed in this task. Their advance was delayed by numerous rivers and creeks. Unlike the Japanese troops, the Indian infantry was not trained to move speedily through this type of terrain. The 2nd/12th FFR suffered about one hundred casualties.[90] Moreover, in the afternoon, Key received an erroneous report that the Japanese were attacking the Kota Bahru airfield.[91] Key did not crosscheck this piece of information. Probably the panicky commander was all the more ready to accept bad news. A detachment comprising thirty-nine Japanese light bombers supported by six fighters again attacked the Kota Bahru airfield. As a result, eleven British aircraft were destroyed.[92]

The Japanese frontline troops equipped with submachine guns, LMGs, and mortars maintained a high volume of fire, which created the impression in the mind of the Allied troops and their commanders that large bodies of enemy with heavy weapons were lurking around.[93] Panic spread upward from the battalions to the senior levels of command. Shortly after 1800 hours on 8 December, Key was informed by Barstow that the defense of Kota Bahru was left to the former's discretion. Barstow warned Key not to lose his brigade in defending the Kota Bahru airfield largely denuded of RAF aircraft.[94] Barstow should have realized that disengaging from an aggressive enemy and carrying out an orderly retreat of inexperienced troops without aerial support was next to impossible. Further, such a move would lower the morale of the men and would dislocate the rickety defensive line along the beaches of northeast Malaya. Retreat by the Allied troops would encourage the Japanese to advance faster. Barstow should have ordered Key to hold on at all costs and rushed troops to Kota Bahru from those sectors not yet engaged. Instead, very early in the campaign, he encouraged his subordinate to withdraw.

Just after 2100 hours, the Japanese infantry infiltrated around the Kota Bahru aerodrome. The 73rd Field Battery by this time had set the airfield on fire. The red glow lit up the whole area, and the Japanese opened a heavy fire. The staccato of Japanese machine-gun fire unnerved the untrained Indian soldiers. The CO and adjutant of the 1st Hyderabad State Infantry were killed. Since the VCOs (who were capable of leading sections and platoons) were not trained for battalion-level command, due to the lack of leadership this battalion disintegrated. As a result, there were some desertions from the 1st Hyderabad State Infantry.[95] Amitav Ghosh in his novel portrays the sense of despair and rumor that spread among the 1st Hyderabad State Infantry. It was rumored that there was leadership failure on the part of the CO and the NCOs. There was a sort of mutiny among the panicky jawans, and they also shot at the officers.[96] One of the weaknesses of the Indian battalion was that once the British officers became casualties, the unit became rudderless and vulnerable.

Soon after the invasion, the 4th/19th Hyderabad Regiment of the 12th Indian Brigade (its other three units were 2nd Argyll and Sutherland Highlanders and 5th/2nd Punjab) was ordered for action in northeast Malaya. Like other Indian battalions, the 4th/19th was weakened due to extensive milking for raising new units. The experienced men were replaced with raw recruits and old reservists. A few weeks before the Japanese attack, this battalion received 240 recruits who had no practice with two-inch mortars, submachine guns, and hand grenades. It must be noted that about 90 percent of the jawans were illiterate, and it was difficult to impart technical knowledge to them. The battalion itself lacked steel helmets, and its rifles were the same as those with which the jawans had fought in East Africa and Persia during the First World War.[97] While marching to the battlefield, this unit's spirit was lowered by a rumor that the brigade commander and the brigade major of 8th Indian Brigade was killed. This information later proved to be false. The 4th/19th Hyderabad finally reached Kettereh (twelve miles south of Kota Bahru) at 1730 hours on 9 December. The Japanese by this time had reached the Kota Bahru airfield. The airfield was actually at Pengkalan Chapa, about five miles east of Kota Bahru town.[98] The 4th/19th Hyderabad witnessed the defeated soldiers of the 8th Indian Brigade streaming back through Kettereh. The men were in bad shape. Most of them were without arms and equipment, and some were without boots.[99] Such a sight was not encouraging to the fighting spirit of the men of Hyderabad. Immediately after arrival, the 4th/19th Hyderabad was ordered that they might have to retreat soon.[100] Obviously such an order resulted in a further drop of morale. Lieutenant Colonel E. L. Wilson Haffenden, CO of the 4th/19th Hyderabad, describes the ensuing chaos in the following words: "Large number of the 8th Brigade had been cut off—the country was intensely thick and intersected by streams which had, owing to the monsoon, flooded a great deal of the country in that area, thus increasing the difficulties of the withdrawing troops. The 4th/19th Hyderabad Regiment . . . in close country without any opportunity to recconoitre tracks, etc. The night was extremely dark and it was impossible to see more than 25 yards and impossible to distinguish friend from foe at more than five yards."[101] The Indian soldiers were not trained for nocturnal operations in the jungle. They developed a feeling of being lost, and incidents of friendly fire broke out. In fact, Ghosh writes that the panicky Indian troops lost fire discipline and fired their Bren Guns madly and wildly. All was in chaos. The Japanese exploited this chaos and because of their training had no problem in advancing through the waterlogged jungles during the night. On 9 December, the 2nd/10th Baluch retreated from the beaches leaving behind the eighteen-pounder guns and much material due to lack of transport. The 2nd/10th Baluch, which had worked so hard to defend the beach, had to withdraw without firing a shot due to withdrawal of the neighboring formations.[102] This pattern would be repeated throughout the Malaya campaign. On the same day, the 8th Indian Brigade had retreated to a line in Kelantan running from Peringot to Mulong.[103] Voluntary withdrawal of the Allied ground units under the panicking British commanders allowed the Japanese to consolidate their control around Kota Bahru. Ugaki was relieved and made the following entry for 9 December: "My headache was the occupation of Kota Bahru. But, according to the 3rd Destroyer Squadron report, they are engaged in hard fighting, their landing craft having drifted away, but the Takumi Force has already occupied the airfield, as was revealed later. I was much relieved at that."[104]

At Kelantan, there were twenty-one aircraft (ten Hudsons, eight Blenheims, two Vildebeestes, and a Swordfish biplane). The Japanese air force attacked this airport twice on 9 December with twenty-seven planes each time. They carried out bombing from a height of three thousand feet. Eight Allied aircraft were damaged, and the ammunition store was hit. After the air raids, the RAF Station Commander vacated this airfield.[105] After a single day of combat, one-third of the 158 operational aircraft of the Allied air force became unfit for use.[106]

The objective of defending north Malaya was to allow the airfields situated there to be used by the RAF. In the absence of RAF aircraft in the airfields of north Malaya, the object was to deny the latter's use to the enemy as long as possible. However, on 10 December 1941, the air force personnel withdrew from Gong Kedah airfield hurriedly, without destroying the materials and the installations. There was lack of coordination between the Allied infantry and the RAF ground crews. And the 2nd/10th Baluch lacked the tools to destroy the airfield. The Japanese took it almost intact and brought it into immediate use.[107] Meanwhile, Kota Bahru airfield was used by the naval Zero fighters.[108]

By 10 December, the Japanese air force had gained air superiority over Kota Bahru and Kedah areas.[109] On 10 December, the 4th/19th Hyderabad made a reconnaissance of the Ketnereh area. By 1500 hours, the two armored cars and six carriers of the battalion arrived. The battalion was short of four carriers, which had broken down due to mechanical faults during training just before the battle and were not replaced.[110]

It was decided to withdraw the 8th Indian Brigade to Machang with the 4th/19th Hyderabad functioning as the rearguard. The 4th/19th Hyderabad with a battery of 4.5-inch howitzers and a section of A/T guns were constituted as a rearguard, and the objective was to withdraw from Kettereh just before dawn. However, due to intense confusion and indiscriminate firing by the troops, the battalion was ordered to withdraw south of Kettereh immediately. It withdrew to Machang. The troops of the 8th Indian Brigade were not informed that the 4th/19th Hyderabad had been withdrawn. Communications among the units within the brigade had already started to break down. Effective staff coordination among the various battalions was extremely poor. At 2100 hours, the other units of the 8th Indian Brigade, fearing that the Japanese had gone behind them, opened fire on the 4th/19th Hyderabad with rifles and three-inch mortars.[111] During the night, the troops were frightened and opened fire at imaginary foes in the Machang village. The 2nd/10th Baluch erroneously believed that they were being fired upon by the Japanese reconnaissance parties. They were probably fired upon by the 4th/19th Hyderabad. The British officers, VCOs, and NCOs failed to control the fright of the men. This incident occurred because most of the personnel were raw, and due to heavy milking, 50 percent of the VCOs and the NCOs were new to their job. John A. English writes that in the combat-effective armies of western Europe (and especially in the German Army), small-group cohesion depended on the corporals. The corporals functioned as father and uncle in the artificial family (closely knit platoon).[112] The fighting spirit of the small units was dependent on the status and quality of the corporals. In the Indian Army, the VCOs and the NCOs took the position of corporals. Further, the jawans were trained for beach defense but not for moving in the jungle.

Actually, only a Japanese jitter party had come between the main body and the rearguard. Pushing a strong advance guard was a characteristic of the IJA in approaching a meeting engagement.[113] At 2100 hours, a Japanese patrol (sixty men) equipped with submachine guns, LMGs, and a couple of three-inch mortars left behind by the Allied coast defense troops made contact with the forward troops of the 4th/19th Hyderabad. The first encounter of this battalion involved shelling by the mortars, and the badly trained personnel of the 4th/19th Hyderabad displayed nervousness. Every company assumed that they were being attacked and outflanked. They opened fire indiscriminately, and rumor spread that the enemy had penetrated at several places.[114] The objective of Yamashita's troops was to provoke fluid running battles repeatedly in order to keep the Allied troops retreating continuously and in a chaotic state, thus offsetting their numerical superiority.[115]

The Japanese infantry spread out and skirmished with the objective of penetration. Inexperienced and badly trained troops are especially vulnerable to rumors. A few Japanese with two to three machine guns would get behind the Allied lines during the night and fire long bursts. It created the impression in the nervous minds of the British and Indian soldiers that the enemy was behind them in large numbers and their LoC had been cut. Sometimes a few Japanese snipers would also get behind the Allied troops. They climbed on the trees and fired blindly. The individual Japanese infantryman was a master at infiltration and camouflage. At times, Japanese infantry also placed machine guns on tree tops to get a wider field of fire. Such firing did not cause many casualties but adversely impacted the shaky morale of the Allied troops by making them think that the enemy was behind them. The British and Indian soldiers, already looking behind their shoulders, were then ordered to withdraw, and another retreat would start.[116] And this process was repeated.

By 11 December, the 8th Indian Brigade was at Chong Dong, twenty-five miles south of Kota Bahru and was withdrawing to the railroad junction at Kuala Krai.[117] On the morning of 11 December 1941, the 2nd/10th Baluch was ordered to take a position west of the road Kota Bahru-Krai near the paddy fields south of Machang. The 2nd/12th FFR was on the east of the road. The 4th/19th Hyderabad was ordered to protect the left flank of the 8th Indian Brigade, which extended from Sungel Nal and the Kelantan River. The battalion had to cover a frontage of eight to ten miles. The region was full of trackless jungle. Patrolling in this difficult region amid incessant rainfall proved exhausting for the sparsely trained troops. One patrol even got lost in the jungle.[118] A Japanese jitter party penetrated among the Indian troops. In sheer anxiety, the brigade blew up the steel-girder bridge over the Kelantan River. Due to breakdown of wireless communication (a common occurrence in Malaya), the various units within the brigade were unable to communicate with each other.[119] This in turn begs the question as to why runners were not used in order to maintain communications between the battalions and the brigade headquarters.

Key writes that due to the monsoon, it was raining continuously, and the men became depressed.[120] Well, the Japanese were not depressed. This was because the British and Indian soldiers were not roughened up by hard physical training. In contrast, the Japanese infantry was trained like the German *Waffen SS*, in a harsh training regimen that resulted in casualties. The cult of emperor worship and the social fabric of Japanese society prepared the Japanese infantry to fight hard and if necessary to die hard.[121] Key writes about the techniques of Japanese warfare: "And the Japs had a habit of slipping through the jungle and forming blocks in the rear."[122] This can be termed as "fish hook" tactics. The Indian and British troops and their British officers lacked the confidence and training to uproot the "hook" by surrounding the Japanese who had established roadblocks at their rear. Maneuver warfare involved lightning thrusts and sudden rushes.[123] This is exactly what the Japanese were doing.

Major H. P. Thomas, who commanded the Mixed Reinforcement Camp in Singapore, summed up the Japanese tactics in the following words: "Briefly, it consisted in locating the areas held and the flanks by drawing fire, working round or through small parties, threatening the road—the vital feature—and causing confusion by shooting from unexpected directions."[124] Heath and Barstow were baffled by the rapidity of the Japanese advance. They and their troops had no counter to the abovementioned Japanese tactics. By 11 December, all the Allied aircraft were withdrawn from northern Malaya.[125] Table 3.1 gives an idea about the dwindling number of various types of Allied aircraft operational in Malaya between 7 and 24 December 1941.

In the night of 11–12 December, Heath decided to leave for Singapore Island to impress upon Percival the necessity of retreating from Kelantan to Kuala Lipis.[126]

Table 3.1. Operationally Serviceable Allied Aircraft in Malaya, 7–24 December 1941

Types of Aircraft						
	Date					
	7 Dec.	12 Dec.	17 Dec.	19 Dec.	22 Dec.	24 Dec.
Bombers (including Torpedo Bombers)	59	45	59	58	49	61
Fighters	72	53	58	53	45	50
Reconnaissance	24	7	12	11	12	13
Flying Boats	3	3	4	4	3	3
Total	158	108	133	126	109	127

Source: Despatch on the Far East by Air Chief Marshal Robert Brooke-Popham, Commander in Chief Far East (October 17, 1940–December 27, 1941), September 8, 1942, Appendix N, CAB/66/28/33, PRO, Kew, Surrey, 72.

Heath should not have left the front at such a critical juncture. He should have stayed to keep an eye on the unfolding architecture of raging battle. How he would counter the Japanese after retreating to Kuala Lipis is a question left unanswered. Heath attempted to justify his nervous actions in the following words: "On the 10th I was in telephonic communication with General Barstow and also General Key most of the time. General Key reported that he had lost both aerodromes, and that there only remained the third aerodrome at Machang, which was not yet in a state to be used. . . . So on the 11th a decision was made . . . to move back the 8th Brigade from Kelantan to Pahang. . . . We had this vulnerable L of C."[127] Heath and his subordinates (Barstow and Key) overreacted to the potential threat posed by the Japanese on the LoC of their troops. They never conceptualized that the British and Indian troops should make an attempt to sever the LoC of the forward-most Japanese troops.

Meanwhile, a naval disaster occurred for the British in the South China Sea that had a decisive impact on the shape of the unfolding ground battle. Admiral Tom S. V. Phillips (nicknamed Tom Thumb for his short stature) who was the vice chief of the Naval Staff from the summer of 1939 onward, was appointed as commander in chief of the Eastern Fleet in October 1941. The RN was hard pressed in the Atlantic and in the Mediterranean. German surface units and U-boats posed a serious threat to the North American and Russian convoy routes. So Churchill decided to send a token force named Force Z to the Far East. This force involved *Prince of Wales* (a battleship), which functioned as the flagship of the detachment, and one old battlecruiser, *Repulse*, commanded by Captain W. G. Tennant. *Repulse* was completed in 1916 and fought in 1917 (also the last time when Phillips had seen action) and was twice modernized in the interwar era. The thirty-six-thousand-ton lightly armored *Repulse*, with 69 officers and 1,240 sailors, carried six fifteen-inch guns and fifteen four-inch guns. For AA defense, this ship had four high-angle -inch guns and four eight-barrel "pompoms." The thirty-five-thousand-ton *Prince of Wales* with twenty-eight-knot speed was commissioned in 1941. It carried 100 officers and 1,502 men and had ten 14.2-inch guns, eight pairs of 5.25-inch heavy AA guns, and six multiple pompom batteries, plus lighter Bofors and Oerlikon AA guns. Compared to *Repulse*, the *Prince of Wales*'s AA defense was better but proved inadequate against the swarm of land-based Japanese bombers. The aircraft carrier *Indomitable*, which was supposed to join this naval detachment, ran aground on the way from the West Indies. Popular historian Dan Van Der Vat claims that the *Indomitable* would not have been able to protect Force Z against the Japanese land-based high level bombers and torpedo bombers.[128] I disagree. At least, *Indomitable*'s fighters would have taken a heavy toll on the attacking Japanese aircraft. And this would have surely discouraged the Japanese from launching successive waves of attacks on Phillips's ships.

Admiral Phillips decided to attack the Japanese transports and warships that had been reported early on 8 December 1941 to be landing troops on the east coast of the Kra Isthmus and at Kota Bahru. Phillips's intent was to attack the Japanese transports at Singora and at Kota Bahru at the dawn of 10 December regardless of the availability of friendly fighter protection. The AOC RAF declared that he was doubtful of providing fighter protection to the Allied ships. Phillip's Force Z comprised the *Prince of Wales, Repulse, Electra, Express, Vampire,* and *Tenedos*. Force Z sailed at 1735 on 8 December and sailed east of the Anamba Islands and then to the northern direction. Phillips believed that a Japanese battlecruiser along with cruisers, destroyers, and submarines was supporting the landing operation at Singora and Patani. Frequent rainstorms and a low cloud on Tuesday (9 December) favored the British ships. However, between 1700 and 1830, the weather cleared, and Japanese naval reconnaissance aircraft spotted Force Z. At 1834, *Tenedos* was ordered to return to Singapore due to its low endurance. After his ships had been sighted, Phillips decided to turn back to Singapore. At the midnight of 9 December, the Japanese submarine *I-58* sighted Force Z and reported its location to the 22nd Japanese Air Flotilla of the JNAF stationed near Saigon.[129]

The Japanese were a bit unnerved about the probable activities of Force Z. They estimated that the two British capital ships were more powerful than *Kongo* and *Haruna*, the two fast battleships under Vice Admiral Nobutake Kondo (commander of the 2nd Japanese Fleet) operating in the South China Sea. So the Japanese were keeping tabs on the movement of Phillips's ships.[130] The Japanese high command knew that a detachment comprising British surface units was advancing toward the landing crafts disgorging IJA troops along the coast of northeast Malaya. Ugaki penned his surprise about the heavy odds against which Force Z was sailing in his diary entry dated 9 December in the following words:

> What can be the purpose of the British fleet's northward voyage? Is it to interrupt our landing at Kota Bahru? Do they intend to find some nice game in attempting guerrilla warfare? Or are they going to adhere to their old principle of fighting the enemy wherever they sight him, and then display their valor after controlling the

enemy? From our point of view, it is too headstrong, but their conduct of outrageous audacity is praiseworthy. I don't know if they know or not that subs, mines, several heavy cruisers, two high speed battleships, and considerably predominant fighter planes are in the southern part of French Indochina.[131]

At midnight on 9 December, Chief of Staff Rear Admiral A. F. E. Palliser sent a message that the Japanese were probably landing at Kuantan. Kuantan was not far off from the return route to Singapore and was considered a key military position that the Allies needed to defend. The nearest Japanese air bases were four hundred miles away at Indochina. Phillips erroneously believed that the Japanese aircraft would not be carrying torpedoes. And he assumed that his capital ships would be able to survive the long-range, land-based Japanese bombers from Thailand. So, at 0052 hours on 10 December, Force Z at twenty-five knots turned toward Kuantan. At 0800 hours, it arrived at Kuantan and found no Japanese landing barges. Then, Force Z turned eastward to investigate some barges.[132] Then, hell struck.

The Japanese possessed fifty-one torpedo bombers, thirty-four high-level bombers, and nine reconnaissance aircraft at Tu Duam airfield in Thailand for attacking Force Z. These aircraft were Mitsubishi Type 96 G3M2 (Nell) and Mitsubishi Type 1 G4M1 (Betty) bombers. Between 0650 hours and 0800 hours, these aircraft took off. Each high-level bomber carried either one 500 kg bomb or two 250 kg bombs. And the torpedo bombers carried modified Type 91 torpedoes.[133] At 1118 hours, nine high-level bombers attacked *Repulse*, but no serious damage occurred. At about 1144 hours, nine torpedo bombers attacked *Prince of Wales*, which suffered serious damage. The torpedoes were dropped from a range of two thousand to one thousand yards, and the torpedoes ran very straight. Some of the aircraft also opened up with machine guns. At 1156 hours, nine torpedo bombers went for *Repulse*. At 1222, two groups of torpedo bombers comprising six and three aircraft, respectively, attacked *Prince of Wales* from her starboard side. The ship, being hit, started slowing down. At 1225 hours, again nine torpedo bombers attacked *Repulse*, and it started sinking. In total five torpedoes and one bomb hit this ship. At 1246, nine bombers targeted *Prince of Wales*. The latter, after being hit by four torpedoes and one bomb, started sinking. Phillips went to the bottom of the sea with his ship. According to one account, he ordered one sailor to bring his most famous cap just before his ship went down. *Electra* and *Vampire* picked up the survivors. However, the Japanese airmen proved to be chivalrous. They did not interfere with the rescue of the survivors.[134] In total, sixty-seven Japanese aircraft actually participated in the battle, and of them only three were lost.[135] Of the 2,921 men of the two capital ships, 840 died.[136]

This naval battle proved beyond any doubt that due to the advent of airpower, the age of the battleship was over. Martin Middlebrook and Patrick Mahoney assert that the small aircraft carrier *Hermes*, which was lying idle in the Indian Ocean, should have joined Force Z. *Hermes* was a small aircraft carrier with a capacity for fifteen aircraft.[137] The presence of fifteen British fighters would not have saved the British battleship and the battlecruiser but would have been able to inflict serious losses on the attacking Japanese high-level bombers and torpedo bombers. Captain W. G. Tennant of *Repulse* noted in his report: "The attacks were pressed home by the Japanese with great determination and efficiency— the high level bomber attacks in close formation at 10,000 feet were remarkably efficient."[138] It was a far cry from the prewar views of the Allied commanders that the Japanese aircrews were inefficient. The Japanese torpedo bombers proved to be more effective than high-level bombing by their bombers. Phillips could be accused of foolhardiness for going to the battle zone without fighter cover. However, if he remained inactive at Singapore with his big-gun ships and later escaped to Ceylon (Sri Lanka), he would have been accused of cowardice. If Phillips had continued to stay in Singapore harbor, the Japanese aircraft would have launched a torpedo attack.[139] Had Phillips succeeded in his ambitious venture of sailing out and destroying the Japanese troopships, he would have gone down in naval history as a "modern Nelson." Rather than Phillips, the responsibility for this disaster rests with Churchill. Due to the demands of the Atlantic and the Mediterranean, he was probably unable to send more ships for Singapore. In that case, no ships should have been sent to the Far East. The token Force Z was the product of Churchill's underestimation of the Japanese military capability and his "strategy of bluff." And it did not work out. As a result of the destruction of Force Z, the Japanese gained naval supremacy both along the east and west coasts of Malaya. So now they could land troops along the east and west coasts behind the rigid, linear Allied defensive lines and outflank them. In addition, the Japanese gained full liberty to induct additional reinforcements to the Malayan theater at their will.

The Japanese troopships carrying the second wave of troops left Camranh Bay on 13 December and landed their troops at Singora and other areas on 16 December.[140] To sum up, the British and Indian forces disintegrated so rapidly against the Japanese thrust because the British command was geared for fighting set piece battle under the colonels' command. The troops were trained to hold a linear line and defend themselves against attacking troops with superior artillery firepower. Counterattacks under superior artillery cover were to be launched in order to repel the invaders and to straighten out the defending line.[141] However, most of the combat occurred at the level of sections, platoons, and companies. And the junior British commanders, along with the Indian VCOs and NCOs, were neither trained nor conceptually equipped to make quick decisions independently on their own for blunting the infiltration and swarming tactics of the light Japanese infantry. As the Japanese surged through the east coast of northeast Malaya, the Allied position on northwest Malaya also started collapsing. And this is the focus of our next section.

From Jitra to Gurun

The III Indian Corps ordered the 11th Indian Division to occupy selected defensive positions on the Singora and Kroh-Patani roads and to send a mobile column toward Singora to obstruct the Japanese. The 28th Indian Brigade was allotted to the 11th Indian Division as reserve.[142] The KROHCOL (an assault column) under Lieutenant Colonel H. D. Moorhead was ordered to check the Japanese advance down the Kroh Road from Patani.[143] KROHCOL comprised the 3rd/16th Punjab Regiment, 5th/14th Punjab, and a 3.7-inch battery. On 8 December at 1400 hours it crossed the Thai frontier.[144] The objective was to advance to the Ledge position and delay the Japanese advance from the Patani beach. The column was held up at Betong on 9 December by Thai police equipped with medium machine guns. On 10 December, KROHCOL encountered the Japanese who had advanced from Patani. On 12 December, the column returned to Kroh after blowing up some bridges. However, the Japanese engineers quickly repaired the damaged bridges, and the Japanese tanks supported by infantry from the 5th Japanese Division started advancing.[145] Japanese infantry advance supported by tanks was facilitated by the assignment of special engineer parties to cooperate with the armored vehicles. The engineer detachments were equipped with picks, shovels, and explosives to blast the A/T obstacles as well as to rebuild demolished bridges.[146]

At 1830 hours on 8 December, the Andrews Column comprising 1st/8th Punjab and a detachment of carriers under Major Eric Robert Andrews crossed the frontier into Thailand. At 2100 hours, the Andrews Column ambushed a Japanese party just north of Sadao. The leading Japanese tank was knocked out by A/T guns, and fire was opened on the Japanese infantry in lorries and carriers with machine guns and mortars. However, the experienced and well-trained Japanese infantry, unlike the Allied infantry, did not panic. The Japanese infantry debussed very rapidly and worked along the flanks of the Allied infantry and destroyed two carriers with mortar fire. Then, the Andrews Column started retreating.[147]

About seventy-five heavy bombers escorted by eighteen fighters bombed the British air bases (Sungei Patani, Alor Star, Ketil, Ayer Tawar, and Penang). Some twenty-three British aircraft were damaged in exchange for three Japanese aerial machines.[148] The attack at Alor Star was made by twenty-seven twin-engine bombers of Army Type 97 and started while the aircraft of No. 62 Squadron were refueling about twenty minutes after the return from their attack on Patani. The Japanese aircraft attacked from a height of about thirteen thousand feet and used highly explosive 150-pound bombs. Four Blenheims were destroyed, and another six were heavily damaged. The fuel dump was set on fire. The four three-inch 20 cwt. AA guns at Alor Star were unable to hit any Japanese aircraft due to the height at which they were flying.[149] The British were paranoid about Japanese fifth columnists (especially the Malays who were supporters of Japan). On the morning of 9 December, seven Malays, including a schoolmaster, were arrested by the military police at Alor Star aerodrome on charges that these men were making signs indicating gun emplacements that were visible from the air. On that day, it was ordered that all the fifth columnists were to be shot.[150] Ghosh, in his novel *The Glass Palace*, writes that a rumor floated among the Allied troops that the Japanese bombers were given information about the disposition of the targets by traitors who happened to be Malays and even Englishmen and personnel within the Allied force.[151]

On 8 December, the 28th Indian Brigade (2nd/1st, 2nd/2nd, and 2nd/9th GRs) under Brigadier W. J. Carpendale was ordered to move north from Ipoh to Alor Star. The 2nd/1st GR was under Lieutenant Colonel Jack Fulton, 2nd/2nd GR was commanded by Lieutenant Colonel G. H. D. Woollcombe, and 2nd/9th GR was under Lieutenant Colonel W. R. Selby.[152] The 2nd/9th and 2nd/1st Gurkhas were ordered to patrol the region south of Alor Star and the aerodrome against a probable landing of Japanese parachute soldiers.[153] Due to nervousness, the Malaya Command was conjuring up phantom threats.[154]

When, at 1330 hours on 8 December, Operation MATADOR was cancelled after the Japanese had landed at Singora, the 11th Indian Division had to revert to the role of occupying and defending Jitra. This sudden change of posture impacted negatively on the morale of the soldiers.[155] Even before the onset of the Far Eastern War, the Malaya Command had suspected that MATADOR might not take off. So they had selected Jitra as a fallback position for the 11th Indian Division. Early in October 1941, Carpendale was ordered to undertake a study of the Jitra defensive position and then report to Murray-Lyon.[156]

The Jitra defense line (Murray-Lyon disliked it and was a supporter of MATADOR) extended from Changlun to Jitra, and it had the Jitra River as a natural barrier behind it.[157] Carpendale spent three days visiting all the sections in the Jitra position. What he found was disheartening. It was planned to hold Jitra with two brigades: the 15th Brigade on the right and 6th Infantry Brigade on the left. The 6th Brigade had the East Surreys on the right, 2nd/16th Punjab on the left, and 2nd/8th Punjab as brigade reserve. The A/T obstacle was in the process of being prepared. The A/T obstacle ran from south Jitra to S. Korok Canal, which ran into the sea. The 15th Indian Brigade had 1st Leicestershire, 1st/14th Punjab Regiment, and 2nd/9th Jat. The 1st/14th Punjab held the south side of S. Bata. The ditch there was part of the A/T obstacle but was not fully dug and was not completed when war broke out. On the right of the defensive position, there were hills covered with thick vegetation. This area proved to be an entry point for the Japanese later. The lane between S. Palong and S. Bata was a tactical gap, and this region was not covered by fire from the flanks. The right flank of the defensive line ended abruptly at a hill named Bk Penia. There was no second reserve position. The area held by 2nd/8th Punjab consisted of a long line of small posts with no depth. In front of them was the paddy field. Carpendale was, however, satisfied with the area held by the Leicestershire. Their flanks were covered with machine guns. Carpendale noted that the COs of the 6th and 15th Indian brigades did not have much confidence in the Jitra defensive position. He opined that it could be infiltrated and turned easily. The whole position had no depth and was too extended, and concentrated fire could not be poured to protect any of the forward defended localities against hostile attack. Worse, the right flank ended three thousand yards short of the main road, which might be the Japanese's main line of approach.[158] Carpendale's fear would be proven right when the Japanese actually attacked.

The Jitra position was selected to protect the Kedah State, which was the granary of Malaya, and also to protect the Alor Star airfield. When the actual Japanese invasion occurred, the rain flooded the shallow trenches and the gun pits.

Many of the field telephone cables hurriedly laid across the waterlogged terrain failed to work.[159] The 155th (Lanarkshire Yeomanry) Field Regiment left Sungei Patani with sixteen 4.5-inch howitzers and reached the so-called prepared positions at Jitra. On their right was the 2nd/9th Jats and on the left were the 1st Leicesters. The 155th Field Regiment found that their observation posts were all flooded.[160] The main defensive line ran from east of Jitra to the west coast in the Kedah State astride the main road and the railway from Malaya to Thailand. The Jitra Line extended for twenty miles and had flooded paddy fields in the center, with jungle country and hilly land in the right. The right flank rested on the jungle-clad hills, which the British commanders erroneously believed to be impassable. There was a prepared position in the south for the protection of the Alor Star airfield. However, the communication trenches and the line signal communications were incomplete. And the position was not wired, nor had A/T mines been laid.[161] Due to high priority given to rubber and tin for exports, civilian labor was not available in required quantities for the construction of the field fortifications and layback positions.[162] The British and the Indian soldiers were still laying down barbed wire along their flimsy defensive positions when the Japanese rushed them.[163] With the aid of hindsight, we can say that the left flank of the Jitra position should have rested on the railway. And the real weakness of the Jitra Line was the ease with which the Japanese could outflank east of the position and race toward Alor Star aerodrome.[164]

On the right was the 15th Indian Brigade under Brigadier K. A. Garrett, and on the left was the 6th Indian Brigade (East Surreys, 1st/8th Punjab Regiment and 2nd/16th Punjab Regiment) under Brigadier W. O. Lay. And the 28th Indian Brigade (2nd/1st, 2nd/2nd, and 2nd/9th GRs) under Carpendale was charged with the protection of Alor Star and Sungei Patani airfields.[165] While the 15th Indian Brigade covered six thousand yards from the road in Kodiang to the railway line at Kangar in Perlis, the 6th Indian Brigade held a stretch about eighteen thousand yards wide from the main road to the coast. On the right of 15th Brigade was the 2nd/9th Jats, deployed in boggy soil covered by paddy fields and bisected by a creek. There was jungle on either side of the creek. The jungle would prove to be an entry point for Japanese infiltrating columns. On their left, separated by two thousand yards of swamps and trees was the 1st Leicestershire Battalion. The swamp would later be crossed by the Japanese troops. During the Malayan Campaign, entire Japanese companies would occasionally hide in the swamps, the men submerged up to their necks for hours waiting for the opportunity to engage the rear and flanks of the Allied units. In the 6th Indian Brigade's sector, the 2nd East Surrey Battalion occupied the position from Kodiang Road to the railway, and the 2nd/16th Punjab covered the remaining distance to the coast. A detachment of the 1st/14th Punjab of the 15th Indian Brigade held Asun (some miles south of Changlun) on the main Singora Road 3 miles north of the main position. The artillery support was provided by the 155th Field Regiment, 22nd Mountain Regiment, and the 80th A/T Regiment.[166]

The morale of the British and Indian troops at Jitra was low. The recent defeats in air and ground had somewhat unnerved them. Further, snakes, leeches, red ants, and centipedes made life unpleasant, especially during the night. Moreover, on 10 December, the rising column of smoke from the Alor Star as the RAF crews evacuated the airfield further undermined the morale of the Jitra defenders. After all, the ground troops were in Jitra to defend the airfield. The confidence of the Allied troops reached rock bottom when toward the end of the day, they received news about the Allied naval disaster along the east coast of Malaya.[167]

On 11 December, the 1st/14th Punjab was holding Changlun in Kedah fifteen miles north of Jitra on the trunk road into Thailand. The Punjabis' A/T weapons consisted of merely two Breda A/T guns of the 4th Mountain Battery. At 0800 hours the Japanese attack started with bombardment by mortars. At 0900 hours on 11 December, the Japanese attack rose in severity.[168] At this stage, the Japanese were using a mere two battalions against the Jitra defensive position.[169] Japanese tactics can be categorized as fluid tactics. Just as water seeps through the perforations in the joints, the Japanese soldiers swarmed between the Allied battalions and within the companies of an Allied battalion. The Japanese displayed remarkable capacity for rapid infiltration along the difficult terrain on the east of the Changlun-Jitra Road. Then they started outflanking the British-Indian defensive position. The Japanese infantry was liberally armed with Tommy Guns and light artillery. They were guided toward the Allied defensive positions by their aircraft, which lighted fires by bombing the British-Indian troops.[170] Coordination and cooperation between Japanese infantry, light artillery, and aircraft was excellent. The Japanese took advantage of the thick jungle on the right flank of the Jitra position. By hacking their position through the jungle, the Japanese surprised the Allied defenders and exploded the myth that the jungle in the Malayan countryside was impassable. The Japanese discovered the location of the flanks of the defended localities and carried out wide turning movements sometimes five miles behind the forward Allied troops. While some Japanese troops on bicycles engaged the Allied troops frontally, their main body carried out a wide outflanking move. With speed they directed mortar fire on the Allied defended localities.[171]

For the time being, the Punjabis were able to hold back the Japanese infantry. A second attack started at 1130 hours. By midday, the Japanese had infiltrated along the right flank of the Punjabis. For deception purposes, some of the Japanese infiltrators were dressed like Malay villagers. The 1st/14thPunjab decided to withdraw behind Asun, which was the outermost ring of the Jitra Line.[172] And this was the signal for the Japanese to launch a heavy attack. Fighting it out was better than to retreat in front of the aggressive Japanese foot soldiers. Toward evening Brigadier Garrett was found missing. And Carpendale was ordered to take over command of the 15th Indian Brigade.[173] Garrett reappeared later and took over his command.

A brigade exercise had been held by the 2nd/8th and 1st/4th Punjab before the Japanese invasion. The 2nd/8th battalion represented the Japanese advancing down the road from Thailand. It carried out an encircling movement and cleared the blocking positions established by the 1st/14th Punjab's companies. While a subsidiary force from the 2nd/8th engaged the 1st/14th frontally, its two companies carried out an encircling movement east of the road behind the rear of the

1st/14th. The Allied commanders, however, failed to draw the necessary conclusion (the futility of clinging to the roads) from this exercise. In the afternoon of 11 December, the Japanese actually carried out such a maneuver. Their envelopment was much deeper than that of 2nd/8th Punjab. And because the bridges were not demolished, Japanese tanks supported by lorried infantry moved deep down along the road.[174]

The Japanese used tanks in support of infantry in direct frontal attacks. Tanks were brought up whenever infantry failed to advance. The tanks attempted to force a passage for the infantry by frontal assault, and if it failed then attacked the hostile flanks. On occasion, the tanks followed the roads with infantry following in trucks. During an occasional effective roadblock by the Allied soldiers, fire from the tanks aided the Japanese infantry to attack the hostile flanks through infiltration tactics. At times, the tanks penetrated to a depth of ten to twelve miles behind the Allied frontline position. Japanese tactical doctrine stressed the use of tanks as a mobile mass.[175] The Japanese tactical treatise notes: "The essence of tank warfare is to take the enemy by surprise and assault him suddenly with concentrated power."[176]

Generally, independent tank units were attached to the infantry detachments in accordance with the needs of the tactical scenario.[177] The Japanese tanks were inferior to the Soviet or German ones. During July–August 1939, at Nomonhan (border of Manchuria-Mongolia), Soviet armor were able to destroy the Japanese armor because of the former's better armament.[178] The problem was that the British had no tanks in the Malayan mainland, and the Allied troops due to inadequate training failed to use their small A/T guns effectively.

Meanwhile, the sky opened up. The Japanese had a penchant for attacking through adverse terrain in adverse weather. In heavy rainfall at about 1630 hours, twelve Japanese medium and light tanks followed by infantry in lorries charged through the rearguard of the retreating 1st/14thPunjabis. As the tanks roared forward, Japanese infantry attacked the 1st/14th Punjab from both sides of the road. Most of the jawans had never before seen a tank. And they were not trained to use A/T weapons, nor had they conducted training in cooperation with A/T artillery. Infantry-artillery cooperation among the Allied force could have contained the Japanese advance, but the British and Indian troops failed in this aspect. This was because of a lack of training in infantry-artillery cooperation. Lieutenant Colonel E. L. Sawyer of the 22nd Mountain Regiment noted that the various infantry units did not carry out joint training with the artillery batteries before the war. He writes: "Going into action in the night time is bad enough but when one goes in with comparative strangers it does not exactly improve matters."[179] Captain Mohan Singh, CO of the Machine Gun Company of 1st/14th Punjab, used a stick to beat the retreating jawans to get them back into the lines. However, the panicky jawans jumped into the trucks to escape the advancing Japanese. The Japanese column broke through the Punjabis and then through the 2nd/1st GR, which had about five hundred personnel.[180] Tanks and aerial supremacy on the part of the Japanese resulted in the complete breakdown of morale of the sparsely trained Indian soldiers. Ironically, Murray-Lyon had assured the 1st/14th Punjab that the Japanese had no tanks in front of Jitra. Not only the Indian soldiers, but also at times the British officers displayed nervousness. Lieutenant Colonel L. V. Fitzpatrick, CO of the 1st/14th Punjab was slightly wounded and temporarily lost his nerve. He was shell shocked and ran away but after some time regained his composure.[181] F. M. Richardson, who served in the Royal Army Medical Corps between 1927 and 1961, noted that the end result of failure of morale is psychiatric casualty. Psychiatric casualty makes a man ineffective in battle because his personality is unable to stand up to the stress of battle.[182] Murray-Lyon's command limitation was exemplified in his failure to send substantial reinforcements to stiffen the outlying position held by the 1st/14th Punjab.

It seemed that the Japanese tanks might cross the Asun Road Bridge. The light Japanese tanks were not panzers supported by mechanized infantry and were actually easy prey to a stout A/T defense. And despite heavy milking and induction of "green" British officers, the Indian battalions were occasionally able to put up a stout defense. The 2nd/1st GR had only two Boys A/T Rifles, and even these had been delivered to them the day before. But they proved to be adequate. A Gurkha company havildar with this weapon was able to dispose of four Japanese tanks.[183] And that was enough to temporarily stop the Japanese tank column from reaching Asun Bridge. Sending parallel columns toward the enemy was another characteristic of IJA's tactics.[184] On 11 December, the Japanese infantry probed the Asun position. The Japanese banzai charges were met with Gurkha *kukris* and bayonets. However, the Japanese infantry crossed the chest-deep "impassable" marsh on the flank of 2nd/1st GR and surrounded its two forward companies.[185] They attacked the Gurkhas from both flanks and the front and overwhelmed them.[186] At 2030 hours, Japanese spearheads confronted and rapidly overwhelmed the Leicestershires and the Jats in Jitra. The first day of fighting on the Jitra Line resulted in some seven hundred Indian casualties.[187]

Early on 12 December, Murray-Lyon lost his nerve and wanted to retreat to Alor Star. Percival ordered him to hold on to Jitra.[188] Reconnaissance aircraft function as eyes of the ground force. On 12 December, Carpendale, in order to get a better "feel" of the situation, requested aerial reconnaissance of the front held by the 15th Indian Brigade. He was curtly told by the divisional headquarters that no aircraft were available.[189]

At noon on 12 December, Major General Saburo Kawamura, CO of the 9th Japanese Brigade of the 5th Japanese Division, ordered the 41st Japanese Regiment to function as advance guard and to attack the eastern side of the main road near Jitra and the 11th Japanese Regiment to attack the western side.[190] At 1530 hours on 12 December, the Japanese launched an attack with heavy mortar fire. One company of the 2nd/8th Punjab when ordered refused to advance. A large body of Japanese penetrated between the main road and south of Jitra. The Sikh soldiers of Major Emsden Lambert's 2nd/16th Punjab deserted.[191] Defeatism was spreading among the jawans, and the novice British officers were losing control over them. The Japanese scouts were excellent, and in the jungle terrain, the Japanese soldiers made better use of their light mortars compared to the heavier cumbersome field artillery of the British.[192] The 1st/8th Punjab's counterattack against the Japanese failed to recapture lost ground.[193] The Japanese technique was to use some units to put pressure by making a frontal attack, while special assault troops infiltrated and attacked the rear and flanks of the defending troops. The assault troops were composed of young soldiers lightly clad in shirts or vests, shorts, and gym shoes armed with mortars, Tommy Guns, and rifles. They were expert stalkers and snipers and were in the tradition of the best light infantry. The heavily laden British and Indian troops had no counter to their infiltrating and outflanking techniques.[194] In accordance with the Japanese plan, Jitra was to be occupied by 12 December,[195] and Yamashita's army actually stuck to this timetable. Besides the Japanese tank blitz, the retreat of the Leicestershires on 12 December, which allowed the Japanese to infiltrate between them and the Jats, resulted in the final collapse of the Jitra position. Murray-Lyon tried to avert criticism of his pathetic leadership by arguing that he would have been successful had he been allowed to implement MATADOR.[196]

The retreat from Jitra was planned in two phases: phase one on the night of 12/13 December to the River Kedah and the second phase on the night of 13/14 December to the Gurun position.[197] The Japanese infantry crossed the paddy fields and attacked the 2nd/2nd GR on the line of the Bata River.[198] Late on 12 December, Murray-Lyon ordered withdrawal further south below the Bata River.[199] On 12 December, KROKOL was forced to retreat. Withdrawal of the transport during the night of 12/13 December proved to be a laborious, nightmarish affair. Carpendale prepared the Iron Bridge for demolition. The 2nd/1st GR did not receive the order for withdrawal.[200] Bad staff work was the culprit. The nervous Indian stragglers fired indiscriminately during the night. The published history of 2nd/9th GR notes: "Towards evening numerous groups of stragglers from the forward units passed through to the rear."[201] However, it must be noted that staunch rearguard action by 2nd/9th GR under Major M. B. Allesbrook covered the withdrawal of the 11th Indian Division from Jitra during the night of 12/13 December.[202] As Richardson notes, confidence in leaders makes a good unit. Good leadership enhances group morale.[203] The bridges at Kepala Batas were blown. And Lieutenant Colonel Selby of 2nd/9th GR was ordered to prepare the position at Gurun.[204] Demolished bridges did not hold up the Japanese for long. The Japanese engineers quickly repaired the bridges with the aid of local labor.[205] Thus, the Jitra Line, which was designed to hold the Japanese for three months, collapsed in two days. The Allied force lost fifty field guns, fifty heavy machine guns, three hundred trucks and armored cars, and a large amount of food, ammunition, and gasoline, which would sustain the Japanese for a month. The Japanese termed the captured bonanza as "Churchill rations."[206]

Gordon Bennett jotted down his impression about the defeat of Jitra in the following words:

> The feat demonstrated that battles are not always won by the big battalions; that a small force of battle-trained men possessing initiative and making use of that most valuable war weapon, "Surprise" can quickly overcome a numerically stronger force which lacks battle experience and also lacks leaders with determination, resolution

and tactical skill. No peace time training can compensate for lack of battle training. Experience in battle is invaluable.... The Japanese troops used in this action were veterans of the war in Manchuria and China.... Battle experienced soldiers... are able to develop a battle cunning that easily tricks the inexperienced and shocked defenders into surrender. Another important lesson learned was that "passive" defense will always succumb to an aggressive attack.[207]

As we will see later, when the edgy Bennett with his inexperienced troops attempted to conduct his so-called aggressive defense in south Malaya, the result was disaster for the Allied troops. Not only did the British and Indian soldiers lack prior combat experience, but they were erroneously trained. Further, their British commanding officers lacked the initiative and capability to make quick decisions independently amid fluid battle scenarios. And the Allied troops, instead of waiting for the Japanese to come against the Jitra Line, should have conducted aggressive patrolling and nocturnal raids and the divisional commander ought to have kept a reserve ready for launching immediate counterattacks. The British commanders conceived the defense line as a linear one with front and rear and emphasized the necessity of maintaining communication between these two parts.[208] This formula failed against the aggressive Japanese irruption tactics, which involved frontal penetration, and simultaneously posing a threat in the rear, encirclement, and outflanking moves.

The Japanese suffered only 110 casualties at Jitra while the 11th Indian Division lost three thousand men as PoWs.[209] The loss of so many Indian soldiers as PoWs raises questions about the state of morale of the jawans. Napoleon Bonaparte used to say that morale is three times more important than the physical. The ancient Greek military theorist cum commander Xenophon conceptualized morale as strength of soul. And for Napoleon, the spirit will always conquer the sword.[210] It might be an overstatement, but there is an element of truth in it. Percival's assessment of the morale of the Indian troops was as follows: "Units varied greatly. Some were extremely good.... Others were not too reliable. There were reasons for this—inexperience, lack of adequate training and lack of leaders.... I think it is true to say that morale was never broken but I would not go so far as to say that it 'stood up magnificently.'"[211]

The Japanese attempt to suborn the loyalty of the Indian soldiers was on high gear. Two VCOs of 2nd/1st GR were captured by the Japanese in the afternoon of 11 December. They were taken by an escort to a headquarters, where two Sikhs in civilian clothes and an arm band questioned them. A Japanese officer told them that they did not wish to fight the Gurkhas but only the British, who had no business in Malaya. Then they were sent back to their unit with orders that they should tell their fellow soldiers to cease fighting for the British. These two Gurkha VCOs reached the Allied line next day and told the whole story to their British masters.[212] The Sikhs probably belonged to the nascent INA or the IIL. Raw, inexperienced, and badly trained Indians were demoralized by defeats and withdrawals. And many of them fell easy prey to Japanese anti-British propaganda. However, the Japanese call for freedom of India from the British did not have much effect on the Gurkhas. This was because the Gurkhas were from semi-independent Nepal, and the national movement of India did not touch their homeland. However, such activities on the part of the Japanese frayed the nerves of non-Gurkha soldiers of the Indian Army.

Meanwhile, the Japanese were dropping leaflets from aircraft. The Japanese message emphasized Asia for the Asians, India for the Indians, "kick out the white devils from the East," etc. Mohan Singh rightly notes that in normal times, nobody would have given much attention to such messages. But it was an abnormal time: the British were being defeated, and the Indian troops were demoralized. And in contrast to the Japanese propaganda, the British did not even give an empty promise of granting freedom to India after the end of the war. Many of the Indian commissioned officers (ICOs) from middle- and upper-class families were influenced by the nationalist current in Indian society, and some of them had personal connections with several Indian nationalist leaders. So anti-British feeling spread among the Indian troops.[213] Ghosh, in his absorbing novel, writes that when the Japanese aircraft dropped the leaflets and the jawans started reading it, an ICO had to threaten the soldiers that if they read the seditious literature, they would face court martial.[214] However, many ICOs were also infected by the rising tide of Indian nationalism and the Japanese promise about Indian freedom. Richardson writes that a soldier's personal/individual morale is strengthened when he fights for his home and family.[215] In case of the jawans and the ICOs, this motivation was lacking.

Some of the early Indian deserters who were asked by Fujiwara *Kikan* to join the fight against the British were as follows: On 8 December, one Subedar Allah Ditta Khan deserted to the Japanese. Captain Fateh Khan of 2nd/9th Jats joined with his company. On 11 December Captain Patnaik, a medical officer of 2nd/1st GR, and Jemadar Puran Singh Khawas surrendered to the Japanese. The Japanese tried to persuade Patnaik to form the nucleus of a volunteer anti-British Indian Army, but he refused. In the afternoon of 13 December, the IIL reported that there was a battalion of Indian troops deployed twenty-five miles east of Alor Star that might surrender due to large casualties it had suffered and because its LoC was cut. This battalion (1st/14th Punjab) was commanded by Lieutenant Colonel Fitzpatrick. Besides him, the other officers of this battalion were Indians. It was an Indianizing battalion. Early in the morning of 14 December, Major Fujiwara, accompanied by the interpreter Otakura and Pritam Singh (a member of the IIIL) set out to establish contact with this battalion. Negotiations for surrender were carried out in a friendly spirit. Pritam Singh established contact with the Indian officers. Captain Mohan Singh was the most senior company commander. Mohan Singh, Captain Muhammad Akram, and Jemadar Sadhu Singh of 1st/14th Punjab would later play an important role in the establishment of the INA. Fujiwara and Pritam Singh continued discussion with Mohan Singh for several days. On 17 December, Fujiwara, Pritam Singh, and Mohan Singh at Alor Star had an interview with Yamashita. Yamashita declared full support for Fujiwara's program. On 19 December, Fujiwara *Kikan* moved to Sungei Patani and then to Taiping. Mohan Singh expressed the opinion that Subhas Bose (an ex-INC politician who was then in Germany) should be brought to Southeast Asia to give leadership to the movement for Indian independence. As a result of the activities of the IIL, local Indians became reconciled with the Japanese soldiers, and many jawans who had deserted after the disastrous Battle of Jitra, discarded their arms and uniforms and came to the Indian PoW barracks established at Alor Star and Sungei Patani.[216]

Murray-Lyon, hotly pursued by the 9th Japanese Brigade, retreated to the Gurun position with only half of its division. The new position at Gurun was between Jitra and the Muda River. This defensive position was not thoroughly prepared because in the absence of civilian labor, the tired troops had to prepare it within three to four days. The Gurun position was six miles wide. The Kedah Peak, which rises to a height of about four thousand feet, is between Gurun and the seashore. The only avenues of approach were the main road and the railway. The depleted and demoralized 11th Indian Division was ordered to perform a delaying role in retarding the southern drive of the Japanese.[217] During the night of 13/14 December, Brigadier Garrett set up his headquarters south of Gurun village. The 15th Indian Brigade concentrated in this region. A detachment of the 6th Indian Brigade held the position left of the main road, and the 28th Indian Brigade was on the right of the road. Not all the Malays were hostile to the Allied soldiers and were pro-Japanese. The 2nd/2nd GR were being fed by the villagers while retreating. The day of 14 December was spent digging and wiring the defensive position. The 28th Indian Brigade took position inside the rubber plantation on the right. The 6th Indian Brigade on the left was deployed in scrub jungle and amid the rubber plantation. The 15th Indian Brigade was in reserve south of Gurun. The weakness of the defense was that the Yen Cross Road was held by the Japanese, and it caused a gap between the 2nd/16th and 2nd/8th Punjab. The 6th Indian Brigade's attempt to capture the crossroad failed.[218] The Japanese had occupied the rubber plantation between the road and the railway. The morale of the British and Indian troops was low at this stage. The Japanese during the night continued to infiltrate on both the flanks of the 6th Indian Brigade and, moving through the jungle, positioned themselves between the brigade headquarters and the East Surrey.[219]

During the night of 14/15 December, a party of Japanese soldiers infiltrated in the rear of the Gurun position.[220] The Japanese struck at 0200 hours of 15 December. Immediately, the Indian soldiers resorted to wild firing. Not only the Indians, but the East Surreys also let go of their rifles in an indiscriminate manner. The Japanese as usual infiltrated between two Allied battalions: in this case between the 2nd/16th and 2nd/8th Punjab. At 0500 hours, Lieutenant Colonel Selby told Carpendale that the East Surreys, 2nd/8th, and 2nd/16th Punjab required transportation for withdrawing.[221] It is to be noted that the Japanese were fighting and advancing rapidly without motor transport. Due to their light equipment, physical fitness, simplicity of rations, and rigorous training, a Japanese soldier was capable of marching even twenty-five miles a day in full battle order.[222] Carpendale noted a bit late about the British and Indian troops: "They must further be trained to carry on without food and sleep for much longer periods than we are used to."²²³ Cooperation between Allied infantry and their field guns was almost nonexistent. At dawn, the British guns by mistake had started shelling the 1st/8th Punjab and the East Surreys. The Japanese had swarmed at the 6th Brigade Headquarters, and luckily Brigadier Lay with a couple of others was able to escape. The 29th Brigade Headquarters was also attacked. Major Bourne, the brigade major, was killed while trying to rally the men.²²⁴ The Japanese seemed to have deliberately attacked the communication nodes of the Allied forces (i.e., brigade headquarters) in order to destroy C3I as per the requirements of maneuver warfare. The counterattack by 2nd/9th GR through the rubber plantation south of Gurun failed. Japanese medium tanks had advanced along the railway crossing. Meanwhile, the road bridge had been blown on the order of an unknown British officer. In the meantime, KROHCOL was amalgamated with the 12th Indian Brigade.²²⁵ The net result after the withdrawal from Gurun position was that the British had lost northern Malaya.

Conclusion

The performance of the British and Indian units was below average. Not only did many Allied soldiers refuse to obey orders, but several ran away and deserted. Before the Japanese invasion, the British and Indian troops got some training in beach defense but none at all in jungle fighting. Again, the beach defense was faulty. It comprised a long, thin line of posts without adequate depth and vulnerable flanks.²²⁶ Just after the Japanese landing when the British and Indian troops had to retreat from the beaches, they were completely at a loss in jungle country and failed to rebuild either a new defense line or to counterattack the Japanese vigorously. Even when a unit was not attacked by the Japanese, to prevent its LoC being cut due to the retreat of the neighboring units, it had to withdraw. And when they discovered Japanese units establishing roadblocks at their rear, instead of thinking of surrounding the advance Japanese elements, the British and Indian troops and their commanders thought themselves to be surrounded and conducted a withdrawal to escape the Japanese net. This process was repeated again and again. A rigid linear defensive barrier like the Jitra-Changlun line was frontally pierced and simultaneously outflanked. Even in static defense, the British and Indian infantry failed to coordinate their action with A/T weapons and field artillery. And their static linear defensive positions were vulnerable to Japanese irruption/infiltration tactics. While retreating without aerial cover amid chaos and confusion, several friendly-fire incidents broke out among the nervous Indian units. This in turn caused further decline of morale. In accordance with the Japanese tactics, while the tanks would dash forward, the infantry mopped up the situation. The Allies did not have tanks, and cooperation between their infantry and A/T guns was substandard. The Japanese tactics could be summed up as: advance, outflank, envelop, and again advance. And the road-bound Allied infantry fell easy prey to the Japanese infantry, who were experts in cross-country movement. What the Japanese had done at Jitra and Gurun, they would repeat on a larger scale at the Slim River, the subject of our next chapter.

Notes

1. Despatch on the Far East by Air Chief Marshal Robert Brooke-Popham, Commander-in-Chief Far East (17 Oct. 1940–27 Dec. 1941), September 8, 1942, CAB/66/28/33, PRO, Kew, London, 19.

2. Ian Morrison, *Malayan Postscript* (London: Faber and Faber, 1942), 25; Lieutenant General A. E. Percival, "Operations of Malaya Command, from 8 December 1941 to 15 February 1942," *Second Supplement to London Gazette*, February 26, 1948 (London: HMSO, 1948), 1245–46.

3. Francis Pike, *Hirohito's War: The Pacific War, 1941–1945* (London: Bloomsbury, 2015), 232.

4. Biographical Sketch of Percival, January 10, 1948, Percival Papers, IWM, London; Clifford Kinvig, "General Percival and the Fall of Singapore," in *Sixty Years On: The Fall of Singapore Revisited*, ed. Brian Farrell and Sandy Hunter (2002; repr., Singapore: Eastern Universities Press, 2003), 241; Robert Lyman, *The Generals: From Defeat to Victory, Leadership in Asia 1941–45* (London: Constable, 2008), 62; Brian P. Farrell, *The Defence and Fall of Singapore 1940–1942* (2005; repr., Stroud: Tempus, 2006), 109–10.

5. Peter Thompson, *The Battle for Singapore: The True Story of the Greatest Catastrophe of World War II* (2005; repr., London: Piatkus, 2013), 12.

6. Andrew Gilchrist, *Malaya 1941: The Fall of a Fighting Empire* (London: Robert Hale, 1992), 22.

7. *History of the Southern Army*, Japanese Monograph No. 24, 9.

8. P. N. Khera, *Technical Services: Ordnance & IEME* (New Delhi: Government of India, 1962), 175–76.

9. Major General B. W. Key, 11th Indian Division, P 456, Key Papers, IWM, 5.

10. T. R. Moreman, *The Jungle, the Japanese and the British Commonwealth Armies at War, 1941–45: Fighting Methods, Doctrine and Training for Jungle Warfare* (London: Frank Cass, 2005), 28.

11. Lyman, *The Generals*, 76.

12. Notes by Lieutenant General A. E. Percival on certain senior commanders and other matters, Percival Papers, 1.

13. *9 Gurkha Rifles: A Regimental History (1817–1947)* (New Delhi: Vision Books, 1984), 159–60.

14. Notes by Lieutenant General A. E. Percival on the Brief Outline Narrative of the Mainland Operations in Malaya 8 Dec. 1941 to 31 Jan. 1942 prepared by the Combined Inter-Services Historical Section (India), June 1947, Percival Papers, 3.

15. Lecture on the Malayan Campaign by General Heath, June 21, 1942, Percival Papers, 4.

16. Pike, *Hirohito's War*, 236.

17. Comments by Lieutenant General A. E. Percival on the Comments by the Official Historians on the Fighting in Singapore Island, December 2, 1953, Percival Papers, 1.

18. Lecture on the Malayan Campaign by Heath, June 21, 1942, Percival Papers, 3; H. Gordon Bennett, *The Fall of Singapore* (1944; repr., New Delhi: Natraj, 1990), 5; A. B. Lodge, *The Fall of General Gordon Bennett* (Sydney: Allen & Unwin, 1986), 70; Colin Smith, *Singapore Burning: Heroism and Surrender in World War II* (2005; repr., London: Penguin, 2006), 57; Lyman, *The Generals*, 77.

19. Pike, *Hirohito's War*, 234.

20. Notes by Percival on the Brief Outline Narrative, 6.

21. Note on the Malayan Campaign by LMH, LMH 5, P 441, Lewis Heath Papers, IWM, 9, 11f.
22. Despatch on the Far East by Brooke-Popham, 20–21.
23. Samuel W. Mitcham, Jr., *The Desert Fox in Normandy: Rommel's Defense of Fortress Europe* (Westport, CT: Praeger, 1997).
24. Timothy Hall, *The Fall of Singapore* (1983; repr., Oxon: Routledge, 2015), 44–45.
25. Operations in Malaya and Singapore, E. E. Bridges, Report drawn up by Major H. P. Thomas, July 27, 1942, WP(42)314, CAB/66/26/44, PRO, Kew, 5.
26. Key, 11th Indian Division, 1–2, 4.
27. Agnes McEwan and Campbell Thomson, *Death Was Our Bedmate: 155th (Lanarkshire Yeomanry) Field Regiment and the Japanese 1941–1945* (Barnsley: Pen & Sword, 2013), 15.
28. Hall, *Fall of Singapore*, 7.
29. Thompson, *Battle for Singapore*, 23.
30. Lieutenant Colonel J. Frith, History of the 2/10 Baluch in the Malayan Campaign, 1973-06-121, NAM, London, 3.
31. Smith, *Singapore Burning*, 131.
32. K. D. Bhargava and K. N. V. Sastri, *Campaigns in South-East Asia 1941–42*, ed. Bisheshwar Prasad, Official History of the Indian Armed Forces in the Second World War 1939–45 (Combined Inter-Services Historical Section India & Pakistan, Distributors Orient Longman, Delhi, 1960), 130.
33. Frith, History of the 2/10 Baluch, 4–5.
34. Major General Prem K. Khanna and Pushpindar Singh Chopra, *Portrait of Courage: Century of the 5th Battalion, The Sikh Regiment* (New Delhi: Military Studies Convention, 2001), 154.
35. Khanna and Chopra, *Portrait of Courage*, 156; John A. English, *On Infantry* (1981; repr., New York: Praeger, 1984), 8.
36. Khanna and Chopra, *Portrait of Courage*, 157–59.
37. Operations in Malaya and Singapore, Bridges, 3; Farrell, *Defence and Fall*, 129.
38. From CGS Australia to War Office, April 3, 1942, L/WS/1/952, OIOC, BL, London.
39. Despatch on the Far East by Brooke-Popham, 21.
40. Lyman, *The Generals*, 17–22.
41. Colonel Masanobu Tsuji, *Japan's Greatest Victory / Britain's Worst Defeat from the Japanese Perspective: The Capture of Singapore, 1942* (1952; repr., Gloucestershire: Spellmount, 2007), 27–28; Lionel Wigmore, *The Japanese Thrust*, vol. 4, Australia in the War of 1939–45, Series 1, Army (Canberra: Australian War Memorial, 1957), 133; Lyman, *The Generals*, 31.
42. Smith, *Singapore Burning*, 108.
43. Ken Kotani, "Pearl Harbor: Japanese Planning and Command Structure," in *The Pacific War: From Pearl Harbor to Hiroshima*, ed. Daniel Marston (2005; repr., Oxford: Osprey, 2010), 31.
44. History of the Southern Army, 10.
45. Henry Probert, *The Forgotten Air Force: The Royal Air Force in the War against Japan, 1941–45* (London: Brassey's, 1995), 34.
46. Air Vice Marshal A. V. M. Paul Maltby, December 28, 1945, Percival Papers.
47. Paul Maltby, "Report on the Air Operations during the Campaigns in Malaya and Netherland East Indies from 8 December 1941 to 12 March 1942," *Third Supplement to the London Gazette*, February 26, 1948 (London: HMSO, 1948), 1350, 1360.

48. Hall, *Fall of Singapore*, 25.
49. Maltby, "Report on the Air Operations," 1355.
50. Comments by Air Chief Marshal R. Brooke-Popham on Major General Percival's Despatch "Operations of Malaya Command," July 1946, Percival Papers, 2.
51. *South-East Area Air Operations Record, Phase I, Nov. 1941–Feb. 1942*, Japanese Monograph No. 55 (Washington, DC: Department of the Army, Office of the Chief of Military History, 1962), 6–7; Lyman, *The Generals*, 32.
52. A. D. Harvey, "Army Air Force and Navy Air Force: Japanese Aviation and the Opening Phase of the War in the Far East," *War in History*, 6, no. 2 (1999): 176.
53. Thompson, *Battle for Singapore*, 12.
54. Lecture on the Malayan Campaign by Heath, June 21, 1942, Percival Papers, 5; Bill Yenne, *The Imperial Japanese Army: The Invincible Years 1941–42* (Oxford: Osprey, 2014), 88.
55. Hall, *Fall of Singapore*, 9.
56. Kyoichi Tachikawa, "General Yamashita and His Style of Leadership: The Malaya/Singapore Campaign," in *British and Japanese Military Leadership in the Far Eastern War, 1941–1945*, ed. Brian Bond and Kyoichi Tachikawa (London: Frank Cass, 2004), 76.
57. Wigmore, *Japanese Thrust*, 133–34; *South-East Area Air Operations Record, Phase I, Nov. 1941–Feb. 1942*, 9–10.
58. Farrell, *Defence and Fall*, 119.
59. Tachikawa, "General Yamashita," 78.
60. Hisayuki Yokoyama, "Air Operational Leadership in the Southern Front: Imperial Army Aviation's Trial to Be an 'Air Force' in the Malaya Offensive air operation," in *British and Japanese Military Leadership*, ed. Bond and Tachikawa, 134–35.
61. Lyman, *The Generals*, 27–28.
62. Yokoyama, "Air Operational Leadership," 140–41.
63. *South-East Area Air Operations Record, Phase I, Nov. 1941–Feb. 1942*, 31, 34–35, 37.
64. Maltby, "Report on the Air Operations," 1363; Masatake Okumiya and Jiro Horikoshi with Martin Caidin, *Zero: The Story of Japan's Air War in the Pacific as Seen by the Enemy* (1956; repr., New York: ibooks, 2002), 93.
65. Lecture on the Malayan Campaign by Heath, June 21, 1942, Percival Papers, 7.
66. Gilchrist, *Malaya 1941*, 119.
67. From Commander-in-Chief China, December 7, 1941, L/WS/1/952 (2), OIOC, BL.
68. Okumiya, Horikoshi, and Caidin, *Zero*, 94.
69. Gilchrist, *Malaya 1941*, 82–83.
70. Operations in Malaya and Singapore, Bridges, 4; *South-East Area Air Operations Record, Phase I, Nov. 1941–Feb. 1942*, 10.
71. Wigmore, *Japanese Thrust*, 135; Hall, *Fall of Singapore*, 53.
72. Notes by Lieutenant General A. E. Percival on Captain Russell Grenfell's Draft, July 1950, Percival Papers.
73. Frith, "History of the 2/10 Baluch," 6.
74. Letter from Shenton Thomas to Percival, May 1, 1947, Percival Papers; Major General Gurbakhsh Singh, *Indelible Reminiscences: Memoirs of Major-General Gurbakhsh Singh* (New Delhi: Lancer, 2013), 37.
75. Harvey, "Army Air Force," 178.
76. Hall, *Fall of Singapore*, 27.
77. Telegram, From Governor Shenton Thomas to Secy. of State for Colonies, December 8, 1941, L/WS/1/952 (2), OIOC, BL.

78. *South-East Area Air Operations Record, Phase I, Nov. 1941–Feb. 1942*, 30.
79. Hall, *Fall of Singapore*, 59.
80. Akashi Yoji, "General Yamashita Tomoyuki: Commander of the Twenty-Fifth Army," and Alan Warren, "The Indian Army and the Fall of Singapore," in *Sixty Years On*, ed. Farrell and Hunter, 191, 273.
81. Thompson, *Battle for Singapore*, 187.
82. Hall, *Fall of Singapore*, 52.
83. Okumiya, Horikoshi, and Caidin, *Zero*, 94–96.
84. Thompson, *Battle for Singapore*, 185.
85. Operations in Malaya and Singapore, Bridges, 5; Lecture on the Malayan Campaign by Heath, June 21, 1942, Percival Papers, 7; Meirion Harries and Susie Harries, *Soldiers of the Sun: The Rise and Fall of the Imperial Japanese Army* (New York: Random House, 1991), 305.
86. Matome Ugaki, *Fading Victory: The Diary of Admiral Matome Ugaki 1941–1945*, foreword by Gordon W. Prange, trans. Masataka Chihaya, with Donald M. Goldstein and Katherine V. Dillon (1991; repr., Annapolis, MD: Naval Institute Press, 2008), 44.
87. Lyman, *The Generals*, 35.
88. *South-East Area Air Operations Record, Phase I, Nov. 1941–Feb. 1942*, 46.
89. Bhargava and Sastri, *Campaigns in South-East Asia*, 132.
90. Khanna and Chopra, *Portrait of Courage*, 160.
91. Wigmore, *Japanese Thrust*, 137–38.
92. *South-East Area Air Operations Record, Phase I, Nov. 1941–Feb. 1942*, 47.
93. Military Intelligence Division, *Notes on Japanese Warfare on the Malayan Front*, Information Bulletin No. 6 (War Department: Washington, DC, 1942), 1.
94. Bhargava and Sastri, *Campaigns in South-East Asia*, 134.
95. Bhargava and Sastri, *Campaigns in South-East Asia*, 134–35.
96. Amitav Ghosh, *The Glass Palace* (New Delhi: Ravi Dayal Publishers, 2000), 389.
97. K. C. Praval, *Valour Triumphs: A History of the Kumaon Regiment* (Faridabad: Thomson, 1976), 103; Tarak Barkawi, "Peoples, Homelands, and Wars? Ethnicity, the Military, and Battle among British Imperial Forces in the War against Japan," *Comparative Studies in Society and History*, 46, no. 1 (2004): 156.
98. Lieutenant Colonel E. L. Wilson Haffenden, History of the 4th/19th Hyderabad Regiment, Operations in Malaya, MISC/707-A/H, MODHS, New Delhi, 1; Smith, *Singapore Burning*, 131; Praval, *Valour Triumphs*, 103.
99. Praval, *Valour Triumphs*, 104.
100. Haffenden, History of the 4th/19th Hyderabad Regiment, 1.
101. Quoted from Haffenden, History of the 4th/19th Hyderabad Regiment, 1–2.
102. Frith, History of the 2/10 Baluch, 7–8; Ghosh, *Glass Palace*, 390.
103. Despatch on the Far East by Brooke-Popham, 39–40.
104. Quoted from Ukagi, *Fading Victory*, 45.
105. Khanna and Chopra, *Portrait of Courage*, 158–59.
106. Jeffrey Grey, *A Military History of Australia* (Cambridge: Cambridge University Press, 1990), 167.
107. Frith, History of the 2/10 Baluch, 7–8.
108. *South-East Area Air Operations Record, Phase I, Nov. 1941–Feb. 1942*, 25.
109. *South-East Area Air Operations Record, Phase I, Nov. 1941–Feb. 1942*, 46.
110. Haffenden, History of the 4th/19th Hyderabad Regiment, 2.
111. Frank Owen, *The Fall of Singapore* (1960; repr., London: Penguin, 2001), 76; Haffenden, History of the 4th/19th Hyderabad Regiment, 2.

112. English, *On Infantry*, 157–58.
113. US War Department, *Handbook on Japanese Military Forces*, with an introduction by David Isby and an afterword by Jeffrey Ethell (1944; repr., Baton Rouge: Louisiana State University Press, 1991), 87.
114. Haffenden, History of the 4th/19th Hyderabad Regiment, 2; Praval, *Valour Triumphs*, 104.
115. Farrell, *Defence and Fall*, 175.
116. General Headquarters, India Military Intelligence Directorate War Information Circular Foreign Armies Non-Operational Intelligence, No. G 15, February 1, 1943, L/MIL/17/5/284, OIOC, BL, 3.
117. Operations in Malaya and Singapore, Bridges, 5.
118. Haffenden, History of the 4th/19th Hyderabad Regiment, 2; English, *On Infantry*, 68–69.
119. Praval, *Valour Triumphs*, 104; Brigadier Jasbir Singh, *Escape from Singapore* (New Delhi: Lancer, 2010), 27.
120. Key, 11th Indian Division, 11.
121. Farrell, *Defence and Fall*, 135.
122. Key, 11th Indian Division, 11.
123. David Hall, "Lessons Not Learned: The Struggle between the Royal Air Force and Army for the Tactical Control of Aircraft, and the Post-Mortem on the Defeat of the British Expeditionary Force in France in 1940," in *The Challenges of High Command: The British Experience*, ed. Gary Sheffield and Geoffrey Till (Hampshire, UK: Palgrave Macmillan, 2003), 120.
124. Operations in Malaya and Singapore, Bridges, 5.
125. Despatch on the Far East by Brooke-Popham, 40.
126. Wigmore, *Japanese Thrust*, 142.
127. Lecture on the Malayan Campaign by Heath, June 21, 1942, Percival Papers, 8.
128. Dan van der Vat, *Standard of Power: The Royal Navy in the Twentieth Century* (2000; repr., London: Pimlico, 2001), 235–36.
129. Van der Vat, *Standard of Power*, 237.
130. Okumiya, Horikoshi, and Caidin, *Zero*, 90–91, 96–97.
131. Ukagi, *Fading Victory*, 46.
132. Vice Admiral Geoffrey Layton, "Loss of HM Ships Prince of Wales and Repulse," *Supplement to the London Gazette*, February 26, 1948 (London: HMSO, 1948), 1237–38.
133. Martin Middlebrook and Patrick Mahoney, *Battleship: The Loss of Prince of Wales and the Repulse* (1977; repr., Middlesex: Penguin, 1979), 162–63.
134. Layton, "Loss of HM Ships," 1239.
135. Van der Vat, *Standard of Power*, 237.
136. Middlebrook and Mahoney, *Battleship*, 284.
137. Middlebrook and Mahoney, *Battleship*, 69–70.
138. Layton, "Loss of HM Ships," 1240.
139. Okumiya, Horikoshi, and Caidin, *Zero*, 96–7.
140. *History of the Southern Army*, 12.
141. Farrell, *Defence and Fall*, 131.
142. Wigmore, *Japanese Thrust*, 140.
143. Lieutenant Colonel Geoffrey Betham and Major H. V. R. Geary, *The Golden Galley: The Story of the Second Punjab Regiment 1761–1947* (1956; repr., New Delhi: Allied, 1975), 224; Operations in the Far East, L/WS/1/952, OIOC, BL.
144. Operations in the Far East, L/WS/1/952, OIOC.

145. Lecture on the Malayan Campaign by Heath, June 21, 1942, Percival Papers, 8–9; Operations in the Far East, 11th Indian Division, Short Summary of Events, L/WS/1/952, OIOC, BL, 44; Pike, *Hirohito's War*, 224.

146. Military Intelligence Service, *Japanese Tanks and Tank Tactics* (Washington, DC: War Department, 1944), 15.

147. 11th Indian Division, Short Summary of Events, L/WS/1/952, 44.

148. *South-East Area Air Operations Record, Phase I, Nov. 1941–Feb. 1942*, 47.

149. Despatch on the Far East by Brooke-Popham, 39.

150. War Diary GS Branch, HQ 9th Indian Division, December 9, Kuala Lumpur, 601/229/WD/Part 2, MODHS, New Delhi.

151. Ghosh, *Glass Palace*, 383, 386.

152. *9 Gurkha Rifles*, 157.

153. Brigadier W. Carpendale, CO 28th Indian Infantry Brigade, Report on Operations of 11 Indian Division in Kedah and Perak, L/WS/1/952, OIOC, BL, 9–10.

154. 11th Indian Division, Short Summary of Events, 44.

155. Note on the Malayan Campaign by LMH, Heath Papers, 4d&f. According to Percival, the order was issued at 1100 hours. Notes by Percival on the Brief Outline Narrative, 3.

156. Carpendale, Report on Operations of 11 Indian Division, 6.

157. Yenne, *Imperial Japanese Army*, 107.

158. Carpendale, Report on Operations of 11 Indian Division, 6–7.

159. Owen, *Fall of Singapore*, 71; Srinath Raghavan, *India's War: The Making of Modern South Asia, 1939–1945* (New Delhi: Penguin, 2016), 186.

160. McEwan and Thomson, *Death Was Our Bedmate*, 18–19.

161. Lecture on the Malayan Campaign by Heath, June 21, 1942, Percival Papers, 6; Wigmore, *Japanese Thrust*, 140.

162. *9 Gurkha Rifles*, 159.

163. McEwan and Thomson, *Death Was Our Bedmate*, 21.

164. Comments by Colonel Harrison on Operations of Malaya Command, Percival Papers, 1.

165. *9 Gurkha Rifles*, 160.

166. Comments by Colonel Harrison on Operations of Malaya Command, Percival Papers, 1; Owen, *Fall of Singapore*, 71–72; Wigmore, *Japanese Thrust*, 146–47; English, *On Infantry*, 160–61.

167. McEwan and Thomson, *Death Was Our Bedmate*, 19–20.

168. *9 Gurkha Rifles*, 160; Mohan Singh, *Soldiers' Contribution to Indian Independence* (New Delhi: Army Educational Stores, 1974), 57; McEwan and Thomson, *Death Was Our Bedmate*, 20.

169. Lyman, *The Generals*, 37.

170. Bhargava and Sastri, *Campaigns in South-East Asia*, 149.

171. Operations in Malaya and Singapore, Bridges, 4, 12.

172. Bhargava and Sastri, *Campaigns in South-East Asia*, 149; Carpendale, Report on Operations of 11 Indian Division, 14.

173. Carpendale, Report on Operations of 11 Indian Division, 12.

174. Carpendale, Report on Operations of 11 Indian Division, 8.

175. Military Intelligence Service, *Japanese Tanks and Tank Tactics*, 10–11.

176. Quoted from *Japanese Tanks and Tank Tactics*, 12.

177. Military Intelligence Service, *Japanese Tanks and Tank Tactics*, 13.

178. Ian Hogg, *Tank Killing: Anti-Tank Warfare by Men and Machines* (London: Sidgwick and Jackson, 1996), 136–37.
179. Lieutenant Colonel E. L. Sawyer, RA, B, 88/33/1, IWM.
180. Bhargava and Sastri, *Campaigns in South-East Asia*, 149; Moreman, *The Jungle*, 29; Singh, *Soldiers' Contribution*, 57–8.
181. Singh, *Soldiers' Contribution*, 59, 61.
182. F. M. Richardson, *Fighting Spirit: Psychological Factors in War* (Dehra Dun: Natraj, 1978), 172.
183. Bhargava and Sastri, *Campaigns in South-East Asia*, 149, 151.
184. US War Department, *Handbook on Japanese Military Forces*, 87.
185. Bhargava and Sastri, *Campaigns in South-East Asia*, 151.
186. Wigmore, *Japanese Thrust*, 148.
187. *9 Gurkha Rifles*, 160–61.
188. *9 Gurkha Rifles*, 161.
189. Carpendale, Report on Operations of 11 Indian Division, 13.
190. Wigmore, *Japanese Thrust*, 149.
191. Carpendale, Report on Operations of 11 Indian Division, 15–6.
192. Lecture on the Malayan Campaign by Heath, June 21, 1942, Percival Papers, 19–21.
193. Notes by Percival on the Brief Outline Narrative, 3.
194. Carpendale, Report on Operations of 11 Indian Division, 24.
195. *South-East Area Air Operations Record, Phase I, Nov. 1941–Feb. 1942*, 52.
196. Lecture on the Malayan Campaign by Heath, June 21, 1942, Percival Papers, 11.
197. Notes by Percival, 3.
198. *9 Gurkha Rifles*, 161.
199. Yenne, *Imperial Japanese Army*, 107.
200. Carpendale, Report on Operations of 11 Indian Division, 17.
201. *9 Gurkha Rifles*, 161.
202. Comments by Colonel Harrison on Operations of Malaya Command, Percival Papers, 4.
203. Richardson, *Fighting Spirit*, 172–73.
204. Carpendale, Report on Operations of 11 Indian Division, 18.
205. Khanna and Chopra, *Portrait of Courage*, 183.
206. Harries and Harries, *Soldiers of the Sun*, 306.
207. H. Gordon Bennett, "Review of The Conquest of Malaya, Singapore, the Japanese Version by Masanobu Tsuji," *Journal of Southeast Asian Studies*, 2, no. 3 (1961): 95.
208. Farrell, *Defence and Fall*, 134.
209. Lodge, *Fall of General Gordon Bennett*, 71.
210. Richardson, *Fighting Spirit*, 1, 3.
211. Notes by Percival, 7.
212. Carpendale, Report on Operations of 11 Indian Division, 15.
213. Singh, *Soldiers' Contribution*, 65–66; Tarak Barkawi, "Culture and Combat in the Colonies: The Indian Army in the Second World War," *Journal of Contemporary History*, 41, no. 2 (2006): 331.
214. Ghosh, *Glass Palace*, 391.
215. Richardson, *Fighting Spirit*, 171.
216. T. R. Sareen, ed., *Select Documents on Indian National Army* (New Delhi: Agam Prakashan, 1988), 16–8, 25, 369; Singh, *Soldiers' Contribution*, 77–78.

217. Lecture on the Malayan Campaign by Heath, June 21, 1942, Percival Papers, 11–12; *9 Gurkha Rifles*, 163; McEwan and Thomson, *Death Was Our Bedmate*, 27.
218. Carpendale, Report on Operations of 11 Indian Division, 19–20.
219. 11th Indian Division, Short Summary of Events, L/WS/1/952, 46.
220. *9 Gurkha Rifles*, 163.
221. Carpendale, Report on Operations of 11 Indian Division, 20–23.
222. English, *On Infantry*, 157.
223. Carpendale, Report on Operations of 11 Indian Division, 24.
224. *9 Gurkha Rifles*, 163.
225. 11th Indian Division, Short Summary of Events, L/WS/1/952, 46–47.
226. War Cabinet, The Malayan Campaign, 4 April 4, 1942, WP(42)145, CAB/66/23/25, PRO, Kew, 2.

4 | Defeat at Slim River

After being forced to withdraw from northern Malaya, the Allied ground forces attempted to delay the rapidly advancing Twenty-Fifth Japanese Army in central Malaya. This chapter focuses on the defeats of the Allied ground forces in central Malaya with special attention to the west coast. The first section traces the retreat from Muda to Ipoh and the second section portrays the wider strategic scenario. The third and last section analyzes the defeat and disaster at Kampar and at Slim River. Overall, it is a depressing story of retreat and further retreat. The reasons behind the Allied failure to check and cause substantial loss to the advancing Japanese are analyzed and integrated within the narrative portrayal of combat. Special attention is given to combat leadership, disciplinary tenor, and the minor tactics of the Allied units.

From Muda to Ipoh

Percival's tactics at this stage involved attempting to hold the main routes and bridges and not to fight a decisive battle of annihilation with the IJA, but to delay the Japanese as long as possible. The Allied troops were trucked from one linear static position to another while they were being successfully outflanked and out-maneuvered by the advancing Japanese.[1] On 15 December, the strategic situation for Percival was not rosy. Kroh was lost, and the road to Ipoh was open. The 11th Indian Division's right flank was vulnerable to Japanese penetration.[2]

The Patani Road forked at Kroh, with one branch running west, the other south, and both branches later joining the main west coast road. The 12th Indian Brigade's task was to protect the Kroh Road. The Japanese, however, pressed along the main west coast road, which threatened this brigade's rear.[3] Brigadier A. C. M. Paris anticipated that the 11th Division might have to withdraw behind the Muda River. Such a withdrawal by the other brigades of the 11th Indian Division would uncover the 12th Indian Brigade in the northwest and eastern directions. So Paris concentrated his troops and decided to retreat.[4] The pattern of Japanese action and the British-Indian troops' reaction had already set in. The Japanese would threaten the flank of one section of the Allied line, and then that section, instead of taking any corrective measures, would withdraw. Since withdrawal of a particular section of the line resulted in uncovering the flanks of the other section of the defense line that was yet to be attacked, the latter section also withdrew to conform with the former section. The Japanese would catch up quickly and repeat this procedure, and the Allied troops would retreat again till they had run out of regions to retreat in the Malayan Peninsula and reached Singapore Island.

On 15 December 1941, the 5th/2nd Punjab Regiment of the 12th Indian Brigade was ordered by Paris to hold the Batu Pakaka Bridge over the Muda River and Koala Ketil Road. The aim was to check the Japanese infantry and tanks advancing from Sungei Patani.[5] The Japanese technique aimed to "feel out" the soft spots in the enemy line.[6] The 5th/2nd Punjab's C (Sikh) Company was at the bridge and A Company at Koala Ketil. The B Company was in support of C, and the D Company was at the left of C Company. On 16 December at 1400 hours, the Japanese detachment that had advanced from Gurun through the inland road attacked the Batu Pakaka Bridge with mortars. Captain I. J. Kiani was CO of the C Company. His leadership during the battle was dismal. He and his company headquarters had vanished for twenty-four hours when the battle was raging. Anne Hoiberg rightly says that in order to be an effective leader, an officer must be willing to share the discomfort and dangers of the men under his command and should demonstrate a heroic fighter spirit or the gladiator leadership style. Soon, Kiani was replaced with Jemadar Pritam Singh as CO of the C Company. One mortar commander picked up his weapon and ran away. Soon C and D companies retreated. An erroneous message came from the C Company that the Japanese had crossed the bridge. In the "fog of war," this was believed.[7] The battalion commander panicked and did not check the veracity of this message. Command at the levels of battalion and subunit (company- and platoon-level command, which was exercised by the VCOs) was inadequate to meet the trying conditions. Probably the loss of trained VCOs and NCOs due to the massive expansion of the Indian Army was partly the reason for the weak command at the subunit level. The fact that newly inducted British officers had a weak command over the jawans' vernaculars further worsened the scenario. Further, the command at the brigade, divisional, and corps levels was also incompetent.

On the morning of 16 December 1941, Heath decided to withdraw the 11th Indian Division to Krian River. He concluded that after the twin defeat at Jitra and Gurun, the 11th Indian Division required a respite. Heath assumed that if the 11th Indian Division withdrew very fast, then the Japanese might not follow up immediately, and it would give the division some time to rest and reorganize. In reality, the Japanese advanced as fast as the division retreated. And the 11th Indian Division got no respite. Another reason for retreat was that Heath figured that a Japanese column supported by armor might outflank the defensive position at Muda River, and such a move could not be contained by the 12th Indian Brigade. Heath thought that the region between the Muda and Krian rivers was suitable for armor. So he wanted his troops behind the Krian River, which, with its extensive swamps, was considered a good antitank obstacle. Heath ordered the 6th (22nd Mountain Regiment, 2nd East Surreys, 1st/8th Punjab, and 2nd/16th Punjab) and 15th (1st Leicestershires, 2nd/9th Jats, 1st/14th Punjab, and 3rd/16th Punjab) Indian brigades to rest and refit at Taiping. The 28th Indian Brigade (2nd/1st, 2nd/2nd, and 2nd/9th Gurkhas) was ordered to hold the position at the road and railway bridge over Krian at Nibong Tebal. To cover the withdrawal from Muda River, the 12th Indian Brigade was ordered to fight a rearguard action along the Titi-Karangan-Selama Road and then join the rest of the 11th Indian

Division at Taiping on 17 December.[8] The order for 11th Indian Division was to keep the Japanese out of Ipoh at least for seven days to allow for the evacuation of the stores.[9]

It is interesting that so early in the campaign, Heath had lost faith in the combat capacity of his troops. He reasoned that his troops required rest. But the Japanese were advancing relentlessly. The Allied generals were soft on their troops. Moreover "tank fear" had clogged Heath's mind. Heath was certain that the Japanese tanks were unstoppable. Whenever Heath anticipated that the Japanese might turn or outflank his position, instead of taking corrective measures, he would retreat. For the time being, he wanted to go behind the Krian River. But what would happen if the Japanese turned the flank of the Krian River position? Then, by the abovementioned logic, he would retreat again. The "retreat/withdrawal" complex had already begun for Heath.

Percival writes about Heath:

> As soon as the operations started, General Heath gave me the impression of developing what might be termed a "withdrawal complex." He always seemed to me to be thinking how soon he could disengage his troops from the enemy and how far he could take them back. I think the fundamental reason for this, at any rate in the early stages, was that he never agreed with the official strategy, laid down in London and endorsed in Malaya, of imposing the maximum delay on the Japanese at every stage so as to gain time for the arrival and deployment of reinforcements. General Heath's conception, as I understand it, was that, as soon as the operations started, we should have withdrawn all our forces to Johore and fought out the battle there.[10]

Percival should have dismissed Heath for disagreeing with the GOC Malaya Command's strategy. Generally, Percival followed the "hands off" command style like Douglas Haig.[11] So, despite frequent disagreement, Percival did not interfere too often with his corps commanders' handling of the battle. On 16 December, the Japanese drove in between the Kroh forces (in Kedah just east of Baling) and the 11th Indian Division.[12] On the night of 16/17 December, the 28th Indian Brigade was ordered to withdraw to Krian River.[13] All the vehicles were abandoned after immobilizing them.[14] One of the essential command skills was the ability to inspire and sustain enthusiasm among the soldiers.[15] Heath's policy of continuous rapid withdrawals reduced his troops' "will to fight."

Rivers posed no obstacle to the advancing Japanese troops. Even when the British and Indian soldiers destroyed the bridges, the Japanese engineers quickly rebuilt them. During the Hainan exercise, Tsuji had trained the troops extensively in bridge-building exercises.[16] Still, the British commanders believed that a river would delay the Japanese columns for quite a long time. Lieutenant Colonel Selby, CO of the 2nd/9th GR, blamed the panicky staff officers for ahead-of-time withdrawals and demolitions.[17] Historian Brian P. Farrell rightly states that the British officers, as part of their delaying actions, were for defending fixed positions to force a set-piece battle emphasizing firepower and numerical superiority. In contrast, fluidity, surprise, and mobility were the three elements integral to Japanese military operations.[18]

Defeat at Slim River

The Krian position was thirty miles long from the coast to the highlands. The troops deployed to hold it were in a sorry state. The 11th Indian Division's brigades had been badly mauled. In the 6th Indian Brigade, the 2nd East Surreys mustered 270 personnel, and the 1st/8th Punjab was represented only by the stragglers. The 1st/16th Punjab had lost 220 men and all its vehicles and mortars. The 15th Indian Brigade had only 600 men in its ranks. The condition of 28th Indian Brigade was similar. The 2nd/9th GR had only one company intact.[19] Krian River was held by 5th/14th Punjab with 3rd Cavalry less one squadron positioned on the right and 28th Brigade on its left.[20]

On 17 December, the 6th and 15th Indian brigades went to Taiping. At 1030 hours, 150 stragglers of the 2nd/16th Punjab came to Kota south of Muda. Transport was sent to collect them. At 1200 hours, the bridge of boats at Butterworth was destroyed. Kepala Batas was bombed in the morning, and the 88th Field Regiment suffered some casualties.[21] Early on 17 December, Paris decided to withdraw the 5th/2nd Punjab of the 12th Indian Brigade from Batu Pekaka.[22] The withdrawal started on 17 December at 0200 hours. The 5th/2nd Punjab suffered eighteen casualties, and the Merbau Pulas Bridge was blown up. During this encounter, Subedar Jiwan Singh ran away from the frontline to the rear.[23] This sort of battlefield behavior stemmed from inadequate training.

For crossing the rivers and streams, the Japanese resorted to the use of collapsible rubber boats, country boats forcibly taken or bought from the local inhabitants, and also rafts made of bamboo poles lashed with rattan. The Chinese *sampans*, each of which was able to carry forty soldiers, were useful in penetrating the mangrove swamps due to their shallow draught.[24] And the Japanese advance parties made liberal use of them. Reconnaissance in the jungle was conducted by picked and specially trained Japanese troops. The objective of the reconnaissance patrol was to gain contact with the enemy. Such parties comprised five to ten men and were equipped with compasses, portable radios, and mapping equipment. When no trail was available for marching, a chopping team preceded the main body for cutting down dense foliage. Generally, four to six miles were covered in a day. In the jungle, the main body was preceded by an advance guard. When the main body was a battalion, the advance guard comprised a company, and when the main body comprised a company, a platoon constituted the advance guard.[25] The Japanese forded the river south of the Merbau Pulas Bridge and opened up with mortars and small arms. They fired standing amid the trees and in the swamps. The 5th/2nd Punjab was aided by the Argylls in checking the Japanese.[26] Lieutenant Colonel C. C. Deakin of the 5th/2nd Punjab writes: "Sometime before midnight I went to visit B (Punjabi Muslim) Company. It was raining and I found the company thoroughly dispirited and all asleep huddled under rubber trees. No sentries, arms lying about, no sign of alertness, all wet and hopeless. I kicked some of them awake into watchfulness, for a bit. Some of them were missing later and it must be because they were apathetically asleep and could not be found in pitch darkness. B was our worst company."[27] Continuous retreat and repeated defeats had killed the fighting spirit of this unit. During the night of 17/18 December, the 12th Indian Brigade crossed the Krian River at Selama.[28]

On 17 December, Heath was thinking of further retreat. The 42nd Japanese Infantry Regiment from Kroh turned south toward Grik with the objective of reaching Kuala Kangsar and cutting the 11th Indian Division's LoC. Instead of throwing all possible units at Kuala Kangsar, Heath thought of retreating to Perak River. Only the 12th Indian Brigade was sent to Kuala Kangsar, and Heath was certain that it would be unable to stop the onslaught of the Japanese. The Perak River ran from north to south instead of west to east, so it was considered unsuitable for a prolonged defense. Heath reasoned that he would have to fall back to Kampar.[29] He emphasized that the Kampar defensive position was good from the A/T and the artillery point of view. In Kampar, argued Heath, the British and Indian troops would be able to utilize their ample artillery, a weapon in which the IJA was deficient as it depended mostly on mortars and light infantry mountain guns.[30]

Heath's superior Percival was also in favor of retreating in the southern direction. But Percival was for making a limited retreat and making a stand at Perak. He rightly realized that the region south of Perak was full of roads and was the center of the tin mining and rubber industry. So the Japanese must be kept away from the region south of Perak as long as possible. Perak rather than the regions further south offered a better chance for defense, to somehow slow down the Japanese advance despite the Perak River flowing from north to south. Percival's strategy at this time was that the III Indian Corps should withdraw behind Perak River and at least temporarily should stop the Japanese.[31]

One of the requirements of mission-oriented command is the presence of subordinates who can be trusted upon to operate with a loose rein and with the same goal in sight.[32] Mutual trust between the commander and his subordinates, a trust founded upon a common doctrine and rigorous training, is a must for the effective functioning of the mission-oriented command system.[33] In fact, as G. D. Sheffield rightly says, for any sort of effective command, trust and mutual understanding between the commanders, his staff, and his subordinates are necessary. Ideally, such trust is founded on personal and working relationships built over a period of time. If this is absent, then what is required is a military culture that generates a common philosophy of decentralized command with appropriate training. But the British Army was rigidly hierarchical and tradition bound.[34] A common doctrine and rigorous training were two aspects missing in the Malaya Command. Further, personal relations between the senior commanders were not good. The relationship between Percival and Heath from the very beginning was tension filled. It all started because Heath, from the Indian Army, despite being senior, was superseded by Percival, his junior from the British Army, and was appointed as GOC Malaya.[35] Heath almost "hated" Percival. The relationship got worse as the military scenario continued to deteriorate. Percival could not rely upon Heath to fulfill his operational goal—that is, retreat up to the Perak River. Heath was looking behind his shoulder and thinking of not conforming to Percival's objective but retreating to Kampar.

On 17 December, when the front was on Krian River and the Grik Road, Heath asked for permission to retreat immediately behind the Perak River, some fifty

Defeat at Slim River

miles back. But Percival refused. On arrival at Ipoh, Percival found that orders for this withdrawal were already drafted but not issued. Due to Percival's direct intervention (very rare), the withdrawal took place only on 22/23 December.[36]

On 17 December, the 5th/2nd Punjab retreated from Lunas to Selama on the Krian River. The regimental history notes: "Fighting rearguard actions, and subsequently withdrawing through thick jungle and swamp, inevitably and regrettably implied that many of the wounded were not brought in. This was a great tragedy, although an unavoidable one; for most of the fighting had to be done in darkness when casualties could not easily be seen and dealt with."[37] This resulted in demoralization of the battalion. In contrast, night attack was a favorite tactical element of the Japanese. Night attacks were employed to extend the success won in daylight actions and seize important tactical features, possession of which facilitated the success of the ensuing operations. Local night attacks were also launched to confuse and distract the Allied troops from the main Japanese effort.[38]

The Japanese had advanced in Kelantan as far as Sungei Nal and Kedah and also attacked detachments of British and Indian troops at Grik. The III Indian Corps was ordered to withdraw behind the line of the Perak River to protect the LoC of the forces north of Kuala Kangsar. The 11th Indian Division was withdrawing from the Muda River to the Krian River in the southward direction and was in the process of linking up with the 28th Indian Brigade. The division's right flank was protected by the 12th Indian Brigade.[39]

Continuous retreat and heavy casualties had killed the spirit of the 5th/2nd Punjab Battalion. On 18 December the battalion was ordered to Kuala Kangsar to rest in billets. This battalion's performance at the Merbau Pulas Bridge was uninspiring. Morale was weak and indiscipline had spread. Three courts of inquiry were held against individuals for bolting during action and one for a self-inflicted wound.[40] Lack of trust between the inadequately trained jawans and the newly inducted British officers who had inadequate control over the vernaculars was the principal reason behind indiscipline and subsequent low combat effectiveness of this battalion. By the dawn of 18 December, the 11th Indian Division was behind the Krian River.[41] If the Allied forces were observed initiating a daylight withdrawal, frontal pressure was increased, and pursuit groups were formed from the reserve Japanese units to turn the enemy's flanks and fall on their rear.[42] The 11th Division at this time included the 12th Indian Brigade and the Composite 6th/15th Brigade.[43]

The 6th and the 15th Indian brigades, due to the heavy losses they had suffered, were reformed as a composite 6th/15th Indian Brigade at Ipoh. Amalgamation of different ethnic units resulted in the weakening of the primary group solidarity of the Indian troops. It must be noted that combat motivation of the Indian soldiery was dependent on religious, caste, regional, and linguistic affinities that were integrated within particular regiments in order to generate regimental ethos.[44] Michael Howard writes that in the British Army the regiment gave the personnel a sense of belonging, and regimental loyalty generated group cohesion. The men liked to be surrounded by personnel whom they knew and commanded by officers with whom they had developed a relationship of trust by serving over a long period.[45] His observation is all the more applicable for the Indian Army. And amalgamation of the different brigades with their attendant battalions under the pressure of war dissolved the distinct regimental group identities, resulting in a drop in the combat motivation of the jawans.

The original task of the 8th Indian Brigade was to defend the airfields near the Kota Bahru region. After the loss of Kota Bahru and the shift of the main weight of Japanese advance along the west coast, the 8th Indian Brigade was shifted to Kuala Lipis, and the 4th/19th Hyderabad attached to this brigade was ordered to rejoin its parent brigade (12th Indian Brigade). The 4th/19th Hyderabad rejoined the 12th Indian Brigade at Kuala Kangsor on the night of 19 December. This brigade's task was to guard against a Japanese breakthrough in the rear of the 11th Indian Division by way of the Kroh-Kuala Kangsor Road. Brigadier Paris, in order to obstruct the advance of the Japanese along this road, had already sent the Argylls and the 5th/2nd Punjab.[46] On that day, Penang Island on the west coast of Malaya was occupied by the Japanese.[47]

On the night of 19/20 December, A Company of 5th/2nd Punjab was sent to the Grik Road area.[48] They took up position at Kota Tampan on the Grik Road to cover the withdrawal of the Argylls. A Company was dispersed along twelve miles of the road with platoon posts near Kota Tampan, Sauk, etc. Armored cars patrolled the area between the platoon posts. This battalion checked a Japanese attack and allowed the Argylls to retreat. This action led to three killed, five wounded, and twelve missing in the 5th/2nd Punjab.[49] The 11th Indian Division reached the Perak River by 20 December.[50] A long stand at Perak was considered impossible by Heath, despite the fact that a large area in the center was protected by swamps. In his eyes, the front was considered too extended, and the thick vegetation along the river banks provided the Japanese with covered approaches.[51] Heath had no counter to the swarming tactics of the Japanese in the swampy jungle-covered terrain. He should have asked himself whether the defensive front at Kampar would be less extensive. And instead of preparing the British and Indian troops to fight it out with the Japanese inside the thick vegetation, the Allied generals and their troops were afraid of encountering the Japanese infantry in thick scrub jungle, especially during the night.

On 20 December, the Japanese reached Selama and the 3rd/16th Punjab was allowed to retreat at its own discretion. This was by no means an example of mission-oriented command as all the battalion commanders were not asked to coordinate their plans and retreat jointly in a timely manner to further the objective of putting up a stout defense somewhere in the Malayan Peninsula. Giving contradictory orders to the various battalion commanders and allowing them to retreat at will without any overarching plan was an example of an incoherent, inefficient, and disjointed command system. As the 3rd/16th Punjab of the 15th Indian Brigade retreated, the 28th Indian Brigade, to conform with the former unit's retreat, also withdrew to Ulu Sapetang. The defense of the so-called Krian River Line was over. Meanwhile, Paris had sent a company of the 5th/2nd Punjab to Kota Tampan (where the Perak River ran close to the road) to protect the LoC of the Argylls, who were on the Grik Road attempting to slow down the Japanese advance toward Kuala Kangsar.[52] The 4th/19th Hyderabad of the 12th Indian Brigade was also sent to Kuala Kangsar.[53] By 20 December, the whole of Kelantan was evacuated by the 8th Indian Brigade.[54] On the same day in a meeting of the War Council, Bennett got the impression that even Percival was suffering from the "withdrawal complex."[55] It must be admitted that Percival, who was indecisive by nature, lacked the personality to carry out a tough fight either with the Japanese or with his subordinates.[56]

Next day, the British and Indian troops of the 11th Indian Division were trying their best to contain the Japanese west of the Perak River and also to prevent their further advance south of the Krian River. The 12th Indian Brigade was protecting Kuala Kangsar and the Grik Road. The Kelantan force (8th Indian Brigade of the 9th Indian Division) was along the railway at Manik Orai. The 22nd Indian Brigade of the 9th Indian Division was at Kuantan.[57]

On 21 December, the 5th/2nd Punjab Battalion suffered another twenty casualties along the Grik Road. Continuous retreat, repeated bombings, and casualties had made the men in this unit jumpy.[58] During the night of 21/22 December, the 5th/2nd Punjab concentrated at Sauk.[59] On 22 December, the RAF attempted to tussle on a large scale with the Japanese air force. The 453rd Squadron's fifteen Buffaloes based at Kuala Lumpur dueled with eighteen Nakajima Oscars of the 59th and 64th *Sentais* (Combat Groups). Only three Buffaloes survived this encounter.[60]

On 22 December, both the 12th and 28th Indian brigades were forced south of Kuala Kangsar. While this was happening on the Perak front, at Kelantan too the 8th Indian Brigade withdrew south of Kuala Krai along the railroad. It was decided to withdraw the 8th Indian Brigade further into central Malaya along Kuala Lipis-Raub area.[61] On this day, the 5th/2nd Punjab withdrew from Sauk. In the German Army, the young officers established authority over the soldiers by displaying personal examples of bravery. The performance of the small subunits depended on resolution and coolness displayed by the officer in the face of danger. During the attack, the section commander functioned as the driving force behind the soldiers' determination to get at the enemy.[62] As John Keegan writes, it is the spectacle of heroism or its immediate report that fires the blood of the frontline soldiers.[63] The performance of the Indian Army's personnel depended on inspirational personalized command by the officers. At times, when the officers displayed inspirational leadership, the jawans responded in kind. To give an example, the D Company under Lieutenant V. J. Chadda was able to repulse two Japanese ambush parties north of Sauk.[64]

On 23 December, because of the Jitra disaster, Murray-Lyon was replaced.[65] The 11th Indian Division fell behind the Perak River.[66] The 5th/2nd Punjab Battalion reached north Salak (near Ipoh). In the morning, the 5th/2nd Punjab was bombed by Japanese aircraft, and it dispersed into the rubber plantation, but not before suffering seven wounded. The battalion moved to the southern part of Siput village.[67] Some men of the 5th/2nd Punjab complained about why no British aircraft were opposing the Japanese.[68] Actually, on that day all the Allied aircraft were withdrawn from the Malayan Peninsula to Singapore.[69] Throughout the day, the road along Blanja Pontoon Bridge and Parit, along with the stretch between Siput and Chemor, was heavily bombed by the Japanese aircraft, resulting in the destruction of numerous motor vehicles. Ipoh was also bombed. A large quantity of ammunition at Ipoh railway station along with the petrol dump was set on fire due to the bombing.[70] A pall of black smoke covered the sky over Ipoh. The Japanese aircraft also bombed the 137th Field Regiment at Sungei Siput, resulting in four killed, six wounded, and two vehicles destroyed. Due to the Japanese bombing, the twenty-five-pounder ammunition in a trailer blew up, killing one and wounding two officers.[71]

The Strategic Scenario

From the battalion level, let us shift our attention to the strategic level. On 15 December 1941, the British Prime Minister, Churchill, told Percival that the troops must be conserved for the defense of Singapore and on no account should they be used up or cut off in the Malayan Peninsula.[72] On 19 December, Churchill also informed the Chiefs of Staff Committee that he along with Field Marshal John Dill (CIGS) and Duff Cooper (Minister Resident for Far Eastern Affairs stationed at Singapore from September 1941 and probably Churchill's spy) had agreed that the Allied troops, after following a scorched-earth policy, should withdraw to Johore and fight the decisive battle for the defense of Singapore there. Churchill was sailing to the United States on the *Duke of York*. He later wrote in his history of the Second World War (quasi autobiography): "A grave strategic choice was involved in the tactical defense of the Malay Peninsula. I had clear convictions which I regret it was not in my power to enforce from mid-ocean."[73] Such a piece of advice must have aggravated Percival's policy of rapid retreat across Malaya.

However, a counterfact can be posed here. Churchill's strategy was the same as that of Heath: a rapid withdrawal to Johore and fight the decisive battle there. What would have happened if Percival had followed such a strategy? Could Singapore have been saved? The answer is no. Churchill, Cooper, and Heath wanted to retreat to the Johore and build up a rigid linear defensive line across the narrow neck of the peninsula. In accordance with the tradition of the British general staff, the British commanders, as well as their troops, were comfortable fighting static battles. They believed that the Japanese frontal attacks on the Johore defensive line would be smashed by massive artillery fire. However, Yamashita would not have obliged them. In case of a short, linear, rigid defensive line across the narrow neck of the Johore Peninsula, Yamashita would have launched frontal probes and, taking advantage of aerial and naval superiority, would have simultaneously landed troops behind the defensive line or even in Singapore Island to outflank the Johore Line. But defense (if Percival was willing to carry out a last-ditch defense somewhat like MacArthur at Bataan) by the Allied troops at Johore would have probably lasted longer than what happened at the Slim and Muar Rivers.

Despite the worsening scenario in Malaya, the War Office on 13 December 1941 reiterated its erstwhile stand that troops could not be withdrawn from the

Middle East to strengthen Far Eastern defense. In other words, the Middle East was a higher priority than Malaya. However, the War Office noted, the troops and equipment that were supposed to go from India to Iraq could be diverted to Malaya. These assets involved the 85th A/T Regiment, 35th Light AA Regiment (twenty-four Bofors with twenty thousand rounds of ammunition), 6th Heavy AA Regiment (sixteen mobile 3.7-inch guns with twenty thousand rounds of ammunition), and sixty-four two-pounder A/T guns.[74] So the War Office at least put the defense of Malaya on a higher plane than the probable Axis threat to West Asia. To counter the threat posed by the Japanese air and ground force to the Allied ground troops, on 16 December, the commander in chief, Far East, wanted 350 A/T rifles and fifty Bofors Guns for the 9th and 11th Indian divisions.[75] On 21 December, Duff Cooper sent a telegram citing that the situation was serious. He requested that aircraft should be sent to Malaya from Burma, Java, and Sumatra. What Cooper did not realize was that Burma, Java, and Sumatra also were coming under heavy Japanese attacks. He cited the minimum requirement of aircraft for immediate use to be four fighter squadrons, four bomber squadrons, one escorting flight, and one transport flight. For ground force, he demanded one division and one brigade, three light AA regiments, and two heavy AA regiments. Cooper failed to realize that Percival had more troops than Yamashita. The real problem was that the Allied troops were untrained and Percival's command was inert. Cooper ended his telegram by requesting fifty light tanks, 350 A/T rifles, five hundred Tommy Guns, and Bofors ammunition.[76]

The political and military authorities in London finally woke up to the fact of decisive Japanese superiority in the air and on land. In order to check the Japanese tank menace, on 18 December 1941 the War Cabinet ordered India to send all the light tanks to Malaya.[77] Such a move would seriously weaken the defense of Burma, another target of Japanese expansion. On 20 December India offered one independent light tank squadron with seventeen Mark IV and thirteen Mark VI light tanks. However, India warned that though these tanks could be shipped in January 1942, there was a serious shortage of spare parts for these armored vehicles.[78] On 23 December, the War Cabinet approved the dispatch of four hundred men of the armored division to man the light tanks sent from India. The War Cabinet also expressed serious concern over the fact that the Japanese fighters were superior to the British ones.[79] On 23 December, London also sent Lieutenant General Henry Pownall (his contribution during the Malaya-Singapore Campaign was of dubious value) as a replacement for Robert Brooke-Popham, who was close to a nervous breakdown.[80] On 27 December, Brooke-Popham was replaced with Pownall.[81] This shuffle in the Allied high command did not have any appreciable effect on the conduct of the Allied operation in Malaya.

On 24 December 1941, the commander in chief of India notified the War Office that the 53rd British Brigade (5th and 6th Royal Norfolks and 2nd Cambridgeshires), with seven thousand personnel, was ready to move from Bombay to Malaya. The London government was to provide the necessary shipping in order to complete this move by January.[82] On the same day, India sent the 45th Indian Brigade, with twenty-six LMGs, thirty-six Thompson submachine guns, four two-inch mortars, six three-inch mortars, six Vickers Guns, and two A/T rifles.[83] However, none of the personnel had tin helmets. Besides the questionable state of training of the 45th Indian Brigade, its A/T weapons and mortar establishments were weak. The War Cabinet in London was unable to realize the true nature of war that had unfolded in Malaya. We have seen that the Allied troops were burdened with excessive motor vehicles, which in turn created not only a logistical logjam especially during retreats, but motor transport itself was more or less useless in the combat conditions of Malaya. Still, the War Cabinet wanted more motor vehicles for the troops in Malaya. On 24 December, the War Cabinet inquired whether India could supply fourteen 30 cwt trucks for the 4th Suffolk Battalion, fifteen 15 cwt. trucks for the headquarters of the 15th Indian Brigade, and eight 15 cwt. trucks for the signal sections of the 18th British Division.[84]

The next day, the London government in a dispatch blamed the native labor for incomplete defensive works. It noted that during a bombing raid, the Malay labor could not be relied upon.[85] The War Cabinet should have asked itself why the Malays would face bombing to serve the needs of their British masters. On 25 December, the commander in chief, India, painted a grim strategic scenario and warned the War Office; commander in chief, Middle East; and commander in chief, East Indies:

> War in Far East has completely altered situation and we are now on defensive until power of USA is developed. Russian recovery has decreased or postponed menace to the Caucasus. Success in Libya has removed danger in that theater. It is vital to secure Burma and India and if possible Singapore even at the expense of operations and preparations elsewhere. Essential requirements are air forces, anti-aircraft and naval forces especially for convoy protection and anti-submarine work. There will be serious shortages of equipment and certain munitions. . . . Request urgent consideration of defense of Sumatra, which is vital to defense of Singapore and naval security in Indian waters.[86]

The commander in chief of India was asking for reinforcement of the Far East, at the expense of the western desert, where he regarded the threat level to be lower, in contrast to the War Office's assessment. He harped on the shortages of equipment as the prime cause for debacle in Malaya but omitted to note that the dismal state of training of Percival's troops and his inept command structure were the reasons for the disaster. Ironically, the defense of the Far East in the eyes of British strategic managers was dependent on the strength and resilience of American power in the Asia-Pacific region.

Back in Singapore, Governor Shenton Thomas was more interested in the economic potential of Singapore, rather than the deteriorating military situation. On 25 December 1941, he noted that the smelter at Singapore required a stock of 500 tons of iron ore but at present the stock was less than 250 tons. This was because Perak production had stopped, and Singapore was still awaiting delivery of iron ore from the Federated Malay States. He continued that it was desirable to maintain the smelting operation at Singapore at the maximum capacity in order to fulfill the American, Australian, Indian, and Russian tin contracts. If, however, circumstances prevented smelting operations, then the iron ore should be shipped to the United Kingdom or the United States.[87] Whether in wartime additional shipping was available for this purpose, when each and every Allied ship was required for bringing troops from the Mediterranean and evacuating personnel from various places in the Far East, is questionable. However, one thing is clear. The weapons promised and already on their way to Malaya would not reach the troops before the disaster at the Slim River due to the speed of the Japanese advance.

Now, let us turn the discussion to Percival's strategy as regards the Malaya-Singapore theater. The situation on the east coast of Malaya was not rosy. On 24 December, the 22nd Indian Brigade was ordered to treat the beach defense as outposts, and in case of a serious Japanese attack, this brigade was to withdraw behind the Kuantan River. Percival did not want this brigade to be destroyed on the beaches. He wanted it intact for combat elsewhere in Malaya.[88] On 27 December, Percival visited Kuantan in the east coast. He rightly noted that due to the Japanese infiltration tactics, a river line could not be held.[89] Still, he and his subordinates would attempt to build a defensive line both at the Slim River and later also along the Muar River. Archibald Wavell has written: "The commander with the imagination—the genius, in fact—to use the new forces may have his name written among the 'great captains.'"[90] Percival lacked imagination to use his force in a creative manner to delay the Japanese. On 30 December 1941, Percival left Singapore by road for Kuala Lumpur in order to assess the ground situation himself. He spent the night with Heath at Kuala Lumpur, and the next day they went to Tapah, the headquarters of the 11th Indian Division. At Tapah, Percival impressed upon Paris, the CO of the 11th Indian Division, that the Japanese must be denied the use of aerodromes in central Malaya till the arrival of the convoy bringing reinforcements. The convoy was to reach Singapore by mid-January 1942. Paris was emphatically told to hold on to the Kampar position as long as possible and not to fall back behind the Kuala Kubu Road junction before 14 January without Percival's permission. In view of this order, Paris still had a depth of about seventy miles to maneuver for the next fortnight.[91] Meanwhile, on the east coast, the Takumi Detachment (which had advanced from Kota Bahru) captured Kuantan on 31 December.[92]

Next, Percival again concentrated his focus along the east coast of Malaya. On 1 January 1942, Percival visited Raub, headquarters of the 9th Indian Division. By road, the distance from Raub to Kuantan was 150 miles. The 22nd Indian Brigade reported that the Japanese soldiers were wearing Indian uniforms to confuse the defenders.[93] Deception and ruses of every possible kind were used by the Japanese: shouting, use of fire crackers, and indiscriminate shooting to simulate strength or conceal the true direction of maneuvers. To conceal their identity, false flags and even civilian dress were used. At times, snipers even lay with the dead and fired upon the unwary Allied troops.[94] At the conference in Raub, possible tactics for stopping the Japanese were discussed. Brigadier Key, who had experience of fighting on the North-West Frontier of India, said that perimeter camps should be set up in the night, as the Indian troops used to do during their frontier campaigns. Heath proposed the idea of leaving behind commando units, comprising volunteers, to disrupt the Japanese LoCs. Heath at last rightly emphasized that the armored carriers were useless, as the Japanese soldiers easily disabled them using armor piercing bullets. Barstow informed Percival about the reluctance of the managers to implement the scorched-earth policy in the Raub gold mine area. Percival emphasized that the policy of the London government was to destroy all the mines. Barstow next brought up the subject of the difficulties of destroying the rubber plantations owned by the Chinese. The European-owned rubber plantations posed no problem, but forcing the Chinese owners to destroy the plantations required strong guard parties. Heath also pointed out the difficulties of implementing the scorched-earth policy for the tin mines along the west coast.[95]

On the first day of January, the 22nd Indian Brigade Headquarters lost all contact with the Garwahl Rifles. A recurring problem of the Allied brigade commanders was the failure to maintain control over the scattered battalions. A Japanese party of fifty men wearing Indian uniforms and tin helmets attacked the surprised Garwahlis near the Kuantan ferry area. Only three hundred Garwahlis were able to filter back to the brigade line.[96] Farrell observes that the 22nd Indian Brigade of the 9th Indian Division fought at Kuantan with determination but lacked clear direction.[97] Barstow had instructed G. W. A. Painter, commander of the Kuantan Force, to deny the Japanese this aerodrome for another five days. Percival insisted that this airport must be held until 10 January. Then, reasoned Percival, the Japanese would be able to use this aerodrome effectively only by mid-January, and by that time the Allied convoy bringing reinforcements would have reached Singapore safely. Percival failed to understand that even if his plan were successful, the Japanese engineers might bring the aerodrome into use earlier. From Raub, Percival returned to Kuala Lumpur. On 2 January, Percival, after visiting Port Swettenham and Port Dickson, was back at Singapore.[98] The 9th Indian Divisional Headquarters reported that the Japanese, instead of launching frontal attacks, were going for deep infiltration and "gangster tactics."[99] Gangster tactics involved establishing roadblocks, conducting ambushes, and using deceptions and ruses, and the British and Indian battalions had no counter to such combat techniques.

The Kuantan airfield was of greater importance for Percival than the Kuala Lumpur airfield. On the morning of 3 January, orders were issued by Heath for the Kuantan Force to retreat to Jerantut.[100] The Japanese troops captured the Kuantan airfield, and the 2nd/12th FFR was able to escape the Japanese encircling troops.[101] The Japanese launched a holding attack frontally, to confuse and distract the enemy. Simultaneously, the Japanese patrols moved to the flanks of the Allied units. The patrols were armed with LMGs and grenades and had compact rations including rice, condensed food, and vitamin tablets. The patrols moved through seemingly impassable terrain to get to the flanks and rear of the Allied positions. At times, the Japanese infiltration patrols dug in and waited for the main body to arrive before launching a coordinated assault.[102] A strong party of Japanese soldiers attacked the headquarters of the 22nd Indian Brigade. Before they could consolidate their gains, Lieutenant Colonel Arthur Edward Cumming of the 2nd/12th FFR immediately counterattacked with a small party. His action allowed the brigade headquarters to withdraw unhurt. Cumming himself received two bayonet wounds and later got a VC.[103] When the British officers displayed "heroic command," the jawans fought vigorously.

By this time, the Japanese air force had gained complete air superiority over northern and central Malaya. While the Japanese bombers attacked the British aerodromes, their fighters engaged the RAF fighters in aerial combat. The bombers flew some distance away from the airfield after the initial attack and waited until the RAF fighters (because of lack of fuel) were forced to land. Then, the Japanese bombers returned and attacked the RAF fighters before their refueling was complete. The RAF was thus unable to intercept the Japanese bombers. The success of this tactic was also partly due to the small number of RAF fighters, which prevented them from launching continuous and intense combat area patrols. After eliminating fighter opposition, the Japanese aircraft also strafed the airfields.[104] The Japanese used bomber aircraft as aerial artillery, when the jungle conditions made it almost impossible to deploy field artillery for supporting the advancing infantry.[105] Percival writes in his memoirs: "During the whole of this time our troops were fighting practically without air support. Those who have a similar experience, when enemy planes seem to be always in the air reconnoitering, bombing, and machine-gunning, and when you never see one of your own planes will know what that means and what a great moral effect it has."[106] Strafing and bombing by the Japanese aircraft psychologically disoriented the Allied ground troops.

On 3 January, about one thousand Japanese troops were in Kuantan. The next day, in the 22nd Indian Brigade, the 5th Sikhs withdrew to the position west of Gambang, and the 2nd Garwahl Rifles and 2nd FFR started withdrawing from Maran.[107] However, Percival's plan of containing the Japanese in central Malaya was thrown into disarray due to the disaster that unfolded at the Slim River; this is the subject of the next section.

From Kampar to the Slim River

The reinforcements promised by Britain and India did not have any immediate effect on the deteriorating ground scenario for the British and Indian troops. Let us take a worm's-eye view of the battle that unfolded on the west coast. On 24 December, Brigadier Paris left the command of the 12th Indian Brigade (which was at Sungei Siput) and became the CO of the 11th Indian Division. Paris was promoted to the new post because he was considered to have had considerable experience in bush warfare. Paris's brigade-level command performance until this time was lackluster and defeatist. Lieutenant Colonel I. A. Stewart of the Argylls assumed command of the 12th Indian Brigade.[108]

Between 24 and 26 December, as a result of a wide turning movement by the Japanese, the 12th Indian Brigade retreated. But its 5th/2nd Punjab fought a good delaying action at Chemor area.[109] On 26 December, the 12th Indian Brigade had taken up position north of Chemor, blocking the road to Ipoh with the 5th/2nd Punjab in the front and the 4th/19th Hyderabad with the Argylls in the rear.[110] The objective was to ambush the Japanese. This attempt by the Argyll and Sutherland Highlanders and the 4th/19th Hyderabad Regiment to ambush the Japanese failed because they lacked the skill to conduct a successful ambush. The result was that the ambush party itself was ambushed by the Japanese. Due to inadequate coordination with the supporting artillery, the D Company of 4th/19th Hyderabad suffered heavy casualties at a feature known as Limestone Rock. The D Company was cut off by the Japanese and then surrounded and captured, but the B Company of 4th/19th Hyderabad was able to escape.[111] Four carriers under Captain L. C. Lind attempted to reinforce the doomed ambush party. This attempt failed after twelve out of the sixteen drivers and crews of the carriers became casualties, and two of the carriers had their radiators punctured.[112] The Bren Carriers were not the ideal tools for fighting the nimble Japanese infantry in the trackless jungle country. The Japanese troops were equipped with Tommy Guns and a large number of automatic weapons that were excellent for close-quarter fighting. In contrast, most of the Allied infantry had rifles. The rifle is an accurate long-range weapon, but in Malaya there was rarely an opportunity for an extended field of fire.[113] Again, the Japanese tactic was that, if the enemy counterattacked, the Japanese advance parties allowed them to pass through and then turned and fired on the flanks and rear of the counterattacking troops.[114] Late during the afternoon, the Argyll and Sutherland Highlanders and the 4th/19th Hyderabad were ordered to withdraw. The Japanese closed up with the rearmost company of the 4th/19th Hyderabad. The only silver lining was that the personnel of the Jat Company held their fire until they were quite close and were able to kill sixty Japanese. As a result, the Japanese did not press on the retreating regiments.[115] The 5th/2nd Punjab Battalion suffered ten killed and wounded. The Japanese attempt to attack the right flank of the A Company of 5th/2nd Punjab failed due to fire support of the 137th Field Regiment. Further, the defensive position was in the open and well dug with good visibility for defensive fire. Another factor for the failure of the Japanese attack was that the Japanese aircraft did not intervene in support of their infantry.[116] When Allied infantry-artillery cooperated, the Japanese infantry attack without air support on prepared Allied defensive positions temporarily stalled. The Japanese were not invincible. The 5th/2nd Punjab and the 4th/19th Hyderabad showed that in positional encounters, they could give a bloody nose to the Japanese but were completely lost in chaotic running battles. There were about 1,200 Japanese at Sungei Seput. The 5th/2nd Punjab retreated before them.[117]

The 4th/19th Hyderabad was to withdraw beyond Chemor and then by vehicles to Gopeng some thirty miles further south. While retreating, 4th/19th Hyderabad's B Company was pursued by the Japanese spearheads.[118] The 5th Japanese Division crossed the Perak River near Blanja, and the Imperial Guards Division crossed near Ipoh. Motorboats that were used for the Singora landing were used to ferry the Japanese troops.[119] The Japanese had no followers like cooks. They (especially the forward troops and the ambush parties) carried with them hard rations, which included balls of uncooked rice, pickles, and dried fish. The ration was tied up in a tube-like cloth container worn around their waist. For fresh supplies and meat requirements, they depended on local resources. And they were trained to forage from the countryside. Since the Japanese were rice eaters, they were able to live off the country and ate the same food that the Malays and the Chinese consumed.[120] This arrangement in turn allowed the Japanese not only to advance quickly, but also sustained their advance over a long period and distance.

Unlike the IJA, the Allied military personnel neither were trained to live off the country nor carried iron rations with them to subsist on, in case the logistical umbilical cord failed to sustain them. The Australian, British, and Indian troops had to be fed at regular intervals by the commissariat. The European troops especially relied on tinned food. And this in turn resulted in a heavy baggage train that slowed the mobility of the forces and also created logistical logjams during rapid withdrawals across the few roads in Malaya.

On 27 December, the jawans of the 5th/2nd Punjab, in accordance with their habit and despite the urgings of their officers, were late in having their breakfast. The Japanese advanced toward them. They gained high ground on the right rear of the A Company and attacked. When Jan Ghulam Aabs (a VCO) of the 8th Platoon was ordered by the Company CO to support the 9th Platoon, he refused to carry out the order. The reason was that both the officer and the VCO were new to the battalion, and they lacked the trust and bonding between them that would hold in the fire field. Then, A Company's right was pushed back, and D Company was ordered to launch a counterattack. The D Company, without any reconnaissance, pushed forward, encountered the Japanese, and was worsted. The battalion suffered fifty casualties, and some trucks and weapons were lost. During the afternoon, the battalion withdrew to Kipang. At 1900 hours both the 12th and 28th Indian brigades started withdrawing to the Kampar position. In the evening, the 5th/2nd Punjab Regiment withdrew to the area north of Dipang. The objective was to cover the withdrawal of the 28th Indian Brigade. The 4th/19th Hyderabad was at Gopeng. And the Argylls were between Gopeng and Dipang.[121]

On 28 December, the 28th Indian Brigade withdrew from Bato Gajah in the southern direction, and the 12th Indian Brigade retreated to Bidor.[122] The 4th/19th Hyderabad withdrew behind the 28th Indian Brigade at Dipang. Later, when the Argyll and Sutherland Highlanders and 5th/2nd Punjab retreated, Japanese tanks caused some confusion. The 11th Indian Division withdrew to Dipang.[123] Ipoh was captured by the Japanese on that day.[124] The next day, after suffering ten casualties, the 5th/2nd Punjab retreated in confusion over the Dipang Bridge along the Kampar Road.[125]

The Kampar position was south of Ipoh. The defensive position was semicircular in shape, covering the Kampar town from the north, west, and southwest on a frontage of four miles. The eastern flank of the defensive position was on the steep rocky feature known as Gunong Bujang Malaka. Near its western slope ran the main road, flanked by rubber plantations. On 21 December, reconnaissance parties from the 155th Field Regiment's Survey Section traveled south from Ipoh to the mountainous outcrop of Gunong Bujang Melaka, near Kampar. There they surveyed the area to the east—the defensive position that was allocated to them to support the 28th Indian Brigade. The next day, advance parties from the 155th Regiment started preparing the gun locations for the 4.5-inch howitzers and the newly acquired twenty-five-pounders. For the first time in the Malayan Campaign, the regiment took up a good defensive position as the valley was bounded on either side by steep cliffs, some two thousand feet high in places. The slopes leading up from the valley floor were covered with rubber and banana trees and long grass, which provided good camouflage and concealment for the guns. So the British gunners called this region "Happy Valley."[126] However, this very landscape offered a choice terrain for the nimble and aggressive Japanese infantry to infiltrate into the British-Indian defensive position. The Kampar position was held by the 6th/15th Indian Brigade. The 28th Indian Brigade held the loop road, which left the trunk road at Kuala Dipang, passed through Sahum, Chenderiang, and rejoined the trunk road north of Tapah.[127]

The Battle of Kampar started on the night of 29 December. During the night of 28/29 December, the B Battery of the 155th Field Regiment fired on predicted targets in the Dipang area, where the Japanese troops were assembling. Fire directions from Captain James Mackenzie in the C Troop Observation Post brought down effective fire on the Dipang Bridge. When the Japanese infantry attempted to infiltrate through the vegetation-covered valley floor, under the directions of Observation Post officers, effective barrages were brought down on them.[128] Spirited defense by the 6th/15th Indian Brigade, supported by a field artillery regiment and a battery of A/T guns, resulted in the blunting of the frontal Japanese attacks.[129] The terrain at Kampar, halfway between Penang and Kuala Lumpur, was unsuitable for tanks. Yamashita decided to apply frontal pressure and simultaneously landed troops further south of Kampar's position along the west coast of Malaya.[130]

By landing a force at Telek Anson, southwest of Bidor, while continuing to push troops along the trunk road, Yamashita outflanked the Kampar position.[131] Yamashita was practicing what in modern terminology is called effects-based operations (EBO). The guiding philosophy is that war is a clash of wills. EBO advocates that the enemy force need not be destroyed, but only threatened. The desired effect/outcome of any action should be identified before the battle is launched. EBO builds on the Observe-Orientate-Decide-Act (OODA) loop. Physical and psychological pressure should be applied on the enemy in order to generate the desired effect on the latter. The assumption is that by making certain tactical-operational moves, the hostile forces when threatened will respond according to the expectations of the commander of the attacking force. And actions at the tactical-operational levels will have an effect on the strategic realm. The objective is to maintain a high tempo by disrupting the enemy's decision-making cycle. The trick is to think and act faster than the cumbersome decision-making cycle of the enemy can react. Yamashita aimed to act quickly, before Percival's commanders could process the information and respond effectively.[132] Yamashita anticipated that if he launched a holding attack on the front and threatened the rear of the Allied forces, the slow British command would be disjointed and Percival's command would order retreat. And when Yamashita launched his operations in such a style, Percival actually conformed to his wishes.

There was a small garrison at Telok, and the region further south was the responsibility of Brigadier R. G. Moir, CO of the LoC of III Indian Corps.[133] On 31 December, Allied air reconnaissance reported a convoy of small steamers with barges in tow moving down the Perak Coast. The convoy anchored for the night in the mouth of the Bernam River, where it landed a force of fifty men.[134] The Japanese continued to land small parties of saboteurs from small crafts to create alarm and disrupt Allied communications with the rear.[135] On 30 December, the 5th/2nd Punjab Regiment moved into Bidor. On 31 December, work on the Bidor position started. The B Company of the 5th/2nd Punjab Regiment linked with the 4th/19th Hyderabad astride the road. The C Company, in support of the B and D companies of 5th/2nd Punjab, were scattered in sectional outposts along the area. The B Company's position was secured with wire, and the D Company had positions along the tin mine area. The C Company was dug in with the river in front. Its position was in the jungle area north of Trolak. Defensive work on this position continued on 1 January 1942.[136]

On 31 December, the Japanese probed in strength along the right flank of the defensive position along Kampar. The men of the 155th Field Regiment were able to establish good rapport with the Gurkha infantrymen despite the limited vocabulary at both parties' disposal. The Gurkhas would grin at the British gunners and yell, "Hello, Johnnie." The British gunners were shocked to find out that the Gurkha soldiers were collecting the earlobes from the bodies of the dead Japanese soldiers. Barbarization was a two-way process. And at this stage of the campaign, the behavior of the Allied soldiers toward the Japanese was also barbaric. Joanna Bourke claims that in the intense heat of combat, the soldiers collected such "souvenirs" (body parts of the enemy soldiers), which strengthened their will to war. The 1st Leicesters and the 2nd East Surreys had suffered so many combat losses that these two units were amalgamated, and the composite unit was called the British Battalion. This unit also participated in the defense of Kampar.[137]

Special detachments of Japanese engineers were in charge of organizing the ferry operations along the west coast. On 1 January, there was a landing at Telok Anson of a Japanese force of about one battalion strong. It had probably come down the Perak River. Later, this force was strengthened. The Allied river reconnaissance found some barges full of Japanese troops stuck on a sandbank in the mouth of the Perak River.[138] Late in the evening, Paris rang up Percival and told him that the Japanese had landed at Utan Melintang at the mouth of the Bernam River, a short distance south of Perak River. The Bernam River was navigable by small craft until the main west coast trunk road. So, reasoned Percival and Paris, the LoC of the 11th Indian Division was again threatened. Instead of ordering Paris to send a strike force to wipe out the Japanese party at the mouth of Bernam River, Paris was given permission by Percival to withdraw at his discretion.[139] Due to the threat posed by Japanese parties at Utan Melintang, the 6th/15th and the 28th Indian brigades withdrew. The 155th Field Regiment provided good fire support, but close country and subsequent lack of observation posts gave them few opportunities to seek out enemy targets in large numbers. The Japanese attacked in the region north of Bidor. The Allied commanders feared that if the Japanese were able to break through, then the artillery and transport fleet of the 12th Indian Brigade would be unable to reach the main road to Trolak.[140] Threats to the rear areas and LoC again forced the withdrawal of the Allied troops.

During the night of 1/2 January 1942, elements from the 11th Japanese Infantry Regiment and a battalion from the 4th Japanese Guards Regiment moved down the coast by boats to points west and southwest of Telok Anson to outflank the Allied defenders and cut the trunk road at their rear. This move forced the withdrawal of the British and Indian soldiers from Telok Anson.[141] The A and C companies of the 5th/2nd Punjab were in the rubber plantation covering the river bridge in south Bidor in Kampar Road. At 0730 hours on 2 January 1942, the Japanese advanced.[142] The Japanese used roads, and when contact was established with the British and Indian troops, they avoided frontal attack and made flanking movements through the rubber plantations.[143] The Germans advocated envelopment or wing attacks. The objective was to hold the enemy frontally and then to turn him and crush the hostile forces. The concept of *Kesselschlacht/Ket telschlacht* (cauldron battle) spread downward from grand strategy to the arena of minor tactics. It involved one-sixth of the force pinning down the enemy frontally and the rest enveloping both the flanks of the enemy.[144] The Japanese minor tactic followed this technique exactly. Whether the Japanese were influenced by German tactics or not cannot be proven, but Japanese infantry tactics to a great extent were similar to those of the Germans.

In the afternoon of 2 January, a Japanese force comprising some steamers with barges in tow appeared off Kuala Selangor. They were driven off by artillery fire.[145] However, one thing is clear. Due to their aerial and naval superiority, the Japanese could move at will along the west coast of Malaya and could land troops behind the Allied formations and cut off their LoCs. On that day, the decision was made to withdraw the 11th Indian Division.[146] The 12th Indian Brigade successfully fought a series of delaying actions and retreated successively from Kroh to Kuala Kangsar and then to Kampar.[147] In the evening, the 12th Indian Brigade withdrew to the Trolak Sector of the Slim River position, and the 6th/15th Brigade took up covering position at Sungkai. The 28th Indian Brigade moved to the Slim River village area.[148] The defensive line at Kampar, like Jitra, comprised a static linear line supported by artillery and infantry. The defense of the Kampar position had lasted for a mere four days. Threat to the LoC had again resulted in the vacating of this defensive position. At this stage the British commanders should have had a mobile strike force behind their defensive position for protection of their forces' LoC. It is to be seen whether the next defensive position at the Slim River would be substantially different.

Simultaneously, the Japanese attempt to turn the Indian soldiers against their British masters continued. On 31 December 1941, Major Fujiwara Iwaichi discussed with Captain Mohan Singh the issue of raising the INA from the Indian PoWs to fight the British in Malaya. The 1st/14th Punjab Regiment was cut to pieces at Jitra. Captain Mohan Singh of this battalion, who was a prisoner of the Japanese, became the "sole Indian spokesman" for the Indian PoWs. Yamashita on that date ordered that all the Indian PoWs were to be handed over to Mohan Singh. The Japanese had captured Indian soldiers belonging to some twenty different battalions. Fujiwara's organization was in touch with the revolutionary Bengali political leader Subhas Chandra Bose in Berlin. Pritam Singh was also interested in getting in touch with Subhas Bose for strengthening the revolutionary movement among the Indians in Southeast Asia. On 3 January 1942, the Fujiwara *Kikan* and the IIL moved to Ipoh. The INA Headquarters followed them, and the IIL opened a branch at Ipoh. In accordance with the wishes of Mohan Singh, the Indian PoWs were concentrated in Ipoh. In the PoW camps, the liaison officers of the Fujiwara *Kikan* worked at high gear. At the request of the INA and the IIL, pamphlets were produced for Indian soldiers and civilians, and they were entrusted to the Fujiwara *Kikan* and the Japanese air units for distribution.[149] From politics let us turn back to the field of military operations.

The British and Indian troops were harassed continuously as they retreated from the Kampar to the Slim River position. On 3 January, the 5th/2nd Punjab was in Trolak Jungle. The Japanese aircraft dive-bombed and machine-gunned the troops. The battalion suffered forty casualties.[150] The Japanese worked their way through the jungle with ease. They displayed considerable initiative, vigor, and physical stamina while moving through trying terrain. The Japanese companies advanced behind one- or two-man patrols that were armed with submachine guns. When the patrols were fired upon, they maneuvered around the flanks of the British and Indian troops with the support of the main body and infiltrated deep into the latter's defensive position.[151] At a company level, a leading platoon would be preceded by six scouts ranging 350 yards ahead. On contact with the Allied force, the two following platoons would attempt a double envelopment. This was achieved through an irruption/infiltration technique that the Japanese infantry had mastered.[152] During the night of 3/4 January, a Japanese detachment of substantial strength landed north of Kuala Selangor. Then, it advanced through the countryside covered with vegetation.[153] The Japanese landing at Telok Anson resulted in the retreat of the Argyll and Sutherland Highlanders and the 5th/2nd Punjab. On 4 January, the 4th/19th Hyderabad joined them. The Japanese dive-bombers caused consternation among the British and Indian soldiers.[154] Japanese pressure from Dipang forced the withdrawal of the 12th Indian Brigade from Trolak.[155]

Percival's plan was to hold the Japanese at Slim River in order to complete the next defensive line at Tah Jong Malim.[156] The 11th Indian Division got three days to prepare the defense of the Slim River position.[157] Three brigades were involved in the Slim River (north of Kuala Lumpur) defense. The defensive position at the Slim River comprised two sectors. The Trolak Sector extended to the north and south of the village, and the Slim River Sector extended from the Slim River railway station along the main road to the road bridge near Mile Stone (MS) 76.[158] While the 6th/15th protected the LoC, the 12th Indian Brigade (4th/19th Hyderabad, 5th/2nd Punjab, 2nd Argyll and Sutherland Highlanders, and 5th/14th

Punjab in reserve) was at the north of Trolak, and the 28th Indian Brigade was near the Slim River village about 6.5 miles south of Trolak.[159] At last the British commanders had detached a brigade-size force for the protection of the LoC unlike in Kampar, and if the two other brigades had held their position against the Japanese attack, then the defensive line might have just held. However, as we will see, the Japanese, in this case as in Jitra, penetrated frontally as well as along the flanks of the rigid linear defense line.

The Indian brigades' A/T weaponry was weak. In the 28th Indian Brigade, no battalion had more than two A/T rifles and some even had none. Only the 5th/14th Punjabis attached to the 12th Indian Brigade had eleven A/T rifles.[160] And we will see that due to weak training, the Indian soldiers were not able to use the A/T rifles against the rushing Japanese tanks with precision. The 11th Indian Division had a stock of 1,400 A/T mines, but for some strange reason, they were not sent forward. For this mishap, the CO of the 11th Indian Division must take the blame. In the Slim River Battle, the 5th/2nd Punjab only had twenty-four A/T mines.[161]

The 12th Indian Brigade was in charge of the Trolak Sector. North of the Slim River railway station, the railway line and the trunk road ran close to each other, and in the northernmost portion of the Trolak Sector, there was very thick jungle that made it impassable for tanks except for the road itself. However, we will see that the British and Indian troops failed to hold even this road. The rest of the Trolak Sector consisted mostly of rubber estates with byroads branching into them from the main road.[162] Within the 12th Indian Brigade, the 4th/19th Hyderabad was deployed at the outpost position ahead of the two other battalions at MS 60. The A and C companies were deployed ahead while B Company was retained in depth. A Company guarded the railway line parallel to the road and was deployed along the high embankment. C Company covered the main road and was positioned atop steep cuttings that seemed impossible for assault by armor. The A/T defense included three A/T guns (two-pounders), some concrete blocks, tar barrels, and desert (Dannert) wire. Concrete blocks, wire, and tar barrels actually proved useless in stopping the Japanese tanks. The battalion was positioned in midst of a thick jungle. Beside the jungle was a rubber estate with numerous byroads and lanes that connected with the main road. As usual, the Japanese infantry would infiltrate along these lanes. The 28th Indian Brigade was deployed in the rear of the 12th Indian Brigade. It held the Slim River Sector extending from the Slim Railway Station along the main road to a road bridge near MS 76.[163] On 5 January, the 5th/14th was transferred from the 28th Indian Brigade to the 12th Indian Brigade.[164]

In the afternoon of 5 January, a large Japanese party advanced down the railway. The 4th/19th Hyderabad engaged the Japanese and inflicted casualties on them. The Ahir (A) -Company of the 4th/19th Hyderabad held their fire until the Japanese were quite close and performed well. The LMGs tore gaps in the Japanese ranks. The flesh of the Japanese soldiers was ripped apart by steel bullets. When the Japanese infantry fled to the jungle, they were fired upon by the two-inch mortars. About 156 Japanese soldiers died in this encounter.[165] The

Japanese withdrew temporarily to lick their wounds. On 6 January, a Tamil refugee informed the Allied troops that Japanese tanks were nearby. In response, twenty-five A/T mines were laid on both sides of the road.[166]

The Tamil refugee's information was indeed right. From midnight of 6 January, the Japanese advance parties clashed with the patrols of the 4th/19th Hyderabad.[167] The surprise night assault was made in two echelons. Night attacks were made by the Japanese just after dusk or before daylight. There were two types of night attack: night attack by surprise without undertaking any extensive artillery preparations and night attack by force. During the latter type of night attack, the use of artillery actually warned the defenders of a forthcoming enemy attack. In the case of a night attack by surprise, initially, a small advance cadre was sent into zones of anticipated hostile mortar and artillery fire. If enemy fire was not encountered, then the attack was pushed forward almost at once.[168]

The next day, on 7 January, at 0300 hours, the Japanese attacked with artillery fire. In the Battle of Slim River, Murphy's Law (if anything can go wrong, it will go wrong) seemed to operate for Percival's troops. Percival's force failed to use the A/T weapons properly; further, the troops lost the "will to fight," and the commanders lost all control over their dispirited troops. A group of thirty tanks (ten light and the rest medium) and twenty armored cars broke through the 12th Indian Brigade and then the 28th Indian Brigade. The Japanese infantry attack was supported by heavy mortars and LMGs. One group comprising Japanese tanks and lorried infantry followed by a marching column swept across the highway and easily disposed of the concrete cylinders that were designed as roadblocks. Another Japanese composite group including tanks and infantry poured along the railway.[169] This form of attack could be categorized as *Kirimomi Sakusen* (driving charge). It meant constant and overwhelming pressure on a narrow front with the objective of constant advance without allowing the enemy an opportunity to rest.[170] In frontal attacks, the principal Japanese effort was made against a sector of the Allied defensive line that was considered to be a soft spot. The objective of this type of attack was rapid and deep penetration of the hostile line and to achieve this, the attack front was deliberately kept narrow.[171] When the terrain was favorable, the Japanese used tanks in wide encircling movements to cut the hostile LoC and strike at the vital rear areas.[172] Yamashita took advantage of launching a surprise night attack, and the Japanese tanks were able to advance seventeen miles inside the Allied defensive position in just two hours.[173] T. R. Moreman writes that the Japanese method of a swift, concentrated, aggressive attack supported by tanks frontally down the road or on the immediate flanks of the Allied troops aiming to split or fillet their force was like boning a fish. The Allied troops were then forced into the surrounding jungle, and their command and control dissolved with the loss of their heavy weapons as well as severance of their LoC. This was known as filleting attack.[174] And the Japanese used this technique both at Jitra and on a larger scale at the Slim River.

The Japanese infantry used several disused loop roads to move behind the Allied defensive position.[175] Not posting guards and absence of flanking patrols along these roads was a gross failure on the part of the British battalion commanders. Captain B. H. Liddell Hart wanted the infantryman to be a stalker, athlete, and marksman. The infantry, through stealth and deadly accurate small arms fire, was to destroy hostile forces.[176] Though Liddell Hart was thinking about the trench-filled Western Front of the First World War, the first two qualities of his model infantryman were present among the Japanese infantry (though not marksmanship; the Japanese soldiers were not good shots). They moved stealthily through trying terrain and brought down a great volume of fire on the Allied defenders. The Japanese infantry, in groups of forty to fifty men riding bicycles, quickly swarmed over the whole area.[177] One report about the Japanese soldiers' use of bicycles to acquire mobility noted: "Can do amazing things with push bikes which they use very extensively and carry big loads on them, also carry bikes if necessary through swamps and across rivers."[178] Unlike the Allied infantry, the forward Japanese units rarely ran out of ammunition because supplies were brought forward in boxes on the carriers of push bikes. The bicycles were brought from Japan and also bought from the Malays.[179] Each Japanese division had a minimum of six thousand bicycles.[180]

The Japanese tanks penetrated to a depth of twenty miles, causing great loss of transport and guns of the Allied troops. Had more A/T mines been available, things might not have gone so smoothly for the Japanese. The presence of A/T guns with the infantry would have stopped the Japanese "tin cans." The B and C companies of 4th/19th Hyderabad had only Molotov cocktails to check the Japanese tanks. At that critical juncture, Paris made an erroneous decision. He ordered the 4th/19th Hyderabad to withdraw from the outpost position and to deploy in the rear of the rest of the two battalions of the 12th Indian Brigade. It was a difficult tactical maneuver to implement in the night, especially when the enemy was lurking nearby. The officiating CO of 4th/19th Hyderabad, Major A. D. Brown, passed the order for the A Company under Second Lieutenant Edmund Loughlin to withdraw down the railway line. The B Company was ordered to wait for the arrival of the C Company and then to retreat along the main road. Attempting to break contact with the aggressive Japanese infantry resulted in heavy casualties, and the battalion was dislocated.[181] Meeting engagements were deliberately sought by the Japanese officers. Japanese tactical treatises define meeting engagements as a collision of two moving forces or the combat that results when a force in motion meets the enemy at rest or not yet installed in prepared defensive positions. In this type of operation, great freedom of decision was left to the subordinate Japanese commanders to seize the initiative and promptly occupy important terrain features.[182] Paris should have ordered the battalion to hold out as long as possible. Such an order would have been better than to order it to retreat when it was engaged in close-quarter combat with an aggressive enemy. The 4th/19th Hyderabad lost four officers, C Company, two platoons of B Company, two platoons of the Headquarters Company, and all unit transport, plus the twenty-five-pounder battery that was supporting this battalion.[183]

Cooperation and coordination between field artillery and infantry was extremely poor on the British-Indian side. The 5th/2nd Punjab held the area between MS 61 and MS 62 with two-pounder guns of an A/T troop. Some eight miles further south, two artillery batteries of the 137th Field Regiment were positioned at Cluny Estate. Some six miles south of the Slim River, the 155th Field Regiment was held in reserve in the rubber estate at Behrang.[184] The 4th/19th Hyderabad withdrew through the 5th/2nd Punjab Regiment. The small number of A/T mines and A/T guns were able to destroy six Japanese tanks. The Japanese tanks rushed through using speed and surprise before the field artillery regiments could be effectively brought into action. Further, the Allied infantry was demoralized. Sant Ram of 5th/2nd Punjab commanding the A/T guns ran away instead of leading his troops to attack the Japanese tanks supported by Japanese infantry on bicycles and lorries.[185] These Indian soldiers had never seen a tank before. In contrast, any Japanese soldier who displayed cowardice was shot dead by the officer.[186] The institutional culture of the IJA emphasized *bushido*, which stood for unswerving loyalty and devotion to the emperor.[187] Percival rightly noted: "Another asset of the Japanese Army is its discipline. This discipline is securely based on the Japanese 'Family System' and on the need of maintaining family honor. It combines with other factors to make the Japanese soldier a strong fighter and enables him to face danger with courage."[188] Not all the Indian NCOs, however, proved to be cowardly. One Jemadar Kabul Singh of the 4th/19th Hyderabad attacked a Japanese tank with grenades.[189] It was useless but a brave gesture indeed. Similarly, Captain Gulzara Singh, the quartermaster of 4th/19th Hyderabad, gathered some drivers and attacked the Japanese tanks with grenades. But the latter had no effect on Japanese armor.[190] The D Company of 5th/2nd Punjab blew up one medium Japanese tank with a fire bottle.[191] However, the majority of the Indian soldiers ran away shouting and firing madly. This was again because of the loss of veteran VCOs and NCOs from the unit due to milking. The 5th/2nd Punjab suffered about two hundred casualties.[192]

Robert Brooke-Popham had rightly harped on the structural weakness of the British and Indian battalions. He noted:

> The majority of the Indian regiments labored under some disability on account of the inexperience of most of their British officers. As a rule there would be two or three senior officers, with fifteen or more years' experience, then a gap until we came to officers who had joined after September 1939. Somewhere about half these officers had experience in India and could talk the language, but having only from one to two and a half years' service they did not carry the weight which more experienced officers would have done. In both British and Indian units there was only a small leaven of war experienced officers and men, and it was under these conditions that young soldiers had to meet the first shock of Japanese attack.[193]

The 4th/19th Hyderabad was ordered to withdraw south of the Slim River. Due to the breakdown of communications, the right forward company was cut off. Captain G. K. Mehta, CO of the Reserve Company, went to its succor and was never heard of again. Only one weak platoon of the Reserve Company under Captain Lind was able to get back behind the river.[194] The battalion commander failed to stabilize the situation. This shows that by this time, the jawans had lost trust in their commanding British officers. The absence of tanks and an inadequate number of A/T guns on the part of the British and Indian infantry enabled the Japanese infantry-tank combination to break through the former's defensive line. By 0830 hours on 7 January, the Japanese had reached the Slim River Bridge.[195]

In the morning of 8 January, the 5th/14th Punjab, which was a reserve battalion of the 12th Indian Brigade, was overwhelmed by the Japanese tanks. The 28th Indian Brigade was also wrecked by the Japanese infantry-armor combine. The A/T tanks and field guns were wiped out before they could fire on the Japanese tanks. By 0900 hours, the 155th Field Regiment, firing at a range of thirty yards, was able to stop the Japanese onrush but only for the time being. Soon this artillery regiment was destroyed.[196] The Japanese infantry mopped up the pockets of Allied resistance left intact after the initial onrush of their tanks.[197] Cohesion was lost among the subordinate formations of the 11th Indian Division, and many units were scattered in the jungle. The remnants of the two Indian brigades (12th and 28th) were withdrawn that night by way of the railway track.[198]

The defeat at the Slim River on 7/8 January 1942 was a first-class disaster for the 11th Indian Division. The 12th Indian Brigade was roughened up and lost most of its officers. The Argylls under Lieutenant Colonel Stewart were left with two intact companies, and the 5th/2nd Punjab was left with only one company, which comprised Punjabi Muslims and one Indian commissioned officer. The 4th/19th Hyderabad Regiment was left with two intact companies. It numbered two officers and 180 men. The brigade was withdrawn to Tyersall Park on Singapore Island for rest and refit.[199] The 28th Indian Brigade was also routed with the loss of all its transport and guns.[200] It was reduced to a third of its strength.[201] The principal reasons for failure were the absence of an adequate number of A/T guns and A/T mines, and inadequate cooperation between field artillery and infantry and between infantry and A/T guns. Added to these, command both at divisional and brigade levels was below average. While Paris made erroneous command decisions, Stewart suffered from what could be termed command paralysis.

Conclusion

Generally, in most of the accounts of the Malaya-Singapore campaign, historians have blamed Percival, but his corps commander escaped the scrutiny of the military historians. Heath's leadership was pathetic and certainly worse than that of Percival. Heath lacked the confidence to delay the Japanese in plain terrain, due to fear of the Nipponese "tin cans," and in swampy, forested regions, he was afraid of the swarming tactics of the Japanese infantry. What sort of terrain was Heath exactly looking for to delay the Japanese? His only agenda was to retreat faster in the southern direction. And continuous retreats bred an inferiority complex among the troops of the III Indian Corps. The Japanese tactics involved infiltration, encirclement, and finally envelopment. Linear static defense against the fluid Japanese combat techniques proved ineffectual. Maintenance of self-contained defensive posts with all-round good views (almost an impossibility in the jungle- and rubber-plantation-covered terrain of Malaya) supported by aggressive reserve could have stopped the Japanese. Compared to Jitra, a greater number of tanks (thirty at one time) was used by the IJA at the Slim River Battle. At Jitra, and at the Slim River, tanks were used admirably in an aggressive dash across the ragtag British-Indian defensive lines.[202] Well-trained infantry with A/T weapons could have made mincemeat of such a tank attack. However, Percival's troops were not well trained, and proper use of the few available A/T weapons was not made. The performance of the 5th/2nd Punjab Regiment, despite it comprising traditional "martial races" like Sikhs and Punjabi Muslims was especially bad. The combat effectiveness of 4th/19th Hyderabad was also nothing great. The overhyped Argylls also did not perform well in the Slim River engagement.

In general the raw British and Indian troops failed to adapt to jungle conditions of warfare and did not adopt the required combat techniques necessary for stopping the Japanese tank thrusts. The commanders of the battalions and their staff deserve poor marks for not being able to maintain contact with the neighboring units during battle. But it must be noted that shortages of signaling equipment and especially telephone wire was also a contributory factor for the breakdown of communication within the units and among various units during battle. Still, one can pose a counterfactual question. Was Allied defeat at the Slim River inevitable? Probably, defeat at the Slim River was not a foregone conclusion. The course of the Slim River Battle would have been different if the 11th Indian Division had strewn its entire stock of A/T mines along the road through which the Japanese tanks made a "mad" rush. After the defeat at the Slim River, the ragtag Allied force started withdrawing toward Muar and Johore, which is the focus of the next chapter.

Notes

1. Francis Pike, *Hirohito's War: The Pacific War, 1941–1945* (London: Bloomsbury, 2015), 218.

2. Lecture on the Malayan Campaign by General Heath, June 21, 1942, Percival Papers, IWM, London, 13.

3. Lieutenant Colonel Geoffrey Betham and Major H. V. R. Geary, *The Golden Galley: The Story of the Second Punjab Regiment 1761–1947* (1956; repr., New Delhi: Allied, 1975), 224–25.

4. Major General S. Woodburn Kirby with Captain C. T. Addis, Colonel J. F. Meiklejohn (succeeded by Brigadier M. R. Roberts), Colonel G. T. Wards and Air Vice Marshal N. L. Desoer, *History of the Second World War, The War against Japan*, vol. 1 (1957; repr., Dehra Dun: Natraj, 1989), 229–30.

5. Lieutenant Colonel C. C. Deakin and Major G. M. S. Webb, 5th/2nd Punjab Regiment, Ch 2, Part 2, 6509-14, NAM, London, 1.

6. Military Intelligence Service, *Soldier's Guide to the Japanese Army* (Washington, DC: Military Intelligence Service, War Department, 1944), 167.

7. Deakin and Webb, 5th/2nd Punjab Regiment, Ch 2, Part 2, 3; Kirby et al., *War against Japan*, vol. 1, 230; Anne Hoiberg, "Military Staying Power," in *Combat Effectiveness: Cohesion, Stress, and the Volunteer Military*, ed. Sam C. Sarkesian (Beverly Hills: SAGE, 1980), 236–37.

8. Kirby et al., *The War against Japan*, vol. 1, 229.

9. 11th Indian Division, Short Summary of Events, December 7–24, 1941, L/WS/1/952, OIOC, BL, London, 46.

10. Notes by Lieutenant General Percival on certain Senior Commanders and other matters, January 8, 1954, Percival Papers, 1.

11. Andrew M. Weist, "Haig, Gough and Passchendaele," in *Leadership and Command: The Anglo-American Military Experience Since 1861*, ed. G. D. Sheffield (London: Brassey's 1997), 78.

12. Despatch on the Far East by Air Chief Marshal Robert Brooke-Popham, Commander-in-Chief Far East (17 Oct. 1940–27 Dec. 1941), September 8, 1942, CAB/66/28/33, PRO, Kew, London, 43.

13. Brigadier W. Carpendale, CO 28th Indian Infantry Brigade, Report on Operations of 11 Indian Division in Kedah and Perak, L/WS/1/952, OIOC, BL, 23.

14. *9 Gurkha Rifles: A Regimental History (1817–1947)* (New Delhi: Vision Books, 1984), 164.

15. Nigel de Lee, "'A Brigadier is only a Co-ordinator': British Command at Brigade Level in North-West Europe, 1944: A Case Study," in *Leadership and Command*, ed. Sheffield, 130.

16. Bill Yenne, *The Imperial Japanese Army: The Invincible Years 1941–42* (Oxford: Osprey, 2014), 108.

17. *9 Gurkha Rifles*, 164.

18. Brian P. Farrell, *The Defence and Fall of Singapore: 1940–1942* (2005; repr., Stroud, UK: Tempus, 2006), 195.

19. *9 Gurkha Rifles*, 165.

20. 11th Indian Division, Short Summary of Events, December 7–24, 1941, L/WS/1/952, 47.

21. Carpendale, Report on Operations of 11 Indian Division, 23.

22. Kirby et al., *War against Japan*, vol. 1, 230.

23. Deakin and Webb, 5th/2nd Punjab Regiment, Ch 2, Part 2, 5.

24. Ian Morrison, *Malayan Postscript* (London: Faber and Faber, 1942), 81–82.

25. Military Intelligence Service, *Soldier's Guide*, 165–66.

26. Betham and Geary, *Golden Galley*, 227.

27. Deakin and Webb, 5th/2nd Punjab Regiment, Ch 2, Part 2, 4.

28. 11th Indian Division, Short Summary of Events, December 7–24, 1941, L/WS/1/952, 47.

29. Kirby et al., *War against Japan*, vol. 1, 230–31.

30. Lecture on the Malayan Campaign by Heath, June 21, 1942, Percival Papers, 13.

31. Kirby et al., *War against Japan*, vol. 1, 231–32.

32. Gary Sheffield, "The Challenges of High Command in the Twentieth Century," in *The Challenges of High Command: The British Experience*, ed. Gary Sheffield and Geoffrey Till (Hampshire: Palgrave Macmillan, 2003), 10.

33. Martin Samuels, *Command or Control? Command, Training and Tactics in the British and German Armies, 1888–1918* (London: Frank Cass, 1995), 18.

34. G. D. Sheffield, "Introduction: Command, Leadership and the Anglo-American Experience," in *Leadership and Command*, ed. Sheffield, 4.

35. Notes by Percival on certain Senior Commanders, January 8, 1954, Percival Papers, 3.

36. Notes by Percival on certain Senior Commanders, January 8, 1954, Percival Papers, 2.

37. Betham and Geary, *Golden Galley*, 228.

38. Military Intelligence Service, *Soldier's Guide*, 150.
39. Despatch on the Far East by Brooke-Popham, 44.
40. Deakin and Webb, 5th/2nd Punjab Regiment, 1–2.
41. Kirby et.al., *War against Japan*, vol. 1, 230.
42. Military Intelligence Service, *Soldier's Guide*, 153.
43. Kirby et al., *War against Japan*, vol. 1, 232–33.
44. David Omissi, *The Sepoy and the Raj: The Indian Army, 1860–1940* (London: Macmillan, 1994), 86.
45. Michael Howard, "Leadership in the British Army in the Second World War: Some Personal Observations," in *Leadership and Command*, ed. Sheffield, 122–23.
46. K. C. Praval, *Valour Triumphs: A History of the Kumaon Regiment* (Faridabad: Thomson Press, 1976), 104–5.
47. *History of the Southern Army*, Japanese Monograph No. 24, 14.
48. Deakin and Webb, 5th/2nd Punjab Regiment, 2.
49. Betham and Geary, *Golden Galley*, 229.
50. Operations in Malaya and Singapore, E. E. Bridges, Report drawn up by Major H. P. Thomas, July 27, 1942, WP(42)314, CAB/66/26/44, PRO, Kew, 5.
51. Kirby et al., *War against Japan*, vol. 1, 235.
52. Kirby et al., *War against Japan*, vol. 1, 235.
53. Lieutenant Colonel E. L. Wilson Haffenden, History of the 4th/19th Hyderabad Regiment, Operations in Malaya, MISC/707-A/H, MODHS, New Delhi, 2.
54. Major General Prem K. Khanna and Pushpindar Singh Chopra, *Portrait of Courage: Century of the 5th Battalion, The Sikh Regiment* (New Delhi: Military Studies Convention, 2001), 160.
55. A. B. Lodge, *The Fall of General Gordon Bennett* (Sydney: Allen & Unwin, 1986), 75.
56. Robert Lyman, *The Generals: From Defeat to Victory, Leadership in Asia 1941–45* (London: Constable, 2008), 59.
57. Despatch on the Far East by Brooke-Popham, 46.
58. Deakin and Webb, 5th/2nd Punjab Regiment, 3.
59. Betham and Geary, *Golden Galley*, 230.
60. Pike, *Hirohito's War*, 224.
61. Despatch on the Far East by Brooke-Popham, 47.
62. John A. English, *On Infantry* (1981; repr., New York: Praeger, 1984), 68–69.
63. John Keegan, *The Mask of Command* (1987; repr., London: Penguin, 1988), 329.
64. Betham and Geary, *Golden Galley*, 230.
65. Yenne, *Imperial Japanese Army*, 117.
66. Praval, *Valour Triumphs*, 105.
67. Deakin and Webb, 5th/2nd Punjab Regiment, 3.
68. Betham and Geary, *Golden Galley*, 231.
69. Despatch on the Far East by Brooke-Popham, 47.
70. 11th Indian Division, Short Summary of Events, December 7–24, 1941, L/WS/1/952.
71. Notes on British and Indian Units in Malaya, WO 106/2592, PRO, Kew, 48.
72. Yenne, *Imperial Japanese Army*, 117.
73. Winston S. Churchill, *The Second World War*, vol. 3, *The Grand Alliance* (1950; repr., Middlesex: Penguin, 1985), 565.
74. From War Office to Commander-in-Chief India, Commander-in-Chief Far East and Commander-in-Chief Middle East, December 13, 1941, L/WS/1/952 (2), OIOC, BL.

75. Cipher Telegram, From Commander-in-Chief Far East to War Office, Commander-in-Chief India and Chief of General Staff Australia, December 16, 1941, L/WS/1/952 (2).
76. Telegram from Duff Cooper, December 21, 1941, L/WS/1/952 (2).
77. Cipher Telegram, From War Office to the Commander-in-Chief India and Commander-in-Chief Far East, December 18, 1941, L/WS/1/952 (2).
78. Cipher Telegram, From Commander-in-Chief India to GOC Malaya and War Office, December 20, 1941, L/WS/1/952 (2).
79. Cipher Telegram from Australian Government, December 23, 1941, L/WS/1/952 (2).
80. Pike, *Hirohito's War*, 235.
81. Timothy Hall, *The Fall of Singapore* (1983; repr., Oxon: Routledge, 2015), 14.
82. Cipher Telegram from Commander-in-Chief India to the War Office, December 24, 1941, L/WS/1/952 (2).
83. Cipher Telegram from Commander-in-Chief India to GOC Malaya and Commander-in-Chief Far East, December 24, 1941, L/WS/1/952 (2).
84. Cipher Telegram, From War Office to the Commander-in-Chief India, December 24, 1941, L/WS/1/952 (2).
85. Cipher Telegram, From War Office to Commander-in-Chief India, GOC Malaya, December 25, 1941, L/WS/1/952 (2).
86. Cipher Telegram, From Commander-in-Chief India to War Office, Commander-in-Chief Middle East, Commander-in-Chief East Indies, December 25, 1941, L/WS/1/952 (2).
87. Cipher Telegram from Governor S. Thomas to the Secy. of State for Colonies, December 25, 1942, L/WS/1/952 (2).
88. Khanna and Chopra, *Portrait of Courage*, 160.
89. War Diary of 9th Indian Division, Rough Précis of Events in the Kuantan Area, December 27, 1941, Appendix 3, 601/229/WD/Part 5, MODHS, New Delhi.
90. General Archibald Wavell, *Generals and Generalship* (London: Penguin, 1941), 29.
91. Lieutenant General A. E. Percival, *The War in Malaya* (1949; repr., Calcutta: Orient Longmans, 1957), 191–93.
92. *History of the Southern Army*, 14.
93. War Diary of 9th Indian Division, Rough Précis of Events in the Kuantan Area, January 1, 1942, Appendix 3.
94. Military Intelligence Service, *Soldier's Guide*, 150.
95. War Diary of 9th Indian Division, Notes on Conference held at 9th Division Headquarters on January 1, 1942, Appendix 5.
96. War Diary GS Branch, Headquarters 9th Indian Division, January 1, 1942, 601/229/WD/Part 2, MODHS, New Delhi.
97. Farrell, *Defence and Fall*, 201.
98. Percival, *War in Malaya*, 194–95.
99. War Diary GS Branch, Headquarters 9th Indian Division, January 6, 1942.
100. Notes by Lieutenant-General A. E. Percival on the Brief Outline Narrative of the Mainland Operations in Malaya 8 Dec. 1941 to 31 Jan. 1942 prepared by the Combined Inter-Services Historical Section (India), June 1947, Percival Papers, 4.
101. Frank Owen, *The Fall of Singapore* (1960; repr., London: Penguin, 2001), 99.
102. Military Intelligence Service, *Soldier's Guide*, 166–67.
103. Notes on British and Indian Units in Malaya, WO 106/2592.
104. Military Intelligence Division, *Notes on Japanese Warfare on the Malayan Front*, Information Bulletin No. 6 (Washington, DC: War Department, 1942), 2.

105. Pike, *Hirohito's War*, 235.
106. Percival, *War in Malaya*, 200-1.
107. War Diary GS Branch, Headquarters 9th Indian Division, January 3-4, 1942.
108. Betham and Geary, *Golden Galley*, 232; Praval, *Valour Triumphs*, 105.
109. Notes by Percival on the Brief Outline Narrative, 4.
110. Praval, *Valour Triumphs*, 105.
111. Brigadier Jasbir Singh, *Escape from Singapore* (New Delhi: Lancer, 2010), 31-34.
112. Haffenden, History of the 4th/19th Hyderabad Regiment, 3.
113. Morrison, *Malayan Postscript*, 80.
114. Military Intelligence Division, *Notes on Japanese Warfare*, 1.
115. Haffenden, History of the 4th/19th Hyderabad Regiment, 3.
116. Deakin and Webb, 5th/2nd Punjab Regiment, Ch 2, Part 2, 3, 8.
117. Notes on British and Indian Units in Malaya, WO 106/2592.
118. Brigadier Jasbir Singh, *Combat Diary: An Illustrated History of Operations conducted by 4th Battalion the Kumaon Regiment 1788 to 1984* (New Delhi: Lancer, 2010), 108.
119. Yenne, *Imperial Japanese Army*, 119.
120. Singapore Island and Johore, 12-22 Aug. Impressions and Facts, P 23, F 47, Percival Papers; Morrison, *Malayan Postscript*, 80; Lieutenant General Harbakhsh Singh, *In the Line of Duty: A Soldier Remembers* (New Delhi: Lancer, 2000), 161.
121. Deakin and Webb, 5th/2nd Punjab Regiment, Ch 2, Part 2, 9-10; Notes by Percival on the Brief Outline Narrative, 4; Betham and Geary, *Golden Galley*, 237.
122. Praval, *Valour Triumphs*, 105-6.
123. Haffenden, History of the 4th/19th Hyderabad Regiment, 4.
124. *History of the Southern Army*, 14.
125. Deakin and Webb, 5th/2nd Punjab Regiment, 4; Betham and Geary, *Golden Galley*, 238.
126. Agnes McEwan and Campbell Thomson, *Death Was Our Bedmate: 155th (Lanarkshire Yeomanry) Field Regiment and the Japanese 1941-1945* (Barnsley: Pen & Sword, 2013), 29.
127. Percival, *War in Malaya*, 196.
128. McEwan and Thomson, *Death Was Our Bedmate*, 30.
129. Lyman, *The Generals*, 43.
130. Pike, *Hirohito's War*, 235.
131. Praval, *Valour Triumphs*, 106.
132. Alan Stephens, "Effects Based Operations and the Fighting Power of a Defence Force," in *On New Wars*, ed. John Andreas Olsen (Oslo: Norwegian Institute for Defence Studies, 2007), 131-49.
133. Percival, *War in Malaya*, 193.
134. The Malayan Campaign, Answers to Admiralty Questions, Percival Papers.
135. Letter from Allen to Percival, February 13, 1950, Percival Papers.
136. Deakin and Webb, 5th/2nd Punjab Regiment, Ch 2, Part 2, 11-12.
137. McEwan and Thomson, *Death Was Our Bedmate*, 30-32; Joanna Bourke, *An Intimate History of Killing: Face-to-Face Killing in Twentieth-Century Warfare* (1999; repr., London: Granta Books, 2000), 39.
138. The Malayan Campaign, Answers to Admiralty Questions, Percival Papers.
139. Percival, *War in Malaya*, 195.
140. Singh, *Combat Diary*, 110.
141. Lodge, *Fall of General Gordon Bennett*, 77.

142. Deakin and Webb, 5th/2nd Punjab Regiment, Ch 2, Part 2, 13.
143. Military Intelligence Division, *Notes on Japanese Warfare*, 1.
144. English, *On Infantry*, 25, 48, 62.
145. The Malayan Campaign, Answers to Admiralty Questions, Percival Papers.
146. Owen, *Fall of Singapore*, 99.
147. Farrell, *Defence and Fall*, 195.
148. Percival, *War in Malaya*, 198–200, 202.
149. T. R. Sareen, ed., *Select Documents on Indian National Army* (Delhi: Agam Prakashan, 1988), 4–6, 13, 19; Mohan Singh, *Soldiers' Contribution to Indian Independence* (New Delhi: Army Educational Stores, 1974), 81.
150. Deakin and Webb, 5th/2nd Punjab Regiment, Ch 2, Part 2, 13.
151. Military Intelligence Division, *Notes on Japanese Warfare*, 1.
152. English, *On Infantry*, 159.
153. The Malayan Campaign, Answers to Admiralty Questions, Percival Papers.
154. Deakin and Webb, 5th/2nd Punjab Regiment, 4.
155. Haffenden, History of the 4th/19th Hyderabad Regiment, 4.
156. McEwan and Thomson, *Death Was Our Bedmate*, 33.
157. Farrell, *Defence and Fall*, 213.
158. Praval, *Valour Triumphs*, 106.
159. Percival, *War in Malaya*, 204–05; Pike, *Hirohito's War*, 236; Alan Jeffreys, "The Indian Army in the Malayan Campaign, 1941–1942," in *The British Indian Army: Virtue and Necessity*, ed. Rob Johnson (Newcastle: Cambridge Scholars Publishing, 2014), 191; McEwan and Thomson, *Death Was Our Bedmate*, 33.
160. Comments by Col. Harrison on Operations of Malaya Command, Percival Papers, 2.
161. Praval, *Valour Triumphs*, 107.
162. Praval, *Valour Triumphs*, 106.
163. Singh, *Combat Diary*, 110–11.
164. A. M. L. Harrison, September 29, Percival Papers.
165. Deakin and Webb, 5th/2nd Punjab Regiment, 4; Haffenden, History of the 4th/19th Hyderabad Regiment, 4; Singh, *Combat Diary*, 112.
166. Deakin and Webb, 5th/2nd Punjab Regiment, Battle at Trolak, 1; Haffenden, History of the 4th/19th Hyderabad Regiment, 4.
167. Singh, *Combat Diary*, 112.
168. Military Intelligence Service, *Soldier's Guide*, 151.
169. Owen, *Fall of Singapore*, 101.
170. Lyman, *The Generals*, 29.
171. Military Intelligence Service, *Soldier's Guide*, 148.
172. Military Intelligence Service, *Japanese Tanks and Tank Tactics* (Washington, DC: Military Intelligence Service, War Department, 1944), 11.
173. Pike, *Hirohito's War*, 236.
174. T. R. Moreman, *The Jungle, the Japanese and the British Commonwealth Armies at War, 1941–45: Fighting Methods, Doctrine and Training for Jungle Warfare* (London: Frank Cass, 2005), 16.
175. Owen, *Fall of Singapore*, 101.
176. English, *On Infantry*, 38.
177. Owen, *Fall of Singapore*, 102–3.
178. Singapore Island and Johore, 12–22 Aug. Impressions and Facts, P 23, F 47, Percival Papers, 6.
179. Morrison, *Malayan Postscript*, 80.

180. Lyman, *The Generals*, 41.
181. Singh, *Combat Diary*, 112–13.
182. Military Intelligence Service, *Soldier's Guide*, 148.
183. Singh, *Combat Diary*, 111.
184. McEwan and Thomson, *Death Was Our Bedmate*, 33.
185. Deakin and Webb, 5th/2nd Punjab Regiment, Battle at Trolak, 1; Haffenden, History of the 4th/19th Hyderabad Regiment, 4.
186. Singapore Island and Johore, 12–22 Aug. Impressions and Facts, P 23, F 47, Percival Papers, 7.
187. Yenne, *Imperial Japanese Army*, 33.
188. Interview with General Percival, November 23, 1942, no. 20, Percival Papers.
189. Haffenden, History of the 4th/19th Hyderabad Regiment, 5.
190. Singh, *Combat Diary*, 115–16.
191. Betham and Geary, *Golden Galley*, 245.
192. Deakin and Webb, 5th/2nd Punjab Regiment, Chapter 2, Part 2, 5, 15.
193. Despatch on the Far East by Brooke-Popham, 53.
194. Haffenden, History of the 4th/19th Hyderabad Regiment, 4.
195. Owen, *Fall of Singapore*, 104.
196. Singh, *Combat Diary*, 116.
197. Military Intelligence Service, *Japanese Tanks and Tank Tactics*, 16.
198. Praval, *Valour Triumphs*, 108.
199. History of the 4th/19th Hyderabad Regiment after the Slim Battle up to Capitulation, MISC/707/H, MODHS, New Delhi, 1; Singh, *Combat Diary*, 116.
200. Owen, *Fall of Singapore*, 105.
201. Praval, *Valour Triumphs*, 108.
202. Operations in Malaya and Singapore, Bridges, 6.

5 | Disaster at Muar and Johore

This chapter discusses the final stages of withdrawal of the Allied forces from the Malayan Peninsula. At this stage of the battle, the Australian troops under Gordon Bennett made their entry on a large scale. The first section of the chapter portrays the overall strategic context, and the second section analyzes the temporary success achieved by the Australians at Gemas. In the third section, the disaster at Muar is charted, and the last section covers the final withdrawal across the Straits of Johore. We focus both at the top to show what the generals were thinking and also at the bottom to portray how the battalions were coping with the reality of Japanese advance due to the limitations of their combat techniques. The interface between operations and tactics is emphasized. An attempt is made to see whether or not the Allied ground units were displaying a learning curve at all.

The Strategic Background

Percival worked long hours, as many as eighteen hours a day. He rose early, received reports from the front, attended to War Council meetings, and traveled to meet with frontline commanders. He had two problematic subordinates: the tired and defeated Heath and the edgy Bennett.[1] The problem with Percival was that he was not a ruthless leader with iron nerves. He failed to bring his subordinates to his line of thinking. Further, Percival was a gentleman but not a leader who was capable of putting steely resolve in the hearts of his soldiers. He lacked the charisma to motivate the soldiers and uplift their morale. What was required was a ruthless commander with an iron will. Instead, Percival would offer advice and then view events from the sidelines. Even when his subordinates refused to obey his orders, he would neither chastise them nor replace or demote them. Percival's umpire-like command was unsuitable against the ruthless Japanese practicing fast-moving warfare. In the ultimate analysis, he was a good staff officer but not a born leader of men.

On 5 January 1942, Percival held a conference at Segamat. It was attended by Heath, Bennett, Brigadier W. O. Lay (CO 45th Indian Brigade), and Lieutenant Colonel Graham. By this time, Percival was aware that the Slim River position might collapse. He emphasized that the Japanese must be kept away from the Kuala Lumpur and Port Swettenham aerodromes for as long as possible. Heath pointed out that the Japanese had fought well in rubber plantations. So the next defensive line must be selected in a terrain which would not suit the enemy's tactics. Heath was in favor of selecting a defensive position on open ground with good visibility. He favored holding the area around Batu Anam. From Batu Anam, a lateral road ran to Muar. Heath and Percival were yet undecided whether the final defensive position should be forward of this road or whether the left flank of the defensive position should be behind the Muar River. However, Heath also discussed the possibility of III Indian Corps retreating into southern Malacca. In the conference, it was decided to strengthen the III Indian Corps with the 45th Indian Brigade.[2]

In light of the Slim River defeat, Percival reassessed his strategy. On 7 January 1942, Percival summed up the strategic scenario. He accepted that the Japanese had naval superiority and they would retain it till the end of January. It is not clear why Percival thought that the Japanese might lose aerial and naval superiority after the end of January or the British and the Americans might regain their naval supremacy in the Asia-Pacific region by the beginning of February 1942. Britain, at least, after the destruction of Force Z was not in a position to send any aircraft carriers and capital ships into the Indian Ocean in the near future. After the destruction wrought by the Japanese on the American battleships at Pearl Harbor, the US Navy was on the defensive in the Pacific Ocean. Percival accepted that the Japanese air force had gained supremacy over northern and central Malaya. Actually the Japanese air force also reigned supreme over southern Malaya. However, Percival was hopeful of getting aircraft from home, and he believed that the RAF would regain air superiority by the end of January 1942. He argued that ground reinforcements would arrive by the middle of February and then a counterstrike was to be launched to regain the Malayan Peninsula. Until that time, the ground forces should contain the IJA by launching local offensives. It is to be noted that from the beginning of the campaign until 6 January, neither Percival nor his subordinate commanders had been able to launch a successful local counterattack against the IJA. They had just retreated in front of Japanese pressure. Percival rightly reasoned that the strike force could only be built up if the convoy bringing the reinforcements were able to reach Singapore safely. The convoy was supposed to reach Singapore between 13 and 15 January. Hence, the Japanese must be denied the use of airports at Kuala Lumpur and Port Swettenham for as long as possible. Once the Japanese acquired these aerodromes, their fighters could cover the bomber attacks on Singapore, and this in turn would make the passage of the troop convoys reaching the island dangerous. Percival warned that if the Japanese were able to capture the aerodromes at Kahang-Kluang and Batu Pahat, then the scale of attack on Singapore and its sea approaches would go up.[3]

Not only the Japanese air force, but also the Japanese ground forces posed a dire problem for Percival. Percival accepted that the Japanese had shown tactical skill in using the tracks and the waterways. He noted that on the east coast of Malaya, a Japanese ground threat might develop along the tracks and waterways that ran inland. He feared that the Japanese might conduct an air-sea attack against Kuantan, the east coast of Johore, or even Singapore Island. On the west coast, there were several roads in southern Selangor, Negri Sembilan, and Malacca, and here the Japanese, noted Percival, might threaten the Allied troops' LoC. The road network in the states of Selangor, Negri Sembilan, and Malacca could be exploited by the Japanese armored columns. Both Heath and Percival were overconscious of the threat posed by the Japanese troops to the LoC of the Allied troops. Interestingly, Percival and Heath accepted that the IJA could pose a threat along the swamps and creeks, and also on the plain terrain with roads. Percival was also worried about probable Japanese landings (thanks to their aerial and naval superiority) on the east coast of Johore and even on Singapore Island. However, he rightly considered the threat along the west coast as more dangerous than the threat along the east coast of Malaya. His strategy was to establish a ring of aerodromes on Singapore Island and to contain the Japanese north of Johore with his ground force until the middle of February. Then, he planned to launch the counteroffensive. He wanted the fresh 18th British Division, which was coming as reinforcement to relieve the 8th AIF, to be used as the counterstrike force. With this objective in view, he forbade any withdrawal south of Mersing-Batu Anam (northwest of Segamat-Muar). He calculated that the III Indian Corps would fall back on northern Johore by 24 January. He was worried that if the III Indian Corps failed to hold the Japanese north of Johore until mid-February 1942, a critical situation would develop.[4]

With the above scenario in mind, Percival reshuffled his assets. One Australian brigade group was left for the defense of the east coast of Johore, and the other was made available for the offensive operation in the Segamat area. One battalion from the 12th Indian Brigade of the III Indian Corps was to take the place of the Australian battalions on Kluang-Kahang Road. The Gordons were to garrison southern Johore. And the Malay Regiment, which he considered of doubtful fighting value, was kept at Singapore Island. He rightly believed that Gordon Bennett would not agree to work under Heath. So, overall, Gordon Bennett was to be in command of eastern Johore, and Lewis Heath was to command western Johore.[5] The situation was further muddied for Percival due to Wavell's intervention.

The date 30 December 1941 is an important one in the history of the Far Eastern War. On that day, the one-eyed (he had lost an eye in 1915) General "Archie" Wavell was asked by Churchill, at the prodding of the Americans to take over the combined American, British, Dutch, and Australian Command (ABDACOM) in the southwest Pacific. This included Malaya, the Netherlands East Indies, and the Philippines. On 4 January 1942, he received the official missive from the Combined Chiefs of Staff in Washington.[6] Wavell was previously relieved of his command in North Africa and then appointed as commander in chief, India, before being appointed as commander in chief of ABDACOM.[7] Wavell, like Percival, lacked the showmanship of Lord Mountbatten and Bernard Montgomery, the cheering and cheerful attitude of Brian Horrocks, or the down-to-earth humanity of "Bill" Slim.[8] But Wavell was an educated general and possessed a sense of history.

On 2 January 1942, Archibald Wavell informed the Chiefs of Staff in London that due to Japanese naval and aerial attacks, and especially taking into account the availability of limited military assets on the part of the Allied powers, the line of Port Darwin-Timor-Southern Sumatra-Singapore could be effectively held. Wavell accepted that northern Sumatra along with Penang was lost to the Japanese.[9]

Wavell left Delhi in the early morning of 5 January to take over his new command. After spending the night in Madras, on 6 January he flew to Colombo and then to Singapore. Wavell arrived at Singapore by air on 7 December. Wavell met Percival and was not impressed, and then he met Duff Cooper. One suspects Cooper's negative views about Percival further strengthened Wavell's negative assessment of Percival. On 8 January, Wavell toured the Malayan front. At that time, the Japanese forward troops were thirty-five miles north of Kuala Lumpur. He did not have to wait long for bad news. He saw some brigade commanders (Stewart and Selby, who were battle shocked) and heard about the Slim River disaster. Neither Heath, the corps commander, nor Paris, the 11th Indian Division's commander, impressed Wavell. Wavell reasoned that the country south of Kuala Lumpur was not suited for delaying actions. He ordered Heath to cover Kuala Lumpur for as long as possible and to delay the Japanese advance by undertaking extensive demolitions. Heath was informed that the III Indian Corps should be withdrawn to Johore for rest and refit. Wavell's general policy more or less was similar to that of Percival. The Japanese should be delayed in Johore till the end of January, and this would enable the arrival of the 18th British Division and the Australian Corps from the Middle East. Then, these new military assets should be used to launch a counterstrike, and the Indian soldiers should be withdrawn to Netherlands East Indies.[10] Actually, the 18th British Division would arrive and fight mainly (rather badly) in Singapore, and the Australian Corps from the Middle East would be diverted to other theaters. In his missive to the Chiefs of Staff dated 8 January 1942, Wavell noted that retreat demoralized the Indian troops.[11] There was no evidence that the jawans became more demoralized due to retreat than the Aussies or the Tommies. Wavell had met with some of the personnel from the 11th Indian Division, and the interactions had strengthened his conviction that the Indians were at the end of their endurance.[12] This was because the Indians had been fighting from the beginning of the Malayan Campaign while the Australians were just about to enter the fray. Unlike Percival, Wavell considered all the Indian soldiers to be second grade and hence not suitable for launching a counterattack against the Japanese in Malaya. At this stage of the campaign, Percival had faith in the Garwahlis and the Dogras but not in the Jats or even British-India's favorite "martial" class, the Sikhs.[13]

Historian Robert Lyman and Percival's biographer Clifford Kinvig assert rightly that Wavell had a jaundiced view of the Japanese and also Percival. Wavell was ignorant of the Asians in general and scorned Japanese military effectiveness. This charge is partly true, for Wavell, as we have seen earlier, had dismissed the Indian soldiers as "soft." Wavell's negative view of Percival partly stemmed from the vicious memo written by Duff Cooper for Churchill. Cooper had erroneously described Percival as a nice, good man who started his life as a schoolteacher and should have remained one.[14] Interestingly, Churchill also viewed Wavell as the manager of a golf club.

Wavell asserted himself vis-à-vis the unassuming, soft-spoken Percival. He did not even consult Percival while preparing the new disposition of troops. During the evening of 8 January, Percival was called by Wavell and made to wait for a long time and then handed over the detailed order for disposition of the troops. The III Indian Corps after delaying the Japanese north of Kuala Lumpur until 11 January was to be withdrawn to Johore by rail and road, leaving sufficient rearguards to cover the demolition scheme. This corps was to take responsibility of the east and west coasts of Johore south of the road Mersing-Kluang-Batu Pahat, leaving Gordon Bennett the responsibility to fight the decisive battle in northwest Johore. So Wavell set up a layered command. While Bennett took up the charge of the frontline troops, Heath was responsible for the rear. Wavell was impressed with Bennett. This was despite the fact that Bennett had no experience of either fighting with the Japanese or commanding Indian troops, who comprised the bulk of the Allied ground forces in Malaya. Wavell was taken in by Bennett's braggadocio. For some strange reason, Wavell assumed that the Australians had trained in appropriate tactics in tune with the Malayan terrain. The 8th AIF less one brigade group in the Mersing area on the east coast was to move to the northwestern frontier of Johore and prepare to fight a decisive battle on the Segamat-Mount Ophir mouth of the Muar River. The 9th Indian Division (comprising the fresh troops of III Indian Corps) and the 45th Indian Brigade (which had arrived in Malaya from India) were to be placed under Gordon Bennett. The 8th AIF was to send mobile detachments to relieve the rearguards of the III Indian Corps.[15]

Like the American Marine Corps, the AIF was comprised of volunteers. The AIF was made up of strongly motivated young men. Moreover, since the AIF battalions recruited locally, the units were able to take advantage of territorial loyalty. Like the American Marines, the AIF personnel served with men from the same town or area. Often friends enlisted together. Again, soldiers who became friends in the service often met each other's families while on leave. This deep cohesion resulted in the generation of "mateship," which in turn strengthened the primary solidarity in the units. The point to be noted is that the Japanese battalions were also locally recruited.[16] The morale of the 8th AIF was indeed high. The men believed that they could lick the "Nips." However, the 8th AIF, as we have seen earlier, was not trained for jungle warfare. Whether they would be able to halt the aggressive and well-trained Japanese infantry remained to be seen. The 9th Indian Division under Gordon Bennett took up position in the Segamat area while the 45th Indian Brigade became responsible for the Muar area.[17] Interestingly, Wavell, was not practicing a "hand's off" command but was interfering aggressively as regards troop deployment, which traditionally lay in the sphere of regional field commander, in this case Percival.

Wavell was aware that his plan allowed the Japanese almost unopposed advance from Kuala Lumpur to the northern boundary of Johore through the provinces of Negri Sembilan and Malacca. But considering the state of III Indian Corps, he realized that in the region south of Kuala Lumpur studded with good roads, it could not fight Japanese armor supported by the infantry. A curious logic indeed! The Allied troops were unable to meet the Japanese either in the swampy jungle terrain or in the plain terrain studded with roads. It is questionable what sort of terrain did suit the Allied troops at this juncture. Percival was rightly forced by Wavell to redeploy troops from southern Singapore, which the latter felt was not threatened at this stage. In fact, Wavell had written about the essential qualities of a good general: "He must have the spirit of adventure, a touch of gambler in him." Percival surely lacked these two qualities. Wavell was for fighting a defensive battle at the Segamat-Muar line. He reasoned that it was the best possible defensible region because the right flank, he wrongly believed, was protected by impenetrable jungle, and the sea was on the left flank.[18] The Japanese would penetrate the "impenetrable" jungle and, using country boats, would land behind the defensive line along the west coast. Heath and Percival should have warned Wavell that no terrain was impassable for the light Japanese infantry. Henry Pownwall became Wavell's chief of staff. Wavell was a busy man. He left for Java on 11 January 1942, and his ABDACOM headquarters came into existence on 15 January, which lasted for forty-two days.[19]

By the beginning of January 1942, the Japanese had gained mastery in the air over the Kuantan area and established dominance over the SLoC along the west coast. This posed a threat to the LoC of the Allied troops. As a result, the 11th Indian Division retreated from Kuala Lumpur to the Johore Sector under cover of rearguards, destroying the roads and bridges along the way. Simultaneously, the 9th Indian Division had to retreat in concert. Following closely, the Japanese forces came in contact with the Allied forces at Gemas.[20]

Gemas

As early as 19 December 1941, Bennett sent Brigadier Maxwell and Colonel J. H. Thyer to reconnoiter a defensive position near Gemas. On 23 December, Bennett held a conference with his brigade and battalion commanders and emphasized that they must not withdraw from western Johore but should attack if pressed by the Japanese. Just before Christmas, Bennett made the 27th AIF Brigade responsible for the defense of north Johore. One battalion was placed in the Gemas-Segamat area, another battalion in Muar, and another battalion as reserve in the Kluang-Ayer Hitam region.[21] After Wavell's reshuffling, Gordon Bennett's WESTFORCE had the responsibility from the mouth of the Muar River to Gemas.[22] The WESTFORCE included the 27th AIF Brigade, two weak Indian brigades (8th and 22nd) of the 9th Indian Division, and the newly arrived raw 45th Indian Brigade. Its mandate was to hold the Gemas-Muar Line.[23] The Australians taunted the battle-weary British and Indian troops for their failure against the Japanese. They just had no idea what the British and Indian soldiers had been up against from the beginning of December 1941.[24]

On 3 January 1942, the 9th Indian Division was ordered to hold the line of Triang-Jerantut-Benta-Raub-Tranum. The 8th Indian Brigade was to hold right of the line, and the 22nd Indian Brigade was to be positioned on the left. On 5 January, a detailed plan with the objective of withdrawing to Johore while inflicting maximum casualties and delay to the Japanese was drawn up. It involved the retreat of the 9th Indian Division in synchronization with the 11th Indian Division in the face of the Japanese threat. Both the 9th and 11th divisions had to synchronize their moves for withdrawal to prevent exposing the flanks to the advancing Japanese. It was planned that by 8 January, the 9th Indian Division was to be concentrated along Triang-Chenor-Temerloh-Mentakab-Jerantut-Lipis-Benta-Raub-Frasers Hill. It was assumed that the 11th Indian Division would be able to hold the crossroads north of Kuala Kubu. While the 8th Indian Brigade was to withdraw in the southern direction, the 22nd Indian Brigade was to move in the westward direction. The withdrawal of the 9th Indian Division from Kuantan to Raub-Tranum-Bentong was to start on the morning of 9 January. The 8th Indian Brigade was ordered to hold the Triang-Temerloh-Jerantut area and cover the retreat of the 22nd Indian Brigade on the west bank of Pahang River. While the 8th Indian Brigade was to destroy the Jerantut Ferry, the 22nd Indian Brigade was to carry out demolitions along the Kuantan Road. In the course of its withdrawal, the 9th Indian Division was ordered to carry out extensive demolitions on the Jerantut Road and to blow up the suspension bridge on Budu Estate and also the Benta Bridge.[25]

In accordance with the plan, on 14 January, the 9th Indian Division was to be along the line of Triang-Temerloh-Chenor-Mentakab-Tranum-Bentong. And the 11th Indian Division was to cover Rasa-Serendah. By 21 January, the 9th Indian Division was to be along Bahau-Simpang-Pertang-K. Pillah, and the rear boundary were to be along Gemas. The 11th Indian Division was to cover Seramban-Port Dickson along Setul Serang Road and Sepang Chuah. By 24 January, the rear boundary of the 9th Indian Division was to be Batu-Anam and Jementan, and the 11th Indian Division was to be along Tampin-Lubok China, and its rear boundary would be along the east border of Malacca. The 9th Indian Division was warned that it might have to make a defensive stand at Gemas. The 9th Indian Division was to retreat to Gemas through Kuala Pillah and Tampin. Further, it might also have to protect its southern flank around Segamat-Tangak-Bandar-Maharani if the 11th Indian Division failed to protect the 9th Indian Division's left flank. The 9th Indian Division was warned that during retreat, its transport assets along the roads might be bombed heavily by Japanese aircraft.[26]

On 8 January, it was decided that the 22nd Indian Brigade was to withdraw from Bentong-Karak to Simpang Pertang during the night of 11/12 January. Kuala Pillah was to be held by this brigade till Tampin was cleared by the 11th Indian Division. And on the night of 11/12 January, the 8th Indian Brigade should leave by rail and road for Batu Anam. During the night of 8/9 January, the 8th Indian Brigade withdrew from Jerantut via road and rail to Raub. And the 22nd Indian Brigade covered Benta.[27] Actually, the retreat occurred earlier than planned.

On 10 January 1942, the 2nd/10th Baluch arrived at Batu Anam railway station. Brigadier Key was promoted to the post of Major General and given command of the 11th Indian Division. Heath pushed for the promotion of Key, and both he and Percival hoped that Key, being an Indian Army officer, would be able to command the jawans better than Paris. And Lieutenant Colonel Frith became the temporary commander of the 8th Indian Brigade (2nd/10th Baluch, 1st/13th FFR, and 3rd/17th Dogra). The 1st/13th FFR and the 2nd/10th Baluch under the personal supervision of Barstow took up extended positions that comprised isolated bare hills held by one company each. The hills were surrounded with thick rubber plantations that provided the ideal route of approach for the nimble Japanese infantry. Again Barstow failed to deploy troops inside the thick rubber plantations. Further, the bare hills occupied by the Indian troops were without water supply and posed an easy target for the Japanese aircraft.[28] It goes without saying that Barstow's positioning of the troops was faulty.

On 11 January, Brigadier Lay of the 6th Indian Brigade took command of the 8th Indian Brigade. He somewhat rectified the exposed defensive positions of the troops. Meanwhile, the 2nd/29th Australians were placed in the rubber plantation north of the road Gemas-Batu Anam and the 2nd/26th was in the rubber plantation south of this road. The 2nd/30th Australians were in ambush position six miles west of Gemas. The 1st/30th FFR was on the western edge of the rubber estate along the road and the railway west of Batu Anam. The 2nd/10th Baluch were defending Batu Anam. The artillery (two twenty-five-pounder batteries and one 4.5-inch howitzer battery) was in Batu Anam. Further, two A/T batteries were dispersed along the road and the railway. The 3rd/17th Dogras guarded the bridge northwest of Buloh Kasap. And the 8th Indian Brigade Headquarters was at Bulow Kasap. The units maintained contact with each other through runners. It was an improvement compared to the past practice. The region was full of rubber estates, and visibility was limited to four hundred yards. The defending units expected the Japanese to infiltrate from Gemas to Buloh Kasap. The day was spent in preparing the defensive position. The 1st/13th FFR laid A/T minefields on the approaches to Gemas, and the 2nd/10th Baluch placed mines on the Tumang Bridge and on the road junction at the Jementeh Road.[29]

There were five million inhabitants in Malaya, and less than half of them were Malays. The rest were Chinese and Indian immigrants.[30] As the Japanese were advancing through the Malayan countryside, the local forces under the British started dissolving. Desertion in the Malay Regiment reached alarming proportions. The 4th Pahang Battalion was disarmed on 12 January 1942.[31] In October 1941, Captain Stephen Hannam of the 2nd/26th Battalion of the 27th AIF Brigade along with two other Australian officers had been seconded to Johore Military Force under Lieutenant Colonel Musa. A British Lieutenant Colonel named Morrison was in charge of training this unit. As the Japanese raced through Johore, the Sultan of Johore wanted this unit to be disarmed and demobilized. Hannam writes: "The Sultan said that while willing for his men to fight on the island he considered it unfair to the families to be separated from their menfolk."[32]

The 5th Japanese Division occupied Kuala Lumpur on 11 January.[33] The next day, the 11th Indian Division withdrew from Seramban. The 28th Indian Brigade was ordered to hold Tampin till the night of 14/15 January. The 22nd Indian Brigade's job was to cover the right flank of the retreating 11th Indian Division. The 22nd and the 28th Indian brigades were ordered to maintain close contact with each other. The 22nd Indian Brigade was ordered to withdraw from Simpang Pertang to Jementah and carry out extensive demolitions along the Simpang Pertang-Gemas Road.[34] Wavell returned to Malaya on 13 January. He motored to Segamat to meet Heath and Gordon Bennett. Wavell knew Heath from Keren in East Africa, where the latter commanded the 5th Indian Division. Bad news was waiting for him. The 9th and 11th Indian divisions had suffered huge losses in the fighting around Kuala Lumpur, and the Japanese advance was far more rapid than he had hoped for. Wavell doubted whether Percival's force would be able to hold the Japanese along northern Johore. An anxious Wavell cabled to the Chiefs of Staff that the Battle for Singapore would be "a close run thing."[35] However, the Japanese were in for a temporary shock due to the trap set for them by Gordon Bennett at Gemas.

On the morning of 14 January 1942, the Japanese advanced into the ambush prepared by the Australians west of Gemas town. The Gemenchen (Jementan) River cut through the main road, and beyond the bridge was a corridor through the jungle. After crossing the Gemencheh Bridge, Colonel Mukaide's infantry, riding on bicycles and advancing in front of the 1st Tank Regiment, were ambushed and killed in large numbers by machine-gun fire. They suffered between eight hundred and a thousand casualties and lost four tanks.[36] At Gemas, the Allied troops were lucky. They held a well-defended position, and the overconfident Japanese walked into the trap because of poor reconnaissance. Here, the Japanese did not try to outflank and outmaneuver the Allied defensive position. The result was a limited Allied victory. However, such local success had no effect on the overall campaign. The Gemas ambush, despite being a local tactical success, displayed two weaknesses. First, Bennett had placed only one Australian company to implement the ambush, and second, this company failed to bring down artillery fire on the Japanese due to the breakdown of communication.[37] This was a case of serious failure as regards cooperation and coordination of various arms. The American, Australian, and British doctrine put much faith in artillery firepower to support the infantry in static defensive positions against hostile attacks.[38] Inadequate infantry-artillery cooperation at Gemas among the Australians was a case of command failure.

At Gemas, the Allied units had dug in, and their defensive positions were covered with wire. The Gemas position was strong frontally but could be turned in the flanks. The Japanese now were once bitten, twice shy. On 15 January, the 27th AIF Brigade outposts were engaged by Japanese advance parties. Later, a Japanese brigade with tanks launched a full-scale attack. During the night, the most forward battalion of this brigade (2nd/30th) withdrew to a line one mile east of Gemas.[39] On 16 January, Yamashita sadly noted in his diary that the Japanese troops at Gemas were careless in their tactics and concentrated on frontal attacks on the Allied forces, which unnecessarily resulted in great casualties.[40] The next day, the Japanese infantry advanced east from Gemas and shelled the Allied positions. Meanwhile, news came that the Japanese had overturned the Muar position, and the Allied troops on the west coast were retreating. On 18 January, the Japanese, by making a frontal attack, pinned down the 1st/13th FFR and worked behind them. It became a standard tactic of the Japanese infantry. Further, the deteriorating situation on the west coast made retreat along the east coast necessary to maintain a continuous front line. By midnight the Australians evacuated their position, leaving the 1st/13th FFR exposed to Japanese assault. It was a standard habit of the Australians to retreat without informing the neighboring

Indian formations. Besides breakdown of communications, racial prejudice was also probably a causative factor behind this sort of behavior. On 19 January, the 2nd/10th Baluch retreated to Buloh Kasap. The 1st/13th FFR less one company was able to make a fighting withdrawal to Buloh Kasap.[41] Thus, the right flank of Bennett's defensive line had collapsed. What happened to the left flank of his much-vaunted defensive line is the focus of the next section.

Retreat from the Muar River

> Our enemies moved too quickly on a simple effective plan and never gave us time to collect the forces necessary to remedy our initial weakness and make headway against them.
>
> General Archibald Wavell[42]

On Friday, 9 January 1942, Ugaki noted that the Allies probably had 134 aircraft at Malaya. He realized that the Allies might further reinforce their air force in Malaya. However, he was confident that the JAAF and the JNAF would be able to destroy the Allied air force.[43] On the same day, the Japanese threatened Kuala Selangor. There was some fighting at the Berjuntai Bridge, and the Japanese were at the north of the river. The Allied troops held the south bank of Kuala Selangor, and the 6th/15th Brigade comprised the rearguard on the road.[44] A. B. Lodge and Carl Bridge assert that both Percival and Bennett underrated the threat posed by the Japanese at Muar.[45] However, Barstow, CO of the 9th Indian Division, was aware of the importance of the Muar front. In fact, Percival himself emphasized that the Muar River Bridge should be defended. Let us see the disposition of the Allied troops at Muar in some detail.

On 13 January, the 22nd Indian Brigade (5th/11th Sikhs, 2nd/12th FFR, and 2nd/18th Garwahl Rifles) was ordered to hold the left section of the 9th Indian Division's front, known as the Muar Sector. The 2nd Loyal Regiment garrisoned Segamat.[46] On 14 January 1942, the 7th/6th Rajputana Rifles (RR) Battalion, along with the 4th/9th Jats and 5th/18th Garwahl Rifles of the 45th Indian Brigade under Brigadier H. C. Duncan, spread along twenty-three miles, were defending the Muar River in Johore State on the west coast of Malaya. The battalions of the 45th Indian Brigade had undergone some training together in Kumbergaon Camp near Poona (Pune). After arrival at Singapore on 3 January 1942, Duncan wanted further training for his semitrained troops. But this opportunity was not given to this brigade, which was rushed to the Muar area. They were soon attacked by the Japanese Imperial Guards Division.[47] By conducting amphibious landings, Colonel Msakazu Ogaki outflanked the Muar defense line.[48] Simultaneously, the Japanese also applied frontal pressure through steady infiltration among the defending Indian units. The shallow, linear, static defensive positions held by unsure troops were easy prey to the infiltrating Japanese. Faced with simultaneous frontal and flanking threats, the Australian, British, and Indian troops retreated as Yamashita hoped. It was again an example of EBO implemented by Yamashita.

The 7th/6th RR Battalion was a partially trained unit. Moreover, what little training this unit had received was suited for combat in the open plain country of the Middle East. The 7th/6th RR had about 170 soldiers (including VCOs) with about twelve to eighteen months of service. And the rest of the six hundred men had service experience between seven and twelve months. Initially, this battalion was destined to travel from Poona to the Middle East in order to complete their training and procure the rest of the equipment, like carriers, there in the next six months. However, they suddenly found themselves in the steaming jungle of Malaya.[49]

Major S. A. Watt of the 7th/6th RR writes: "Now we found ourselves preparing to defend an area 14 miles wide and 5 or 6 miles deep in country where average visibility was 30 yards. The terrain included rubber estates, mangrove swamp, thick scrub and jungle, and between our forward companies and two rear ones was a tidal river 400 yards wide with no bridge across it."[50] Not only did the 7th/6th RR Battalion's position lack depth, but the scattered defensive positions were not even deep and linked together. Any attempt to dig holes more than two feet in depth as in the Jitra position resulted in them filling with water due to the low-lying nature of the terrain. The unit found that whatever little training was imparted to it for warfare in the open desert plains was completely irrelevant in the close jungle country with reduced visibility. Not only was the unit widely dispersed in the jungle, but they had to operate the only ferry across the Muar River themselves, as the Malays had fled due to the Japanese bombing. Further, communication among the battalion was difficult due to shortage of telephone wires. There was only adequate wire available for laying the connection to the nearest company. The battalion had trucks, but they were useless in the jungle for communication purposes. And even on the roads, these trucks were sitting targets for Japanese aircraft as they were painted in bright Western Desert colors. For proper camouflage, the trucks should have been painted in accordance with the color of the Malayan landscape—that is, dark green.[51]

The British officers were making the same mistake in attempting to hold the Muar position as they had made at the beginning of the Malayan Campaign, while attempting to contain the Japanese along the beaches. They were attempting to construct a thin crust of linear defense with infantry battalions that were broken by the Japanese at the position they chose to concentrate their strength. And the rest of the widely dispersed small static positions were bypassed, surrounded, and attacked from the rear. This resulted in not only the defensive line being broken at the first contact with the enemy, but also a large number of troops remaining behind the advancing enemy formations without waging any sort of sustained combat. These troops became demoralized stragglers and often prisoners of the Japanese. The British officers were not learning from their past mistakes. Rather, the British high command should have left a light covering screen of troops in the front backed by mobile reserves. This scheme would have been at least more effective in containing or slowing down the Japanese.

Worse, the Malaya Command, to strengthen the morale of the defenders, followed the faulty policy of underestimating its opponent. The 7th/6th RR

Battalion, despite their confrontation with the veteran well-trained Japanese units, was told that the Japanese soldiers were neither well equipped nor highly trained for jungle warfare, but were like clever gangsters and dacoits. The jawans were informed that the Japanese soldiers dressed in civilian clothing, infiltrated along the defensive lines, and made a lot of noises, even mimicking machine-gun fire. The troops were told that all would be well if they just ignored the childish trickery of the Japanese.[52]

This sort of deliberate misinformation was a standard policy of the Malaya High Command. We have noted earlier that the 5th/11th Sikhs were also deliberately misinformed about the capability of the IJA. Soon, the Japanese attack developed, and the Indian troops were in for a great shock. Williamson Murray claims that honest after-action reports from the lowest level and learning lessons at the tactical level play a crucial part in battlefield success. The military organization has to discern what is occurring in the battlefield through honest reporting from the bottom up, and then these lessons have to be translated into coherent programs to remedy the principal deficiencies.[53] The Malaya Command was doing the opposite. It engaged in a game of dishonesty and deliberate misrepresentation of the enemy's combat capacity. Rather than trying to learn honestly, the Malaya Command was engaging in distortion of facts, which backfired soon on its own troops. So we can conclude that the Malaya Command functioned as an obstruction as regards the learning curve.

Major General B. W. Key gave high marks to the performance of the Japanese divisions. He accepted that the British and Indian soldiers carried a lot of unnecessary equipment that slowed them down, and as a result they were unable to move quickly through the jungle. Once inside the jungle, the Allied troops lost their way and the dispirited troops soon dumped the LMGs, wireless sets, and so on.[54] In contrast, the light Japanese infantry, unlike the unwieldy, heavily laden Allied units, had perfected the art of moving quickly through the jungle.

The left forward company of the 7th/6th RR Battalion, the D Company under Second Lieutenant S. J. Warren, held a front of five miles. The company headquarters was at Kesang, five miles by road north of Muar Ferry. Warren was ordered to conduct an active patrolling and to prevent the enemy from reaching the north bank. He kept a platoon in the company headquarters, and two platoons were engaged in patrol work. Warren's small force was unable to keep the Japanese advance parties from reaching the north bank of Muar. However, there were four Australian twenty-five-pounder guns in support of the D Company. The problem was that the Forward Observation Officer (FOO), who was to direct the fire of the four guns in support of the infantry, was stationed in the company headquarters. His link with the battalion headquarters was by the gunner wire. And the gunner wire ran under the water through the river bed. Frequently, the wire went dead. In this case, the wire went dead forty-five minutes after the beginning of combat.[55] Communication among the various battalions and within each battalion was bad, and this in turn jeopardized the construction of a coherent defensive line.

The right forward B Company of 7th/6th RR under Second Lieutenant A. T. Chilman held a front of nine miles, and on its right were the 4th/9th Jats. The

4th/9th Jats under Lieutenant Colonel J. Williams had sailed from Bombay on 21 December 1941. This battalion was initially trained for deployment in the Caucasus region to aid the Russians. Only during the voyage was the unit informed that it was intended for deployment in Malaya. On 3 January 1942, this unit reached Singapore. On 5 January 1942, this battalion disembarked at Singapore and was ordered to Malacca on the west coast of Malaya.[56] All its vehicles were painted in white with grey stripes. Captain F. E. Mileham of the 4th/9th Jats recorded: "All our trucks were camouflaged for snow conditions and made a beautiful target for any aircraft."[57] In the afternoon of 9 January, this battalion reached Malacca. The adjutant, Captain B. Lee, informed the battalion that there was nothing to worry about, as the Japanese were still 150 miles north of Malacca. However, this battalion was in for a rude shock. In the evening, the CO informed the men that the Japanese were landing nearby. During the night of 9/10 January, the 4th/9th Jats' B Company exchanged shots with a party of twenty Japanese. The battalion was ordered to Muar because reinforcements were needed there.[58]

On 11 January, the 4th/9th Jats took position at Muar. On 12 January, the A, B, and C companies were spread out along an eight-mile front. Communications among these companies was already breaking down. The company commanders had no idea about where the Japanese were lurking but expected an attack at any time. Heavy rainfall further depressed the British officers.[59] However, the Japanese officers were not depressed by the heavy rainfall in Malaya. Mileham of the 4th/9th Jats complained: "It was impossible in this type of country to hold a line of such length."[60] The British officers were trained to think of holding a continuous front as in the First World War. It was a cognitive failure on their part to prepare to hold a long stretch of ground with concentrated mobile strike forces rather than spreading out the troops thinly in a continuous line.

South of the Muar River on the right was the C Company of 7th/6th RR under Second Lieutenant E. A. P. Larter. It held position from Jorak to S. Abong. The area was full of rubber trees and difficult scrub. And on the left was the A Company of 7th/6th RR under Lieutenant R. V. C. Martyn. Its defensive position extended from S. Abong to the mouth of the Muar River. The Muar River at its mouth was between a 0.25 and 0.5 miles wide. The south bank of the river was the waterfront of the Muar town.[61]

The Japanese had boats (including "native" country boats), and enjoyed naval and aerial superiority. So they could cross at any point and land behind the defending Indian units. In order to guard against the small Japanese parties laying ambush and causing disorganization in the rear area, the three carriers of the 7th/6th RR Battalion were employed in patrolling the roads leading into Muar from the south. The point to be noted is that the carriers were received just thirty-six hours before the battle started. And only six men in the battalion had completed a rush course (three days) at Ahmadnagar in India during the week before the battle in driving the carriers. The carriers were equipped with LMGs taken from the AA platoon and these vehicles were vulnerable to grenades thrown by the Japanese infantry.[62] In the enclosed jungle terrain, patrolling was of crucial importance. Patrolling was necessary to gather information about the hostile forces, to seize the initiative, to disorganize hostile encircling operations, and finally, by dominating the countryside, to implement encirclement techniques against the enemy.[63] And foot patrols were more effective than patrolling by wheeled carriers. But the Allied troops were not adept in patrolling and scouting in jungle conditions.

Sudden night attacks by the Japanese depended on the advantages of surprise to compensate for the absence of artillery preparations. They were made by companies and even platoons. If a company made an attack, a reconnaissance patrol of five to ten men was sent ahead, and forward lookout points were established. Several patrols were also pushed forward to ascertain the position and strength of the hostile forces. Soon after dusk on the night selected for attack, another patrol was sent forward to lay out a line of approach that followed the easily recognizable terrain features. The approach continued with maximum stealth until the Japanese troops were within rushing distance of the Allied troops.[64] The Japanese nocturnal jitter tactics was designed to spread alarm, confusion, and demoralization among the Indians. The Japanese infiltrators used noisy firecrackers and shouted in English and Urdu, which in turn provoked wild, unaimed fire from the jawans that revealed their positions to the Japanese and also resulted in unnecessary expenditure of ammunition by the defenders.[65] On the night of 14/15 January 1941, Japanese infiltration through the light defensive front created by the Indian companies started. At 0930 hours on 15 January, a small Japanese party worked its way between the inexperienced B and C companies of 7th/6th RR, which were spread out along a front of fourteen miles. Soon the D Company of 7th/6th RR was attacked, but the FOO could not bring fire support, as the gunner wire went dead.[66] The Allied commanders instead of clinging to rigid linear defense should have resorted to elastic defense in depth, which was introduced by the Germans in 1917 in the Western Front. Elastic defense in depth involved a sprinkling of self-supporting defensive points centered on interlocking machine guns instead of a linear static line.[67]

The Japanese conducted frontal and flanking attacks simultaneously. On 15 January, the Japanese arrived in strength on the north bank of the Muar River, and later that day, Japanese troops landed from the sea at a point about ten miles south of Muar and also at Batu Pahat. The Japanese actually landed at Telaga Jetty on the west coast near Batu Pahat. The forces landed to the south of Muar were about one battalion strong with light artillery.[68] During the night of 15 January, the CO of the 7th/6th RR Battalion ordered every man to remain alert in order to prevent any nocturnal infiltration by the Japanese among the widely dispersed positions of the battalion. This order prevented the men from catching any sleep. And there was no battalion reserve available. Further, the men were unable to conduct patrolling effectively in the jungle terrain during the night.[69] In contrast, the Japanese were trained in jungle craft, which included observation, concealment, and silent movement in the jungle.[70] One can say that the night belonged to the Japanese. Major S. A. Watt asserts that with little training and some experience, the men could have patrolled better and would have been able to contact the advancing Japanese before they suddenly burst on the defenders. During the night, small Japanese parties moved around the 7th/6th RR's C Company's position between Muar and Jorak.⁷¹ The Japanese nocturnal swarming and infiltration tactics were indeed succeeding.

G. W. Seabridge exposes the limitations of the Allied troops in the following words:

> A contributory factor to the demoralization of our troops was the complete inability to counter the Japanese infiltration tactics, and that inability arose mainly from the greater mobility of the enemy. We were not under-equipped in Malaya; we were over-equipped. Our men were over-burdened. We had motor transport everywhere and a large amount of it had to be abandoned. The Japanese soldiers were clad in singlet and shorts and sandshoes. They carried a light Tommy Gun or rifle and a small bag of ammunition. They also carried small rations and a supply of quinine or atebrin and many of them wore rubber belts which could be inflated to enable them to cross rivers. They used bicycles freely and transported light mortars in parts on these bicycles.⁷²

In fact, the Japanese Nambu LMG was suited for jungle combat. The Nambu fired a .256 caliber bullet, which left an ugly wound on the recipient. Because of the light charge used, the gun hardly emitted any flash or smoke while firing. Hence, the Japanese machine gunners lurking in the jungle could not be located by the Allied soldiers. Compared to the Nambu, the Browning Automatic Rifle (BAR) used by the American troops required diligent maintenance and cleaning (which was not possible in the muddy and slushy tropical theaters); otherwise it jammed. The Australian and the British infantry used the Bren Gun, which was heavier than the BAR.⁷³

Late on 15 January, the Japanese broke through the 7th/6th RR Battalion. The D Company of the 4th/9th Jats was ordered to clear the Muar-Lenga Road, which was blocked by the Japanese with felled trees. The Jat Company, without making any prior reconnaissance, walked blithely into the ambush set up by the Japanese and suffered thirty casualties.⁷⁴

The next morning, Lieutenant Colonel Woolridge of the 5th Garwahlis, which was in reserve at Bakri, visited Watt. While going back he was killed by an ambush that was set up by the Japanese parties that were landed by boats behind the position of the 7th/6th RR Battalion during the previous night.⁷⁵ On the same day, a Japanese convoy, including barges and special landing craft, landed troops at the mouth of the Muar River near the lighthouse. Percival feared that the Japanese might also land troops at Malacca.⁷⁶ Japanese advance patrols armed with Tommy Guns worked toward an objective, sometimes for days, often lying low in the dense undergrowth to conceal themselves from the Allied soldiers. They made an intimate study of the terrain and knew every road and path. A number of advance units were sent to attack the same objective, so even if some failed to reach, the other parties slipped through and reached their designated objective.⁷⁷

The Japanese fighting technique was to put pressure at one point of the British-Indian defensive line, and when it cracked, the rest of the defending British and Indian units either left their positions to plug the gap in the defensive line or retreated back in order to create another defensive line. There was no mobile tactical or operational reserve on the part of the Allies to plug the gaps and maintain intact the defensive line if it was ruptured at one point. Between 0800 and 0900 hours on 16 January, the tired troops of the C Company of 7th/6th RR, who had spent a sleepless night, cried for help, and its A Company was pulled out to aid it. While moving without prior reconnaissance toward the C Company, the A Company was itself attacked by the Japanese, and it scattered amid rubber and scrub jungle. The leadership quotient of the A Company failed miserably in its ability to conduct a reconnaissance before moving out. This failure seems to have been common among the Allied battalions. The untrained and partially trained Allied soldiers were completely confused in close-quarter battles amid rubber trees and dense scrubs. While the British and Indian troops were physically and conceptually tied to the roads and tracks, the Japanese, by moving readily and easily through the jungle and rubber plantations, enjoyed a greater degree of freedom. Around two in the afternoon, news came that the wheeled carriers were ambushed, and as a result one vehicle was lost near Dumpar Tinggi. Wheeled carriers without infantry escort were not ideal vehicles to patrol roads surrounded by rubber plantations and scrub jungle. The 7th/6th RR had no reserve to deal with this threat at their rear.[78] At this stage of the campaign, the British battalion commanders, knowing the penchant of the Japanese to go behind the units and cut their LoCs, should have kept a mobile reserve ready at their rear.

The British command culture was to look behind their back to their superiors even during a battle for detailed and precise orders. In such critical times, communication between the higher headquarters and fighting formations might be cut, or the commanding officer might be absent. Like the 4th/9th Jats, the 7th/6th RR did not know what to do and were at a loss. The British-officered Indian units were accustomed to restrictive control that involved detailed planning and strict obedience to precise orders from top. This was due to structured decision making designed to eliminate uncertainty in battle. War is a complex, nonlinear phenomenon, and chaos and uncertainty are inherent in it. Murray rightly says that of all the activities in which mankind engages, it is the conduct of war that envelops it with the greatest degree of uncertainty, ambiguity, and friction. Unintended consequences and unforeseen second- and third-order effects bedevil the most logical and carefully thought out approaches to war.[79] Ironically, that very uncertainty and chaos prevented the structured decision-making command apparatus of Malaya Command from operating effectively. In the prevailing context, there was neither time nor opportunity for the Indian battalions to operate within the centralized command apparatus. What was required was decentralized control (a mission-oriented command system) that involved coordination of the activities of the subordinates exhibiting initiative to deliver the required effect. By decentralizing the very decision making to lower levels, the mission command system reduces uncertainty and exploits it.[80] The 7th/6th RR looked to the brigadier for succor, but he was not in the brigade headquarters. Worse, there were only fourteen men present there. In other words, the whole brigade had no reserves.[81] The rigid, upward-looking command culture seemed to be the main culprit. This was not unique to Percival's force but was also present, for instance, in Bernard Montgomery's Eighth Army in North Africa in 1943.[82]

In contrast, the Japanese practiced a decentralized command system. Small groups of men were asked to make their way as best as they could to a point a number of miles ahead. It was then up to them how to get there. They set off through the jungle quietly picking their way, sometimes lying concealed for hours. After arriving at the designated point, they regrouped. Contact with the rear units was maintained through portable wireless apparatus.[83] Murray writes that decentralized command and control practiced by the Germans during the two World Wars, which encouraged the platoon and company commanders to make tactical decisions on their own is a necessity for being successful in modern combat.[84] The command culture of the British-Indian Army in 1941–42 was not prepared for this sort of decentralized command setup. Soon the brigadier, with Captain Alderman and thirty men of the 7th Rajputana, moved toward Dumpar Tinggi, and they were ambushed. The brigadier and Alderman were killed.[85] The Japanese soldiers were well trained in laying ambushes. Further, the cross-country capability of the Japanese troops equipped in a light uniform of cotton shorts and rubber soled shoes was remarkable.[86]

On 16 January while patrolling the B Company's position, the carriers of the 4th/9th Jats found a roadblock established by the Japanese. The Japanese were in the trees. They had tied themselves with ropes and were armed with an ample supply of hand grenades. They dropped the grenades like ripe plums on the Bren Gun carriers. Quite late, it dawned upon Mileham, Carrier Platoon commander of 4th/9th Jats, that "in this type of country a Bren Gun Carrier was a very vulnerable vehicle."[87] By the evening, the 7th/6th RR was ordered to evacuate Muar Line. In the absence of proper communications, contacting the scattered sub-units and conducting an orderly withdrawal was next to impossible.[88] The Japanese captured Muar town.[89] They crossed the Muar River in strength. The 45th Indian Brigade attempted to withdraw to Bakri. But, its battalions, dispersed over some seventeen miles along the Muar River, failed to retreat properly.[90] On that day, the 1st/4th Japanese Guard Battalion landed southwest of Batu Pahat.[91]

In order to shore up the retreating and disorganized 45th Indian Brigade, the 2nd/29th AIF Battalion was shifted from Segamat to Bakri, and the 2nd/19th AIF Battalion was sent from Jemaluang on the east coast.[92] On 17 January, the 4th/9th Jats were ordered to join up with the 29th AIF Battalion at MS 101 on the Bakri-Muar Road. The 4th/9th Jats moved through a rubber track toward Bakri. While doing so, it came under fire from the Japanese. In the confused situation, communication with higher headquarters was cut, and the men and their officers seemed to be at a loss about what to do. The British and Indian battalions were not trained to operate semiautonomously and display initiative when in the chaotic combat conditions communication links between higher headquarters and lower formation commanders were severed. The panicky situation in the 4th/9th Jats was described by Mileham in the following words: "I sent three separate messages by motor cycle dispatch riders to inform Battalion Headquarters of the situation, but none of these returned. Presumably they were killed by the Japanese, who by this time had taken over the track and one Viceroy's Commissioned Officer said that he had seen the CO and Adjutant killed. We told him not to say anything to the rest of the men, who by this time appeared to be very concerned."[93]

During the night of 17/18 January, the 7th/6th RR took up a position a mile east of Bukit Muar. The 5th/18th Garwahl Rifles passed through the position of 7th/6th RR to Parit Jaws.[94] The 2nd/29th AIF Battalion arrived at Bakri-Muar. The 4th/9th Jats were at the right of the 7th/6th RR Battalion, but there was no contact between these two units. Breakdown of communications between the neighboring units was due to bad staff work and the failure of their COs to send reconnaissance patrols and runners for contacting the neighboring units. At 1900 hours, four Australians from the 29th AIF turned up to the 4th/9th Jats. They told Mileham that the Japanese were in control of the rubber track that the 4th/9th Jats intended to use to reach MS 101. Consequently, the 4th/9th Jats decided to go to MS 96 down the Muar-Bakri Road. It was a rare case when an Australian unit was taking the trouble to inform their neighboring Indian formation about the battle situation. The 4th/9th Jats at this time numbered two hundred men and under Major Kidd set out for their new destination. On 18 January, the 4th/9th Jats moved through the swamps and met some wounded Australians. Panic spread among the battalion as the Australians told the story of how the Allied troops had suffered a great reverse at Muar. The men heard firing in the north. Instead of marching to the sound of the guns, the battalion decided to bypass the Japanese and escape to Parit Sulong.[95]

Meanwhile, discipline disintegrated in the 4th/9th Jats. The VCOs who were in charge of maintaining discipline among the jawans suffered from nervous breakdowns. News reached them that the Japanese held the Parit Sulong Bridge. Mileham narrates: "The men were extremely tired as they had no food for three or four days. . . . A subedar in our party tried to make trouble telling me he was going to take some of the men down the road. I told him to obey orders and keep quiet whereupon he became very rude. I put him in charge of Jemadar Ram Swarup and another VCO and I didn't see him again and think he was probably disposed of quietly."[96] The journey continued, and now the 4th/9th Jats numbered only 150 men.[97] Probably many had escaped into the rubber plantation with the idea of surrendering to the Japanese.

The day of 18 January was not good for Percival. Two Japanese divisions were advancing: the Imperial Guards Division on the coast road from Muar to Batu Pahat and the 5th Division along the main trunk road, which ran across via Segamat and Yong Peng to Singapore. The Japanese attack on Bakri was supported by tank columns. Finally, the Japanese battalion of the 4th Guards Regiment, which had landed from the sea south of Batu Pahat had moved inland into the jungle, where it posed a grave threat to the LoC of the Allied force occupying Batu Pahat. Percival realized the dangers of holding on to Segamat and north Johore. If the Japanese Imperial Guards Division advanced east from Bakri and captured the crucial road junction at Yong Peng, the III Indian Corps would be trapped between the Japanese pincers. This would leave central Johore undefended and the road to Singapore wide open. By hook or by crook, the Imperial

Guards Division had to be stopped until 24 January, by which date the III Indian Corps could retreat through the bottleneck of Yong Peng.[98]

Percival regrouped his forces for holding Batu Pahat and the Bukit Belah-Pelandok defile position, which was essential for the defense of the Yong Peng position. For this, he had to use the 53rd British Brigade, which had been detached from the 18th British Division. It had sailed from the Middle East and had just landed at Singapore after a sea voyage of twelve weeks. By this time, two Japanese battalions had occupied the seven miles of road between the defile position and Parit Sulong and were poised to attack both places.[99] On 18 January, the 9th Indian Division was ordered to withdraw to the east bank of Muar. The 8th Indian Brigade functioned as the rear guard at Buloh Kasap, and the 27th AIF Brigade withdrew to the east bank of south Segamat.[100]

On 19 January, the Japanese detachment that had landed on 15 January south of Muar attacked and captured Bukit Paying defile and Parit Sulong. Consequently the Allied force's LoC at Bakri was cut off.[101] By the morning of 19 January, the 7th/6th RR was withdrawn from Bakri-Parit Jawa Road and entrusted with the defense of the western part of the Bakri crossroads. The 7th/6th RR was attacked at 1300 hours by the Japanese infantry equipped with automatic weapons. At 1600 hours, the 4th/9th Jats, after suffering heavy losses (including their CO Lieutenant Colonel John Williams killed), was able to join up with the 7th/6th RR. By that time, the 2nd/19th AIF had also joined the 7th RR.[102] The retreat from Muar led to the subsequent Battle of Yong Peng. In fact, these two battles were interconnected. Whether the whole III Indian Corps would be bagged or not by the Japanese depended on the Yong Peng encounter.

On 19 January, the codeword DRAGON was issued. In accordance with it, the 27th AIF Brigade was to hold Segamat till 20/21 night. The 22nd Indian Brigade was to take up a reargruard position along Segamat-Labis Road. And the 8th Indian Brigade was to be at the east of Segamat. The 8th Indian Brigade's 1st FFR encountered Japanese cyclists equipped with mortars. The 2nd Loyal withdrew to Yong Peng.[103]

Between 18 and 23 January, the Battle of Yong Peng was fought. The 53rd British Brigade jostled with the Japanese Imperial Guards Division. The 6th Norfolk was given the unenviable task of holding the Bukit-Belah-Pelandok defile position, essential for retaining Yong Peng.[104] The British battalion started to dig slit trenches, and the companies were widely dispersed in the thick country. The troops were trained to establish defensive positions with clear field of fire, but this was not possible in the dense jungle country. Major Robert Hammond of 6th Norfolk writes about the dismay of the battalion regarding the terrain they had to defend: "The jungle was a completely strange and seemingly hostile environment to most officers and men of the Norfolk, the majority of whom never moved far from their homes. The enervating heat, the mosquitoes and strange jungle noises at night deprived them of sleep and aggravated the softening effects of their long sea journey."[105] A lengthy period of acclimatization was required to introduce the troops to the physical strain of life in the jungle and to the specialized arts of jungle lore, which involved finding potable water, identifying edible plants, constructing shelters from local materials, tracking, and manufacturing booby traps.[106]

The two forward companies, C Company on Bukit Pelandok and D Company on Bukit Belah, had to be positioned on the forward slopes of the defile position, as the higher ground was covered with thick scrub jungle. The British soldiers were not comfortable taking up defensive positions inside dense scrubs. The reserve platoon of C Company guarded the top of Pelandok. The 6th Norfolk's order was to hold the defile so that the 45th Indian Brigade and the 2nd/19th and 2nd/29th Australian battalions, who were retreating from Muar, could escape. Further, the battalion was tasked to stop the Japanese forces on the west coast from advancing to Yong Peng to prevent any interference with the withdrawal of the III Indian corps. Lastly, the 6th Norfolk was to deny the Japanese an important road junction west of the defile, from which a road ran south to Batu Pahat. In the evening of 18 January, a report came that Japanese troops were advancing on the road leading from the defile to Batu Pahat. A patrol was sent out and it was ambushed. Two patrols were sent to guard the bridge at Parit Sulong to cover the Allied forces retreating from Muar.[107]

In the afternoon of 19 January, the B and C companies of 6th Norfolk were attacked. The Japanese had emerged like phantoms from the Batu Pahat Road and then in the east along the Bukit Pelandok Ridge where they overran the C Company's reserve platoon and attacked the company from the rear. They definitely had a penchant for moving fast unseen, and the reconnaissance of the 6th Norfolk was sloppy. However, the 6th Norfolk received some reinforcements. The B Company of the 2nd Battalion of the Loyal Regiment had arrived. Brigadier C. L. B. Duke decided to use the Loyals, who had seemingly more experience in jungle warfare than the Norfolks, to turn the Japanese flank at Bukit Pelandok. But the new British battalion that had come as reinforcement developed cold feet. The 2nd Loyals judged the Japanese as too strong to attack. So the ambitious scheme of turning the flank of the attacking Japanese came to nothing. Meanwhile, the 6th Norfolk's position was threatened due to the slow and steady infiltration by the Japanese. In the evening, the Japanese were behind the D Company's position at Belah and severed their LoC with the battalion headquarters.[108]

At the dawn of 20 January, the 3rd/16th Punjab (a weak battalion comprising also survivors of the 2nd/16th) attacked Bukit Belah. When they reached the crest of the hill, they came under withering fire. The CO of 3rd/16th Punjab, Lieutenant Colonel H. D. Moorhead, was killed, and the leading company was almost wiped out. Once the British officers were killed, the inability of the VCOs to take up company-level command (for which they were not trained), led to the disintegration of the Indian battalions. As the 3rd/16th Punjab retreated, the Japanese counterattacked and overran the 6th Norfolk's D Company Headquarters. Under pressure of Japanese attack, the D Company scattered. The survivors of two platoons were able to reach Batu Pahat on 22 January and linked up with the 2nd Cambridgeshires. The two small standing patrols of the 6th Norfolk at Parit Sulong Bridge were cut off, and they withdrew to Batu Pahat. On 20 January, a battalion of the Japanese Imperial Guards Division occupied Parit Sulong in an attempt to trap the 45th Indian Brigade retreating from Muar.[109]

At the dawn of 19 January, the 45th Indian Brigade was organized into a box formation, somewhat like the Duke of Wellington's squares at the battlefield of Waterloo. The wounded and the transport elements were placed in the middle of the "box." The box formation with advance guard, flank guards, and rear guard moved slowly through the rubber plantation. This was a tactical innovation of great import. Later, in 1944, "Bill" Slim would use the box formation supported by aerial resupply with great effectiveness in delaying the Japanese advance toward Imphal-Kohima. Mileham's party of 4th/9th Jats held the northern perimeter of the box. The 7th/6th RR Battalion formed the rearguard and later formed the flank protection column. The Japanese unsuccessfully tried to penetrate the perimeter of the box by sending small parties armed with automatic rifles. When they failed, the Japanese sent light tanks. With the aid of two twenty-five-pounder guns and another A/T gun plus the guns of RA, eleven tanks were knocked out. Against the resolute defense by troops organized in box formation, the Japanese light infantry's lightning attacks failed. What was required for a successful box formation defense to succeed was strong leadership and battle-hardened troops who could implement infantry-artillery coordination. The Japanese rushed in infantry, who disembarked from the lorries and country buses. Against the wounded Allied soldiers, the Japanese showed no mercy. A request was made to the Japanese to allow the trucks with severely wounded to pass through the Japanese lines to Singapore. The Japanese refused this request, and the men in the trucks that were captured were slaughtered.[110]

The next day, the 45th Indian Brigade retreated from Bakri with the objective of withdrawing to Yong Peng. Meanwhile, the men went without hot meals, and this fact somewhat demoralized them. They subsisted on *atta*, condensed milk, pineapples, coconuts, and biscuits. The Japanese soldiers due to their rigorous training were able to continue subsisting on their dry packed provision. During the retreat to Yong Peng, the Japanese repeatedly attacked with a combination of infantry, tanks, and aircraft.[111] Thanks to the simplicity of the supply of ammunition, the advancing Japanese soldiers rarely ran out of ammunition. The Japanese did not require a large number of trucks and carriers for supplying the frontline troops with ammunition. The ammunition boxes were carried as shoulder packs, which left their arms free for negotiating difficult terrain and permitted greater freedom of action under fire.[112] The 45th Indian Brigade's ordeal was to continue.

In the night of 20/21 January, the 27th AIF Brigade moved to Yong Peng. The 22nd Indian Brigade moved to Paloh. Steps were taken to demolish the road between Segamat and Yong Peng and to blow up the railway bridges at Bekok and Labis.[113] On 21 January, the threat to LoC of the Segamat Force, which had developed from Muar, forced withdrawal to the Labis area.[114] On 21 January, the 8th Indian Brigade took position in the southern part of Socfin Palm Oil Estate near Kampong Chaard. The objective was to keep the Japanese away from Yong Peng Road junction, as this was the nodal point of the LoC for the two brigades operating toward Muar on the west coast road.[115] There were several roads through the Socfin Palm Oil Estate, and through them the Japanese tanks and cyclists infiltrated.

On 21 January, the 45th Indian Brigade, after retreating to Parit Sulong, found the bridge was occupied by the Japanese. The brigade attacked but failed to dislodge the Japanese. In response, the Japanese tanks attacked its rear. The brigade was compressed into an area of two hundred by three hundred yards—a perfect killing ground for the Japanese attackers. On 22 January, the Japanese launched a ground attack supported by aerial bombing. Lieutenant Colonel C. G. W. Anderson of the 2nd/19th AIF (he had taken charge after the brigade commander, Duncan, was killed on 20 January while leading a bayonet charge against Japanese infantry and tanks), realizing that the end was near, ordered the destruction of all heavy guns and vehicles, and the men were ordered to reach Yong Peng as best as they could by foot. This meant the virtual disintegration of the brigade. Of its four thousand personnel, only about nine hundred were able to escape. Many of the wounded who had to be abandoned were killed by the Japanese soldiers.[116] Thus, the luckless 45th Indian Brigade, already battered at Muar, almost ceased to exist while attempting to escape the advancing Japanese jaws. The destruction of the 45th Indian Brigade formally marked the end of the Muar Battle.

On 22 January, while the Japanese cyclists advancing along the main road pinned down the defenders frontally by firing, other Japanese infantry units started infiltrating through the jungle astride the road among the various battalions of the 8th Indian Brigade. About 1,200 Japanese equipped with mortars and machine guns infiltrated on the left of the 1st/13th FFR and 3rd/17th Dogras. Then, the Japanese infiltrated to the rear of the 2nd/10th Baluch Battalion's Headquarters. It goes without saying that the Japanese infantry was highly skilled in moving through uncharted territory and appearing behind the Allied units. As a result of Japanese pressure, the 2nd/10th Baluch withdrew six miles to Sungei Gerchok.[117] While the 8th Indian Brigade withdrew after blowing up the bridges, the Japanese quickly repaired them and crossed the rivers and streams. The Japanese infantry, equipped with mortars, appeared at the flanks and rear of the British and Indian units, and the latter then retreated further south.[118] In fact, the highly portable light two-inch mortars (each of which was operated by two men) along with hand grenades used by the Japanese were ideal instruments for carrying out ambush.[119] In the Solomons and in New Guinea between 1942 and 1944, mortars and grenades caused almost half of the casualties.[120] The same applies for Malaya in early 1942. When threatened at the flank and rear, the British and Indian units did not stand their ground and fight it out, but fearing threat to their LoC, retreated again and again. On 22 January, the 22nd Indian Brigade evacuated the Labis position.[121]

On 23 January, 2nd RGR reported that the Japanese were making a wide encircling movement at Paloh. The Japanese would occasionally shout, "Don't shoot; we are wounded." And when the unwary Indian troops would go near them, they would shoot at the latter. However, credit is due to the 2nd RGR, which in an ambush was able to kill a hundred Japanese soldiers.[122] On the same day, the 8th Indian Brigade withdrew through Yong Peng, which was held by the 2nd/30th

AIF Battalion.[123] And the 6th Norfolk was ordered to retreat from the defile position to Yong Peng.[124] Hammond describes the chaotic withdrawal by the 6th Norfolk, the 2nd Loyal, and the 3rd/16th Punjab:

> Withdrawal during daylight is a delicate operation even in the best of circumstances; in close contact with the enemy, in thick country, where troops are exhausted and where control is difficult to maintain because of poor communications, confusion and disaster are never far away. Things began to go sadly wrong with this carefully timed withdrawal. At 1230 hours, Japanese infantry, supported by heavy mortar and machine-gun fire, attacked the Punjabis just as the latter were preparing to pull back, and also swept on to the positions held by . . . 2nd Loyals and their carriers. As the Punjabis were driven off their positions and came streaming back ahead of their scheduled time of withdrawal, the Japanese overran the Loyals. . . . Survivors . . . took to the jungle and made their way back to Yong Peng as best as they could, but they did not pass through the 6th Norfolk as planned who were thus unaware that they had gone and their right flank was now undefended.[125]

Major Hammond of the 6th Norfolk blamed poor communications and low visibility for the chaotic retreat, which was caused by being deployed in thick jungle country. However, these very factors worked to the advantage of the Japanese. The reasons for chaos and confusion among the Allied units during the retreat were centralized command and inadequate training. Due to lack of training, the British and Indian troops' combat effectiveness was reduced in the dank, damp environment of hot and humid jungle. On the other hand, the Japanese, in accordance with their doctrine and training in maneuver warfare, exploited chaos. The morale of the British soldiers had indeed reached rock bottom. John McEwan, a twenty-one-year-old gunner noted in his autobiography: "We had the chilling thought that they might even be watching us at that very moment from the cover of the thick jungle foliage and might be about to annihilate us all."[126]

The 6th Norfolk was attacked by Japanese tanks.[127] Hammond describes the situation in the following words:

> It was becoming a race against time; the Japanese were moving down off the hills into swamps flanking the causeway in the rear of 6th Norfolks. If they were to succeed in capturing part of the causeway and in establishing a road-block, the Norfolks would be trapped and destroyed. Doggedly they fought their way slowly back and it was with a sense of relief that, in the darkness, the battalion finally cleared the end of the dangerous causeway and set out to march to Yong Peng which they reached at midnight, after blowing up another two bridges in their rear.[128]

During the night of 23/24 January, WESTFORCE retreated to the Kluang-Ayer Hitam line. The 2nd/30th AIF took covering positions north of Yong Penh Road junction. The 53rd British Brigade was ordered to clear Yong Peng by 2400 hours.[129] The 4th/9th Jats took the road to Singapore from Batu Pahat.[130] The senior Allied officers were relieved when the rearguard of the III Indian Corps passed through Yong Peng during the night of 23/24 January. The Japanese captured this place the next day.[131]

Disaster at Muar and Johore 167

A battalion of the Japanese Imperial Guards Division advanced toward Yong Peng.[132] The Japanese streamed down the roads in bicycles and, when checked, went to the ground and sent flanking columns that worked around the rear of the Allied troops. They were very successful in cutting off a large number of transports and Allied units that failed to detach aggressive patrols for protecting their flanks and rear.[133] After narrowly avoiding several small Japanese parties riding on bicycles and small Japanese detachments equipped with two-pounder guns and a large dose of automatics moving through the jungle tracks, the depleted 4th/9th Jats reached Batu Pahat and linked up with the Cambridgeshire Battalion. On 24 January, Japanese advance parties moved toward Batu Pahat but were temporarily driven back by mortar fire from the 2nd Cambridgeshire Battalion. On that day, the 4th/9th Jats were machine-gunned and bombed by low flying Japanese aircraft.[134]

Overall, the Muar Battle was fought by the 45th Indian Brigade and from 18 January onwards by two Australian battalions supported by Australian field and A/T artillery. The Japanese tanks played no part in the action at Kampar but played an important but not decisive role in the Muar Battle.[135] Some four thousand Indian troops were engaged in Muar Battle, and of them only eight hundred remained intact. The rest had become casualties (killed, PoW, and missing).[136] Percival accused Gordon Bennett's faulty dispositions in front of Muar for the debacle. He had written that the four Indian companies that were deployed north of Muar were not strong enough to check the Japanese and were overwhelmed unnecessarily.[137] Brian P. Farrell asserts that Gordon Bennett's positioning of one-third of the strength of the 45th Indian Brigade north of Muar River spelled disaster for the defense of the Muar Line.[138] True, but even if Bennett had concentrated all the available troops on the south bank of Muar, it is doubtful whether the Japanese thrust would have been checked or not. The real cause of the Muar defeat was the inadequate training of the 45th Indian Brigade and the 53rd British Brigade plus the Australians' inability to respond effectively to the frontal pressure of infiltrating Japanese infantry and the threat posed to their rear by the Japanese parties that were landed behind their lines. The Allied defensive line was penetrated frontally and outflanked simultaneously. The Allied troops failed even to contain the frontal attacks of the Japanese. Percival noted: "In Malaya, nearly all the fighting took place in close country—jungles, swamps and rubber plantations—where visibility is limited and where movement is often a difficulty. For this type of warfare, the training and tactics of the Japanese Army were well adapted."[139] Mark Johnston writes that to the Australians their Japanese opponents were especially frightening because they seemed less than human. The jungles in which the Japanese were encountered increased the terrors of life-and-death struggle. Again, the screaming sound of low-flying Japanese aircraft and the bombs dropped from above further spread the sense of dread among the Australian soldiers.[140] This observation is equally applicable for the British and Indian troops also. However, the Allied commanders and their troops deserve some credit for not being surrounded at Yong Peng.

Retreat to Johore Causeway

> the Japanese troops undoubtedly out-maneuvered ours by their superior mobility, training and preparation.
>
> General Archibald Wavell[141]

By the end of third week of January 1942, Gordon Bennett's (on whom Wavell had placed high hopes) plan of fighting a defensive battle with the Japanese in the Gemas-Muar region was in complete ruin. Gordon Bennett was by then a broken man. He was no longer confident of stopping the Japanese onrush. Much of his enthusiasm had ebbed away. He realized that he and his troops were no better than Heath and the III Indian Corps.[142] The Aussies' initial enthusiasm about confronting the "Japs" had also ebbed away. Wavell visited Singapore on 20 January. His plan of holding the Segamat-Muar line till the whole of the 18th British Division had landed and the 11th Indian Division had been rested and refitted was in shambles. The raw and untrained 45th Indian Brigade had failed to hold the Muar line and was cut off along with two Australian battalions east of the river. The 53rd British Brigade had to be thrown into battle before the arrival of the rest of the 18th British Division. Wavell was planning to hold the Mersing-Kluang-Batu Pahat line but was not sanguine. He was aware of the probability that the Allied troops might be thrown back from Johore to Singapore Island. And the northern part of Singapore Island was still without extensive defensive works.[143] The issue was whether the defeated Allied forces would be able to escape to Singapore Island by avoiding the advancing Japanese forces.

On 24 January, Percival put Heath's III Corps in overall command of the EASTFORCE, WESTFORCE, and the 11th Indian Division on the west coast.[144] On that day, the EASTFORCE was in contact with the Japanese along the Mersing River. In the central front, WESTFORCE, with the 9th Indian Division (8th and 22nd Indian brigades), was out of touch with the Japanese temporarily. On the west coast, 11th Indian Division had the 15th Indian Brigade at Batu Pahat and the 28th Indian Brigade at Pontian Kechil/Keehil. The 53rd British Brigade was retreating from Skudai to Benut. All these fronts were under the III Indian Corps.[145] The 11th Indian Division was worsted and exhausted. B Battery of 155th Field Regiment was attached to the 15th Indian Brigade. The 53rd British Brigade (which had arrived at Singapore on 13 January) had two weak battalions: 6th Norfolk and 3rd/16th Punjab. And the 28th Indian Brigade had 2nd/2nd GR, 2nd/9th GR, and 5th/14th Punjab. The 135th Field Regiment (Hertfordshire Yeomanry) under Lieutenant Colonel P. J. D. Toosey, with the 344th Battery under Major Peacock, provided fire support to the brigade. The 336th and 499th batteries were in reserve in the Skudai Road.[146] The senior British commanders hoped that unlike the Indian troops, the 53rd British Brigade would fight well. Their assumption was that unlike the colonial Indian soldiers, the British soldiers would be motivated to fight and die for defending their empire.[147] As we will see, the 53rd British Brigade's performance proved to be below average. Despite possessing substantial numbers of field batteries, the brigades of the 11th Indian Division (including the 53rd) were unable to use them properly. Wavell emphasized that the Mersing-Kluang-Ayer Hitam-Batu Pahat line must be held as long as possible. Wavell was worried that due to the aerial superiority of the Japanese and the large number of small craft at their disposal (which could be used to make landings behind the Allied defensive line), ultimately the III Indian Corps might have to fall back to Singapore Island.[148]

The 28th Indian Brigade had arrived at Pontian Keehil on 24 January. The coastal road from Pontian Keehil to Senggarang was narrow and flanked by marshes. The only dry ground for the vehicles was the villages. The Skudai Road ran through rubber and pineapple plantations. The G. Pulai Reservoir, which supplied water to Singapore that was carried in pipes across the Johore Causeway, was near this road. The abovementioned brigade was engaged in watching the coast. Further, it constructed a defensive position known as the Boulder on the Skudai Road just below the reservoir. On 24 January, the 2nd/2nd GR was responsible for the area from Pontian Keehil to Benut and the 2nd/9th GR from Benut to Koris. The 3rd Cavalry was in charge of patrolling the whole road. And the 5th/14th Punjab was in reserve at Benut.[149]

Between 22 and 24 January, elements from the Japanese Imperial Guards Division had cut the Batu Pahat-Ayer Hitam Road and also attacked Batu Pahat.[150] At 0100 hours of 24 January, the Japanese launched an attack against the A Company of 2nd Cambridgeshires along the Bauxite Mine Road. The attack was repulsed for the time being. Simultaneously, B Company in Batu Pahat town was attacked from the rear. The 15th Indian Brigade's Headquarters was at the cemetery one mile south of Batu Pahat. Meanwhile, a large number of Japanese started crossing the Ayer Hitam Road.[151]

At this stage, the 11th Indian Division's plan was to hold Mersing-Ayer Hitam-Batu Pahat. The 53rd British Brigade moved to take responsibility of the Pontian-Keehil Road from Senggarang to Benut. The 15th Indian Brigade was at Benut. Brigadier B. S. Challen CO of the 15th Indian Brigade was afraid of a repeat of the Muar disaster and wanted to withdraw immediately but was refused permission by the 11th Indian Division's CO, who displayed some spine. Colonel A. M. L. Harrison, GSO 1 of 11th Indian Division (who later wrote the unpublished history of the 11th Indian Division), informed Challen that the Muar disaster was because the 45th Indian Brigade was too spread out to provide concentrated defense. But, in this case, the 15th Indian Brigade at Batu Pahat was only fourteen miles from Senggarang. Moreover, from 25 January onward, there would be further support from the 53rd British Brigade. So, for the time being, Batu Pahat must be held.[152] Heath visited the 15th Indian Brigade at Batu Pahat on 21 January. Then, Brigadier Challen reported to him that the Japanese had cut both the Ayer Hitam and the coast roads and suggested a limited withdrawal. For once, Heath was against retreat. He somewhat rhetorically asserted that Batu Pahat should become a "Tobruk" and ordered the town to be stocked with ten days' supplies. Heath argued that by holding Batu Pahat, the Japanese advance down the trunk road would be disorganized.[153] Actually, despite Heath's rhetorical order, Batu Pahat would eventually be evacuated by the Allied troops in record time.

Meanwhile, the 5th Norfolk's counterattack under Lieutenant Colonel Eric Prattley on Hill 127, which rises from Pontian Keehil Road to the jungle-clad hills of Soga Range, failed because of inadequate support by the artillery. Infantry–artillery cooperation and coordination were yet to become a reality. Further, the infantry were bogged down in the swampy ground on which the Japanese concentrated mortar and light automatic fire. By 1500 hours, the Japanese were around the east flank of Batu Pahat. In the evening, Brigadier Challen ordered Major Most's company to withdraw from the Bauxite Mine Road, and it came back into battalion reserve. Meanwhile, the Japanese were probing the brigade's LoC at Benut. Due to the confused situation in the night, the sparsely trained Indian and Malay troops opened fire on each other because of nervousness. The B Company of the 1st/14th Punjab opened fire at the Johore Military Forces near the G. Pulai Causeway, erroneously believing that the latter were infiltrating Japanese.[154] Casualties due to friendly fire were also common among the Allied forces who fought in the jungles of South Pacific. Friendly-fire casualties occurred mostly during the night due to firing by the "green" troops. However, all the cases were not reported as it was feared that it would result in a drop of morale.[155]

At that time, the WESTFORCE held the railway and the trunk road between Kluang and Ayer Hitam. And the 22nd AIF Brigade held Mersing.[156] On 24 January, the 8th Indian Brigade arrived at Rengam. At 0830 hours, Major General A. E. Barstow ordered that since the 22nd Indian Brigade was in difficulty north of Kluang, the 8th Indian Brigade must help them. The 8th Indian Brigade in Australian transport was taken forward to aid the withdrawal of the 22nd Indian Brigade. The 2nd/10th Baluch took position on the west of Kluang, the 3rd/17th covered the northern approaches, and the 1st/13th FFR was at the south of Kluang.[157] On that day, the two Indian brigades experimented with a new tactical mechanism. At Kluang, the 8th and 22nd Indian brigades formed a perimeter for night defense against Japanese infiltration techniques.[158] The Indian units in North-West Frontier, while fighting the Pathans, used to set up perimeters for defending their camps during the night. By the end of 24 January, the Japanese controlled the roads from Muar to Yong Peng, from Muar to Batu Pahat, and between Batu Pahat and Ayer Hitam.[159] On the same day, two thousand untrained Australian recruits landed at Singapore.[160]

On 25 January, Heath was given control of the operations in southern Johore. He planned daily withdrawals, which were too long and too fast.[161] On 25 January 1942, the 8th Indian Brigade withdrew from Kluang.[162] On that day, the 6th Norfolk was at Senggarang and Rengit. Senggarang Bridge was of vital importance to the Batu Pahat force's LoC because Senggarang River was quite deep at this place.[163] At 0400 hours on 25 January, the 53rd British Brigade reached Benut. The 3rd/16th Punjab was at Benut supported by the 336th Field Battery. At 0800 hours, the Japanese were moving toward the Pontian-Keehil Road. The 6th Norfolk was failing in its task of keeping the road between Batu Pahat and Senggarang open as the Japanese started infiltrating. A platoon of the 6th Norfolk was ambushed south of Senggarang.[164] During the night of 24/25 January, the Japanese continued their harassing fire with mortars against the 15th Indian Brigade at Batu Pahat. After 0700 hours, the Japanese put up a roadblock between Senggarang and Pontian Keehil. Throughout the day, the Japanese continued mortar fire and occasional sniping.[165]

By this time, Major General Key had lost his nerve. He rang up the corps headquarters and asked permission for withdrawal. He emphasized that if withdrawal was contemplated from Mersing, Ayer Hitam, and Batu Pahat, then the 15th Indian Brigade must be allowed to retreat immediately. Key was ordered to attend a conference called by Percival at WESTFORCE Headquarters which was to start at 1400 hours. Heath promised to put up the issue of withdrawal to Percival during the conference. A nervous Key again called up the corps headquarters and asked for permission to allow the 15th Indian Brigade to withdraw. It was refused, and Key left for the conference.[166]

In the conference on 25 January, Gordon Bennett reported that the 22nd Indian Brigade at Kluang was engaged, and the 5th Sikhs had launched a successful counterattack. In a conference on 20 December 1941, Gordon Bennett had spoken contemptuously of the Indians. His attitude had changed due to the successful performance of the 5th/11th Sikhs at Niyor.[167] At south Niyor, the 5th Sikhs engaged two hundred Japanese cyclists and were able to inflict heavy casualties on them.[168] On the trunk road, the 2nd/30th AIF Battalion was slightly under pressure. In contrast, Heath as usual pointed out the danger of the road being cut behind the 15th Indian Brigade. He seems to have been influenced by Key's defeatism. Key and Heath argued that this brigade should be withdrawn from Pontian Keehil immediately. Percival, whose nerves had been frayed, topped the situation by noting that the whole force should withdraw to Singapore. A. Wavell, in his *Generals and Generalship*, has written about the essential quality of a good general: "He must have what we call the fighting spirit, the will to win." Percival definitely lacked this quality. Thirty-one January was fixed as the date on which the force would cross the causeway. After the conference ended, Key communicated to the 15th Indian Brigade the codeword "Nuts"—the signal for retreat. This brigade was ordered to reach Benut on 27 January. Brigadier Challen ordered the withdrawal to start at 2030 hours.[169] The 1st/14th Japanese Battalion was at Batu Pahat. At 2030 hours on 25 January, the 15th Indian Brigade, taking advantage of the darkness of the night, was able to disengage from the Japanese without much difficulty at Batu Pahat. And at 0500 hours, the 2nd Cambridgeshires had reached Senggarang.[170]

Major General Barstow visited the 5th/11th Sikhs on 26 January and the CO, Lieutenant Colonel Parkin, was informed that soon all the troops would be withdrawn to Singapore. The 9th Indian Division was to withdraw along the railway between Rengam and Kulai. The 27th AIF was to retire along Ayer-Johore Road. And the 11th Indian Division under "Billy" Key was to retreat along the main western coastal road from Batu Pahat. Since the withdrawal of the 11th Indian Division would expose the western flanks of the 9th Indian Division, the latter also had to retreat in synchronization with the former.[171]

The 53rd British Brigade was ordered to open the road from Rengit to Senggarang in the morning of 26 January. The column named BANCOL detailed to open the road consisted of a troop of Volunteer Armored Car Company under Second Lieutenant Archer, two carriers of the 5th/16th Punjabis, and two carriers of the 6th Norfolk. Key gave orders to Brigadier C. L. B. Duke, CO of the 53rd Brigade, that BANCOL would come under Brigadier Challen, CO of the 6th/15th Indian Brigade.[172] On 26 January from 0900 hours, the Japanese started sniping and opened mortar fire at Rengit. They had blocked the road with tree trunks and barrels. The infantry of BANCOL was mowed down in their lorries. Instead of remaining in the trucks, the infantry should have marched on either side of the road while approaching the roadblock. And when fired upon by the Japanese ambush party, the Allied infantry failed to disembark quickly from the lorries and then take cover in the surrounding vegetation and fight back. Major C. F. W. Banham evaded the carnage by escaping in a carrier driven by Naik Bakhtawar Singh of 3rd/16th Punjab.[173] Major Banham's ill-fated force was an unwieldy assortment and lacked cohesion. Moreover, most of the British officers were raw and lacked combat experience.[174] After reaching Senggarang, Banham, in a state of anxiety, informed the brigadier that the Japanese had cut the road and no wheeled vehicles would be able to get through to Rengit. He continued that Rengit itself was heavily attacked and he had heard that the Johore Causeway would be blown in two to three days.[175] Information received by a commander during battle represents only disparate, chaotic fragments of the reality. The commander's job is to filter and analyze it into a rough depiction of what appears to be happening.[176] However, the brigadier failed to analyze critically the information supplied to him by Major Banham. Both Banham and Challen agreed that a night march would be a sure recipe for disaster.[177] The British officers had no confidence in engaging the Japanese in nocturnal attacks. The establishment of a roadblock not only undermined morale of the partially trained Allied troops but also resulted in paralysis of command and control.[178] Challen reported that there were six roadblocks established by the Japanese between his position and Rengit. Each such roadblock was held by a Japanese company at the most. A brigade with artillery support could have easily brushed past them.[179] The failure to do so reflects the low morale of the brigade commander and the personnel under him.

Further, Japanese equipment like knee mortars and rifles were handy for combat in the wooded regions. The Japanese infantry was mainly armed with the Arisaka Model 38 rifle. Historian Eric Bergerud writes that this rifle was aptly suited for jungle warfare. It fired a .25-caliber bullet that was smaller than the .30- or the .303-caliber bullets of the Springfield and Lee Enfield Mark III rifles used by the Western armies. So Japanese rifle ammunition was lighter in comparison to the Western counterparts. The Japanese chemists had produced very good smokeless powder. The long barrel of the Arisaka rifle (the rifle was 50.25 inches in length without the bayonet and was 6 inches longer than the Springfield), and smaller round of the Model 38 with smokeless powder resulted in a small flash and almost no smoke. This was extremely advantageous to the Japanese in jungle combat. In the jungle, due to low visibility, a soldier rarely had a clear visual target. A puff of smoke in daylight or an inch of flame in the night coming from the barrel identified the location of the hostile rifleman. During a firefight, the Japanese infantrymen aimed at the smoke and flame generated due to firing by the Allied riflemen. As the soldiers held the stocks of the rifles against their chests, Japanese rifle rounds hit mostly their heads or upper portion of their bodies. In addition, the Arisaka had a mild recoil. So a Japanese soldier who was firing prone or supporting the rifle on some object (stone or ground) could easily get off a second round quickly. The Springfield of the Marines in contrast had a high recoil. Further, the .25-caliber bullet had an advantage. Firing a light round with a high velocity caused the round to wobble slightly in flight, a condition known as yaw in ballistics. This created a cracking sound and not a loud noise when the round passed overhead or struck nearby. Hence, it was very difficult to tell where the round came from. The crack-like sound seemed that it was the breaking of a twig or a branch. So the Allied soldiers had to fire blind.[180]

At 1400 hours on 26 January, Japanese mortars hit the Senggarang Bridge. The Japanese infantry guns fired indiscriminately and snipers fired from the thick vegetation around the road. Some snipers also climbed up the trees for a good lookout and to shoot at the Allied soldiers. The roadblock was held by one Japanese company.[181] At 1800 hours, the bridge over Senggarang was blown and the 6th Norfolk retreated. As night fell, Senggarang was brilliantly lit up by the numerous burning vehicles strewn across the road, and occasional explosions occurred as the ammunition lorries blew up.[182]

The British and Indian detachment at Rengit was waiting for the 15th Indian Brigade. At 1530 hours, after two hours of mortaring and sniping, the Japanese launched a heavy attack on the 6th Norfolk and the D Company of 3rd/16th Punjab at Rengit. The Japanese swarmed from the thick vegetation surrounding the village and concentrated toward the water tower in the south. To create confusion among the defenders, the Japanese resorted to wild firing and made liberal use of grenades and crackers. The Japanese attack continued till midnight. At that time, D Company of 3rd/16th Punjab was driven out, and the Japanese advanced from the flank. On that day, the 22nd AIF Brigade had retreated from Mersing without any untoward incident, and the WESTFORCE had reached Rengam. The 22nd AIF Brigade and the 2nd Gordon held the trunk road, and the 9th Indian Division was across the railway.[183]

Percival, without consulting Wavell, had already made the decision to retreat to Singapore Island on 25 January. Two days later, Wavell's decision tallied with that of Percival. Wavell's cable to Percival dated 27 January noted: "Primary objects are to gain time and cause maximum loss to the enemy. You must judge when withdrawal to island is necessary to avoid disorganization and unnecessary losses of men and material which may prejudice defense of the island, which you must be prepared to hold for many months."[184] Wavell was thinking of conducting a long-term attritional defense of Singapore. On 27 January, Brigadier Duke was given the discretion to destroy the bridge at Benut and was ordered to hold the village till the morning of next day. It was still hoped that the "lost" 15th Indian Brigade might come within this time. The much-depleted 53rd British Brigade (which included the weak 3rd/16th Punjab) was ordered to withdraw five miles north of Pontian Keehil. They were to occupy this position till 28 January and then retreat to the Boulder position.[185]

Even when defeat was looming large in the face of Percival's force, Gordon Bennett maintained his attitude. In his communication to F. M. Forde, the minister of the Australian Army, Bennett accused everybody except himself. He poured abuse on the British military leaders (especially Percival and Heath), their military system, and especially the Indian troops. He accused the 53rd British Brigade of low military efficiency and equated the performance of the 45th Indian Brigade with frightened "schoolgirls." This is unfair because at Muar, the 45th Indian Brigade fought as badly as the Australian and British troops. Bennett continued that things would have been right if he had been put in overall charge. In fact, he asked Forde to promote him so that he could confront Percival face to face and prevent further retreat. Bennett emphasized that the British only respect rank. So, with a higher rank in case he was promoted, his decision would carry more weight with Percival. Bennett concluded that, with two more Australian brigades, he would be able to contain the Japanese at Johore and with two Australian divisions would be able to throw the Japanese out of Malaya. This was Bennett's rhetoric at its best. Bennett concluded his letter in the tone of a popular general: "When I get depressed, I go amongst the Diggers. They always fill me with confidence... they are always cheery."[186]

While the 5th Japanese Division confronted the WESTFORCE, the Japanese Imperial Guards Division was advancing against the 11th Indian Division. The EASTFORCE under Brigadier H. B. Taylor held the line Jemaluang-Sedili Boom and Kota Tinggi. The WESTFORCE was around Rengam. The WESTFORCE was vulnerable to Japanese infiltration from south Pontian, Ayer Hitam, and north of Pulai because these regions were uncovered due to the hasty withdrawal of the 11th Indian Division. The 15th Indian Brigade, keeping in touch with the 53rd British Brigade, was withdrawing from Senggarang. On the night of 25/26 January, the EASTFORCE was opposed by only three hundred Japanese in the Mersing area. However, at 0700 hours on 26 January, a Japanese convoy was reported off Endau. It was assumed that two Japanese regiments were being landed in that area.[187] Aviation fuel and ammunition were landed at Endau, and the Imperial Guards Division blocked a minor Allied counterattack at Bahabat.[188]

On 27 January, a detailed plan was issued concerning the retreat of the Allied ground force. The 15th Indian Brigade of the 11th Indian Division was to start from Senggarang-Rengit in the night of 26/27 January and reach Benut next day. On 28/29 January, it was to reach Sebatang. The next day, it was to retreat to P. Kechil. On 30/31 January, this brigade was to reach KG Peng Raja, and on 31 January, it was to move to Singapore. The WESTFORCE was to start from Benut on the night of 26/27 January. On the night of 29/30 January, it was ordered to reach Sedenak. And on 31 January, it was to be withdrawn to Singapore. The EASTFORCE was to start from Jemaluang during the night of 26/27 January. It was to retreat through Lombong and Kota Tinggi. And on 31 January, it was to reach north of Ulu Tiram.[189] It remained to be seen if this plan could be disrupted by the Japanese advance units.

On 27 January, the 5th/11th Sikhs was south of Layang Layang. By 1300 hours, the Japanese started shelling the Layang Layang village with heavy artillery. By 1600 hours, the 8th Indian Brigade had withdrawn. The Japanese soldiers emerged from the surroundings like phantoms and attacked the B Company of 5th/11th Sikhs with mortars and infiltrated toward the headquarters.[190] Two things stand out: the reconnaissance and patrolling of the 5th/11th Sikhs were below standard, and Japanese capacity to advance under camouflage was remarkable.

Gradually stragglers of the 15th Indian Brigade came pouring in on 27 January. Several Indian commissioned officers displayed weak leadership. One example could be given. At noon, Lieutenant Zarif Khan with thirty-six men reached Benut. He had left Rengit when two of his platoons suffered heavy casualties and ran out of ammunition. Zarif Khan claimed that he had lost contact with his third platoon, which was under Jemadar Atta Muhammad Khan and was positioned across a marsh. Sometime later, Atta Muhammad arrived with twelve men of Zarif Khan's third platoon. Zarif Khan's decision not to wait for Atta Muhammad's platoon or to make any attempt to aid the latter was an example of a panicky and inefficient command decision. Atta Muhammad reported that the Japanese had occupied Rengit. At 1800 hours, one Mr. Wallace of the Malay Police who reached Benut reported that he had seen an exhausted party of 1,200 men of the 15th Indian Brigade some seven miles east of the road. Major General Key ordered Brigadier Duke to hold on to Benut until the stragglers from the 15th Indian Brigade arrived. Key also set up a stragglers' post at Skudai and sent fifty-four lorries to Benut to bring back the stragglers when they reached Benut.[191] Even at this stage of battle, when the Japanese were marching and advancing, the British and Indian soldiers required transport for evacuation. Ian Morrison's observation about the British soldiers could be applied to the Indian troops: "He had also been trained to be very dependent on his vehicular transport and this complicated, if it did not impede, movement. One used to see British troops seemingly immobilized by their own transport."[192] Around 2230 hours, further news came in that 1,500 men of the 15th Indian Brigade were at Ponggor on the coast not far from Rengit under Lieutenant Colonel Morrison, but Brigadier Challen was missing.[193]

The tired personnel of the 15th Indian Brigade had started their trek westward along the boggy south bank of Senggarang River at 1815 hours on 26 January. The brigade was organized in two columns. Lieutenant Colonel Prattley commanded the rearguard. Even without enemy pressure, the brigade was unable to retreat properly in the dark. It seems that the British and Indian soldiers had no training as regards marching in order in the dark. During midnight, the rearguard lost contact with the main body of the brigade. Prattley with his men was able to reach Benut in the early hours of 28 January. The rest of the brigade was only able to reach Benut in the afternoon of 28 January. During the retreat, the brigade had lost 30 percent of its rifles and 80 percent of its light automatics. Had the Japanese followed them up in the night, the retreat would have become a rout. Anyway, the demoralized brigade was taken to Skudai and then to Singapore.[194]

By the evening of 27 January, the Jat/Punjabi Battalion rejoined the 11th Indian Division after being attached to the 22nd AIF Brigade for fifteen days.

At Kahang, the strength of this battalion was raised to five hundred men due to reinforcements, including some from the 2nd Jats. Due to heavy casualties and lack of adequate reinforcements from particular ethnic groups, the different ethnic units of the Indian Army were amalgamated together as an emergency measure. This resulted in a sharp drop in combat motivation of the Indian troops. The influx of new entrants and mixing of the different ethnic communities in the Jat/Punjabi Battalion, due to the exigencies of combat, weakened the primary group solidarity of this unit. After all, the Indian units' combat motivation to a great extent depended on their ethnic solidarity, especially on their caste, clan ties, and mutual acquaintance. Colonel Charles J. J. J. Ardant du Picq noted that four brave men who do not know each other would not dare attack a lion. But four less brave men who know each other well, sure of their reliability and mutual aid, would attack resolutely.[195] Picq's observation applies all the more to the Indian units. Kahang had already been evacuated by the RAF personnel on 20 January.[196] The RAF personnel were several steps ahead of the Allied ground units in retreating. The 8th Indian Brigade withdrew through the 22nd Indian Brigade in Sedenak, while the Japanese shelled with mortars and 70 mm artillery.[197]

The Japanese patrols approached Benut in the night of 27/8 January. The 3rd/16th Punjabis supported by the 499th Field Battery blew up the bridge and withdrew. At 1300 hours, they passed through the 28th Indian Brigade and occupied the Boulder position with 3rd Cavalry. On their right flank was the B Company of 1st/14th Punjab.[198]

After getting Wavell's cable on 27 January, Percival officially informed him the next day that he intended to withdraw the troops to Singapore Island during the night of 30/31 January. Wavell at this stage feared the landing of fresh Japanese troops at Endau and approved Percival's decision.[199] In the morning of 28 January, the troops received orders that all of them would cross the Johore Causeway during the night of 30/31 January. The 11th Indian Division was made responsible for holding Skudai till the retreat of the WESTFORCE. After the safe withdrawal of the WESTFORCE, the 11th Indian Division would retreat through two bridgeheads. The outer bridgehead was to be held by 22nd AIF Brigade and 2nd Gordon, and the inner bridgehead was the responsibility of the 2nd Argylls and two marine companies. The 53rd British Brigade, which now comprised the much reduced 3rd/16th Punjab and the Jat/Punjabi Battalion, was ordered to retreat to Singapore during the night of 29/30 January. After receiving this order, Key ordered the 28th Indian Brigade to hold Pontian Keehil until the dusk of 29 January.[200]

On 28 January, Colonel J. R. Broadbent, quartermaster general of the 8th AIF, analyzed the reasons behind the collapse of the Australian troops in particular and the British and Indian soldiers in general. Bombing and machine-gunning of the Allied troops from the air reduced their morale to rubble. Again, the Allied units had too many vehicles. And the infantry had almost forgotten how to march. They were overdependent on the vehicles for transportation, and the latter were a liability in Malaya. Instead of transport vehicles, more riflemen were required. But most of the infantry reinforcements were not trained adequately to handle their arms properly. The men were unable to shoot quickly and straight. Even though gas equipment was withdrawn, still the infantry carried too much impedimenta, which caused fatigue in the hot and humid climate. Broadbent understood that the heavy Allied infantry needed to be transformed like the light Japanese infantry. The soldiers were fed with bully beef and biscuits, which turned sodden in the damp climate. Broadbent wanted small, light packets of raisins, chocolates, and rice as soldiers' rations. However, Broadbent's point that heavy rainfall in Malaya demoralized the Indians[201] is tinged with racial bias. The hot, humid, and damp conditions along with heavy rainfall also demoralized the Australians and the British.

On 28 January, the 22nd AIF Brigade withdrew from Kota Tinggi Road without any pursuit by the Japanese. But that was not the case with the WESTFORCE. The Japanese interposed themselves between the two brigades of the 9th Indian Division along the railway and had cut off the 22nd Indian Brigade, which was north of Layang Layang. Barstow, the divisional commander, went forward to ascertain what had happened to this brigade. On 28 January, Barstow was shot dead by a Japanese patrol, and the Japanese infiltrated between the 8th and 22nd Indian brigades. While the Japanese soldiers would creep and belly crawl through thick vegetation, the Indian soldiers had difficulties in retreating through the region filled with dense vegetation, and in this terrain the British officers lost control over their men.[202]

With the aid of artillery fire, the 2nd/2nd GR were able to escape the pursuing Japanese. Toward the closing stage of the campaign in the Malayan Peninsula, in the battalion level at least, some form of artillery-infantry cooperation was emerging. And this allowed the retreating battalions to escape the Japanese nets. The 2nd/2nd GR passed through the 5th/14th Punjabis at Pontian Keehil at 1845 hours. Meanwhile, the Japanese attempted an outflanking movement to cut off the Skudai Road in the rear of the 28th Indian Brigade. For once, the British and Indian troops were ready, and the Japanese were not successful in their venture. The 2nd/2nd GR's D Company under Lieutenant Smith held the Pumping Station from which the track to Skudai Road via the G. Pulai Reservoir took off. One platoon of Smith's and C Company of 5th/14th Punjab protected the northern flank of the brigade's withdrawal up to 1850 hours, and then Smith's party withdrew via the reservoir.[203]

After the loss of Rengit and Benut, the 6th Norfolk had ceased to be an operational battalion. The remnants of the 6th Norfolk moved across the mangrove swamps toward the sea on 28 January. They spent two to three days on the shore before the RN evacuated them. The 6th Norfolk was lucky that they were able to escape from Senggarang. The Japanese did not pursue them hotly, because they were busy in repairing the bridges and roads, and their large-scale movement was somewhat blocked by scores of disabled Allied guns and vehicles.[204]

Meanwhile, the Japanese continued their attempt to suborn the loyalty of the Indian troops, and their policy showed some success. By 15 January, the IIL and Fujiwara *Kikan*'s headquarters had moved to Kuala Lumpur where they remained till 12 February. As the Japanese forces advanced, the IIL opened branches at

Kuala Lumpur, Seremben, Malacca, Muar, and Johore. The IIL established contact with the influential Indians and took care of the interest of the Indians under Japanese occupation. Some two thousand Indian PoWs were collected at Kuala Lumpur and at Muar. From them, volunteers for INA were requested.[205] An Indian Medical Service Officer was captured by the Japanese south of Layang Layang on 28 January. He was released with a letter written in English for the Indian troops. The letter stated that the Japanese were friends of Indians and did not wish to fight them. The Indians were urged not to fire at the Japanese but to surrender with the promise that they would be well treated.[206] The call of the Japanese to the Indians to declare themselves against the British found more traction with the Sikhs than with the Gurkhas, and many of the former would join the Japanese-sponsored INA after the surrender at Singapore.

By 29 January, the Japanese Imperial Guards Division was in control of the road from Batu Pahat to Benut.[207] Early on this day, the 8th Indian Brigade retreated to Sendak. During the night, the brigade was ordered to withdraw to Singapore Island.[208] A small party of 4th/9th Jats was able to reach the west coast near the tip of Johore. Some personnel of the Malay Regiment were also present there. They were evacuated by boats. However, panic spread like an epidemic among the Allied troops. Mileham describes the scene: "Soldiers from the Malay Regiment were endeavouring to jump into the boats without orders."[209] This incident reflected the loss of control of the officers over their men.

Next day, Japanese aircraft were actively bombing and machine-gunning the Allied troops. In the Philippines too, the Japanese enjoyed aerial superiority, but the American troops, unlike the Indian soldiers, made full use of camouflage and cover.[210] At 0930 hours, seven Japanese bombers encountered a group of Buffalo fighters over Singapore city. A large Japanese bomber formation also bombed the convoy bringing reinforcements to Singapore.[211] The Japanese Army 97 (Nate) aircraft were more maneuverable than the Buffaloes. Due to the Buffaloes' slow rate of climb, these aircraft were unable to implement the "dive and zoom" tactics to escape the more maneuverable and faster Japanese aircraft. Not only the Japanese aircraft but the Japanese pilots were more skilled than the Allied pilots. The average flying experience of the JNAF and JAAF pilots who fought in Malaya and the Philippines during 1941 and 1942 was between five hundred and six hundred hours, and the squadron and flight commanders had much more flying experience. In contrast, the Allied pilots had ten to twenty hours flying experience at the OTUs. Further, 50 percent of the JAAF pilots had combat experience against the Chinese and the Soviets.[212] Wavell again flew to Singapore on this day with Air Marshal Richard Peirse, chief of air staff ABDACOM. Wavell met the governor, Percival, Pulford, Major General Simmons, and finally Heath and Gordon Bennett at Johore. Wavell ordered the withdrawal of the remaining fighters from Singapore to Sumatra. He rightly argued that events in Crete had shown that maintenance of a weak aerial force in close range of a stronger enemy resulted in the ultimate destruction of the former.[213] It is to be noted that on 13 January 1942, sixty-six Hurricanes had arrived at Singapore. But they were too few to win back air superiority from the Japanese aviation.[214] Moreover, the Hurricanes were slower than the Zeros below twenty thousand feet and were less maneuverable at all heights. Within two weeks, seventeen had been destroyed, nine were damaged, and only twenty-five were serviceable.[215]

On 30 January, the battalion commanders were officially notified that the troops would be evacuated to Singapore Island. The fact that the last fifty miles of the Malayan Peninsula would not be contested demoralized some of the British commanding officers. But the argument was given by the Malaya Command that the troops required some rest and reorganization. And it was further assumed, somewhat erroneously, that such a quick evacuation would surprise the Japanese.[216] Quick retreat at Kampar and Perak did not work to the advantage of the Allied troops. Rather, it encouraged the Japanese to advance far more quickly. If anything, such an evacuation without fighting strengthened Japanese morale and demoralized the defenders.

The Allied commanders were worried that their retreat would be seriously interfered with by the Japanese air force.[217] The threat posed by the Japanese ground forces cannot be ignored either. The 5th Japanese Division and the Imperial Guards Division arrived at Johore Channel on 30 January.[218] At 1330 hours, the 8th Indian Brigade discovered that the Australians had left their positions at Kulai village without informing them. As a result the left flank of the 8th Indian Brigade was in the air. In the near future at Singapore Island too, the Australian units would repeat this sort of unilateral withdrawal without informing the neighboring Indian units. As the 8th Indian Brigade left Kulai village, the Japanese cyclist troops, making a wide outflanking movement, attacked the 1st/13th FFR.[219] During the final withdrawal of the two brigades of WESTFORCE (8th Indian Brigade and 27th AIF Brigade) and the 11th Indian Division, the Japanese made no attempt to follow them closely.[220]

On 31 January 1942, the 2nd/10th Baluch reached the Singapore Island.[221] The A Company of 5th/11th Sikhs surrendered. Most of the others were either missing or casualties. The rest of the 5th/11th Sikhs (four British officers and thirty jawans) underwent a tactical innovation. They formed a square and retreated through the rubber plantations. The Japanese attacked the flanks but were unable to break in.[222] The stragglers finally managed to reach Singapore. At 0730 hours on 31 January 1942, the 2nd Argylls crossed the Johore Causeway with their pipes playing.

The Johore Causeway, which linked the Singapore Island with the mainland of Malaya, had been completed in 1924 and was 1,155 yards in length, averaged 16 yards in width during low tide, and carried a road, two rail lines, and big water pipes.[223] Initially, the Public Works Department (PWD) was charged with demolition. The PWD expressed its inability to execute the order. The causeway was constructed of pitched block masonry, and it was necessary to excavate to a lower depth for setting the demolition charges. The nature of masonry precluded the use of boring and power tools and required the use of manual labor. The demolitions were finally carried out by Lieutenant Colonel H. M. Taylor of the Royal Engineers. The lock gates at the northern end of the Johore Causeway were destroyed. A seventy-five-foot gap was blown after all the troops had crossed over. Further,

Table 5.1. Allied Casualties in Malaya until 31 January 1942

Units	Killed	Wounded	Missing or Prisoner	Total	Remarks
Indian Army					
Officers	28	29	60		
BORs	11	25	28		
VCOs, NCOs and Jawans	612	1,230	6,533		
Total				8,556	
Local Forces					
British	6	17	19		
Eurasian			111		
Asians	6	15	3,223		Most of the missing Asians went back to their homes
Total				3,397	
British Army					
Officers	13	27	73		
ORs	179	426	1,586		
Total				2,304	
Australian Imperial Force					
Officers	14	16	25		
ORs	159	313	656		
Total				1,183	
Malay Regiment					
British Officers					
Malay ORs	6	4	15	25	
Total	1,034	2,102	12,329	15,465	
Probable Additions			1,251	1,251	They belonged mostly to the 22nd Indian Brigade
Grand Total	1,034	2,102	13,580	16,715	

Source: Malaya, Army Casualties to 31 Jan. 1942, L/WS/1/952, OIOC, BL, London.

the Johore Causeway was also blocked with two hundred yards of wire entanglements sown with mines and booby traps on the Singapore side of the breach.[224]

The 22nd Indian Brigade, which had remained on the Malayan Peninsula, reached the Johore Causeway on 1 February. Finding the Causeway blown and Johore Bahru held by a Japanese division, Brigadier Painter and most of his depleted brigade surrendered.[225] The Battle for the Malayan Peninsula was over, and the Battle of Singapore was about to begin.

Table 5.1 shows the casualties suffered by the Allied forces from the beginning of the campaign until they retreated across the Johore. For the Indian troops in particular and all the Allied troops in general, a large number of missing or prisoners compared to the number killed or wounded show that the demoralized, nervous troops, when outflanked and surrounded, surrendered quite easily rather than carrying out last-ditch struggles. The Indian troops were demoralized due to continuous defeat and retreats, Japanese-IIL propaganda, and bad handling by the "green" British officers. The campaign in the Malay mainland cost the IJA a mere 4,565 casualties.[226]

Conclusion

> The Japanese tactics are leading to a savage warfare of movement, ambush, surprise, and encirclement. United States War Department 1942[227]

Gordon Bennett's assertion of 19 December 1941: "Of one thing you may be sure, the AIF will stand firm and will not retreat one yard, no matter what the opposition,"[228] proved to be hollow. Combat performance of the Australian, British, and Indian troops (especially the 53rd British Brigade and 45th Indian Brigade) was below average, as they failed to adapt to jungle conditions and adopt the necessary countermeasures. Many junior and midlevel British officers fell prey to Japanese ambushes. The loss of these officers hampered the British command over the Indian troops. The Allied commanders could only think of conducting battle with fixed lines and clear front and rear. The Australian, British, and Indian soldiers were capable of conducting set-piece positional defensive battles but were completely lost in chaotic mobile battles. The Japanese combat techniques were simple to conceive but difficult to execute in the jungle terrain. The techniques involved fixing the Allied troops frontally and simultaneously to either encircle their defensive position or undertake an envelopment operation designed to occupy a section of the Allied troops' LoC. Implementing such techniques in the difficult jungle terrain required highly skilled troops and a decentralized command culture. The Allied troops failed to respond effectively to the Japanese tactics of establishing roadblocks and ambushes along their LoCs. And the Japanese infantry arms like light mortars, grenades, semiautomatics, and Arisaka rifles were especially well suited for the close-quarter jungle combat that unfolded in the Malayan Peninsula. However, the Japanese penchant for bayonets did prove to be useless. Bayonets did not prove to be an effective weapon in jungle combat either in Malaya or in the South Pacific.[229]

In general, the raw Indian troops failed to adapt to jungle conditions of warfare, but toward the end of the campaign, they adopted the defensive box formation/square formation and implemented perimeter defense during the night against Japanese infiltration techniques with some success. And in the final stage of withdrawal across the Johore, infantry-artillery cooperation at the battalion level achieved some success. Partial adoption of these combat techniques enabled the retreating battalions to escape the Japanese encircling moves and continue further withdrawals. However, the 45th Indian Brigade, already defeated at the Muar Battle, was almost annihilated during the retreat. Further, two Indian brigades (15th and 22nd) were worsted during the retreat to Johore Causeway. Extensive demolitions carried out by the retreating Allied ground forces failed to delay the Japanese for long. But some credit is due to the Allied generals for extricating their forces successfully from southern Johore to Singapore. However, the operational-strategic scenario was horrendous. By the end of January 1942, Percival's plan of holding a defensive line in Johore and bouncing back with a counterattack was completely shattered. There could be no question of launching a counterattack against the Japanese. Rather, the question is whether the Allied troops could hold out on Singapore Island itself. The next chapter will address this issue.

Notes

1. Clifford Kinvig, *Scapegoat: General Percival of Singapore* (London: Brassey's, 1996), 186.
2. Notes on Conference held by GOC Malaya at Segamat 5 January 1942, Percival Papers, IWM, London.
3. Appreciation and Plan, GOC Malaya, January 7, 1942, Percival Papers; LieutenantGeneral A. E. Percival, *The War in Malaya* (1949; repr., Calcutta: Orient Longmans, 1957), 189.
4. Appreciation and Plan, GOC Malaya, January 7, 1942, Percival Papers; Frank Owen, *The Fall of Singapore* (1960; repr., London: Penguin, 2001), 109; Percival, *War in Malaya*, 191.
5. Appreciation and Plan, GOC Malaya, January 7, 1942, Comments by Lieutenant General Percival on the Official Historians' Comments on the Fighting in Johore, Chapters 19 to 20, November 30, 1953, Percival Papers, 1.
6. General Archibald Wavell, Despatch on Operations in South-West Pacific 15 Jan.–25 Feb. 1942, Appendix A, CAB 106/38, PRO, Kew, London, 1.
7. Jeffrey Grey, *A Military History of Australia* (Cambridge: Cambridge University Press, 1990), 167.
8. Ronald Lewin, *The Chief: Field Marshal Lord Wavell, Commander-in-Chief and Viceroy, 1939–1947* (London: Hutchinson, 1980), 21.
9. Wavell, Despatch on Operations in South-West Pacific, 1.
10. Wavell, Despatch on Operations in South-West Pacific, 2; Kinvig, *Scapegoat*, 178.
11. Lewin, *The Chief*, 162.
12. Agnes McEwan and Campbell Thomson, *Death Was Our Bedmate: 155th (Lanarkshire Yeomanry) Field Regiment and the Japanese 1941–1945* (Barnsley: Pen & Sword, 2013), 41.
13. Kinvig, *Scapegoat*, 179.
14. Robert Lyman, *The Generals: From Defeat to Victory, Leadership in Asia 1941–45* (London: Constable, 2008), 60–61; Kinvig, *Scapegoat*, 176.
15. Kinvig, *Scapegoat*, 179; Wavell, Despatch on Operations in South-West Pacific, 2–3; Comments by Lieutenant General A. E. Percival on Remarks by the Panel on his Comments on Chapters 19 and 20, January 3, 1954, Percival Papers, 2.
16. Eric Bergerud, *Touched with Fire: The Land War in the South Pacific* (1996; repr., New York: Penguin, 1997), 237–39.
17. Percival, December 14, 1945, Comments by Percival on Remarks by the Panel on Chapters 19 and 20, 2.

18. Wavell, Despatch on Operations in South-West Pacific, 3. For Wavell's concept of generalship, see General Archibald Wavell, *Generals and Generalship* (London: Penguin, 1941), 23.

19. Percival, *War in Malaya*, 188; Wavell, Despatch on Operations in South-West Pacific, 1.

20. Operations in the Far East, L/WS/1/952, OIOC, BL, London, 3.

21. A. B. Lodge, *The Fall of General Gordon Bennett* (Sydney: Allen & Unwin, 1986), 74–75.

22. Owen, *Fall of Singapore*, 111.

23. Lecture on the Malayan Campaign by General Heath, June 21, 1942, Percival Papers, 16; Carl Bridge, "Crisis of Command: Major-General Gordon Bennett and British Military Effectiveness in the Malayan Campaign, 1941–42," in *British and Japanese Military Leadership in the Far Eastern War, 1941–1945*, ed. Brian Bond and Kyoichi Tachikawa (London: Frank Cass, 2004), 70.

24. McEwan and Thomson, *Death Was Our Bedmate*, 42.

25. War Diary of 9th Indian Division, Operation Instruction No. 23, Appendix 11, MODHS, New Delhi.

26. War Diary of 9th Indian Division, Memorandum by CO 9th Division, January 5, 1942.

27. War Diary of 9th Indian Division, Appendix 20, Record of Conversation between GOC 9th Division and BGS 3rd Corps, January 8, 1942, Appendix 22.

28. Lieutenant Colonel J. Frith, History of the 2/10 Baluch in the Malayan Campaign, 1973-06-121, NAM, London, 20; Kinvig, *Scapegoat*, 179–80.

29. Frith, History of the 2/10 Baluch, 20–21.

30. Andrew Gilchrist, *Malaya 1941: The Fall of a Fighting Empire* (London: Robert Hale, 1992), 23.

31. War Diary of 9th Indian Division, 12 January 1942.

32. Captain S. Hannam, 2nd/26th Battalion, 1–2, P 470, IWM. The quotation is from page 2.

33. *History of the Southern Army*, Japanese Monograph No. 24, 15.

34. War Diary of 9th Indian Division, Appendix 24.

35. Wavell, Despatch on Operations in South-West Pacific, 5; Lewin, *The Chief*, 162.

36. Frith, History of the 2/10 Baluch, 22; War Cabinet, The Malayan Campaign, April 4, 1942, WP(42)145, CAB/66/23/25, PRO, Kew, London, 2; Francis Pike, *Hirohito's War: The Pacific War, 1941–1945* (London: Bloomsbury, 2015), 236–37.

37. Lecture on the Malayan Campaign by Heath, June 21, 1942, Percival Papers, 17.

38. Bergerud, *Touched with Fire*, 243.

39. War Diary GS Branch Headquarters 9th Indian Division, January 15, 1942, 601/229/WD/Part 2, MODHS, New Delhi.

40. Lyman, *The Generals*, 43.

41. Frith, History of the 2/10 Baluch, 22–23.

42. Wavell, Despatch on Operations in South-West Pacific, 16.

43. Matome Ugaki, *Fading Victory: The Diary of Admiral Matome Ugaki 1941–1945*, foreword by Gordon W. Prange, trans. Masataka Chihaya, with Donald M. Goldstein and Katherine V. Dillon (1991; repr., Annapolis, MD: Naval Institute Press, 2008), 71.

44. Notes by Lieutenant-General A. E. Percival on the Brief Outline Narrative of the Mainland Operations in Malaya 8 Dec. 1941 to 31 Jan. 1942 prepared by the Combined Inter-Services Historical Section (India), June 1947, Percival Papers, 5.

45. Lodge, *Fall of General Gordon Bennett*, 77; Carl Bridge, "Crisis of Command: Major-General Gordon Bennett and British Military Effectiveness in the Malayan Campaign, 1941–42," in *British and Japanese Military Leadership,* ed. Bond and Tachikawa, 71.

46. War Diary of 9th Indian Division, Special Instructions to CO 22nd Brigade, January 13, 1942.

47. Account of the Malayan Campaign by Captain F. E. Mileham 4/9th Jat Regiment, D1196/33, OIOC, BL, London; Comments by Percival on the Official Historians' Comments on the Fighting in Johore, Chapters 19 and 20, November 30, 1953, Percival Papers, 1.

48. Pike, *Hirohito's War*, 237.

49. Major S. A. Watt, 7th Rajputana Rifles in Malaya, 1977-09-62, NAM, London, 1.

50. Quoted from Watt, 7th Rajputana Rifles in Malaya, 1.

51. Watt, 7th Rajputana Rifles in Malaya, 1–2.

52. Watt, 7th Rajputana Rifles in Malaya, 2.

53. Williamson Murray, *Military Adaptation in War: With Fear of Change* (Cambridge: Cambridge University Press, 2011), 125.

54. Major General B. W. Key, 11th Indian Division, P 456, IWM Archives, London, 15.

55. Watt, 7th Rajputana Rifles in Malaya, 3–4.

56. Account of the Malayan Campaign by Mileham 4/9th Jat Regiment, The Voyage, Singapore.

57. Account of the Malaya Campaign by Mileham 4/9th Jat Regiment, Road to Malacca.

58. Account of the Malaya Campaign by Mileham 4/9th Jat Regiment, Road to Malacca, Segamat.

59. Account of the Malaya Campaign by Mileham 4/9th Jat Regiment, The Road to Muar.

60. Quoted from Account of the Malaya Campaign by Mileham 4/9th Jat Regiment, The Muar River.

61. Watt, 7th Rajputana Rifles in Malaya, 4; Comments by Percival on the Official Historians' Comments, 2.

62. Watt, 7th Rajputana Rifles in Malaya, 5.

63. T. R. Moreman, *The Jungle, the Japanese and the British Commonwealth Armies at War, 1941–45: Fighting Methods, Doctrine and Training for Jungle Warfare* (London: Frank Cass, 2005), 15.

64. Military Intelligence Service, *Soldier's Guide to the Japanese Army* (Washington, DC: Military Intelligence Service, War Department, 1944), 150–51.

65. Moreman, *The Jungle*, 27–28.

66. Watt, 7th Rajputana Rifles in Malaya, 6.

67. Williamson Murray, *War, Strategy, and Military Effectiveness* (Cambridge: Cambridge University Press, 2011), 89.

68. The Malayan Campaign, Answers to Admiralty Questions, Percival Papers; Major R. Hammond, Appendix 1, 88/34/1, IWM, London; McEwan and Thomson, *Death Was Our Bedmate*, 42.

69. Watt, 7th Rajputana Rifles in Malaya, 7.

70. Moreman, *The Jungle*, 15.

71. Watt, 7th Rajputana Rifles in Malaya, 8.

72. G. W. Seabridge, Report on the Fall of Singapore, April 25, 1942, WP(42)177, CAB/66/24/7, PRO, Kew, Surrey, 3.

73. Bergerud, *Touched with Fire*, 303–4.
74. Account of the Malaya Campaign by Mileham 4/9th Jat Regiment, The Muar River.
75. Watt, 7th Rajputana Rifles in Malaya, 8.
76. The Malayan Campaign, Answers to Admiralty Questions, Percival Papers; Hammond, Appendix 1.
77. Military Intelligence Division, *Notes on Japanese Warfare on the Malayan Front*, Information Bulletin No. 6 (Washington, DC: War Department, 1942), 9.
78. Watt, 7th Rajputana Rifles in Malaya, 9; Moreman, *The Jungle*, 38–39.
79. Murray, *War, Strategy*, 3–4, 8.
80. Patrick Rose, "Indian Army Command Culture and the North West Frontier, 1919-1939," in *The Indian Army, 1939-47: Experience and Development*, ed. Alan Jeffreys and Patrick Rose (Surrey: Ashgate, 2012), 32.
81. Watt, 7th Rajputana Rifles in Malaya, 9.
82. Chris Mann, "The Battle of WadiAkarit, 6 April 1943: 4th Indian Division and its Place in 8th Army," in *The Indian Army*, ed. Jeffreys and Rose, 108.
83. Ian Morrison, *Malayan Postscript* (London: Faber and Faber, 1942), 82.
84. Murray, *Military Adaptation in War*, 13.
85. Watt, 7th Rajputana Rifles in Malaya, 10.
86. Morrison, *Malayan Postscript*, 78.
87. Account of the Malaya Campaign by Mileham 4/9th Jat Regiment, The Muar River.
88. Watt, 7th Rajputana Rifles in Malaya, 11.
89. Pike, *Hirohito's War*, 237.
90. Hammond, Appendix 1.
91. Official History of the Second World War, Percival Papers, P 22, F 47, 521.
92. Hammond, Appendix 1.
93. Account of the Malaya Campaign by Mileham 4/9th Jat Regiment, The Muar River.
94. Watt, 7th Rajputana Rifles in Malaya, 11.
95. Account of the Malaya Campaign by Mileham 4/9th Jat Regiment, The Muar River.
96. Quoted from Account of the Malaya Campaign by Mileham 4/9th Jat Regiment, The Muar River.
97. Account of the Malaya Campaign by Mileham 4/9th Jat Regiment, The Muar River.
98. Hammond, Appendix 1.
99. Hammond, 242.
100. War Diary of 9th Indian Division, January 18, Appendix 36.
101. The Malayan Campaign, Answers to Admiralty Questions, Percival Papers.
102. Watt, 7th Rajputana Rifles in Malaya, 12.
103. War Diary GS Branch Headquarters 9th Indian Division, January 18, 1942; War Diary of 9th Indian Division, January 19, 1942.
104. Hammond, 242.
105. Quoted from Hammond, 243.
106. Moreman, *The Jungle*, 14.
107. Hammond, 243–44.
108. Hammond, 244–45.
109. Hammond, The Yong Peng Battle, January 16–23, 1942, 245–46.
110. Account of the Malaya Campaign by Mileham 4/9thJat Regiment, The Muar River.
111. Watt, 7th Rajputana Rifles in Malaya, 13–16.
112. Military Intelligence Division, *Notes on Japanese Warfare on the Malayan Front*, 8.

113. War Diary of 9th Indian Division, January 21, Appendix 39.
114. Notes by Percival on the Brief Outline Narrative, 5.
115. Frith, History of the 2/10 Baluch, 25.
116. Hammond, 246–47.
117. Frith, History of the 2/10 Baluch, 26; War Diary GS Branch Headquarters 9th Indian Division, January 22, 1942.
118. Frith, History of the 2/10 Baluch, 27–28.
119. Morrison, *Malayan Postscript*, 80–81.
120. Bergerud, *Touched with Fire*, 284.
121. Frith, History of the 2/10 Baluch, 26.
122. War Diary GS Branch Headquarters 9th Indian Division, Klunag Area, January 23, 1942.
123. Frith, History of the 2/10 Baluch, 27.
124. Hammond, 248.
125. Quoted from Hammond, 249.
126. John McEwan, *Out of the Depths of Hell: A Soldier's Story of Life and Death in Japanese Hands* (1999; repr., Barnsley: Pen & Sword, 2014), 34.
127. Hammond, 250.
128. Quoted from Hammond, 251.
129. War Diary of 9th Indian Division, January 23, Appendix 42.
130. Account of the Malaya Campaign by Mileham 4/9th Jat Regiment, The Muar River.
131. Hammond, 251.
132. Hammond, The Yong Peng Battle, January 16–23, 1942.
133. Colonel J. R. Broadbent to Major-General Rowell, January 28, 1942, Gordon Bennett Papers, PR 90/111, AWM, Canberra, 2.
134. Account of the Malaya Campaign by Mileham 4/9th Jat Regiment, The Muar River.
135. Notes by Percival on the Brief Outline Narrative, 5–6.
136. Major General Gurbakhsh Singh, *Indelible Reminiscences: Memoirs of Major-General Gurbakhsh Singh* (New Delhi: Lancer, 2013), 50.
137. Comments by Percival on the Official Historians' Comments, 2.
138. Brian P. Farrell, *The Defence and Fall of Singapore: 1940–1942* (2005; repr., Stroud, UK: Tempus, 2006), 263.
139. Interview with Percival, No. 20, November 23, 1942, Percival Papers.
140. Mark Johnston, *At the Frontline: Experiences of Australian Soldiers in World War II* (Melbourne: Cambridge University Press, 1996), 29–30.
141. Wavell, Despatch on Operations in South-West Pacific, 17.
142. Notes by Lieutenant General A. E. Percival on certain Senior Commanders and other matters, January 8, 1954, Percival Papers, 4.
143. Wavell, Despatch on Operations in South-West Pacific, 10.
144. Kinvig, *Scapegoat*, 188.
145. Official History of the Second World War, Percival Papers, 520.
146. Col. A. M. L. Harrison, History of the 11th Indian Infantry Division in Malaya, 1941–42, CAB 106/57, PRO, 421; Wavell, Despatch on Operations in South-West Pacific, 8.
147. Kinvig, *Scapegoat*, 183.
148. Wavell, Despatch on Operations in South-West Pacific, Appendix A, 13.
149. Harrison, History of the 11th Indian Division, 422–23.
150. Hammond, The West Coast Battle, January 16–28, 1942.
151. Harrison, History of the 11th Indian Division, 424.
152. Harrison, History of the 11th Indian Division, 425.

153. Remarks on Notes submitted by Lieutenant General A. E. Percival, Percival Papers, 1.
154. Harrison, History of the 11th Indian Division, 426–29.
155. Bergerud, *Touched with Fire*, 379–80.
156. Harrison, History of the 11th Indian Division, 429.
157. Frith, History of the 2/10 Baluch, 27.
158. War Diary GS Branch Headquarters 9th Indian Division, January 24, 1942.
159. Hammond, The Yong Peng Battle, January 16–23, 1942.
160. Grey, *Military History of Australia*, 169.
161. Notes by Percival on certain Senior Commanders 2.
162. Frith, History of the 2/10 Baluch, 27–28.
163. Hammond, The West Coast Battle, 252.
164. Harrison, History of the 11th Indian Division, 430; Hammond, The West Coast Battle, 253.
165. Harrison, History of the 11th Indian Division, 433.
166. Harrison, History of the 11th Indian Division, 434.
167. Major-General Prem K. Khanna and Pushpindar Singh Chopra, *Portrait of Courage: Century of the 5th Battalion, The Sikh Regiment* (New Delhi: Military Studies Convention, 2001), 175.
168. War Diary GS Branch Headquarters 9th Indian Division, January 25, 1942.
169. Harrison, History of the 11th Indian Division, 434–35. For Wavell's quotation see Wavell, *Generals and Generalship*, 23.
170. Harrison, History of the 11th Indian Division, 440; McEwan and Thomson, *Death Was Our Bedmate*, 42.
171. Khanna and Chopra, *Portrait of Courage*, 175.
172. Harrison, History of the 11th Indian Division, 436–37; Hammond, The West Coast Battle, 254.
173. Harrison, History of the 11th Indian Division, 438–40.
174. Hammond, The West Coast Battle, 259.
175. Harrison, History of the 11th Indian Division, 445.
176. Murray, *War, Strategy*, 4.
177. Harrison, History of the 11th Indian Division, 446.
178. Moreman, *The Jungle*, 27.
179. Comments by Percival on Remarks by the Panel, 2.
180. Bergerud, *Touched with Fire*, 283–88.
181. Harrison, History of the 11th Indian Division, 444; Morrison, *Malayan Postscript*, 81.
182. Hammond, The West Coast Battle, 257.
183. Harrison, History of the 11th Indian Division, 448–51.
184. Wavell, Despatch on Operations in South-West Pacific, Appendix B.
185. Harrison, History of the 11th Indian Division, 451.
186. Gordon Bennett to F. M. Forde, January 27, 1942, AIF Malaya, AA 1974/398, AWM.
187. War Diary of 9th Indian Division, WESTFORCE Operation, Instruction No. 4, January 27, 1942.
188. *History of the Southern Army*, 15.
189. War Diary of 9th Indian Division, WESTFORCE Operation, Instruction No. 4, January 27, 1942.
190. Khanna and Chopra, *Portrait of Courage*, 176.
191. Harrison, History of the 11th Indian Division, 452–53.
192. Morrison, *Malayan Postscript*, 82.

193. Harrison, History of the 11th Indian Division, 453.
194. Harrison, History of the 11th Indian Division, 454–55.
195. Taken from John A. English, *On Infantry* (1981; repr., New York: Praeger, 1984), 182.
196. Harrison, History of the 11th Indian Division, 462.
197. War Diary GS Branch Headquarters 9th Indian Division, January 27, 1942.
198. Harrison, History of the 11th Indian Division, 462–63.
199. Wavell, Despatch on Operations in South-West Pacific, Appendix C, 13.
200. Harrison, History of the 11th Indian Division, 463–64.
201. Broadbent to Rowell, January 28, 1942, Gordon Bennett Papers, PR 90/111.
202. Frith, History of the 2/10 Baluch, 29; Harrison, History of the 11th Indian Division, 464.
203. Harrison, History of the 11th Indian Division, 465–66.
204. Hammond, The West Coast Battle, 257–58.
205. T. R. Sareen, ed., *Select Documents on Indian National Army* (Delhi: Agam Prakashan, 1988), 20.
206. Khanna and Chopra, *Portrait of Courage*, 181.
207. Hammond, The West Coast Battle, January 16–28, 1942.
208. Frith, History of the 2/10 Baluch, 30.
209. Account of the Malaya Campaign by Mileham 4/9th Jat Regiment, The Muar River.
210. Colonel Milton A. Hill, "Lessons of Bataan," in *How the Jap Army Fights*, ed. Lieutenant Colonel Paul W. Thompson, Lieutenant Colonel Harold Doud, and Lieutenant John Scofield (1942; repr., New York: Penguin, 1943), 90.
211. Lieutenant D. J. Glanfield, 118th Royal Artillery Field Regiment, 90/15/1, IWM, 13.
212. Peter Preston-Hough, *Commanding Far Eastern Skies: A Critical Analysis of the Royal Air Force Air Superiority Campaign in India, Burma and Malaya 1941–1945* (Solihull: Helion, 2015), 111, 129.
213. Wavell, Despatch on Operations in South-West Pacific, 10–11.
214. Michael Dockrill, "British Leadership in Air Operations: Malaya and Burma," in *British and Japanese Military Leadership,* ed. Bond and Tachikawa, 124.
215. Preston-Hough, *Commanding Far Eastern Skies*, 115; Kinvig, *Scapegoat*, 188–89.
216. Frith, History of the 2/10 Baluch, 30–31.
217. War Diary of 9th Indian Division, January 30, 1942, Appendix 46 (B).
218. *History of the Southern Army*, 15.
219. Frith, History of the 2/10 Baluch, 31.
220. Harrison, History of the 11th Indian Division, 468.
221. Frith, History of the 2/10 Baluch, 31.
222. Khanna and Chopra, *Portrait of Courage*, 182–84.
223. Morrison, *Malayan Postscript*, 25.
224. Destruction of the Singapore Causeway, Percival Papers.
225. Harrison, History of the 11th Indian Division, 469.
226. Lyman, *The Generals*, 33.
227. Military Intelligence Division, *Notes on Japanese Warfare on the Malayan Front*, 9.
228. Gordon Bennett to Forde, December 19, 1941, AIF Malaya, AA1974/398, AWM.
229. Bergerud, *Touched with Fire*, 290–91.

6 | Endgame on Singapore Island

This chapter analyzes the collapse of Allied defense and the subsequent surrender of the Australian, British, and Indian troops at Singapore Island. The first section analyzes the state of defensive forces in Singapore, and the next section deals with the Japanese attack on the island. The third section portrays the final surrender of the Allied forces. The factors behind the rapid collapse of Singapore's defense against the Japanese invasion are analyzed. Special attention is given to the state of discipline of the Indian troops, their arms and equipment, and their command and control arrangements, along with the deficiencies of their defensive postures. While discussing combat, this chapter pays due attention to the sphere of minor tactics. Due to the importance of the INA in post–Second World War South Asian historiography, the last section focuses on the evolution and impact of the Japanese-sponsored Indian liberation force.

Singapore Island was linked to the Malayan mainland by a causeway. In the south, the Strait of Malacca separates the island from the Dutch East Indies (now Indonesia). The Johore Strait northeast of Singapore was up to five thousand yards across, but west of the causeway the water body was only between eight hundred and two thousand yards wide.[1] Singapore Island at its maximum is thirteen miles from north to south and twenty-seven miles from east to west. In total, the island covers 220 square miles. On the southern coast of the island, Singapore town stretched for six miles along the waterfront.[2] While the naval base was at the northeast, the great cantonment of Changi, which was a complex of barracks and defense sites, was in the east.[3] Most of the island was flat and covered with rubber plantations. There were occasional patches of secondary and primary jungle. At the center of the island was the highest point, known as the Bukit Timah (Silver Mountain). This mountain is only 581 feet high.[4] Communication within the island was good. There were several metalled and unmetalled estate roads. The main highway was the Bukit Timah Road, which ran northwest out of the city through Bukit Timah village and then turned north to join up with the causeway. It then became the main trunk road that ran through Malaya to Thailand and Burma. The main railway line crossed the Johore Causeway and went to the port and city of Singapore.[5] By early February 1942, Singapore was showing symptoms of "war fever." It became increasingly difficult to get regular meals at Raffles Hotel or at Adelphi. Cyrano's restaurant was forced to shut down.[6]

Defensive Forces in Singapore

> I was concerned to find that no defenses had been made or even planned in detail on the north side of Singapore Island, although it was obvious by now that we might be driven back into the Island and have to defend it.
>
> General Archibald Wavell, 9 January 1942[7]

The coast defense armament comprised guns varying from 15-inch to 6-inch caliber. There were twenty-nine such guns, which were distributed in batteries of two to three guns over a frontage of over thirty miles, from Pengerang on the eastern side of the channel of entry to the naval base, to the western end of Singapore Island.[8] The island had forty heavy 3.7-inch AA guns that were capable of firing at targets over twenty thousand feet.[9] The 6-inch battery at Pasir Laba was sited to protect the west channel from the seaward side.[10] These guns had limited traverse and were mostly ineffective against land targets, as they fired armor-piercing shells.[11]

Percival had about eighty thousand troops, but many among them were in the ancillary services. These troops were bolstered by six RA field regiments and two A/T regiments. The ammunition situation was not very rosy. The stock of twenty-five-pounder guns' ammunition was limited.[12] Percival noted: "Not only were there no reserves of weapons. There were far from enough to equip units to field service scales. Many units, for instance, did not have more than 50 per cent of their establishment of light automatics. Some had far less."[13] Further, extreme shortage of telephone wire due to loss in the mainland was a problem in establishing a communication net with the various units.[14] On 1 February 1942, the 100th Light Tank Squadron arrived under Major Alford. This squadron had obsolete tanks, and the men were semitrained.[15] Yamashita had more tanks than Percival's force.[16] Since the Japanese enjoyed aerial and naval superiority and they could possibly land anywhere along the coast of Singapore Island, Percival was forced to guard all along the coastline.

The island had a coastal perimeter of seventy miles, which actually increased further due to frequent salients caused by numerous creeks.[17] Let us analyze the state of the different Commonwealth formations (Indian units in particular and non-Indian units in general) deployed for defense of Singapore Island and the nature of defense prepared by them. The 18th British Division was positioned on the right, the 11th Indian Division was at the center, and the 8th AIF was at the left. The Australians were at the north and west side of the island. The 8th AIF Division with two brigades (22nd and 27th) was in charge of the area between Jurong River and the causeway. It had the 44th Indian Brigade under its command. The 18th British Division was in charge of the Seletar to Changi. The 11th Indian Division was in charge of the naval base and the Seletar aerodrome. The 11th Indian Division had under its command the 15th and 28th Indian brigades. During the campaign in the Malayan Peninsula, the 9th Indian Division had lost one of its brigades. The 9th Indian Division, due to the heavy losses suffered in the Malayan mainland, was amalgamated with the 11th Indian Division. On 1 February 1942, the 11th Indian Division received the 8th Indian Brigade from the 9th Indian Division, which was broken up. Then, in the first week of February 1942, the 15th Indian Brigade became part of Malaya Command Reserve. The Singapore town and the docks were under the Southern Area.[18]

As early as 20 January 1942, Wavell had told Percival that the 18th British Division (which the former considered as the most combat effective) should be placed along the northwest coast of the island. For Wavell, the Japanese attack from the mainland would be focused on that part of Singapore Island.[19] Why Wavell considered the 18th British Division as more combat effective than the Australian division or the Indian units is a mystery. Probably, Wavell's reasoning was the product of British prejudice. Gordon Bennett and Percival considered the 18th British Division as poor.[20] In fact, most of the soldiers of this British division had no training, and their morale was below average. Many of them would surrender to the Japanese even without firing a single shot. When the young and novice troops of the 18th British Division landed at Singapore, the veteran British soldiers who had fought the Japanese in the Malayan mainland and escaped to Singapore felt sorry for them.[21] Percival himself believed that the principal Japanese attack would come at the northeast of the island, while Paris assumed that the principal Japanese attack would be on the west coast of the island. As Carl von Clausewitz says, in war most things are uncertain, and calculations have to be made with variable quantities.[22] In this case, Paris and Wavell's reasoning proved closer to the mark as the Japanese attacked northwest part of Singapore.[23] Percival attempted a postwar justification about his disposition in the following words: "I put the Australians in the North West chiefly because I thought it was the most vulnerable area and that as the Australians had had experience of fighting on the main land and training in bush warfare, it would be better to put them there than the newly arrived 18th Division. . . . To give them a little time to get acclimatized."[24] The Japanese landed at the northwest area of the island, since the strait was narrowest on this part (only six hundred meters) and also because this part of the island was covered with salt water mangrove swamps, criss-crossed with rivers and creeks—the terrain that suited Japanese light infantry's infiltration tactics.[25]

The 18th British Division with three brigades (53rd, 54th, and 55th) under Major General M. B. Beckwith-Smith, was in charge of the region from Fairy Point to south Seletar, a frontage of nineteen thousand yards. This division suffered from a shortage of weapons (especially A/T guns) because most of their equipment, which had been carried by the *Empress of Asia*, had been sunk by the Japanese. Eastward of the dockyard lay the 53rd Brigade, which on its left had the 2nd/2nd GR of the 28th Indian Brigade.[26] The 54th British Brigade under Brigadier Beckhouse, with the 4th and 5th Suffolks and 4th Northfolk, covered the point from Fairy Point to Punggol. The 55th British Brigade under Brigadier Messey-Beresford, with the 1st Cambridgeshires, 5th Bedfordshires, and Hertfordshires, plus 1st/5th Sherwood Foresters, covered the area between Punggol and south Seletar. This division had the 9th Northumberland Fusiliers (a machine gun battalion), 118th and 148th Field regiments, plus the 122nd A/T Regiment.[27]

The Northumberland Fusiliers had in total thirty-six officers and 795 other ranks. During the sea voyage, the limited deck space on the ship that had transported them was used in every way to carry out training of the companies. The troops also heard lectures by the training officers. However, the value of such training on board is questionable. This battalion held the region between Seletar, Punggol Point, and Tampinis River.[28] Lieutenant Colonel H. S. Flower of the 9th Battalion Royal Northumberland Fusiliers noted: "Tactically the whole of the island, except the built up areas in the south, was covered with vegetation, either rubber plantations or thick mangrove swamps along the coast. Defense works along the Johore Strait hardly existed, no clearing of the undergrowth for fields of fire or coordinated systems of digging and wiring had been carried out."[29] On 7 February, the X Company headquarters was in Serangoon village, and the Y Company headquarters was in the control room of the Seletar airport. On 8 February, the W Company was deployed south of Seletar aerodrome. Lieutenant Colonel Thomas was ordered to use this battalion to prevent infiltration along the Punggol Creek. It was decided that they would dig in and construct pill boxes. However, at 1100 hours on 8 February, orders came in to put the Z Company under Captain Thornhill at the disposal of the 11th Indian Division. This company came under the command of the 28th Indian Brigade. Hence, work on the construction of strong points ceased.[30] Thus, we see that this battalion lacked time to construct elaborate static defensive positions. How far they would have been effective in checking the irruption of Japanese infantry is another question altogether. The 118th Field Regiment RA was a territorial force and comprised young recruits from the Eltham and Blackheath districts. They started from Britain in November 1941 and arrived in January 1942 just before the beginning of the Battle of Singapore.[31]

On the night of 28 January, Colonel A. M. L. Harrison, GSO1 of the 11th Indian Division, came to Singapore Island. During the next two days, he inspected the region (the area between the mouth of Seletar and the naval base), which was to be held by the 11th Indian Division. On 29 January, Harrison went to a conference at Fort Canning that was chaired by Paris. The latter was in charge of making the preliminary arrangements for the defense of the Island.[32] When Harrison asked whether there was any plan for withdrawal to a smaller perimeter in case of an enemy breakthrough, he was told there was none. Then, Harrison asked for a map detailing the plan of the naval base but was told there were none in Fort Canning. Harrison found out that searchlights, barbed wire, and layouts for defending machine gun fire plans were yet to be set up. Paris led him aside and said: "I'm sorry, old boy; I quite understand what you expected to find, but it just doesn't exist."[33] Harrison concluded: "Singapore Island is completely without defenses except for a few heavy batteries sited to hold the two entrances to the Johore Straits or to stop a landing on the south coast. There's absolutely nothing laid on the north, west and south except for pill boxes and wire on the eastern half of the south coast."[34] Paris himself believed that the Allied defense of Singapore would last only for a fortnight.[35]

The state of field defense was extremely poor. Churchill was of the opinion that the Kranji-Jurong Switch Line was without any prepared defensive structure.[36] The Kranji-Jurong Switch Line (Kranji River flows into the Johore Strait, and the Jurong flows southward into the Singapore Strait) was part of the prewar defense scheme. It was cleared of bush and undergrowth to a depth of two to three hundred yards. However, digging and wiring were not complete.[37] A Chinese contractor was in charge of preparing defensive works along this line. And whenever the Japanese bombers arrived, his workers also vanished. Further, the edgy Gordon Bennett was not eager to strengthen this line. He believed that construction of a defensive line would exhibit withdrawal complex. Bennett was back in his element. Despite Wavell's assertion that Singapore's northern land defense was weak, Percival claims that on 19 January, he was informed by the ABDACOM commander that defensive preparations were to be kept entirely secret, and only some preparations, such as establishment of obstacles, etc., were to be carried out. Probably, Wavell was concerned that the undertaking of defensive measures openly would hamper the morale of the troops and the citizens. A hapless Percival noted that if defensive preparations were to be kept entirely secret, then very little could actually be done on the ground. The issue is why Percival had not prepared field defense on the northern side of Singapore Island before the Japanese invasion of Malaya started. Percival's chief engineer, Brigadier Ivan Simson, had repeatedly emphasized the need for constructing defenses in northern Johore. But both Percival and Brooke-Popham believed erroneously that construction of defensive work would give rise to "Maginot mentality/fortress complex" and would also result in loss of precious man hours on the part of the troops.[38] Percival lacked the authority to conscript civilian labor to work on the field defense under direction of the military officers. Actually, Percival was confident that even if the Japanese attacked, they would be stopped far away either in north or central Malaya. During January 1942, when the Japanese infantry was advancing through central Malaya, Percival should have ordered the construction of field fortifications along the northern shore of Singapore Island.

The 11th Indian Division under newly promoted Major General "Billy" Key was sandwiched between the 18th British Division on its right and the 8th AIF Division on its left. The 11th Indian Division had to defend the region from Seletar to Bukit Timah Road. The Bukit Timah Road was the road from the causeway through Bukit Timah to Singapore. Besides defending the coastline, the 11th Indian Division was also ordered to defend Sembawang aerodrome, which was three miles from the coast behind the naval base. The 15th Indian Brigade under Lieutenant Colonel Morrison held 6,500 yards of coastline. The British battalion under Major Harvey was on the right, the 3rd/16th Punjab was in the center, and the Jat/Punjabi battalion was in the dockyard. This brigade was backed up by the 155th Field Regiment (less B Battery), 22nd Mountain Regiment (less 4th and 21st mountain batteries), and one section of the 137th Field Regiment (equipped with 75 mm guns), plus one troop of the 2nd A/T Battery. The 155th Field Regiment was ordered to bombard the mouths of S. Masai and S. Lumehoo on the Johore coast to harass Japanese concentration and also to aid the 18th British Division during the battle.[39] The morale of the 155th (Lanarkshire Yeomanry) Field Regiment was low. John McEwan, a young gunner of this unit, notes in his autobiography: "Even lowly gunners and privates knew that the battle for Malaya and for the island of Singapore had been lost some time ago back on the mainland."[40]

When the 15th Indian Brigade left the 11th Indian Division, to form part of the Malaya Command Reserve on 7 February, it included the British Battalion, 3rd/16thPunjab, and the Jat Battalion under Lieutenant Colonel A. E. Cumming. The Jat Battalion was formed from the survivors and reinforcements of 2nd Jats,

4th Jats (45th Indian Brigade), and 2nd FFR, plus newly arrived drafts.⁴¹ Captains F. E. Mileham and Henry Watson were the only British officers from 4th/9th Jats to reach Singapore. About 150 personnel from this unit had been able to reach Singapore. They were amalgamated with the 2nd/9th Jats, which had suffered heavy casualties during the retreat from north of Kuala Lumpur to Segamat.⁴² The composite Jat Battalion numbered sixteen British officers (from different battalions hence unknown to the men) and 605 VCOs and jawans. Besides the British officers, the VCOs were also new to the jawans. The mixing of different ethnic communities (Jats and Punjabi Muslims) resulted in the heterogeneous composition of the Jat Battalion, which in turn was detrimental to its combat effectiveness. Combat motivation of the Indian soldiers depended on regimental loyalty. The latter was the product of pride in belonging to a unit with a long historical tradition and knowing the other personnel well and being known by them, in having strong roots in a well-loved and well-known community. All these elements were missing in the newly formed composite battalion. And the new drafts were without any sort of training. In the context of the *Wehrmacht*, Edward A. Shils and Morris Janowitz write that primary group solidarity was essential for combat effectiveness of the units. Comradeship, solidarity, and subordination to junior officers were essential elements of strong primary group solidarity. And for the genesis of primary group solidarity, it was essential that NCOs should have adequate time to promote the growth of strong identifications between themselves and their men. We have seen earlier that in the absence of ideological motivation, strong primary group solidarity was all the more essential for proper functioning of the Indian units. But this solidarity was very weak in the Jat Battalion. Worse, the Jat Battalion was inadequately equipped. Cumming's Jat Battalion suffered from a shortage of boots, steel helmets, Bren and Tommy guns, two-inch mortars, and medical and signal equipment. This battalion had only four three-inch mortars, and only six jawans were trained to use them. The Jat Battalion's camp was situated three miles from the Singapore town on the Serangoon Road behind the Bidadari Christian Cemetery. The camp site was waterlogged, and it was impossible to dig slit trenches more than six inches deep without striking water.⁴³

The 28th Indian Brigade defended six thousand yards of seafront between the dockyard and the causeway. B Company of 1st/14th Punjab held the small bay west of the dockyard, and the 2nd/2nd GR, with Machine Gun Company of the Manchesters, covered the rest of the seafront. Their left flank, linked with the right flank of 2nd/30th Battalion of the 27th AIF Brigade, was positioned four hundred yards east of the causeway. From 1 February onward, the 2nd/9th GR was at Sembawang airport three miles south of the dockyard. The 5th/14th Punjab was in brigade reserve. The 135th Field Regiment (less 336th Field Battery) with the 4th Mountain Battery (equipped with two six-inch guns) under Lieutenant Colonel P. J. D. Toosey and one troop of the 273rd A/T Battery were in support of this brigade. The 135th Field Regiment was given the task of harassing the mouth of S. Skudai and Johore Bahru. Toosey was also under obligation to support the 27th AIF Brigade in the upcoming battle.⁴⁴

Thus, the above two brigades of the 11th Indian Division had good artillery support. Whether they would be able to use it with effectiveness during actual battle was another issue. The divisional reserve comprised the 2nd/9th GR at Sembawang aerodrome and the 8th Indian (Bareilly) Brigade. The aerodrome itself was protected by a detachment of Kapurthala Infantry and 3rd Cavalry. The latter received its first issue of carriers (only six) on 6 February 1942.[45] The 8th Bareilly Brigade (under Brigadier Trott) personnel were dug in with ten days' supplies of food and ammunition.[46] Trott was ordered to prepare a position astride the Thomson Road near Simpang village. In the case of a Japanese attack, Trott was ordered to counterattack either toward the mouth of Seletar along the right flank of the 15th Indian Brigade or toward the left flank of the 28th Indian Brigade as circumstances dictated. Trott's 8th Indian Brigade included the 1st FFR under Lieutenant Colonel Gilbert, 2nd Baluchis under Major Parker, and the Bhawalpur Infantry (which at this stage had two companies) under Lieutenant Colonel Tyrrell. Later, this brigade received the Garwahl Battalion and 1st/8th Punjab. The Garwahl Battalion was raised from the survivors and reinforcements of the 2nd Garwahlis (22nd Indian Brigade) and the 5th Garwahlis (45th Indian Brigade). The Garwahl Battalion under Lieutenant Colonel Smith joined the 8th Indian Brigade in the morning of 8 February and took up position on the high ground north of MS 13 on the Mandai Road, thus forming the defensive flank behind the 28th Indian Brigade.[47] The 1st/8th Punjab was reformed as a separate unit from the Jat/Punjabi Battalion.[48] These new battalions comprising different ethnic groups mixed indiscriminately did not have any long-standing regimental traditions. Hence, their military effectiveness was very low. In the Indian Army, combat motivation was to a great extent the product of the jawans' bonding with the unit. This is known as esprit de corps or regimental spirit. Long-term personal interactions among the personnel of a regiment build up unit cohesion. The soldiers took pride in the unit's history and felt a sense of responsibility to maintain the heroic tradition of the unit.[49] All these elements were missing in the agglomeration of men into the newly created ad hoc units. The cohesiveness of these newly created units and hence their combat effectiveness was also low.

The 8th AIF Division was in charge of the area from the causeway and Bukit Timah Road till Jurong, a front of 40,500 yards. The 22nd AIF Brigade under Brigadier H. B. Taylor defended the area from Bulim Village, including Chor Chir Keng, to S. Berih. It held 17,000 yards of the coast with the 2nd/18th and 2nd/20th AIF battalions, which were tired after their combat at Mersing. This brigade also had the 2nd/19th AIF Battalion, which had been shattered at Muar.[50] The 22nd AIF Brigade's deployment was in part faulty. The left part of this brigade was not deployed along the beaches but several hundred yards in the rear.[51] Mangrove swamps in its area were erroneously considered impassable by the Japanese troops.[52] The 27th AIF Brigade under Brigadier D. S. Maxwell took over the region from South Kranji.[53] This brigade included the 2nd/26th AIF Battalion from Queensland, 2nd/29th from Victoria, and the 2nd/30th from New South Wales.[54] It held 5,500 yards of the coast, with the 2nd/30th AIF Battalion on the right and the 2nd/26th AIF Battalion on the left.[55] The brigade headquarters was established at Mandai Junction. The 2nd/26th AIF Battalion's A Company faced the Johore Straits between Kranji Road and Kranji River. The region was full of mangrove forest. The defensive positions were established behind the mangrove forest in the dry region. This was a mistake, as the Japanese would later penetrate through the mangrove forest. The Allied commanders after their experience in the Malayan mainland should have known better. The Johore Strait at this point was 2,000 yards wide. Captain Stephen Hannam of 2nd Battalion 26th AIF Brigade had arranged with the 2nd/10th Field Regiment to lay down a barrage in front of the mangrove forest in case of a Japanese landing.[56] The 2nd/29th Battalion of the 27th AIF Brigade was in divisional reserve. Most of the reinforcements that the two Australian brigades received to bring them to strength were semitrained.[57] Some of the Australian recruits were enlisted from the jails. They had spent two to three weeks in a recruiting depot and knew nothing of soldiering. The men were seasick and their officers disorientated.[58] The Australian soldiers deployed in New Guinea and in Malaya-Singapore had a high opinion about themselves before coming in contact with the Japanese. The Australians initially displayed racist contempt for the "little toothy buggers with glasses."[59] However, after the initial encounters, their morale declined, and the Japanese were regarded as jungle supermen.

The 44th Indian Brigade was formed in Poona in July 1941 as part of the 17th Indian Division. It comprised the 6th/1st, 6th/14th, and 7th/8th Punjab regiments. These battalions were raised during the autumn of 1940. When they arrived in Poona, they were all under strength, averaging 650 men each. These units included trained regular soldiers, reservists, and recruits straight from the training battalions in equal proportion. One company of the 6th/1st Punjab Regiment joined its parent battalion only in November 1941. Training till the end of November was carried out near Poona and from 1 December 1941 onward in a training camp seventy miles southeast of Poona. However, training was carried out with an eye for deployment in the Middle East. The brigade was informed that it was destined for Iran-Iraq in early 1941, where they would be given further training. Another problem was that some men were sent away to form new battalions as soon as they were trained. And the new drafts had to be trained from scratch again. Between July and December 1941, each battalion of the 44th Indian Brigade had to donate 250 trained men and forty-five VCOs and NCOs for raising new units. Of the 250 recruits received in December in their place, most of them were under eighteen years old and had been in the army for four to five months. Another two hundred recruits joined when the brigade moved to Bombay, in the first week of January 1942, before sailing for Singapore. The net result was that there was a gross shortage of trained VCOs and NCOs, and most of the jawans had less than three months' military service with their respective battalion.[60] The 44th Indian Brigade had many personnel who joined directly from the training battalions when the brigade was en route for Malaya.[61] As regards the British officers in each of the Indian battalions, less than three were regulars, and the rest were ECOs from outside India. The latter had a maximum of approximately twelve months' service with the Indian troops. They were unaware of the customs and languages of the jawans.[62] Thus, the loyalty bond between the sahibs and the sepoys was extremely weak in this brigade.

The different ancillary units of the infantry brigade group were raised from scratch between August and October 1940. And the brigade signal section was completed only in December 1940, just before the brigade sailed to Malaya. One sapper company was earmarked for this brigade, but it was never raised. The brigade suffered from a shortage of Bren Guns and A/T weapons. There were only four A/T Rifles per battalion, and the holdings of the Bren Guns were 30 percent short of the authorized strength. In terms of equipment and training, the 44th Indian Brigade was worse than its sister formation, the 45th Indian Brigade, which was overwhelmed at the Muar River.[63] The principal Japanese thrust in Singapore came against the 44th Indian Brigade, which was actually much less trained and experienced than the 45th Indian Brigade. Wavell accepted that the 44th and the 45th Indian brigades had actually received no training in jungle warfare and were quite new to the conditions of Malaya-Singapore. These two brigades were originally prepared for deployment in the Middle East. When they were ordered to Malaya, it was believed that they would get time for training.[64] This did not happen, however. And whatever training was given to them was erroneous. Lastly, the internal cohesiveness of the battalions of these two brigades was destroyed due to extensive milking. Kinvig blames Wavell for sending the 45th and 44th Indian brigades to Malaya and Singapore against the advice of his director of military training. Instead, Wavell should have sent the 48th Indian Brigade (comprising the Gurkha regiments).[65]

On 7 January 1942, the 44th Indian Brigade sailed from Bombay for an unknown destination. After a few hours at sea, the news was revealed to the personnel that they were destined for Malaya. The convoy sailed through the Sunda Strait and passed the Bank Island without any mishap and reached Singapore on 21 January. On the same day, the troops disembarked. Japanese air interference during the disembarkation of the troops was minor. However, due to the desertion of the local labor, disembarkation of the transport elements of the brigade took a few days.[66]

The 44th Indian Brigade was given the task of defending the southwest region of Singapore Island from S. Berih (on the right flank) to S. Jurong (on the left flank). The length of the beach held by this brigade came to be about ten miles. The 44th Indian Brigade came under the command of the 8th AIF Division. The Indian brigade was given the tall order that at all costs, the enemy should be contained at the beaches. Under no circumstances should the Japanese be allowed to consolidate their position on the beaches and move inland. To prevent enemy penetration deep into the island and to destroy them at the beaches, it was ordered that reserves should be created and used immediately for launching local counterattacks. Whether the untrained brigade and its inept command structure would be able to carry out rapid counterattack was another question. There was no defensive work constructed in this brigade's sector, and even a reconnaissance of the beach was not carried out. Between 21 January, when the 44th Indian Brigade arrived, and 8 February 1942, when the Japanese actually attacked, the personnel were kept busy rehearsing mock local counterattacks. Local counterattacks by the battalion and brigade reserve were planned and practiced. By 31 January 1942, the 44th Indian Brigade had under its command a twenty-five-pounder field regiment, one Australian company of machine guns (excluding them, the brigade had sixteen machine guns), one Australian troop of A/T guns, and six eighteen-pounder and 75 mm beach defense guns. However, these guns were not mobile. They had to be manhandled across the country and were drawn by lorries with trailers across the road. These guns somewhat bolstered the firepower punch of the Indian brigade. The 5th Field Regiment covered all the beaches in the area of the 44th Indian Brigade and also the beaches in the western region held by the 22nd AIF Brigade.[67]

On 8 February 1942, within the 44th Indian Brigade, the 6th/14th Punjab comprised the right battalion, the 6th/1st Punjab constituted the center battalion, and the 7th/8th Punjab less two companies was the left battalion. The beaches in the zone of the 6th/14th Punjab were few in number and difficult for landing. This battalion's personnel patrolled the few beach areas and the swamps. The 6th/1st Punjab defended the region between S. Tengeh and S. Benwi and Lowyang village. Most of the personnel of this battalion covered the beaches, and only two platoons were held for launching a possible counterattack. The whole Machine Gun Company and the A/T troops were allocated to this battalion's sector. And four beach defense guns were also deployed in support of this battalion. The 7th/8th Punjab held the area from S. Berwi to S. Jurong, and this region was full of beaches. Almost all the men in this unit were detailed for patrolling the beaches, and very few were available as reserves for launching a counterattack. The brigade headquarters was located at Hill 70. The brigade reserve was negligible: only two companies of the 7th/8th Punjab.[68] The mistake that the British officers had made in defending the Muar River was repeated in Singapore. Most of the units except the 6th/14th were spread out in the front line, with negligible reserves being kept for launching counterattacks. So when the Japanese attack came, substantial reserves were not available for containing the enemy.

Major General F. Keith Simmons was in command of the Singapore Fortress Troops. Their area of responsibility covered fifty thousand yards from south Jurong to the Torpedo Base (Fairy Point). He had the two Malay brigades, the Singapore Volunteers, and the 122nd Field Regiment. The 1st Malay Brigade under Brigadier G. G. R. Williams had the 1st and 2nd Malay battalions, 2nd Loyals, and one Machine Gun Company. The 1st Battalion of the Malay Regiment was assigned beach defense in the west coast sector. Their area stretched from the end of Keppel Harbour to Jurong River and contained a large number of concrete beach defense posts. The A Company's sector was further west, around Pasir Panjang. Sandbag posts were built in this area.[69] On their right were the 2nd Battalion of the Malay Regiment and the 2nd Battalion of the Loyal Regiment.[70] The 2nd Malay Brigade under Brigadier Fraser defended the region from Singlap to Fairy Point. It had the Manchesters, Gordons, 2nd Dogras, the much-depleted 3rd Dogras, and the Mysore Battalion. The Singapore Volunteer Brigade under Colonel Grimwood had three battalions and defended the region from Jardine

Steps to Siglap.⁷¹ Several British officers of the Malay battalions had been planters before the onset of the war.⁷² The absence of prewar regular officers resulted in reduced combat effectiveness. Pillboxes and wire entanglements were erected along the coast between Buona Vista and Fairy Point.⁷³

The DALFORCE, which was twenty thousand strong, comprised Chinese members of the Communist Party under British officers. This force was named after the Special Branch British officer John Dalley, who commanded it. The Chinese personnel called this force Singapore Overseas Chinese Volunteer Army. The volunteers were laborers, clerks, students, etc. Many Chinese women also wanted to enlist in this force. After the Japanese atrocities in China, the overseas Chinese were eager to fight the Japanese. The military effectiveness of the Chinese irregulars in regular war was negligible. Due to the sinking of the transport ship *Empress of Asia* by Japanese bombers, there was a shortage of arms, and not all the members of the DALFORCE could be adequately armed. In fact, many were armed with sporting guns.⁷⁴ Brigadier G. C. Ballentine, CO of the 44th Indian Brigade, noted: "Some 250 Chinese, armed with anything from a rifle to a knife, were sent into brigade area. They were used to patrol and watch mangrove swamps as we were under the quite false impression they would be quite at home in such primeval surroundings. Actually they were city based folk, who had never been nearer swamps. . . . They proved very trigger-happy and a constant source of alarm and unease."⁷⁵

The Command Reserve comprised the one-thousand-strong 12th Indian Brigade under Brigadier Paris, the 53rd British Brigade, the Volunteer Armored Car Company, and the 100th Light Tank Section of the 44th Cavalry.⁷⁶ The 12th Indian Brigade was refitting in Tyersall Park. Its British battalion, the 2nd Argyll and Sutherland Highlanders, had only 100 experienced men out of a ration strength of 800 personnel.⁷⁷ Hence, its military effectiveness was below average. In addition, the 12th Indian Brigade had the 5th/2nd and 4th/19th Hyderabad under its command. On 25 January, 400 young, inexperienced draftees arrived from India to replace the losses that the 4th/19th Hyderabad had suffered at the confrontation at the Slim River.⁷⁸ In total, the 4th/19th Hyderabad now numbered 680 personnel.⁷⁹ The unpublished official history of the 4th/19th Hyderabad describes the state of this unit quite vividly:

> The morale of the troops was extremely low. The numbers of sick were excessive, the common complaint being skin infection picked up in the jungle. Most of the equipment had been lost. A skeleton signal section was raised, two Vicker gunners and two guns were available, one to two LMGs could be manned, but no crews for the mortars existed. Each man had a rifle and ammunition, but little else. The reinforcement of 400, were young inexperienced men of about an average of one year's service. The sight of the tired and worn out soldiers had a bad effect. The impression they created on the new arrivals was one of despair and futility. It was hoped that a month would be available to refit and train up the new men.⁸⁰

Not only the Indian troops but the Australian soldiers also suffered from cramp, fatigue, and skin disorders.⁸¹ Demoralization was not confined to the Indian troops but had spread among the other section of the Allied troops. A report dated 28 February 1942 by G. W. Seabridge, editor of the *Straits Times* noted "the almost complete demoralization of the defending troops; the striking lack of any offensive spirit; the widespread acceptance of the view that the Battle for Singapore was a forlorn hope; and in isolated cases, an actual refusal to fight."[82]

Mortars and machine guns were essential for close-quarter combat, and the 4th/19th Hyderabad was especially weak in this regard. The battalion was composed of untrained drafts and demoralized survivors, and the Japanese would not give them a respite of even one month to regain their composure. In the context of the Second World War, Richard Holmes writes that the excellent fighting spirit of the German troops was partly due to the fact that they were given basic training lasting from twelve to sixteen weeks. And this basic training was what the jawans lacked. Nor were the jawans aided by defensive works. No wires were laid on the northern sector from Jurong River to Changi. Neither were trenches dug, nor were gun positions reconnoitered. The tired troops were astonished to find out that most of the defenses of Singapore Island were facing south. Brigadier Paris, CO of the 12th Indian Brigade, was given the task of coordinating the defensive positions. Although the stores were full of wire, sandbags, and tools, Paris found it almost impossible to requisition them and to use Chinese labor to construct the defensive positions. The 4th/19th was deployed in front of the causeway, the Argylls were in the Tyersall Park to continue with their training, and the 5th/2nd was near MRG BIDDHADARI/Bidadari. Continuous air raids further demoralized the troops. In the next seven days, a tank trap was prepared with bulldozers, flame thrower pits were constructed, and mines and booby traps, along with roadblocks, were laid. However, there remained an undefended gap of several miles between the causeway and the Jurong River.[83]

After the retreat from Muar, the 7th/6th RR Battalion comprised two British officers and 320 jawans (including those in the hospitals). On 8 February 1942, they were amalgamated with the 3rd Battalion of the Dogra Regiment.[84] We have seen earlier that the motivation of the Indian units was based on distinct caste, clan, ethnic, and regimental pride. So amalgamation of the different communities from different battalions due to wartime emergencies lowered the cohesiveness of the newly formed units. John A. English observes that unlike the German soldier, who was willing and able to fight under the direction of any officer, the British soldier displayed a narrow loyalty to his particular unit.[85] This observation was all the more applicable to the Indian Army's units due to the ethnic structure of their regiments. Omer Bartov opines that in the absence of primary group solidarity, ideological motivation (be it nationalism or any other secular ideology) is necessary in order to strengthen the soldiers' "will to war."[86] The Indian battalions with weak primary group solidarity did not have any ideological backup to strengthen their determination to fight hard and if necessary, to die hard.

The loyalty of the Indian troops was also wavering. This was partly because most of the British officers were new and barely knew the language of the jawans.[87] So the British officers could not establish any personal bond with the Indian troops. Again, by means of radio and pamphlets dropped from aircraft, the Japanese emphasized the point that the British were using the Asiatic troops as cannon fodder. Between 8 December 1942 and 31 January 1942, the IJA captured ten thousand Indians as PoWs.[88] The Indian PoWs captured during the Malaya Campaign had been taken at Penang, where they were treated well by the Japanese, and after being deprived of arms, were set free, provisioned with some food and medicines. In many cases, the Indian PoWs spoke in the microphones to their fellows asking them to surrender to the Japanese.[89] Fujiwara persuasively spoke to the Indian PoWs regarding the Japanese aim to free the Asian people from western domination. The Greater East Asia War was portrayed as a crusade against the European colonizing powers. Captain Mohan Singh along with many other PoWs believed in the Japanese propaganda. News of Japanese successes and Allied setbacks along with the germ of independence among the Indian PoWs encouraged them to tilt toward the Japanese. By the time the Japanese were preparing to invade Singapore Island, Mohan Singh was able to raise a party of two hundred Indians to fight the British.[90]

The above account shows that overall the field defenses constructed were sloppy and not very effective. The morale of the troops was wavering, and their equipment was not up to the mark. The details of dispositions of troops discussed shows that Percival had scattered the troops unevenly throughout the whole island. He had placed most of the combat-effective troops along with artillery units in the northern part of the island. Nevertheless, he had kept a substantial number of troops along the southern part of the island fearing a Japanese amphibious attack that never came. And along the northern part of the island, Percival had concentrated on the northeastern part. The Japanese duped him and attacked the northwestern part of the island. Overall, Percival did not keep substantial numbers of central reserves. When the Japanese attack came as we will see, not only did he fail to shift unengaged troops rapidly from the southern and northeastern parts of the island, but the lack of central reserves also hampered the Allied effort to launch a vigorous counterattack after the initial Japanese landing.

The provision of air-raid shelters was insufficient. Construction of such shelters was a near impossibility because the water level was close to the surface. In most places, the digging of trenches was not only useless but also dangerous because they soon filled with water and became a breeding place for mosquitoes. Many of the streets were narrow, and there was little space available for the building of air-raid shelters. Apart from blocking traffic, the medical authorities advised against building shelters in the streets on the grounds that the circulation of air would thereby be stopped, thus leading to epidemics.[91]

At long last Malaya Command believed that it had hit upon the right tactics to fight the Japanese. On 3 February 1942, Malaya Command advised the III Indian Corps, the AIF, and the Southern Area that the Japanese soldiers would not stand up to bayonet charges, so launching bayonet charges was the best way to defeat them.[92] In a directive dated 3 February 1942, Brigadier H. C. Phillips, belonging to the General Staff of Malaya Command, in a rhetorical manner advised the formation commanders that offense is the best defense. In such an attack, firepower weapons were considered secondary, and the bayonet was regarded as the primary weapon. And what was required was aggressive spirit among the defending troops. The directive continued: "All ranks must be imbued with the spirit of the attack. It is no good waiting for the Japanese to attack first. The endeavour of every soldier must be to locate the enemy and, having located him, to close with him. The soldier should, if exposed, cover his advance with fire, either from Tommy Gun, rifle or light automatic, until he is able to attack with the bayonet. If every soldier is determined to kill at least one Japanese the enemy will not have a chance."[93] There is a cliché that generals prepare for the wrong war. The Malaya Command believed that the defense of Singapore Island would be a rerun of the infantry battles of the First World War or similar to the late nineteenth-century imperial campaigns that were won by the "thin red line" launching bayonet charges against the "savages." Nowhere in the campaign in the Malayan Peninsula were the Allied troops successful in defeating the Japanese by launching bayonet charges. It was wishful thinking that the Japanese would wait passively to receive a bayonet charge by the Allied troops.

The Invasion

Yamashita had sixty thousand troops (thirty thousand were combat personnel), 132 guns of varying calibers, sixty-eight AA guns, forty armored cars, tanks, three engineer regiments, three companies of bridging troops, and three companies of river-crossing troops. He was supported by 459 aircraft of III Air Corps and 158 JNAF aircraft.[94] Yamashita selected the palace of the Sultan of Johore as his headquarters. It had a five-story observation tower at the eastern end.[95]

On 6 February 1942, Japanese shelling of Sembewang aerodrome was so heavy that the RAF declared it nonoperable. On 7 February, Japanese artillery concentrated on the front of the 11th Indian Division and on the left flank of the 27th AIF Brigade.[96] On 8 February, the tower in Johore Bahru was perforated with shells, and an observation balloon hovered over the town of Johore Bahru. At noon, Japanese shelling reached a crescendo. It focused on the 27th AIF, and shelling of the 11th Indian Division's positions slackened. The pattern of Japanese artillery bombardment before the actual invasion was thus contradictory and did not give any indication of the region in which the Japanese would actually land. The gunners of the 11th Indian Division also opened up during the afternoon and swept the creeks along the Johore Coast and the far end of the causeway. The 135th Field Regiment especially concentrated on the mouth of south Skudai. However, Allied bombardment did not cause many casualties to the Japanese, who were concentrating further inland hidden from the Allied observers. At 1930 hours, Japanese shelling reached its highest pitch, and it was concentrated on the 8th AIF Division. At 2200 hours, Lieutenant Colonel Toosey telephoned the 11th Indian Division's Headquarters and said that he had seen red and blue lights being fired on the front of the 22nd AIF Brigade. He presumed that it was an SOS signal, and he further said that he had not heard any firing by the guns under the Australians.[97] The 11th Indian Division Headquarters should have asked its brigade which was closest to the Australians as to what was going on. Or at best, it should have sent

Endgame on Singapore Island 203

a reconnaissance patrol toward the sector held by the 8th AIF Division. The colored signals that Toosey had observed were actually fired by the invading Japanese troops. Had the 11th Indian Division followed the abovementioned steps, it would have been clear that the Japanese were just coming ashore. In such a scenario, a vigorous joint counterattack by the 8th AIF Division and the 11th Indian Division would have thrown Yamashita's troops back from the beaches to the Johore Strait. It was probably the turning point of the battle for Singapore.

The Japanese massed the experienced 5th and 18th divisions within a front of twelve thousand yards from Kranji, on the west of the causeway to the Berih River on the west of the island. The Imperial Guards Division was on the eastern part and was ordered to carry on a feint (which succeeded with Percival's earlier reasoning that the main attack would come on the northeast part of Singapore) to deceive the Allied commanders as regards the focal point of their principal attack.[98] In the early hours of 8 February, Percival signaled to Wavell that the Japanese would probably attack the northeastern part of Singapore Island.[99] On the night of 8/9 February, the bulk of the 5th and 18th Japanese divisions poured against Brigadier Taylor's 22nd AIF Brigade (and especially the 2nd/20th Battalion). The Japanese crossed Johore Strait in small motorboats, launches, and barges.[100] A Japanese source describes the amphibious landing in the following words:

> By the 8th February our launches (which included many armored landing craft) and hundreds of heavy guns had been collected. At zero hour the engines began to beat softly and fifteen minutes after midnight the red and blue signal rockets went up, indicating that the first group was over. The Matsui and Mutaguchi units had been given the Tengah Aerodrome as their mutual objective. The Japanese . . . losses were unexpectedly heavy . . . the final outcome, however, was never in doubt, for there simply were not enough British guns to cover the two fronts on which the Japanese were attacking.[101]

The motor launches were transported in lorries from Singora to Penang, and from the latter place they sailed to Batu Pahat; from there again they were loaded on lorries and transported down the coastal road to south Skudai, south Malayu, and south Pendas.[102]

The Japanese landed west of Kranji River. The defensive positions here were poor, and the mangrove swamp extended up to the river's edge. Taylor had dispersed his two forward battalions along the coast, and one battalion was kept as a mobile reserve.[103] In the evening of 8 February, the 2nd/26th AIF Battalion of the 27th AIF Brigade heard firing on their left, west of the Kranji River. The invasion had begun. Napoleon's dictum was that troops should march to the sound of guns. But neither on their own initiative nor in the absence of orders from above did this battalion march to aid the neighboring units.[104] In contrast, in the German Army in accordance with *Auftragstaktik* (mission-oriented decentralized command system), both the officers and the men were trained to display a high degree of initiative in battle.[105] From the very beginning of the Japanese attack, there was no communication and coordination between the two Australian brigade commanders and no direction from Bennett's headquarters. Neither did Bennett attempt to coordinate the action of two Australian brigades nor did he activate the 44th Indian Brigade under his command. It seems that each battalion was fighting their separate battles. About five thousand Japanese soldiers landed during the first night.[106] Percival still had a chance to concentrate all his troops and push them back to sea. However, Percival, though personally brave, was neither dynamic nor inspiring and was timid and hesitant when it came to making tough decisions.[107] In Clausewitzian language, Percival lacked moral courage.

At about 0600 hours, some one hundred Australian stragglers without arms and equipment passed the 44th Indian Brigade Headquarters in small groups. They were collected and kept out of sight of the Indian troops to prevent the latter's demoralization. Later, the Australians were sent back in lorries.[108] Major H. P. Thomas asserts that by 8/9 February the fighting spirit and discipline of the Australians had withered away.[109] The 7th/8th Punjab (less eighty jawans), along with the A/T troops, were moved out of the southern beaches and placed in reserve. Percival should have thrown this battalion immediately against the Japanese in the northwest of the island. Patrols were sent out from the 6th/14th and 7th/8th Punjab toward Bulim Road and Choa Chir Kang.[110]

The Japanese tactics have been aptly described by an Indian commissioned officer who was in Singapore: "The Japanese, as always, seemed to be everywhere—in front, behind, on either side, infiltrating swiftly behind disorganized pockets of our troops cut off from their colleagues. Carefully avoiding any frontal attack they sought out the gaps in the Australian lines and pushed through behind them and attacked from the rear. Swarming through the close, intricate country, each Japanese party was led by an officer with a compass strapped to his wrist."[111] These were the same infantry tactics that the Japanese had implemented in Hong Kong and in combat in the Malayan Peninsula.

Early on 9 February, the 11th Indian Division Headquarters received the message from the corps headquarters that the Japanese had landed in front of the 22nd AIF Brigade.[112] On the morning of 9 February, the 12th Indian Brigade was ordered to Bukit Panjang village in support of the 22nd AIF. The 5th/2nd Punjab Regiment remained as a reserve, and the 4th/19th along with the Argylls moved to a position west of the village and north of the road running to Tengah airport. The men assembled under the rubber trees, and there was no time to dig trenches. The Japanese bombers arrived and bombed the 4th/19th, which suffered some seventy casualties. Since a lot of Allied troops were now concentrated in the comparatively smaller area of Singapore, the Japanese bombers had a target-rich zone to bomb. The bombing and subsequent large numbers of casualties had an unnerving effect on the new drafts in the regiment.[113]

The 8th AIF division now had the 44th Indian and the 12th Indian brigades under its command, and these two brigades were yet to be committed to battle. In the northwest of the island, the two Australian battalions holding the area from Kranji Creek to Sungei Berih were retreating due to Japanese pressure. The reserve Australian battalion was badly shelled and bombed and was in no position to carry out a counterattack. The 44th Indian Brigade remained unengaged on the left of the Australians. The 8th AIF Division's CO and his staff should have immediately sent the 44th Indian Brigade in support of the 22nd AIF Brigade. Further potential reinforcements were available. The 12th Indian Brigade at Tengah airport should have been ordered to the beaches where the 22nd AIF was being worsted. However, the 8th AIF divisional commander bungled, and there was no contact or coordination between his staff and the different subordinate brigades. There was no contact or coordination between the different brigade commanders either. Communication between the divisional headquarters and brigade headquarters and also between the various brigades had broken down on the very first day of the Japanese onslaught. What had happened in the Malayan Peninsula was being repeated on Singapore Island. As the 22nd AIF retreated, the 44th Indian Brigade on their left had to retreat without firing a shot to maintain a continuous front line.[114] If one portion of the defensive line broke, instead of launching a counterattack to sort it out, withdrawal of the neighboring formations in order to maintain a linear defensive line had become an obsession with the Allied commanders. As in the Malayan mainland, the Allied commanders in Singapore also were conceptually unprepared to replace linear defense with elastic defense.

Overall, both Percival and Bennett had failed to concentrate their forces against the Japanese landing. Two Australian battalions were decimated by almost two Japanese divisions. Even then, 40 percent of the total casualties suffered by the IJA in Singapore occurred during their initial phase of landing.[115] An invading force was most vulnerable when it was disembarking on the beaches. What would have happened if Percival and Bennett had been able to concentrate their force during the night of 8 February and early 9 February remains one of history's greatest "what ifs."

In the morning of 9 February, the 22nd AIF Brigade withdrew without informing the 44th Indian Brigade on their left. Again communication between the front and rear elements within a brigade and between different brigades disintegrated very early after the onset of the fighting. To give an example, only at 0500 hours did information reach the headquarters of the 44th Indian Brigade that the 22nd AIF Brigade had been driven some two thousand yards back from the western beaches. Only then did the field guns start firing. But by then it was too late to stop the Japanese penetration.[116]

Breakdown of communications within the battalions of the 12th Indian Brigade, which were not yet heavily engaged, was also complete. Lieutenant Colonel Gurbakhsh Singh, CO of Jhind Infantry Battalion (an Indian States Force unit), writes: "Our communication with the brigade headquarters remained snapped during the night. It was only in the morning that we could discover that the position had been abandoned and we had been left exposed on all sides. Eventually we decided to fall back too."[117] In postindependent India, Gurbakhsh would rise to the rank of major general. He was the elder brother of Harbakhsh Singh of the 5th/11th Sikhs. Jhind Infantry had some experience of fighting along the North-West Frontier. In Singapore, the Jhind Infantry was in charge of guarding Kalang and Tengah airfields. These two airfields were ten miles apart, and the headquarters of this battalion was established at Tengah. On 8 February, this battalion was put under the 12th Indian Brigade. When Tengah airfield was surrounded by the Japanese, the Jhind company guarding this airfield retreated to the Jurong Line. The company complained that the Australians had retreated without informing them.[118] The failure of the brigade commanders and their subordinate battalion commanders to maintain contact patrols and liaison officers and to use artillery effectively was a gross failure in the sphere of command.

Throughout the day, nothing of much importance occurred in the 18th British Division's sector. But the troops and their commanders remained inactive. They were not rushed by Percival to the danger spots along the northwest part of the island. The inactive personnel witnessed the smoke from the burning oil tanks, which hung like a black pall over the island.[119] This sight must have demoralized the defenders. Later, on 9 February, the 15th Indian Brigade was ordered to the Race Course and Cumming's Jat Battalion remained as the corps reserve.[120] These troops were not utilized by Percival against the Japanese landing.

On 9 February, the 11th Indian Division also remained inactive. During the evening, this division, despite the protests of Key, was given the responsibility of blowing up the three munition dumps near Nee Soon. Strangely, somebody had withdrawn the demolition parties that were composed of the fortress engineers. This incident was symptomatic of the command confusion among the Allies by the end of the first day of fighting in the Singapore Island. Key was informed that after completing the demolitions, the 11th Indian Division might have to withdraw to the siege perimeter.[121]

During the night of 9 February, the Japanese soldiers in boats started crossing in the 2nd/26th AIF Battalion's sector. The Australians opened up on the boats with machine guns. The Japanese artillery started shelling the road and cut the telephone wires, which severed this battalion's connection with the 2nd/10th Field Regiment. Captain S. Hannam (2nd IC A Company of 2nd/26th AIF) tried to fire his Very Pistol in order to signal the supporting artillery to open fire on the Japanese. However, he found out that due to dampness the cartridges had swollen, and the pistol was not working. In desperation, Hannam sent a runner to contact their supporting artillery. Soon the 2nd/26th AIF received orders to retreat to the Mandai Junction.[122] It was a rerun of the previous actions in the Malayan Peninsula. Just after the Japanese attack parties had been encountered, fearing penetration in a particular sector, all the units along the defensive line were ordered to retreat. Hannam describes the scenario in the following words:

> Here (Mandai Junction) the battalion assembled and we were informed that due to the previous night's attack against the 22nd AIF Brigade and Indian brigades, they had withdrawn and together with the civilian population were jamming the one access road from the west to Bukit Timah Road. The battalion then made its way along the sides of Bukit Timah Road to Yew Tee Village. There was an oil tank firm at Yew Tee and Jap planes were bombing the farm continuously and they went on doing so even though black smoke was enveloping the whole scene and black rain fell from the sky. It was at this point that our battalion was diverted from Bukit Timah Road to follow the pipeline to MacRitchie Reservoir.[123]

On the night of 9 February, the Australians abandoned the Tengah airport and held a line near Bulim village and the upper reaches of the Tengal Creek. The 2nd/29th AIF Battalion, Gordon Bennett's only reserve was deployed there. Behind them the 12th Indian Brigade was deployed with the Argylls on the right and 4th/19th Hyderabad on the left. The 4th/19th Hyderabad held 1,400 yards of the Hui Estate with only two machine guns. This battalion had no other automatics. The unpublished regimental history notes: "The depression of the day's operations was increased by rain, which started in the afternoon and continued throughout the night."[124] The incessant rain did not depress the Japanese, because they were superbly trained and were winning and continuously advancing. The 44th Indian Brigade had retreated from the coast and held Jurong River south of Jurong Road, and the 15th Indian Brigade was at the north of Jurong Road. Gordon Bennett was in command of the 12th and the 15th Indian brigades.[125]

About 0400 hours on 10 February (Tuesday), small arms fire was heard in the marshes near Hill 85 opposite Pulau Ubin. The 9th Royal Northumberland Fusiliers sent a patrol but did nothing more. The Allied battalions were generally inactive and did not display any initiative. In the morning, Lieutenant Colonel L. C. Thomas of the 9th Northumberland Fusiliers was ordered to take command of a composite force known as the TOMFORCE. It was to operate on the left of the 8th AIF and drive back the Japanese. This force comprised the 4th Royal Norfolks, 1st/5th Sherwood Foresters, 18th Battalion of the Reconnaissance Corps, six twenty-five-pounder guns, and 4.5-inch howitzers.[126]

During the early hours of 10 February, the 27th AIF Brigade panicked. It had on its right the 2nd/2nd GR. At 0430 hours on 10 February, the British officer in command of the left platoon of the D Company of 2nd/2nd GR was given a scrap of paper by two Australians. On this piece of paper was scribbled: "Position on Mandai Road near Bt. Mandai 195 features near 12 MS." The latter position was three miles south of the southern end of the causeway. This piece of paper was passed on to Captain R. D. H. Bucknall, CO of D Company, and he sent a patrol into the area that was supposed to be held by the 2nd/30th AIF Battalion. It was found that the region was empty and the Australians had retreated. This development demoralized the Gurkhas, who expected a fight to the finish along the beaches. The CO of the 27th AIF Brigade deserves criticism for initiating a unilateral retreat, which in turn dislocated the defensive line. He should have contacted the CO of the 28th Indian Brigade before starting to retreat. The 2nd/2nd GR reported the situation to Brigadier Selby, who in turn reported it to the 11th Indian Division's Headquarters. When the 8th AIF Division was contacted by Colonel Harrison, GSO1 of the 11th Indian Division, by telephone, Colonel Thyer (Bennett's chief of staff) said that he had just heard that the 27th AIF Brigade had withdrawn from its position. Thyer overestimated the strength of Japanese infiltrating units and replied that it was impossible to reoccupy the original position with the few troops that were available. The 11th Indian Division and later the 2nd GR were informed that the 27th AIF Brigade would try to hold the Mandai Road village near MS 13.[127] On 10 February, the 27th AIF Brigade was ordered to withdraw to Mandai village. The 2nd/30th AIF Battalion was in contact with the Japanese at Kranji Inlet. The new position in Mandai was taken up in support of the retreating 22nd AIF Brigade.[128] The above incident shows that the 8th AIF Divisional headquarters had no contact and control over its subordinate brigades.

Colonel Harrison writes:

> This was serious news. The enemy was now free to cross the Johore Strait west of the Causeway undisturbed by small-arm fire as the Causeway would defilade his passage from the fire of the 2nd/2nd Gurkhas, whose flank was now exposed and overlooked by the hills vacated by the 2nd/30th Battalion. This vacated area was covered with rubber and scrub through which the enemy could move unobserved, and they were also free to penetrate west of the Bt. Timah Road and thence through the rubber and scrub south of the Naval Base in rear of the 28th Indian Brigade.[129]

A gap appeared between the 27th AIF Brigade and the 2nd/2nd GR on their right. Some junior British officers at least displayed initiative, but they were few and far between. One such officer was Captain Bucknall. He led his reserve platoon along the railway line behind the naval base toward Hill 95, which was previously occupied by a machine-gun detachment of the 27th AIF Brigade. However, the hill was strongly occupied by the Japanese, and they had surrounded their defensive position with wires. The Japanese infantry also infiltrated between Hills 125 and 95. Worse, the Japanese were irrupting between B Company and the battalion headquarters of 2nd/2nd GR. After 1000 hours, the 5th/14th Punjab arrived in an attempt to occupy Hill 95.[130]

Meanwhile, the senior British officers were taking some steps for damage control. Major General Key, CO of the 11th Indian Division, called Trott to the divisional headquarters and emphasized the necessity to fill the gap to prevent infiltration of the Japanese on the left flank of the 28th Indian Brigade, which would result in cutting off all the Allied troops in the naval base. In the afternoon of 10 February, the 8th Indian Brigade was ordered to plug in this gap. The 135th Field Regiment was to support the 8th Indian Brigade's attack. Trott's plan was that the Garwahl Battalion would lead the attack, followed by the 1st FFR. And the 2nd Baluch were to advance north of MS 13. The Garwahl Battalion was able to advance to Sembawang Estate.[131]

The 44th Indian Brigade was at the left flank of the 4th/19th Hyderabad Regiment. The 4th/19th Hyderabad held the northeast corner of the junction of the Tengal and Bukit Timah roads at Bukit Panjang village. The Jhind Infantry, less two companies, which was guarding the Tengah airport, retreated to a position on the left flank of the 4th/19th Hyderabad and occupied Bukit Panjang village. The Argylls and the Australians retreated in confusion and refused to stop when their commanding officers ordered them to stand fast. Command and control by the officers over their battalions were dissolving. The Australians had left many of their guns at Kranji Creek. The right flank of the 4th/19th Hyderabad was exposed. If the Japanese had probed here, it would have been a sure recipe for disaster. Brigadier Paris's order was to hold the present position and delay the enemy as long as possible and inflict on them as many casualties as possible, but on no account was the battalion to be cut off by hostile advance.[132] The last part of the order actually gave autonomy to the battalion commanders to withdraw as and when they wished.

During the afternoon of 10 February, the 4th/19th Hyderabad was attacked by Japanese aircraft that relentlessly dive-bombed and machine-gunned the troops. Then from 1500 to 1900 hours, the battalion was heavily shelled. At 1930 hours the battalion was ordered to occupy the lower slopes of Bukit Panjang in order to establish contact with the Jhind Infantry. The 4th/19th Hyderabad was lucky, because throughout the day its right flank was in the air, but no Japanese troops had probed this weakness.[133]

However, the 4th/19th Hyderabad had had enough. In the dark, the officers failed to control the unnerved men, and the latter begun to slip back. First the C Company (Kumaunis) and then the D Company (mixed) and then B (Jats) fell back. However, the A Company (Ahirs) with sixty men stood firm. Most of the trenches were deserted. It would be wrong to argue that only the Indian troops were unnerved. In the morning the Indians had witnessed that the Australians and the British were streaming back in utter disorder. The Japanese added to the terror of the night by throwing hand grenades and opening up with small arms. A Company failed to maintain its own position. Even worse, all contact between this subunit and the Jhind Infantry headquarters had vanished. All the battalions were fighting their own separate battles without any idea of how the neighboring and supporting formations were faring. The Jhind Infantry evacuated Bukit Panjang village without informing the 4th/19th Hyderabad. It was symptomatic of command disintegration as the two neighboring Indian battalions were not in touch with each other. Firing occurred on the left and rear of the A Company of the 4th/19th Hyderabad. But the men were not sure whether this was done by friend or foe. The nocturnal situation was further enlivened when a single Japanese light tank attacked the A Company. At 0230 hours the A Company of the 4th/19th Hyderabad reached Tyersall and got a few hours' sleep.[134]

Historian Mark Johnston writes that combat not only produced tiresome exertion but also loss of sleep. And retreat was especially tiresome both mentally and physically. Sleep deprivation resulted in loss of concentration and sapped their powers of logical thought. Frontline soldiering is a battle against fatigue as much as against the enemy. Many Australian soldiers in Singapore had only three to four hours of sleep every day. And several Australian soldiers actually died of exhaustion.[135] The Japanese, in contrast, due to their hardy training and experiences of continuous victories and advance, exhibited high morale. Late during the day, stragglers (all of them were very young and semitrained) from the 8th AIF and 44th Indian Brigade passed through the lines of the 1st Battalion Malay Regiment. And this had an adverse impact on the Malay soldiers.[136] On 10 February, the 1st Battalion was withdrawn from the beach and formed the left of the line that started at Pasir Panjang and continued through rear defense locality.[137]

During the midnight of 9/10 February, the Jat Battalion was ordered to join the 15th Indian Brigade at Bukit Timah. This battalion reached the village in the morning of 10 February and marched westward along the Jurong Road. The 15th Indian Brigade's headquarters was at de Souza Avenue, a mile from Bukit Timah. South of the 15th Indian Brigade was the severely mauled 44th Indian Brigade. Throughout the day, the Jurong Road was heavily bombed by Japanese aircraft. Later, during 10 February, many Australians and men from the 44th Indian Brigade who had filtered back were rounded up to strengthen the position held by the Jat Battalion.[138] And the Jat Battalion, comprising four hundred men under Lieutenant Colonel A. Cumming stationed at Serangoon Road, remained inactive.[139]

On 10 February, Wavell visited Singapore and strongly impressed upon Percival the necessity to launch a counterattack to contain the Japanese, who were making rapid progress with their usual infiltration tactics. Wavell, displaying a high degree of personal courage, had come to Singapore despite Percival's warning that a flight to Singapore at this stage was unsafe. Wavell was encouraged by the minor counterattack launched by the 11th Indian Division to restore the dangerous situation that had been caused by the premature withdrawal of the 27th AIF Brigade. Wavell and Percival visited the 11th Indian Division's Headquarters in a car profusely perforated by bomb splinters. Wavell appeared satisfied with the steps that Key was taking to restore the situation. Generally, when a subordinate explained things to him, Wavell would merely say, "I see." But, this time, he was a bit excited. Wavell said, "Well done. That's what I want. Attack the enemy, and don't give him time to exploit any advantage he has temporarily gained."[140] However, even the minor counterattack planned by Key failed. The 5th/14th Punjab was halted. The 1st FFR was ordered to attack Hill 95 at 1800 hours after ten minutes of preliminary bombardment by the 135th Field Regiment.[141] At 1900 hours, the 27th AIF Brigade, which had lost all communication with Bennett's headquarters, was put under Key's command. Maxwell informed Key that the 2nd/30th AIF Battalion was holding Mandai Road village. Key stressed to Maxwell: "If it goes, the Japs will be free to advance straight down the Bukit Timah Road and cut in behind the 8th Division on the Choa Chu Kang and Jurong roads. We know that he's ferrying across a large force west of the Causeway during the day."[142] Wavell left Singapore on the morning of 11 February without much confidence that Percival would be able to conduct a prolonged defense.[143]

After the end of the Second World War, Percival asserted that even without Wavell's prodding, he was already thinking of launching a counterattack with Bennett's troops to regain the Jurong Switch Line. More interesting is that Wavell had offered Percival the 11th Armored Brigade. Percival answered that it was uncertain whether the armored brigade, due to Japanese aerial supremacy, could be landed before the Japanese could launch their main attack against Singapore. Percival was of the opinion that the armored brigade could be better utilized either in Burma or in Java.[144] This armored brigade would later be used quite effectively in Burma. Percival at this stage was not sure whether he could hold Singapore long enough before the armored brigade could be brought into play. It seems that the gentlemanly Percival had already accepted defeat. Had Percival conducted an aggressive and active prolonged defense, and if the armored division had been landed on Singapore Island, Yamashita's troops would have been in a soup. Archie Wavell's order issued in Singapore on 10 February rhetorically stated:

> It is certain that our troops in Singapore heavily outnumber the Japanese troops who have crossed the Straits. We must destroy them, our whole fighting reputation is at stake and the honor of the British Empire. The Americans have held out in the Bataan Peninsula against far heavier odds. The Russians are turning back the picked strength of the Germans. The Chinese with almost complete lack of modern equipment have held the Japanese for four and a half years. It will be disgraceful if we cannot hold our boasted fortress of Singapore to inferior enemy forces.... Please see that the above is brought to the notice of all senior officers and through them to all the troops.[145]

Wavell was somewhat pushed to issue such an order after getting Churchill's last-ditch order to him. The prime minister had a prejudiced view of the Indian Army. He emphasized that the 18th British Division had a chance to make history by fighting heroically against the Japanese.[146] Despite Churchill's faith in the British division, it had fought badly. At 0600 hours on 11 February (Wednesday), the 4th/19th Hyderabad mustered only 160 men. The rest had melted away. Even the remaining personnel were considered unreliable by their CO, who told Brigadier Paris that his men would not stay in their positions.[147] Already from 9 February onward, there were desertions from the Australian units, and many Australian soldiers refused to go back to the front line.[148] The morale of the Allied defenders was crumbling. On 11 February, the combined 7th Battalion–3rd Battalion Dogra Regiment was given the task of defending the Bukit Timah crossroads. They were relieved on 13 February and then held the Cluny Hills in the west of the suburbs of Singapore City until the ceasefire in the evening of 15 February 1942.[149]

By 11 February, the Race Course was lost, and the Allied troops retreated to the Adams Road.[150] The Japanese infiltrated into the naval base area from the west. At about 2200 hours, the 9th Battalion Royal Northumberland Fusiliers withdrew to the north of Nee Soon village to support the Indian troops there.[151] As long as the Allied forces held the Singapore side of the causeway, their artillery fire could sweep across it, and the Japanese were unable to repair the breach. However, the retreat of the Allied troops from the southern side of the causeway gave the Japanese the opportunity to repair it. On 11 February, the Japanese engineers repaired the breach at Johore Causeway, and the Imperial Guards started crossing over toward Nee Soon village.[152]

Even as late as 11 February, Percival described the IJA as an army of "clever gangsters."[153] Percival had failed to comprehend the tactical skill of the IJA and hence could not evolve any effective countermeasures. In the morning of 11 February, Bennett had under his command his two Australian brigades and the 44th Indian Brigade.[154] In the late evening of 10 February, a counterattack was planned by Percival and Bennett after Wavell's prodding with the aim of driving the Japanese back from the Sungei-Jurong-Sungei Kranji line. The order for this counterattack was issued at 2230 hours on 10 February. In phase one, the Jat Battalion under Cumming and the 16th Punjab were to occupy the high ridge west of the Bukit-Timah-Bukit Panjang Road. Phase two was to start at 0600 hours on 11 February and the Jat Battalion was to capture Hill 72. No artillery support was to be available during phase one and two. However, artillery support would be available during phase three, when the 15th Indian Brigade in the center, the 12th Indian Brigade on its right, and the 44th Indian Brigade on the left would attack. The commanders of the above-mentioned brigades were notified that no air support would be available during the counterattack.[155] Percival noted that if this counterattack failed, then the 8th and 11th divisions were to be withdrawn to a perimeter around Singapore City. Heath and Colonel Harrison were against this withdrawal. For the first time, at least Heath was not advocating retreat. They believed that if the troops were ordered to withdraw, it would be the end of Singapore's defense. They reasoned that it would be better for the troops to defend where they stood even if the counterattack failed. In the end, they fell in line with Percival's wish.[156]

This counterattack never materialized. Only one Indian brigade (the 15th Indian Brigade) at the southern end of the line reached its start line almost unopposed. However, due to failure by its sister formations to support it, this brigade had to withdraw.[157] Even if the counterattack had succeeded in stabilizing the Jurong Switch Line, it would not have altered significantly the nature of the battle in Singapore. The Jurong Line was only four thousand yards long. Yamashita's troops had already consolidated their beachheads and penetrated deep into Singapore Island. But why did even the limited counterattack fail? Percival believed that the counterattack would have succeeded had the Japanese not anticipated it by launching their own attack.[158] Why did Percival assume that the Japanese would remain inactive? Weak leadership by the British and Indian officers was also an important contributory factor in the failure of this projected counterattack. For instance, the Jat Battalion was ordered to capture Hill 220, which overlooks the Bukit Timah Road. Cumming failed to maintain control over the four companies. During phase one of the operation, the A Company under Captain A. G. Khan retreated. The D Company under Captain Watson got separated from the other companies of the Jat Battalion.[159] At 0700 hours of 11 February, the battalion advanced with fixed bayonets. While proceeding up the hill, the men were bombed by Japanese aircraft. Since they had no cover, they suffered some casualties. However, they were able to reach the top of the hill. Then, they waited for further orders, which never came due to a breakdown of communications with higher headquarters. CO Cumming could not conceptualize that he and his battalion should, without waiting for orders, exploit the limited victory gained by them. This was because the British officers were not trained in mission-oriented command. The next day, the battalion (ten British officers and 240 VCOs and jawans) witnessed that the Japanese positioned a battery of guns at their rear and started shelling Singapore City.[160] The men survived by foraging and collecting food from the Chinese villages.[161] The men and their officers remained passive actors. In the absence of orders from above, they decided to do nothing. They should have acted on their own and attacked the Japanese battery.

By 11 February, the 8th AIF casualties numbered roughly seven thousand killed and missing and two thousand in the hospitals. They had suffered most of the casualties in the three days between 8 and 11 February.[162] The 18th British Division retreated from the Northern Sector, and the 11th Indian Division retreated from the naval base.[163] Percival blamed Heath for giving up control of the MacRitchie Reservoir, the main source of water supply for Singapore City.[164] The Bedfordshires and the Hertfordshires at Ayer Raja Road on the right of the 1st Battalion, Malay Regiment, started firing indiscriminately. Panic spread like an epidemic. Seeing such indiscriminate firing, the personnel of the 1st Battalion also started firing blindly. In fact one British officer had written about the Bedfordshires and Hertfordshires: "The regiment was part of 18th Division who had only been in Singapore a few days and were much frightened of rubber trees let alone jungle, than they were of the Jap."[165] During the night of 11/12 February, the 11th Indian Division was ordered to withdraw from the naval base to a line running from Nee Soon to Simpang village in order to protect the left flank of the 18th British Division. The 28th Indian Brigade came into divisional reserve north of Nee Soon, and the 2nd/2nd GR was positioned north of this village. The 8th Indian Brigade, moving eastward along the Mandai Road, took position on the west of Nee Soon.[166]

TOMFORCE's attempt to retake Bukit Timah village from the eastern direction on 11 February failed due to Japanese mortar fire and aerial bombing. On 12 February, the Japanese attacked with light tanks, and the TOMFORCE was pushed back to Adam-Syme Road. In the evening, the TOMFORCE was dissolved. The much-vaunted 18th British Division's hand-picked troops, on whom Wavell and Churchill had put great store, had failed to drive back the Japanese, like Percival's other Allied troops. The W Company of 9th Battalion Royal Northumberland Fusiliers retreated to the east of the MacRitchie Reservoir Broadcasting Station, and its X Company withdrew to the east end of Malcolm Road. The Z Company remained under the 11th Indian Division north of Nee Soon village. The 13th Platoon of the Z Company aided the withdrawal of the 2nd/10th Baluch.[167] On this day, the 11th Indian Division was ordered to withdraw to a position east of Singapore City.[168]

On 12 February (Thursday), leaflets were dropped by Japanese aircraft exhorting the defenders to surrender.[169] The message from Yamashita for Percival is reproduced here:

> Many fierce and gallant fights have been fought by your gallant men and officers.... But the developments of the general war situation has already sealed the fate of Singapore and the continuation of futile resistance would only serve to inflict direct harm and injuries to thousands of non-combatants living in the city, throwing them into further miseries and horror of war, but also would add nothing to the honor of your army. I expect Your Excellency accepting my advice will give up this meaningless and desperate resistance and promptly order the entire front to cease hostilities.[170]

Yamashita was generous in assessing the performance of Percival's troops. The troops of Malaya Command had fought neither fiercely nor gallantly. About seventy-five thousand demoralized troops, all mixed up, were concentrated in a narrow perimeter (of a four-mile radius), which extended from Nee Soon village to the outskirts of Singapore City. The 2nd/2nd GR took position near MS 5 on the Thomson Road near the eastern end of the MacRitchie Reservoir.[171] The 4th/19th Hyderabad, 4th/11th Sikhs, and 2nd/12th FFR in Tyersall Park were bombed and mortared by the Japanese. So many Indian battalions had taken refuge in this park that they presented a good target for the Japanese mortars and aircraft. Percival should have organized a counterattack at them at all costs. On that day, Colonel Gough assumed command of the 12th Indian Brigade.[172] The AIF and parts of the 2nd/15th Indian Brigade comprised the perimeter near the Reformatory Road. On the left, the 44th Indian Brigade extended the defensive line to Pasir Panjang. Bennett accused the 44th Indian Brigade of melting away.[173] Bennett's Australian troops were not in good shape either. The Australian soldiers escaped from the front line and engaged in pillage and plunder in Singapore City. Many broke into the shops selling alcohol. In fact, in several cases, the Australian officers were literally afraid of their men.[174] Both in Malaya and in Bougainville, individuals and small groups of Australians refused to go back to the front line. Mark Johnston writes that the rate of discharge in the Australian force was quite high (above 13 percent of the total strength). In fact, many men were discharged even though they had not suffered combat stress. This was because many men who were incapable of standing the stress and strain of battle had been included in the force. Desertion in the Australian Army was four times higher than in the British Army.[175] Petrol and food were not rationed in Singapore even then. On 12 February, Bennett accepted that Singapore could not be held any longer.[176] One can say that Percival's handling of the city under siege was loose. The "gentlemanly" Percival, exercising "umpire"-like command, had failed to establish a tight grip on the situation as well as on his subordinate commanders.

Capitulation

> The vaunted Fortress of Singapore was no Fortress. It was an undefended tropical island, its coast indented with creeks and belted with mangrove swamps. The enemy had proved that he know how to exploit these swamps. Our troops had shown that they were at sea in them.
>
> Colonel A. M. L. Harrison, GSO 1 of 11th Indian Division[177]

Percival challenged Harrison's assertion that Singapore was an undefended tropical island. Its seaward defense, Percival commented, was impressive, and the army had spent four million pounds in constructing field defense.[178] But, alas, the Japanese launched a land invasion against Singapore from the north instead of a seaborne invasion, and the army's so-called field defense proved inadequate in stopping the Japanese onrush. T. R. Moreman writes that in Singapore, the focus was on beach defense, and not much attention was paid to the fact of jungle warfare. A coherent tactical doctrine among the three different contingents of the Malaya Command (Australian, British, and Indian) for guiding the troops was absent.[179] But, even in beach defense, the Allied troops underperformed. Not only along the coast, but in the course of fighting along the plain terrain also, the Japanese proved that they were masters of the battlefield. After the end of the Second World War, Colonel Ichiji Sugita remarked: "Your forces are not so aggressive as we expect them . . . we easily attacked and occupied the northern parts of Singapore Island."[180]

The day of 13 February was known as Black Friday. Singapore City was heavily shelled and bombed continuously, resulting in severe civilian casualties. Several parts of the city burned intensely, and the situation was so hellish that it reminded many of Dante's *Inferno*. Japanese bombing and shelling caused a series of fires that could not be doused effectively due to a shortage of water.[181] The defense perimeter was just three miles from Fort Canning. The Allied troops held Kalang airfield, Bidadari, Adams Road, and Singapore City.[182] From right to left, the III Indian Corps' 11th Indian Division was on the right, and the 18th British Division was on the left. The 11th Indian Division had taken up a position on the right of the 18th British Division astride the Serangoon Road south of Payar Lebar. The 28th Indian Brigade was in the rear in the rest area between Payar Lebar and Singapore City.[183] The 18th British Division and the 11th Indian Division's headquarters were established in the Chancery Lane-Thompson Road area. The W Company of 9th Battalion Royal Northumberland Fusiliers held the position east of Thomson Road north of the Police Club, and X Company was at the southwest end of Mount Pleasant Road.[184] After the 18th British Division came the 8th AIF on its left and then the Southern Area. The 8th AIF held the area from the junction of Adam and Bukit Timah Roads to Tanglin Halt. The Southern Area was responsible for the seaward front and for the islands of Pulau Bukum, Blakang Mati, Pulau Brani, and Tekong. The inactive Allied troops continued to be bombed, and their officers listlessly looked upward.[185] Probably, Percival lacked the confidence to do anything positive with such dispirited troops.

At 1400 hours on the morning of 13 February, at the request of Heath, Percival summoned a conference of the senior commanders at Fort Canning. In this conference, Percival suggested launching an attack, but all his subordinate commanders unanimously claimed that the situation was hopeless.[186] Percival sent a grim telegram to Wavell:

> Enemy now within five thousand yards of sea front which brings whole of Singapore town within field artillery range. We are also in danger of being driven off water and food supplies. In opinion of commanders troops already committed are too exhausted either to withstand strong attack or to launch counterattack. We would all earnestly welcome the chance of initiating an offensive even though this would only amount to a gesture but even this is not (repeat not) possible as there are no troops who would carry out this attack. In these circumstances it is unlikely that resistance can last more than a day or two.[187]

Percival had lost the will to fight. In this telegram, he continued on to say that all his commanders agreed that further resistance would result in unnecessary hardship to the civilians and destruction of civilian property.[188] In fact, Percival was indirectly asking Wavell to give him permission to surrender in this telegram. Wavell was taken aback by the rapid advance of the Japanese troops on Singapore Island. His idea of conducting a many-months-long attritional defense of Singapore was in ruins. Wavell was worried that the fall of Singapore would free a substantial number of Japanese forces, which could then advance toward Dutch East Indies and British Burma.[189]

On 14 February, the Japanese pincers closed round Bukit Timah and Holland roads. On the western front of the Southern Area, the Allied troops were driven back to the line of Gillman Barracks and Keppel Golf Course. The III Indian Corps was driven back from the Singapore Golf Course to the Chinese Cemetery. In the east, along the Serangoon Road, the Japanese advance elements were only five hundred yards away from the vital Woodleigh Pumping Station.[190] On that day, Singapore City was shelled heavily by the Japanese.[191] Singapore by this time had become a nightmare city. The streets were littered with burnt-out cars, broken glass, tangled telegraph wires, and mangled victims of air raids.[192] Japanese parties with small arms frequented north of Pasir Panjang Road and the Buona Vista corner.[193]

At least some of the Allied battalions were still full of fighting spirit. All the companies of the 9th Battalion of the Royal Northumberland Fusiliers acted as collecting posts for the stragglers, gave them food and tea, and organized them into rifle companies for checking further Japanese irruption.[194] The behavior of the Australian troops toward the latter part of the campaign set a very bad example to the Indian soldiers.[195] On 14 February, news spread among the Indian troops that the Australians were running wild in the city with Tommy Guns, looting and refusing to go back to the front line. However, the 2nd/30th AIF Battalion remained intact. Many Indian soldiers also deserted and threw away their guns and wandered about or hid in the dugouts.[196] One Ms. H. Dane, wife of the general manager of Perak River Hydro Electric Company, however, emphasized that the behavior of some of the Indian troops was very good.[197] On that day, the Jhind Infantry came under the 1st Malay Infantry Brigade.[198] Percival, Heath, and their subordinate commanders had lost all control over their troops as the end neared in Singapore.

Occasionally the victorious, overconfident Japanese met with defeat, though it had no effect on the overall course of the battle. A party of Japanese marched from Buona Vista along Pasir Panjang Road without carrying out prior reconnaissance. When they were within 150 to 100 yards of the Alexandra Road corner, the 1st Battalion Malay Regiment and the 2nd Loyals opened up on them.[199] In a short time, ninety-four Japanese lay dead. At times, Japanese marching discipline (as was previously proved during the Gemas ambush) was very poor.

The day of 14 February stands out for the tragic incident at the three-story Alexandra Military Hospital. It was the principal hospital for the British troops in Singapore, flanked by the Admiralty Oil Tanks of Normanton. A partially prepared defensive position was established on 7 February for the defense of the Depot Area of Alexandra. The Depot Area was east of the Alexandra Road, which in this area ran from north to south. And Alexandra Hospital was located west of the Alexandra Road. On 13 February, the 1st Malay Brigade had withdrawn to the Depot Area. The hospital was full of battle casualties, and patients from Changi Hospital were evacuated to there as well. The Japanese bombers concentrated on the Normanton Oil Tanks from 9 February onward. On 11 February, the medical orderlies destroyed all liquor (whisky and brandy) in the hospital. By 12 February, the front line almost touched the Alexandra Hospital. The sound of machine-gun firing was heard from the west. On 13 February, a few bullets hit the walls of the Alexandra Hospital. On 14 February, Alexandra Hospital's date with history, the Japanese bombers and artillery targeted the area around this region. A thick black pall of smoke rose from the Normanton Oil Tanks. An advance patrol from the 55th Japanese Regiment of the 18th Japanese Division entered the hospital and murdered the patients and orderlies in cold blood. Despite the fact that the orderlies were wearing Red Cross bands, they were shot, and the patients were bayoneted. Some Japanese soldiers dashed upward looking for food and loot. The Japanese later claimed that some Indian soldiers stationed in the Alexandra Hospital had fired on them. Sometime later, a Japanese officer posted a guard at the hospital, but the massacre continued. The rest of the patients were taken out and shot. About two hundred died in the hospital. On 15 February, the Japanese released the doctors and the orderlies who had been locked downstairs. In the afternoon, the 1st Malay Brigade withdrew to the line that ran across Bukit Cherman-Mount Washington and Henderson Road. This line was a mile east of the hospital. The next day, a high-ranking Japanese officer visited the hospital and apologized for the "grievous mistake." The senior Japanese officer provided assurance that food and water would be supplied to the hospital. After the end of the Second World War, Alexandra Hospital continued to function as a civilian hospital. A room where fifty patients were massacred was believed to be haunted.[200]

The population of Singapore during peacetime was 560,000 but rose to over a million during the war due to the influx of the refugees.[201] Key emphasized that Percival had no alternative but to surrender because of the water problem. There was no water in the reservoir, and the water mains had burst, and the PWD was unable to rise to the occasion.[202] The water pipes were close to ground level and hence vulnerable to aerial bombing.[203] In his telegram to Wavell on 13 February, Percival had mentioned the water problem. He himself claimed that on 14 February, he was warned by the director general of Civil Defence that a complete failure of the water supply was imminent. Water was not rationed until 10 February. But Seabridge challenged the issue that water shortage forced Percival to surrender. There were several reservoirs (Seletar, Peirce, etc.) close to the town and in the town itself. A large number of people had dug private wells.[204] Percival could have continued to fight until at least the water supply really failed. To sum up, there might have been a water shortage for the public at large, but Percival had enough water for his troops to carry out fighting for a few more days if he wanted. Even without the water problem, Percival's troops were in a mess. The water issue was probably a pretext that Percival required to surrender. Heath also believed that further resistance would be useless. Probably, Heath was distraught because his young wife (a nurse) was in Singapore and was suffering from aplastic anemia.[205] Heath had previously asked Percival's permission to leave Singapore but was not granted his wish.

Percival did not carry out Wavell's order, which stated that no mercy was to be shown in any shape or form. Wavell emphasized that there must not be any thought of sparing the troops or the civil population. Senior officers must lead the troops and if necessary die with them. Wavell ended his order by noting that there should not be any thought of surrender, but the troops should fight it out to the end in close contact with the enemy.[206] Percival and Shenton Thomas did not even carry out a thorough demolition of the military and other installations at Singapore.[207] About the issue of incomplete demolitions, Percival noted:

> It is true that demolitions at the Singapore Base were far from complete. I have no knowledge of scheme being cancelled.... Admiral Spooner informed me at the meeting of Far East War Council one morning early in February that he had arranged with the GOC 11th Indian Division to carry out the demolitions for him. I understood from what he said that his men had already left the Naval Base. I told him that the responsibility for demolitions in the Naval Base was his and that it could not be delegated to anybody else. I asked him to reoccupy the Naval Base and to resume responsibility.[208]

Percival should be blamed for failing to ensure obedience on the part of his subordinates. For this failure, Percival attempted to pass the buck to Admiral Spooner. Percival had failed to maintain a steel grip over his wavering subordinates. Further, Percival and his subordinates like Bennett and Heath lacked the guts to carry out a Stalingrad-like defense amid the rubble of Singapore City.

Wavell's 10 February order ordering defense to the last was superseded by another order issued on 15 February, which somewhat passed the buck on to Percival, as regards the issue of the further defense of Singapore. Wavell's 15 February order stated: "So long as you are in a position to inflict losses and damage to enemy and your troops are physically capable of doing so you must fight on.... When you are fully satisfied that this is no longer possible I give you discretion to cease resistance."[209] At 0930 hours on 15 February, another conference was called at Fort Canning. The meeting lasted for barely twenty minutes. The food reserves were available for a few days. The ammunition for twenty-five-pounder guns was low, and the ammunition of the Bofors AA guns was exhausted. All of Percival's subordinate commanders informed him that further resistance was hopeless and that surrender was the only option.[210] At that time, the Allied troops held the Kalang airport, the Tarlat air strip, the junction of the Serangoon and Braddell roads, the junction of the Braddell and Thomson roads, the broadcasting station, Bukit Brown, Flagstaff House, the Raffles College area, the Tyersall area, the Tanglin area, the Biscuit Factory, Mt Faber, and the eastern end of the Keppel Golf Links.

The surrender meeting between Percival with his staff officers and Yamashita with his staff took place at the Ford Factory north of Bukit Timah village. At 1810 hours on Friday, 15 February, Percival signed the instrument of surrender. The fighting was to cease at 2030 hours, and the order to this effect was to be issued after 1900 hours.[211] The instrument of surrender laid down that there would be unconditional surrender on the part of the Allied troops. All the troops were to remain in positions occupied at the time of cessation of hostilities. Further, all weapons and military equipment and documents were to be handed over to the IJA. And to prevent looting and disorder in Singapore City, a force of one hundred British armed men were to be left temporarily in the urban area until relieved by the Japanese.[212]

On 15 February, Lieutenant Colonel Glelough, CO of the 4th/19th Hyderabad, wrote: "In our area all our guns had ceased to fire, yet the enemy's seemed to have increased. We had no AA fire and the planes did what they liked—bombing, machine-gunning, observing and photographing—all at low altitudes. We were in a state of complete despair."[213] Not all the British officers were in a state of despair, however. For instance, Lieutenant A. G. Mackenzie of the 1st Battalion Malay Regiment woke up on 16 February, took a bath, and then, late in the day, married a lady named Sybil who worked in the General Hospital.[214]

At 1000 hours on 15 February, the 9th Battalion of the Royal Northumberland Fusiliers received a message ordering the destruction of all remaining liquor. The men realized that the only option before them was surrender, as there was no other place left for retreat, and adequate shipping to evacuate the Singapore garrison was just not available. As the Japanese held all the water reservoirs, orders were issued regarding the greatest economy for the use of water. On this day, W Company fired some 21,000 rounds within a range of one thousand yards. The Japanese infiltrated and drove a wedge between the Y and Z companies. At 1330 hours, a message was received from 18th British Division that all firing was to cease at 1600 hours.[215] Cumming ordered the Jat Battalion to break up into small parties and attempt to escape.[216] At 1510 hours on 15 February, the 4th/19th Hyderabad received a message that an armistice was asked for from 1600 hours. By 1800 hours, it was all quiet. This unit received a message that a ceasefire would be at 2030 hours. At the same time, the Jhind Battalion received orders to stop fighting.[217] The 2nd/26th AIF Battalion also received the same message. They were instructed to remain in their positions and not to fire unless fired upon. The next day, they marched to the University of Singapore on Bukit Timah Road.[218] On 16 February, the Jat Battalion broke up into small parties under the different British officers and the VCOs. Some attempted to escape, but the bulk of the personnel surrendered.[219] On 17 February, the jawans and Indian officers were separated from the British officers. Many British officers broke down as they marched into captivity.[220]

On 16 February, Percival got the news that Gordon Bennett had vanished, and he appointed Brigadier C. A. Callaghan as the CO of the 8th AIF. The 15,395 survivors (including three thousand sick personnel) of the 8th AIF Division were taken into captivity.[221] On 17 February, Fujiwara took charge of the combatant Indian PoWs from the British staff officer Lieutenant Colonel Hunt at Farrar Park.[222] In total, some seventy-five thousand Allied troops surrendered at

Singapore.²²³ The Japanese were shocked and surprised that so many Allied soldiers had surrendered. In accordance with the Japanese military culture, surrender was inconceivable.²²⁴ The IJA suffered only 1,713 killed and 3,378 wounded in Singapore.²²⁵

Origins and Consequences of the INA

The INA was called *Azad Hind Fauj* (Liberation Army of India) by the Indians. Contemporary British officers dismissed the INA as JIFs (Japanese Indian Forces). Nevertheless, British military intelligence was anxious about the existence of this force and tried to block all news of it from contaminating the Indian Army and the people of the Indian subcontinent. Actually, there were two INAs. The first INA was commanded by Captain (promoted to General by the Japanese) Mohan Singh. However, due to differences between Mohan Singh and the Japanese high command, the former was arrested, and the force was dissolved. Then, the Indian revolutionary leader Rash Behari Bose, living in Japan, came to Southeast Asia and took control over this force. The second INA was formed by ex-INC leader Subhas Chandra Bose. While Mohan Singh and Subhas Bose wanted to use the INA primarily as a combat instrument along the India-Burma border, the Japanese mostly wanted to use the INA as a propaganda tool to undermine the loyalty of the British-officered Indian Army fighting the IJA in Burma and also to spark rebellion in British-occupied India. Though Subhas Bose wanted to widen the social base of the INA by recruiting from the Indian diaspora in Southeast Asia, the Indian PoWs captured during the Malaya-Singapore Campaign comprised the core of the INA. In the following paragraphs, we discuss the motives of the Indian PoWs for joining the INA, how many of the PoWs actually joined, and the legacies of this Japanese-supported Indian front.

On 17 February, about forty-five thousand Indian PoWs were separated from their British officers and concentrated in Farrar Park, where they were subjected to Japanese propaganda about India's independence. Major Fujiwara, then attached to Yamashita's headquarters along with Mohan Singh, asked for volunteers to join the INA, and many Indians responded to their call. It is to be noted that the Indian PoWs were separated from their British officers so that the latter could in no way influence or persuade them to remain loyal to the oaths they had taken on behalf of the British king-emperor. And the jawans' sense of isolation increased when their *mai-baps* (father figures; i.e., the British officers) were taken away from their presence. On 7 April, several companies with 323 men each were formed. And the companies were brigaded into three brigades named Azad Brigade, Nehru Brigade, and Gandhi Brigade.²²⁶ The point is that both Fujiwara and Mohan Singh, by naming the INA brigades in accordance with the names of leading INC politicians, were attempting to justify and legitimize the existence of the Japanese-sponsored Indian liberation force.

Discontent and disaffection among the Indian soldiers due to harsh British treatment, racial discrimination, inept handling of the Malaya-Singapore Campaign by the British officers, and the prospect of better treatment at the hands of the Japanese motivated many of the PoWs to join the INA.[227] Due to differences with the Japanese high command, Mohan Singh ordered the disbanding of the INA and was arrested in December 1942. Rash Behari Bose came from Tokyo and became the supreme commander of the INA and the IIL. Lieutenant Colonel J. K. Bhonsle of the 5th Marathas became the GOC of the INA. After returning from Germany in July 1943, Subhas Bose took command of the INA from Rash Behari Bose.[228] Due to the greater charisma, standing, and personality of Subhas Bose compared to Mohan Singh, a larger number of PoWs joined the second INA. Bose had been, after all, a noted nationalist politician who had been the All India Congress Committee's chairman and had also founded the Indian Legion in Germany from the Indian PoWs captured by *Afrika Korps* in North Africa in 1942. In contrast, Mohan Singh was only an officer in the Indian Army promoted from the ranks. Historian Chandar S. Sundaram writes that some forty-five thousand PoWs (including those captured in Burma in 1942) joined Subhas Bose's force.[229] As a point of comparison, only fifteen thousand PoWs had joined the first INA of Mohan Singh.[230]

And not all the Indian PoWs who joined the first INA were volunteers. Between April and December 1942, those Indian commissioned officers, with the aid of some VCOs who had joined the INA, used violence to force the jawans to change sides. Those jawans who refused to join the INA were denied medical treatment and food and were even sent to work in the Japanese "death camps" (labor camps) in New Guinea. One example is that of John Baptist Crasta, who was born on 31 March 1910 near Mangalore in south India. He was an Indian Christian. In 1933, he joined the Indian Army in the noncombatant branch. In March 1941, the 12th Field Battalion in which Crasta was serving was ordered to Singapore. As head clerk, Crasta was in charge of supplying rations to the 11th Indian Division. According to him, torture of the nonvolunteers started under Mohan Singh's direction from late March 1942 onwards.[231] In Crasta's own words:

> Near Bidadare, a camp was created to torture non-volunteers. Although given the innocent name of Separation Camp, it was actually a concentration camp where the most inhuman atrocities were committed by the INA men on their non-volunteer Indian brethren. Subedars Sher Singh and Fateh Khan were put in charge of this notorious prison. High ranking officers who refused to have anything to do with the INA were thrown into it without clothing or food, made to carry heavy loads on their heads, and to double up on the slightest sign of slackness. . . . They would be caned, beaten, and kicked.[232]

However, Subhas Bose never used violence to compel the PoWs to join the second INA. Nevertheless, the Indian PoWs were subjected to virulent propaganda in order to ensure their compliance to join the INA.[233] Subhas Bose attempted to widen the social base of the INA by recruiting from the Indian diaspora in Malaya and Burma. In fact, he set up a women combatant unit known as the Rani Jhansi Regiment. In his conceptual framework, Indian women were to adopt a goddess Durga-like active role rather than a Sita-like passive role (as M. K. Gandhi advocated) in the Indian national movement.[234] Lakshmi Sahgal, the commander of the Rani Jhansi Regiment, remembered Subhas Bose's objective many years after the Second World War:

> He frankly told me that it was his ambition and dream to form a regiment of women who would be willing to take up arms and fight just as the men were going to fight on the battle front.... That was something which had never been contemplated in any other phase of the Indian struggle till then.... He knew that there were limitations to women's physical power, but he felt that psychologically it would have a tremendous effect on Indian men, soldiers as well as Indians inside India, and he cited the example that other countries had been using women as fighting forces and he saw no reason why Indian women also could not take part in a fighting unit.[235]

In fact, the Red Army used women as combatants during their Great Patriotic War. Further, Subhas Bose did away with the British regimental structure (discussed in chap. 2) that organized the jawans on the basis of caste, clan, and religion. All the ethnic communities were mixed even within the companies.

Partly due to pressure from Subhas Bose, during the 1944 Japanese campaigns in the Arakan and in Imphal-Kohima, INA units were used. Lightly equipped, they were mainly designed to incite rebellions in the British-led Indian Army. However, the INA failed in its purpose because the GoI, by providing large amounts of material incentives both to the jawans and their families and opening up the commissioned officers' cadre to the university-educated Indian urban middle class, kept both these groups happy.[236] During the Japanese retreat to Rangoon in the first half of 1945, they were forced to deploy INA units in defensive battles like that in Mount Popa. But without armor and artillery support, the INA failed miserably, and many personnel also deserted to the British side.[237] Though the INA failed in its purpose in wartime, it succeeded in the immediate postwar era in weakening the legitimacy of the Raj.

Between 3 November and 31 December 1945, the GoI attempted a public trial of three high-profile INA officers—one Hindu, one Muslim, and one Sikh—at Red Fort in Delhi. Red Fort was symbolic to Indian national consciousness because it was here that the last Mughal Emperor, Bahadur Shah, was imprisoned during the 1857 uprising. It was a gross political mistake on the part of the British. The imperial attempt to punish the three officers who had forsaken the oath of loyalty taken to the British ruler resulted in generating unity among the three communities of the Indian subcontinent. The public in general was angry with the GoI because of high inflation and a scarcity of necessary goods. Further, from August 1945 onward, the Indian Army started demobilizing the jawans. Its size shrunk from 2.5 million to only 800,000 men. Young Indians had joined the army with the objective of gaining permanent military service in a society rampant with unemployment. Further, long-service Indian military personnel expected that the Raj would provide them with land grants after the war. However, the cash-strapped GoI was not in a position to provide either permanent jobs or land to the demobilized Indian soldiers. Moreover, the young commissioned Indian officers realized that if the British officers left the Indian Army, then their promotion prospects would brighten. At a critical juncture, both the jawans' and the commissioned Indian officers' interest turned against their British masters. Hence, the sword arm of the Raj turned against the "white" sahibs. And the Indian politicians released after long imprisonment whipped up public sentiment in pursuit of their anticolonial agenda. Public and military grievances converged and were further stoked by the Indian politicians. And the INA became a symbol of legitimizing the anticolonial grievances. Overnight, the INA personnel were transformed into heroes and heroines of India. While the INC took up the cause of the Sikh and Hindu soldiers of the INA and the Indian Army, the AIML supported the Muslim personnel. General discontent with the British plus the INA issue had an adverse impact on the Indian armed forces. In 1946, mutinies occurred in the Royal Indian Air Force and in the Royal Indian Navy at Karachi and Bombay (Mumbai).[238] The days of the Raj were numbered.

The INA personnel took part in the Partition riots in Punjab during 1946–47. While the Muslim personnel, acting on the behest of AIML, attacked the Hindus and the Sikhs in west Punjab, the Hindu and Muslim personnel acting for the *Rashtriya Swayamsevak Sangh* (Hindu National Volunteer Organization) and the *Akali Dal* (party of the Sikhs) attacked the Muslim civilians in east Punjab. The military experience of the INA personnel made them essential for the Hindu, Sikh, and Muslim political parties, which organized mass communal riots. After the departure of the British from the Indian subcontinent in August 1947, two independent states, India and Pakistan, came into existence. The armed forces of these two countries did not allow entry of the INA personnel in their ranks. Partly this was because those Indian officers who had remained loyal to the Raj during and after the Second World War got promotions in the armed forces of India and Pakistan. And they did not want any competition that would have resulted if the INA officers were inducted into their armies. Jawaharlal Nehru (who became India's first prime minister) asked some Indian commissioned officers like Brigadier (later General) J. N. Chaudhuri and others (who had remained loyal to the British) about their views on the INA. The commissioned Indian officers responded negatively about the INA men who had broken their oath.[239] After 1947, India and Pakistan maintained comparatively small armies. So the jawans also did not want any competition that would result had the doors been opened to the INA personnel. Further, Nehru was warned by Lord Mountbatten (then commander of South East Asia Command and later the last viceroy of British India) that if the former allowed the INA to serve in the independent Indian Army, then it would result in politicization of the force. And a politicized army, emphasized Mountbatten, might also turn against the Nehru government in the near future. In March 1946, Nehru visited Singapore and wanted to lay a wreath on the memorial for the INA. Mountbatten commented:

> Doubtless you think that the Indian National Army are all like Subhas Chandra Bose, devoted patriots, who have sacrificed everything for their own country. In fact that is not how any of us, who have been in the war, regard them. . . . They were used, to torture those Indians who remained loyal to their oath. When you get your independence and have your own army, the people you want are those who remain

loyal to their oath, and who will stay with you, and not the people who just change according to political opportunism. Otherwise you will find that if you become unpopular in your own country one day, the opposition party will call on the army to turn you out. You want people who will stick to their oath.[240]

Mountbatten's warning did not prevent Nehru from using the INA issue in mobilizing the masses against the Raj in 1946, but it did stop him from attempting to integrate the ex-INA personnel into postindependent India's army. Neither Nehru nor Jinnah could afford to alienate the commissioned officers and the jawans who had remained loyal to the British during the Second World War and comprised the independent Indian and Pakistani armies. It is to be noted that both the Indian and the Pakistani armies rejected the innovative regimental organization introduced by Subhas Bose and did not employ women combatants. Even today, the armies of India and Pakistan retain the regimental structure of the British-Indian Army.

Conclusion

> Well, if you try to put troops into that position who had probably never fired a round in their lives up to that time it wouldn't stop the Japs.
>
> Major-General B. W. Key[241]

So why then did Singapore Island fall so easily? Akashi Yoji writes that the Indian and the Gurkha troops did not get along well in Singapore, which somewhat reduced the combat effectiveness of Percival's force.[242] The Indian Army had a lot of limitations, but the lack of bonhomie between the Gurkhas, Hindu, Muslim, and Sikh troops was not one of them. Key's observation noted at the beginning of this section holds water. Not only were the Australian, British, and Indian troops untrained, but they were also defeated in details. While the Allied soldiers were scattered in small packets, the Japanese infiltrated between these bodies of troops and were able to concentrate their strength at selected points of their own choosing.[243] The morale of the Allied units was also questionable. Racial discrimination of the British as noted in chapter 2 had already weakened the morale of the Indian soldiers from the beginning of the campaign. And as the Battle of Malaya unfolded badly for the British, the Indian soldiers' morale dampened further. And this further encouraged the Indian troops to believe in Japanese propaganda. A large number of desertions occurred from the Baluch battalion, and for the last four days the Jat Battalion under Cumming remained inactive and did not attack the Japanese.[244] Fighting by day and retreating during the night continuously drained the combat spirit of the Allied soldiers. The weak performance of the Allied units was compounded by several other factors.

Before the Japanese invasion of the island, construction of static defensive works was abysmal. The assumption was that the Japanese ground force would not be able to advance quickly along the length of the Malayan Peninsula and threaten the north side of Singapore Island. Tactical leadership on the part of Percival left much to be desired. Percival and his subordinates seemed to have been gripped by command paralysis. He was slow to respond to the Japanese threat. To use a modern terminology, rather than going inside the enemy's Observe, Orient, Decide, Act (OODA) loop, Percival was almost inert. Historian Alan Warren asserts that on the morning or at least by noon of 9 February, Percival should have shifted the troops from northeast and southern parts of Singapore Island to the northwest part where the Japanese attack was developing.[245] Such a tactical move probably could not have saved the island from Japanese invasion but would have delayed the time table of the Japanese and certainly would have caused them a lot more casualties.

Not only operational cum tactical leadership on part of the senior Commonwealth commanders like Percival, Heath, and Bennett left much to be desired, but also command at the brigade level was of low quality. Interbrigade cooperation and communication broke down because Percival's force was of heterogeneous character and also due to a lack of joint training and staff exercise among the different brigade commanders. The Australians retreated repeatedly without notifying the neighboring Indian infantry units, which left the latter's flank in the air. And through this gap, the Japanese infantry infiltrated.[246] The newly enlisted British officers failed to exercise control over the heterogeneous mass of raw, inexperienced jawans at the battalion level. Inferior tactics, incompetent command, and racial discrimination of the Indian soldiers were the chief culprits. All these weaknesses were evident during the campaign in the Malayan Peninsula, and Percival and his commanders were unable to rectify them during their last battle on Singapore Island.

Notes

1. Alan Warren, *Britain's Greatest Defeat: Singapore 1942* (2002; repr., London: Hambledon Continuum, 2002), 213.

2. Warren, *Britain's Greatest Defeat*, 211. According to Colin Smith, Singapore Island covers about 240 square miles. Colin Smith, *Singapore Burning: Heroism and Surrender in World War II* (2005; repr., London: Penguin, 2006), 1.

3. Timothy Hall, *The Fall of Singapore* (1983; repr., Oxon, UK: Routledge, 2015), 21–22.

4. Warren, *Britain's Greatest Defeat*, 211.

5. Compton Mackenzie, *Eastern Epic*, vol. 1, *September 1939–March 1943* (London: Chatto & Windus, 1951), 376; Hall, *Fall of Singapore*, 20; Warren, *Britain's Greatest Defeat*, 211.

6. Operations in the Far East, L/WS/1/952, OIOC, BL, London, 27.

7. General Archibald Wavell, Despatch on Operations in South-West Pacific 15 Jan.–25 Feb. 1942, CAB 106/38, PRO, Kew, London, 3.

8. Note on the Malayan Campaign by LMH, Heath Papers, 1–2.

9. Warren, *Britain's Greatest Defeat*, 203.

10. Account of Brigadier G. C. Ballentine Commander 44th Indian Infantry Brigade, 1973-09-2, NAM, London, 3.

11. Major-General Gurbakhsh Singh, *Indelible Reminiscences: Memoirs of Major-General Gurbakhsh Singh* (New Delhi: Lancer, 2013), 31.

12. History of the 11th Indian Division in Malaya, Comments by Lieutenant General A. E. Percival, Percival Papers, IWM.

13. Notes by Lieutenant General A. E. Percival on Singapore 1942, Percival Papers, 1.

14. Operations in Malaya and Singapore, E. E. Bridges, Report drawn up by Major H. P. Thomas, July 27, 1942, WP(42)314, CAB/66/26/44, PRO, Kew, Surrey, 16.

15. Col. A. M. L. Harrison, History of the 11th Indian Infantry Division in Malaya 1941–42, CAB 106/57, PRO, Kew, 487.

16. Percival's figure that Yamashita had three hundred tanks is certainly an overestimate. Letter from Percival to the Under-Secy. of State for War, London, May 3, 1948, Percival Papers.

17. Harrison, History of the 11th Indian Infantry Division in Malaya 1941–42, CAB 106/57, 479.

18. History of the 4/19th Hyderabad Regiment after the Slim Battle up to Capitulation, MISC/707/H, MODHS, New Delhi, 2; Major General B. W. Key, 11th Indian Division, P 456, IWM, 17.

19. Warren, *Britain's Greatest Defeat*, 213.

20. War Cabinet, The Malayan Campaign, April 4, 1942, WP(42)145, CAB/66/23/25, PRO, 2.

21. John McEwan, *Out of the Depths of Hell: A Soldier's Story of Life and Death in Japanese Hands* (1999; repr., Barnsley: Pen & Sword, 2014), 35.

22. Williamson Murray, *War, Strategy, and Military Effectiveness* (Cambridge: Cambridge University Press, 2011), 48.

23. Karl Hack and Kevin Blackburn, *Did Singapore Have to Fall? Churchill and the Impregnable Fortress* (2004; repr., Oxon, UK: Routledge, 2008), 1; Harrison, History of the 11th Indian Infantry Division in Malaya 1941–42, CAB 106/57, 474.

24. Percival, December 14, 1945, Percival Papers.

25. Hall, *Fall of Singapore*, 23–24.

26. The Official History of the Second World War, The War against Japan, vol. 1, Part 2, Comments by Lieutenant General A. E. Percival, December 2, 1953, Percival Papers, 4; Brigadier E. V .R. Bellers, *The History of the 1st King George V's Own Gurkha Rifles (The Malaun Regiment)*, vol. 2, *1920–1947* (Aldershot, UK: Gale & Polden, 1956), 129.

27. Harrison, History of the 11th Indian Infantry Division in Malaya 1941–42, CAB 106/57, 481.

28. The Diary of Lieutenant Colonel H. S. Flower, 9th Battalion Royal Northumberland Fusiliers, Outward Voyage, at Singapore, Compiled by R. C. Fenwick, 86/87/1, IWM.

29. Quoted from The Diary of Lieutenant Colonel H. S. Flower, February 8, 1942.

30. The Diary of Lieutenant Colonel H. S. Flower, February 7 and 8, 1942.

31. Lieutenant D. J. Glanfield, 118th Royal Artillery Field Regiment, 90/15/1, IWM.

32. Harrison, History of the 11th Indian Infantry Division in Malaya 1941–42, CAB 106/57, 471–72.

33. Quoted from Harrison, History of the 11th Indian Infantry Division in Malaya 1941–42, CAB 106/57, 473.

34. Quoted from Harrison, History of the 11th Indian Infantry Division in Malaya 1941–42, CAB 106/57, 473–74.

35. Harrison, History of the 11th Indian Infantry Division in Malaya 1941–42, CAB 106/57, 474.

36. Letter from Henry Pownall to Percival, March 31, Percival Papers.

37. Letter from Percival, April 4, 1950, Percival Papers; Hall, *Fall of Singapore*, 22.

38. The Official History of the Second World War, The War against Japan, vol. 1, Part 2, Comments by Percival, December 2, 1953, Percival Papers, 1; Clifford Kinvig, *Scapegoat: General Percival of Singapore* (London: Brassey's 1996), 195, 197, 204.

39. Harrison, History of the 11th Indian Infantry Division in Malaya 1941–42, CAB 106/57, 472, 479, 484.

40. McEwan, *Out of the Depths of Hell*, 35.

41. Harrison, History of the 11th Indian Infantry Division in Malaya 1941–42, CAB 106/57, 488.

42. Account of the Malayan Campaign by Captain F. E. Mileham 4/9th Jat Regiment, Singapore, D1196/33, OIOC, BL.

43. Lieutenant Colonel A. E. Cumming, The Fall of Singapore, L/WS/1/952, OIOC, BL, 1-2, 6; Stephen D. Wesbrook, "The Potential for Military Disintegration," in *Combat Effectiveness: Cohesion, Stress, and the Volunteer Military*, ed. Sam C. Sarkesian (Beverly Hills: SAGE, 1980), 259; Edward A. Shils and Morris Janowitz, "Cohesion and Disintegration in the Wehrmacht in World War II," *Public Opinion Quarterly* 12, no. 2 (1948): 299, 306.

44. Harrison, History of the 11th Indian Infantry Division in Malaya 1941–42, CAB 106/57, 484–85; Bellers, *History of the 1st King George V's*, 129.

45. Harrison, History of the 11th Indian Infantry Division in Malaya 1941–42, CAB 106/57, 485.

46. Key, 11th Indian Division, 17.

47. Harrison, 11th Indian Division Malaya, Chaps. 24–25, CAB 106/58, PRO, 496.

48. Harrison, History of the 11th Indian Infantry Division in Malaya 1941–42, CAB 106/57, 485–86.

49. Wesbrook, "Potential for Military Disintegration," 252–53.

50. Harrison, History of the 11th Indian Infantry Division in Malaya 1941–42, CAB 106/57, 480.

51. Account of Ballentine Commander 44th Indian Brigade, 5.

52. Operations in Malaya and Singapore, Bridges, 15.

53. Account of Ballentine Commander 44th Indian Brigade, 3.

54. Captain S. Hannam, 2nd/26th Battalion, P 470, IWM, 1.

55. Harrison, History of the 11th Indian Infantry Division in Malaya 1941–42, CAB 106/57, 479.

56. Hannam, 2nd/26th Battalion, 2–3.

57. Harrison, History of the 11th Indian Infantry Division in Malaya 1941–42, CAB 106/57, 480, 482.

58. C. Bayly and Tim Harper, *Forgotten Armies: The Fall of British Asia, 1941-1945* (London: Allen Lane, 2004), 133.

59. Mark Johnston, *At the Frontline: Experiences of Australian Soldiers in World War II* (Melbourne: Cambridge University Press, 1996), 37.

60. Account of Ballentine Commander 44th Indian Brigade, 1–2.

61. Major S. A. Watt, 7th Rajputana Rifles in Malaya, 1977-09-62, NAM, 17.

62. Account of Ballentine Commander 44th Indian Brigade, 2.

63. Account of Ballentine Commander 44th Indian Brigade, 1–2.

64. Summary of Comments by Lord Wavell on General Percival's dispatch on Operations of Malaya Command, Appendix B, Percival Papers, 1.

65. Kinvig, *Scapegoat*, 176, 178.

66. Account of Ballentine Commander 44th Indian Brigade, 2.

67. Account of Ballentine Commander 44th Indian Brigade, 2–5.

68. Account of Ballentine Commander 44th Indian Brigade, 4–5.

69. Lieutenant D. H. Webber, 1st Malay Regiment, 88/33/1, IWM, 27; Lieutenant S. E. Bell, "Hospital in No Man's Land: The Atrocity at Alexandra Hospital, Singapore,"

88/63/1, IWM, 1; Harrison, History of the 11th Indian Infantry Division in Malaya 1941–42, CAB 106/57, 480.

70. Lieutenant A. G. Mackenzie, 1st Malay Regiment, 90/15/1, IWM, 1.

71. Harrison, History of the 11th Indian Infantry Division in Malaya 1941–42, CAB 106/57, 480.

72. Mackenzie, 1st Malay Regiment, 1.

73. Harrison, History of the 11th Indian Infantry Division in Malaya 1941–42, CAB 106/57, 481.

74. Kinvig, *Scapegoat*, 201–2; Bayly and Harper, *Forgotten Armies*, 136.

75. Account of Ballentine Commander 44th Indian Brigade, 5.

76. Harrison, History of the 11th Indian Infantry Division in Malaya 1941–42, CAB 106/57, 481.

77. The Story of Singapore by George Sansom in Current Affairs, January 1942, Percival Papers, 5.

78. History of the 4/19th Hyderabad Regiment after the Slim Battle up to Capitulation, 1.

79. Brigadier Jasbir Singh, *Escape from Singapore* (New Delhi: Lancer, 2010), 41–42.

80. History of the 4/19th Hyderabad Regiment after the Slim Battle up to Capitulation, 1.

81. Hall, *Fall of Singapore*, 32.

82. G. W. Seabridge, Report on the Fall of Singapore, April 25, 1942, WP(42)177, CAB/66/24/7, PRO, 2.

83. History of the 4/19th Hyderabad Regiment after the Slim Battle up to Capitulation, 1–2; Richard Holmes, *Acts of War: The Behaviour of Men in Battle* (1985; repr., New York: Free Press, 1989), 36–37.

84. Watt, 7th Rajputana Rifles in Malaya, 17.

85. John A. English, *On Infantry* (1981; repr., New York: Praeger, 1984), 69.

86. Omer Bartov, "Daily Life and Motivation in War: The Wehrmacht in the Soviet Union," *Journal of Strategic Studies* 12, no. 2 (1989): 200–14.

87. A Statement by Ms. H. Dane, L/WS/1/952, OIOC, BL, 72.

88. Sibylla Jane Flower, "Allied Prisoners of War: The Malayan Campaign, 1941–42," in *Sixty Years On: The Fall of Singapore Revisited*, ed. Brian Farrell and Sandy Hunter (2002; repr., Singapore: Eastern Universities Press, 2003), 208.

89. Seabridge, Report on the Fall of Singapore, 2–3; *India's Freedom Struggle and the Great INA: Memoirs of Major-General Mohammad Zaman Kiani* (New Delhi: Reliance, 1994), 42.

90. *India's Freedom Struggle and the Great INA*, 41–2.

91. Despatch on the Far East by Air Chief Marshal Robert Brooke-Popham, Commander-in-Chief Far East (17 Oct. 1940–27 Dec. 1941), September 8, 1942, CAB/66/28/33, PRO, 26.

92. H. C. Phillips, Secret, Appendix 49, General Staff Malaya Command to III Indian Corps, Southern Area and AIF, February 3, 1942, Percival Papers.

93. Quoted from Phillips, Secret, Appendix 49.

94. Robert Lyman, *The Generals: From Defeat to Victory, Leadership in Asia 1941–45* (London: Constable, 2008), 34.

95. Meirion and Susie Harries, *Soldiers of the Sun: The Rise and Fall of the Imperial Japanese Army* (New York: Random House, 1991), 307.

96. Harrison, History of the 11th Indian Infantry Division in Malaya 1941–42, CAB 106/57, 494–95.

97. Harrison, 11th Indian Division Malaya, Chaps. 24–25, CAB 106/58, 496–97.
98. H. Gordon Bennett, "Review of The Conquest of Malaya, Singapore, the Japanese Version by Masanobu Tsuji," *Journal of Southeast Asian Studies* 2, no. 3 (1961): 98.
99. Kinvig, *Scapegoat*, 204.
100. Warren, *Britain's Greatest Defeat*, 224–25.
101. Quoted from Harrison, 11th Indian Division Malaya, Chaps. 24–25, CAB 106/58, 498.
102. Harrison, 11th Indian Division Malaya, Chaps. 24–25, CAB 106/58, 498.
103. History of the 4/19th Hyderabad Regiment after the Slim Battle up to Capitulation, 3.
104. Hannam, 2nd/26th Battalion, 3.
105. English, *On Infantry*, 68.
106. Seabridge, Report on the Fall of Singapore, 6.
107. Lyman, *The Generals*, 59.
108. Account of Ballentine Commander 44th Indian Brigade, 6.
109. Operations in Malaya and Singapore, Bridges, 17.
110. Account of Ballentine Commander 44th Indian Brigade, 6–7.
111. Singh, *Indelible Reminiscences*, 60.
112. Harrison, 11th Indian Division Malaya, Chaps. 24–25, CAB 106/58, 497.
113. History of the 4/19th Hyderabad Regiment after the Slim Battle up to Capitulation, 3–4.
114. History of the 4/19th Hyderabad Regiment after the Slim Battle up to Capitulation, 4.
115. Bayly and Harper, *Forgotten Armies*, 141.
116. Account of Ballentine Commander 44th Indian Brigade, 6.
117. Quoted from Singh, *Indelible Reminiscences*, 57.
118. Singh, *Indelible Reminiscences*, 57.
119. The Diary of Lieutenant Colonel H. S. Flower, February 9, 1942.
120. Cumming, The Fall of Singapore, 2.
121. Harrison, 11th Indian Division Malaya, Chaps. 24–25, CAB 106/58, 499.
122. Hannam, 2nd/26th Battalion, 3.
123. Quoted from Hannam, 2nd/26th Battalion, 4.
124. History of the 4/19th Hyderabad Regiment after the Slim Battle up to Capitulation, 4.
125. Harrison, 11th Indian Division Malaya, Chaps. 24–25, CAB 106/58, 499–500.
126. The Diary of Lieutenant Colonel H. S. Flower, 9th Battalion Royal Northumberland Fusiliers, 10 Feb. 1942; Harrison, 11th Indian Division Malaya, Chaps. 24–25, CAB 106/58, 509.
127. Bellers, *History of the 1st King George V's*, 132; Harrison, 11th Indian Division Malaya, Chaps. 24–25, CAB 106/58, 500–1.
128. History of the 4/19th Hyderabad Regiment after the Slim Battle up to Capitulation, 5.
129. Quoted from Harrison, 11th Indian Division Malaya, Chaps. 24–25, CAB 106/58, 501.
130. Harrison, 11th Indian Division Malaya, Chaps. 24–25, CAB 106/58, 502.
131. History of the 4/19th Hyderabad Regiment after the Slim Battle up to Capitulation, 5; Harrison, 11th Indian Division Malaya, Chaps. 24–25, CAB 106/58, 503.
132. History of the 4/19th Hyderabad Regiment after the Slim Battle up to Capitulation, 4–5.
133. History of the 4/19th Hyderabad Regiment after the Slim Battle up to Capitulation, 5.

134. History of the 4/19th Hyderabad Regiment after the Slim Battle up to Capitulation, 6.
135. Johnston, *At the Frontline*, 13–5.
136. Mackenzie, 1st Malay Regiment, 1.
137. Webber, 1st Malay Regiment, 29.
138. Cumming, The Fall of Singapore, 3.
139. Account of the Malayan Campaign by Mileham 4/9th Jat Regiment, Singapore.
140. Quoted from Harrison, 11th Indian Division Malaya, Chaps. 24–25, CAB 106/58, 504; Lieutenant General G. N. Molesworth, *Curfew on Olympus* (Bombay: Asia Publishing House, 1965), 198; Kinvig, *Scapegoat*, 207.
141. Harrison, 11th Indian Division Malaya, Chaps. 24–25, CAB 106/58, 505–6.
142. Quoted from Harrison, 11th Indian Division Malaya, Chaps. 24–25, CAB 106/58, 508.
143. Wavell, Despatch on Operations in South-West Pacific 15 Jan.–25 Feb. 1942, 13.
144. Percival, December 14, 1945, Percival Papers.
145. Copy of General Wavell's last Order issued in Singapore, Percival Papers.
146. Kinvig, *Scapegoat*, 206.
147. History of the 4/19th Hyderabad Regiment after the Slim Battle up to Capitulation, 7.
148. Seabridge, Report on the Fall of Singapore, 2.
149. Watt, 7th Rajputana Rifles in Malaya, 17–18.
150. Operations in the Far East, L/WS/1/952, OIOC, BL.
151. The Diary of Lieutenant Colonel H. S. Flower, February 11, 1942.
152. Letter from Henry Pownall to Percival, February 9, 1950; Letter from Percival to Pownall, February 12, 1950, Percival Papers.
153. GOC Malaya Command 11 Feb. 1942, Percival Papers.
154. Clifford Kinvig, "General Percival and the Fall of Singapore," in *Sixty Years On*, ed. Farrell and Hunter, 259.
155. Cumming, The Fall of Singapore, 3.
156. Harrison, 11th Indian Division Malaya, Chaps. 24–25, CAB 106/58, 510.
157. Operations in Malaya and Singapore, Bridges, 18.
158. Notes by Lieutenant General A. E. Percival on Singapore 1942, Percival Papers, 2; Kinvig, *Scapegoat*, 206.
159. Cumming, The Fall of Singapore, 3.
160. Account of the Malayan Campaign by Captain F. E. Mileham 4/9th Jat Regiment, Singapore; Cumming, The Fall of Singapore, 3–4.
161. Cumming, The Fall of Singapore, 5.
162. Operations in Malaya and Singapore, Bridges, Appendix A, 20.
163. Operations in the Far East, L/WS/1/952.
164. Notes by Lieutenant General A. E. Percival on certain Senior Commanders and other matters, Percival Papers, 2.
165. Mackenzie, 1st Malay Regiment, 1.
166. Bellers, *History of the 1st King George V's*, 133–34.
167. The Diary of Lieutenant Colonel H. S. Flower, February 10 and 12, 1942.
168. Bellers, *History of the 1st King George V's*, 134.
169. Hannam, 2nd/26th Battalion, 5.
170. Singh, *Indelible Reminiscences*, 69.
171. Bellers, *History of the 1st King George V's*, 134–35.
172. History of the 4/19th Hyderabad Regiment after the Slim Battle up to Capitulation, 7.

173. War Cabinet, The Malayan Campaign, April 4, 1942, 4.
174. Bayly and Harper, *Forgotten Armies*, 138, 149.
175. Johnston, *At the Frontline*, 55.
176. Seabridge, Report on the Fall of Singapore, 1–2.
177. Harrison, History of the 11th Indian Infantry Division in Malaya 1941–42, CAB 106/57, 483.
178. History of the 11th Indian Division in Malaya, comments by Percival, Percival Papers.
179. T. R. Moreman, *The Jungle, the Japanese and the British Commonwealth Armies at War, 1941–45: Fighting Methods, Doctrine and Training for Jungle Warfare* (London: Frank Cass, 2005), 13; Alan Jeffreys, *Approach to Battle: Training the Indian Army during the Second World War* (Solihull: Helion, 2017), 131.
180. Colonel Ichiji Sugita, 2839/03, IWM, 2.
181. Singh, *Indelible Reminiscences*, 66.
182. Operations in the Far East, L/WS/1/952.
183. Bellers, *History of the 1st King George V's*, 137.
184. The Diary of Lieutenant Colonel H. S. Flower, February 13, 1942.
185. History of the 4/19th Hyderabad Regiment after the Slim Battle up to Capitulation, 8; Report on the Circumstances under which Major General Gordon Bennett vacated the Command of the Australian Imperial Force, Malaya, October 18, 1945, Percival Papers, 1.
186. From CGS Australia to War Office, 2 April 1942, L/WS/1/952; Report on the Circumstances, Percival Papers, 1.
187. Quoted from Telegram, Percival to Wavell, February 13, 1942, P 23, F 47, Percival Papers.
188. Telegram, Percival to Wavell, February 13, 1942, P 23, F 47, Percival Papers.
189. Wavell, Despatch on Operations in South-West Pacific 15 Jan.–25 Feb. 1942, Appendix D, 14.
190. Report on the Circumstances, Percival Papers, 2.
191. History of the 4/19th Hyderabad Regiment after the Slim Battle up to Capitulation, 8.
192. Meirion and Susie Harries, *Soldiers of the Sun*, 309.
193. Mackenzie, 1st Malay Regiment, 6.
194. The Diary of Lieutenant Colonel H. S. Flower, February 14, 1942.
195. Operations in Malaya and Singapore, Bridges, Appendix B, 24.
196. History of the 4/19th Hyderabad Regiment after the Slim Battle up to Capitulation, 8.
197. A Statement by Ms H. Dane, L/WS/1/952, OIOC, BL, 72.
198. Singh, *Indelible Reminiscences*, 67.
199. Mackenzie, 1st Malay Regiment, 7.
200. Bell, "Hospital in No Man's Land," 1–9.
201. Hack and Blackburn, *Did Singapore Have to Fall?*, 15. Warren notes that the population of Singapore during capitulation rose from 769,216 to about 900,000 men: *Britain's Greatest Defeat*, 211.
202. Key, 11th Indian Division, 19.
203. Harrison, History of the 11th Indian Infantry Division in Malaya 1941–42, CAB 106/57, 482.
204. Seabridge, Report on the Fall of Singapore, 2; Report on the Circumstances, Percival Papers, 2.

205. Lewis Heath Papers, October 19-20, 1942, LMH 11, P 442, IWM.
206. Copy of General Wavell's Last Order issued in Singapore, Percival Papers.
207. Letter from Allen to Percival, March 22, 1950, Percival Papers.
208. The Malayan Campaign, Answers to Admiralty Questions, Percival Papers.
209. Notes by Percival on Singapore 1942, Percival Papers, 2.
210. From CGS Australia to War Office, April 3, 1942, L/WS/1/952; Singh, *Indelible Reminiscences*, 71.
211. Report on the Circumstances, Percival Papers, 3-4; Singh, *Indelible Reminiscences*, 73.
212. The Instrument of Surrender of Singapore, February 15, 1942, Percival Papers.
213. History of the 4/19th Hyderabad Regiment after the Slim Battle up to Capitulation, 8.
214. Mackenzie, 1st Malay Regiment, 9-10.
215. The Diary of Lieutenant Colonel H. S. Flower, February 15, 1942.
216. Account of the Malayan Campaign by Captain F. E. Mileham 4/9th Jat Regiment, Singapore.
217. Singh, *Indelible Reminiscences*, 73.
218. Hannam, 2nd/26th Battalion, 5.
219. Cumming, The Fall of Singapore, 5-6.
220. History of the 4/19th Hyderabad Regiment after the Slim Battle up to Capitulation, 8.
221. Report on the Circumstances, 4; Despatch on Operation of Malaya Command, 8 Dec.-15 Feb. 42, by Major General A. E. Percival, January 27, 1947, Percival Papers; Jeffrey Grey, *A Military History of Australia* (Cambridge: Cambridge University Press, 1990), 169.
222. T. R. Sareen, ed., *Select Documents on Indian National Army* (Delhi: Agam Prakashan, 1988), 20-21.
223. Raymond Callahan, *The Worst Disaster: The Fall of Singapore* (1977; repr., Singapore: Cultured Lotus, 2001), 11.
224. Sugita, 2839/03, IWM, 7.
225. Lyman, *The Generals*, 359.
226. Lieutenant Colonel E. L. Sawyer, Royal Artillery, 22nd Mountain Regiment attached to the 11th Indian Division, The Growth of the Indian National Army and the General Conditions of Indian Prisoners of War in Singapore from 1942 to 1943, 88/33/1, IWM.
227. Chandar S. Sundaram, "The Indian National Army, 1942-1946: A Circumstantial Force," in *A Military History of India and South Asia: From the East India Company to the Nuclear Era*, ed. Daniel P. Marston and Chandar S. Sundaram (Westport, CT: Praeger, 2007), 123.
228. Kaushik Roy, "Axis Satellite Armies of World War II: A Case Study of the *Azad Hind Fauj*, 1942-45," *Indian Historical Review* 35, no. 1 (2008): 149; Sawyer, The Growth of the Indian National Army and the General Conditions of Indian Prisoners of War in Singapore from 1942 to 1943, 2-3.
229. Sundaram, "Indian National Army," 129.
230. Roy, "Axis Satellite Armies," 152.
231. John Baptist Crasta, *Eaten by the Japanese: The Memoir of an Unknown Indian Prisoner of War* (1998; repr., Bangalore: Invisible Man Publishers, 1999), 1-24.
232. Quoted from Crasta, *Eaten by the Japanese*, 25-26.
233. Sawyer, The Growth of the Indian National Army.

234. Carol Hills, "Nationalism and Feminism in Late Colonial India: The Rani of Jhansi Regiment, 1943–1945," *Modern Asian Studies* 27, no. 4 (1993): 741–60.

235. Oral History Interview with Dr Lakshmi Sahgal, Kanpur, November 17, 1973, by S.L. Manchanda, Acc No. 277, NMML, New Delhi, 11–12.

236. Kaushik Roy, "Military Loyalty in the Colonial Context: A Case Study of the Indian Army during World War II," *Journal of Military History* 73, no. 2 (2009): 497–529.

237. 28th Army Operations, Operations KAN 2 & 3, Dec. 1944–April 1945, CAB 44/203, PRO, Kew.

238. Daniel P. Marston, "End of the Raj, 1945–1947," in *A Military History of India and South Asia*, ed. Marston and Sundaram, 131–38.

239. Oral History Interview with General J. N. Chauhduri, New Delhi, March 23, 1973, by B. R. Nanda, Acc No. 426, NMML, 12–13.

240. Oral History Interview with Lord Mountbatten, London, July 26, 1967 by B. R. Nanda, Acc No. 351, NMML, 4.

241. Key, 11th Indian Division, 20.

242. Akashi Yoji, "General Yamashita Tomoyuki: Commander of the Twenty-Fifth Army," in *Sixty Years On*, ed. Farrell and Hunter, 195.

243. Key, 11th Indian Division, 20.

244. History of the 11th Indian Division in Malaya, Comments by Percival, Percival Papers.

245. Warren, *Britain's Greatest Defeat*, 231.

246. Key, 11th Indian Division, 16.

Conclusion

Including noncombatants (administrative personnel and LoC troops), the Japanese used some 75,000 soldiers in the Malaya-Singapore Campaign. Percival in total had 138,000 soldiers (including LoC personnel and administrative support personnel) fighting against them.[1] The Malaya-Singapore Campaign cost the Japanese 9,600 casualties (3,500 dead and 6,100 wounded).[2] The Japanese aircraft losses were substantial. Some 331 aircraft were damaged, and 270 were received as replacements. Some of the damaged aircraft were returned to frontline duties after minor repair. Overall, the Japanese used some 560 aircraft, and the Allied side fielded 246 aircraft in total against them.[3] The 8th AIF Division suffered 1,700 killed and 1,300 wounded, and 15,000 became PoWs.[4] The 18th British Division suffered 612 killed, 1,065 missing, and 1,232 wounded; the rest of the personnel of this division became PoWs. The total British casualties (including killed, wounded, missing, and PoWs) numbered 38,297 personnel. About 60,000 Indian soldiers of the III Corps became PoWs. In total, Percival's force had about 8,000 fatalities and more than 11,000 were wounded, and the rest became PoWs.[5]

Racial prejudice and the tendency to denigrate the qualities of non-Western military organizations led the Americans and the British to highly underestimate the capabilities of the Japanese war machine. This explains, to an extent, the complacency of the British commanders in Malaya before the onset of the Japanese invasion. Tsuji admits that the Japanese made a mistake in underrating the strength of the Allied forces in Malaya.[6] Still, the Japanese came out victorious. How was this possible? Murray writes that the willingness to be self-critical enables a military organization to perform successfully in a war.[7] Never once was the Malaya High Command being self-critical. Percival blamed Churchill for the disaster in Malaya-Singapore. After the Second World War, Percival argued that Churchill believed that the Japanese would not go to war until it was too late.[8] British grand strategy in late 1941 was faulty, but that does not explain why the Allied troops on the ground fought so miserably. Percival stated that he was defeated due to the vast numerical superiority of the Japanese. He erroneously believed that five Japanese divisions attacked him.[9] He wrongly argued that Yamashita had three hundred thousand troops backed by 940 aircraft.[10] After the end of the war, Lewis Heath, in a long note on the Malaya Campaign, attempted to exonerate himself and his troops. He speaks of fifth column support for the Japanese.[11] G. W. Seabridge rightly challenged the assumption that the Japanese won due to fifth column support. In fact, the Malays, he rightly said, remained more or less neutral. There were only a few pro-Japanese Malays.[12] If the Japanese received support from the locals, the British only had their racial prejudice and the nature of colonial administration to blame. The support of the locals to the Japanese is probably overstated. In fact, Ian Morrison, correspondent of *The Times* asserted that if a few Malays aided the Japanese, many more aided the British.[13]

Heath says that the defeat in Malaya was because of the loss of aerial and naval superiority and absence of an arm for maneuver (tanks).[14] Both Heath and Key considered that defeat in Malaya was inevitable because of the abovementioned factors.[15] None of the Allied commanders accepted that they and their troops fought badly in Malaya. In fact, Heath, who suffered from "withdrawal mania" during the campaign, in a postwar note says that credit is due to him for conducting the withdrawal across the Malayan Peninsula, which enabled him to save the army from Yamashita's pincers. Heath says that his plan was to fight a battle at the concentrated area of Johore. The battered III Indian Corps failed to fight even an attritional battle at Johore and escaped from the Malayan Peninsula only to surrender ignominiously in Singapore. In the confused close-quarter combat that occurred in the rubber plantations and jungles, the Allied forces were unable to utilize their superiority in artillery fully. Heath and Bennett write that in the dense jungles of Malaya, reduced visibility and restricted fields of fire created problems for the defenders.[16] The jungle did not create problems for the Japanese. However, the jungle was a problem for the Allied troops because they were badly trained. Both theoretically and practically, the Allied commanders and their troops had no adequate response to the three elements of Japanese fish hook/filleting tactics: infiltration, encirclement, and roadblock.

The jungle terrain suited the Japanese military machine, with its light field artillery and its lack of motorized transport. The ability of the Japanese troops to live off the country and advance quickly compensated the weak logistical structure of the IJA.[17] Obsolete aircraft, numerical inferiority, and inadequate warning systems in the exposed airfields resulted in the Japanese gaining aerial superiority early in the campaign, and they maintained it until the fall of Singapore.[18] Murray, in the context of the German campaign in Poland in 1939, writes that CAS for the German troops had a negative impact on the enemy's morale, rather than causing massive destruction of hostile military assets.[19] This also holds true in case of the Japanese air force's CAS to their ground troops against Percival's force. Wavell also accepted that the Japanese air force, rather than causing extensive material damage to the Allied troops, had an adverse psychological effect on the latter.[20] Again the Japanese tanks generated psychological pressure rather than massive losses among the Allied troops. On the Eastern Front from late 1943 onward, with a lesser number of tanks and dwindling Luftwaffe support, the numerically inferior German infantry fought magnificently. The Allied troops, being badly trained and badly led, were unable to stand up to the intense psychological pressure generated by the Japanese tanks and aircraft. After the end of the war, Percival admitted that the Japanese blitz tactics and Japanese air force to a great extent were responsible for the Allied force crumbling in Malaya-Singapore.[21] Francis Pike terms the Japanese advance along Malaya as a "bicycle blitzkrieg."[22] This is partly true, as the Japanese soldiers also marched rapidly along the Malayan mainland besides using bicycles.

Besides inefficient command and control, the instrument at Percival's disposal displayed several structural flaws. The Australian, British, and Indian units were not trained to fight in conditions when the enemy might enjoy air superiority, and the troops did not learn to camouflage their positions and movements. Murray states that when small-unit training reaches a satisfactory level, larger-scale battalion and regimental training should start.[23] The Allied ground units were deficient in all levels of training. Being deficient in general training, they were unable to adapt in jungle terrain and adopt specialized jungle warfare techniques. Bennett and Heath's troops were not ready to fight any type of war, let alone jungle warfare.[24] The Japanese aircraft created pandemonium by bombing the road junctions. But the thickly vegetated Malayan countryside should have provided cover to the Allied troops. After all, Malaya was not an open country like the Western Desert. However, the raw and nervous Allied infantry were unable to take cover in the jungle against the marauding Japanese aircraft. Allied training in jungle warfare proved woefully inadequate for the task at hand.

Andrew Gilchrist rightly states that the best battalions of the Indian Army were deployed in the Middle East. The raw, partially trained Indian units in Malaya-Singapore were officered by newly inducted British officers, who knew nothing about the customs of the jawans and spoke no Indian languages.[25] Quick expansion of the Indian Army resulted in dilution of the Indian Army's trained ranks. NCOs were leaders, trainers, and educators. In the Indian Army, the VCOs supplemented the work done by the NCOs. And the Indian units lost a large number of veteran NCOs and VCOs due to the breakneck expansion of the Indian Army. The German Army, while fighting in the forest of central Russia in the summer of 1941, found out that units got split in the dense vegetation, resulting in several scattered small-unit actions. And this in turn requires the unit commanders to be further forward for effective command of the troops.[26] In the absence of experienced NCOs and VCOs, the Indian battalions, when divided by forest regions, were unable to conduct effective small-unit actions within the framework of a cohesive plan. Moreover, the Australian and the British battalion and regimental commanders, instead of displaying ingenuity and initiative, always looked behind to the brigade headquarters. Not only were the brigade and battalion headquarters out of touch with the rapidly changing scenario, but very often communications with them were severed.

Noted historian Michael Howard asserts that most military organizations prepare for the wrong war.[27] At least this is true for Percival's heterogeneous army in the case of Malaya during 1941–42. The ground units were partly trained and for the wrong war—that is, war in the open desert country, rather than in the closed jungle country. Their equipment was not suitable for warfare in the jungle country. The faulty British defensive policy of constructing a static linear defense, instead of elastic defense, further worsened the scenario. The British commanders' attempts to build up defensive lines along the rivers proved faulty, as there were various approaches to the rivers, and all of them could not be effectively guarded. Defensive tactics remained inflexible and inelastic. The British officers' attempt to build up linear defenses would have worked well within the confined space of Singapore City in case of urban combat with Japanese infantry. But such combat did not occur. Percival and his subordinates lost heart and surrendered before conducting a last-ditch defense within the urban concrete jungle. The Japanese, however, displayed creativity. This was possible because they were trained to conduct maneuver warfare, and their officers were inculcated in a mission-oriented command system. For instance, whenever the Japanese tanks moved across a single road or in a defile, they suffered losses from the A/T guns.[28] Then, the marching Japanese foot soldiers, as well as cycle-borne infantry, would outflank and outmaneuver Allied defensive positions by moving through the innumerable small tracks across the rubber plantations and even through scrub jungle. To sum up, Percival's untrained force (except a few Indian battalions) did not display any significant learning curve during the fighting in Malaya-Singapore.

Percival and his subordinate commanders throughout the campaign only reacted to Japanese moves, and the latter always held the initiative. Yamashita always called the shots. The Japanese were able to maintain a higher tempo, thanks to their mission-oriented command culture and mobility.[29] They used speed and surprise to get inside the Allied high command's decision-making cycle, thus causing a paralysis of will that further compounded Percival's problems. Yamashita to a great extent conducted an effects-based maneuver campaign against Percival and his subordinate commanders, who attempted to fight a linear attrition war. The attrition-oriented approach is characterized by firepower and by little movement once battle is started.[30] Taking advantage of a higher tempo, the Japanese aimed at the weakness of the Allied troops; they fought in certain terrain where the Allied soldiers were unable and unwilling to fight and concentrated their troops at certain places before Percival could generate his own force.

A decentralized mission-style command system is a must for waging maneuver war. Percival presided over a loose command set up, not a decentralized one. Percival failed to lay down an objective, and often his subordinates did things without informing him. Like Ian Hamilton at Gallipoli, Percival followed a consensual command style. It depended on eliciting a full spectrum of opinions in collaborative discussions before a decision emerged.[31] However, such a process was time consuming in the case of Percival; in contrast Yamashita took quick decisions and got inside Percival's decision-making loop. Kinvig's argument that Malaya-Singapore could not have been saved even if Percival had been replaced by another "better" commander is probably true. But a more determined, aggressive, and charismatic commander would have been able to inflict more casualties on the IJA and would have seriously delayed Yamashita's timetable. Moreover, unlike Hamilton, Percival was served by quasi-disloyal subordinates like Heath and Bennett. Heath and Bennett were greater "culprits" than Percival. The low state of staff work in the III Indian Corps and in Bennett's AIF further increased Percival's problems.[32] For instance, Heath had never been to the staff college.[33] Weak, disjointed, and inefficient leadership from top, which merely gave orders for withdrawals and further withdrawals increased the demoralization of the Allied troops during the Malaya-Singapore Campaign. Morale is not static but fluctuates with the changing conditions in battle. Had the top leadership displayed more resolute leadership, then it is probable that the morale of the Allied troops (especially the Indian soldiers, who were suffering from racial discrimination and were targets of Japanese propaganda attempts) might have soared or at least remained intact. Overall, the Australian, British, and Indian troops displayed the same level of military incompetence.

The combat performance of the Allied troops in the Malaya-Singapore Campaign needs to be placed within the broader context of the British Empire's troops' performance in the various outposts of Asia. Absence of long-term acquaintance with the local environment and inadequate training caused their rapid collapse against the Japanese onslaught. For instance, in Hong Kong, where combat lasted from 8 December 1941 until Christmas Day, the Japanese infantry, under their protective aerial cover, used the same infiltration and encirclement along the flanks formula to overwhelm the British, Canadian, and Indian defenders. Franco David Macri turns the spotlight on the Canadian C Force under Brigadier General J. K. Lawson, which fought in Hong Kong during December 1941. The C Force comprised volunteers drawn from the cities of Winnipeg and Quebec. It is to be noted that the jawans were also volunteers but drawn from the countryside. Being volunteers, the Canadians' spirits were high, and they were willing to fight and die to save the British Empire from the Japanese. For many Canadians and the Indian soldiers, deployment overseas was a great adventure. A number of Canadians, like the Indians, had joined the army to tide over economic difficulties. Nevertheless, there was some divergence. While the Canadians developed a moral hatred against the Axis powers, this feeling was absent among the Indians. Even when the fate of Hong Kong was sealed, the Canadians launched counterattacks in the belief that they were gaining precious time for the British Empire to mobilize and also to inflict the maximum possible casualties on the Japanese invaders. However, the Canadians and the Indians, both in Hong Kong and in Malaya-Singapore, were hampered by lack of combat experience and absence of realistic training.[34]

The German blitzkrieg formula comprised aerial bombing of soldiers and civilians, breakthrough by armored formations, and deep envelopments by motorized units in a lightning war.[35] The Japanese used light and medium tanks with verve in Malaya, Singapore, the Philippines, Burma, and Guadalcanal.[36] But they never implemented a tank-armored infantry, self-propelled artillery ground attack aircraft in combined arms assaults like the Wehrmacht.. The Japanese paradigm of war in Malaya centered on infantry-centric blitzkrieg. The infantry marched rapidly through the jungle and on bicycles in the road, and they easily outmaneuvered and outflanked the road-bound Allied troops. The Japanese frequently used a tank-infantry combination with devastating effects, for instance at Jitra and at the Slim River. The presence of tanks in the Allied inventory would have definitely slowed down the Japanese advance. In fact, use of tanks by the American-Australian force in New Guinea surprised the Japanese.[37]

However, it is questionable whether the partially trained Allied troops in Malaya would have been able to evolve combined arms techniques with tanks, infantry, and A/T artillery. A larger number of A/T guns would probably have decelerated the Japanese advance. But, even when A/T guns were present, cooperation with infantry was not always of a high order. And the Australian units' penchant for unilateral withdrawal without informing the neighboring formations, a feature that was present both during the retreat in the Malayan Peninsula and on Singapore Island, further reduced the coherence of the defensive lines. In Burma, the Japanese repeated the same successful formula based on infiltration, encirclement, and outflanking moves by light infantry. For the Allied troops, it was déjà vu again. The learning curve proved too steep for them at least until early 1944. After the debacle at Singapore, the Indian Army absorbed the lessons of defeat and generated training manuals to counter jungle warfare.[38] Their effect became visible only during Imphal-Kohima in 1944.

Notes

1. Andrew Gilchrist, *Malaya 1941: The Fall of a Fighting Empire* (London: Robert Hale, 1992), 63.
2. Tomoyuki Ishizu and Raymond Callahan, "The Rising Sun Strikes," in *The Pacific War: From Pearl Harbor to Hiroshima*, ed. Daniel Marston (2005; repr., Oxford: Osprey, 2010), 55.
3. Gilchrist, *Malaya 1941*, 63; *South-East Area Air Operations Record Phase I, Nov. 1941–Feb. 1942*, Japanese Monograph No. 55 (Washington DC: Department of the Army, Office of the Chief of Military History, 1962), Table of Planes Damaged and Replaced for the 3rd Air Group during the Malaya Operations.
4. David Horner, "The ANZAC Contribution: Australia and New Zealand in the Pacific War," in *The Pacific War*, ed. Marston, 144.
5. Brian P. Farrell, *The Defence and Fall of Singapore: 1940–1942* (2005; repr., Stroud, UK: Tempus, 2006), 451; Alan Warren, *Britain's Greatest Defeat: Singapore 1942* (2002; repr., London: Hambledon Continuum, 2002), 302; F. A. Crew, *History of the Second World War United Kingdom Medical Services, The Army Medical Services, Campaigns*, vol. 2 (1954; repr., Uckfield: Naval & Military Press, n.d.), 106.
6. Colonel Masanobu Tsuji, *Japan's Greatest Victory / Britain's Worst Defeat from the Japanese Perspective: The Capture of Singapore, 1942* (1952; repr., Gloucestershire: Spellmount, 2007), 27.
7. Williamson Murray, *Military Adaptation in War: With Fear of Change* (Cambridge: Cambridge University Press, 2011), 126.
8. Notes by Lieutenant General A. E. Percival on Captain Russell Grenfell's Draft, July 1950, Percival Papers, IWM, London.
9. Notes by Percival on the Brief Outline Narrative of the Mainland Operations in Malaya 8 Dec. 1941 to 31 Jan. 1942, Prepared by the Combined Inter-Services Historical Section (India), June 1947, Percival Papers, 2.
10. Letter from Percival, July 4, 1948, Percival Papers.
11. Note on the Malayan Campaign by LMH, Part 2, Lewis Heath Papers, P 441, LMH 5, IWM, 8.
12. G. W. Seabridge, Report on the Fall of Singapore, April 25, 1942, WP(42)177, CAB/66/24/7, PRO, Kew, London, 3.
13. Ian Morrison, *Malayan Postscript* (London: Faber and Faber, 1942), 79.
14. Note on the Malayan Campaign by LMH, p. 4c, Part 2, 10.

15. Major General B. W. Key, 11th Indian Division, P 456, Key Papers, IWM, 39.
16. Note on the Malayan Campaign by LMH, Part 2, 6, 10, 13, 15.
17. Military Intelligence Service, *Soldier's Guide to the Japanese Army* (Washington DC: Military Intelligence Service, War Department, 1944), 164–65.
18. Ishizu and Callahan, "The Rising Sun Strikes," in *The Pacific War*, ed. Marston, 57.
19. Murray, *Military Adaptation in War*, 140–41.
20. Despatch on Operations in South-West Pacific 15 Jan.–25 Feb. 1942 by General Archibald Wavell, CAB 106/38, PRO, Kew, London, 16.
21. Notes by Lieutenant General A. E. Percival on the Brief Outline Narrative, 2.
22. Francis Pike, *Hirohito's War: The Pacific War, 1941–1945* (London: Bloomsbury, 2015), 215–42.
23. Murray, *Military Adaptation in War*, 133–34.
24. Note on the Malayan Campaign by LMH, Part 2, 8.
25. Gilchrist, *Malaya 1941*, 24.
26. Jesse J. Miller, Jr., "Forest Fighting on the Eastern Front in World War II," *Geographical Review* 62, no. 2 (1972): 190.
27. Murray, *Military Adaptation in War*, 1.
28. Note on the Malayan Campaign by LMH, Part 2, 2, 4.
29. J. J. A. Wallace, "Manoeuvre Theory in Operations Other Than War," *Journal of Strategic Studies* 19, no. 4 (1996): 209.
30. For maneuver and attritional warfare see John Kiszely, "The British Army and Approaches to Warfare since 1945," *Journal of Strategic Studies* 19, no. 4 (1996): 179–81.
31. For Ian Hamilton's case see Geoffrey Till, "The Gallipoli Campaign: Command Performances," in *The Challenges of High Command: The British Experience*, ed. Gary Sheffield and Geoffrey Till (Hampshire: Palgrave Macmillan, 2003), 50.
32. War Cabinet, The Malayan Campaign, April 4, 1942, WP(42)145, CAB/66/23/25, PRO, 2.
33. Notes by Lieutenant General A.E. Percival on certain Senior Commanders and other matters, Percival Papers, 3.
34. Franco David Macri, "Canadians under Fire: C Force and the Battle of Hong Kong, December 1941," *Journal of the Royal Asiatic Society Hong Kong Branch* 51 (2011): 237–56.
35. Jurgen Forster, "From 'Blitzkrieg' to 'Total War,'" in *A World at Total War: Global Conflict and the Politics of Destruction, 1937–1945*, ed. Roger Chickering, Stig Forster, and Bernd Greiner (Cambridge: Cambridge University Press and German Historical Institute, Washington DC, 2005), 97.
36. Military Intelligence Service, *Japanese Tanks and Tank Tactics* (Washington, DC: Military Intelligence Service, War Department, 1944), vii.
37. General Headquarters, India, Military Intelligence Directorate, War Information Circular Foreign Armies Non-Operational Intelligence, No. G 15, February 1, 1943, L/MIL/17/5/284, OIOC, BL, London, 1.
38. Alan Jeffreys, *Approach to Battle: Training the Indian Army during the Second World War* (Solihull, UK: Helion, 2017), 143–47.

BIBLIOGRAPHY

Archival Sources

Australian War Memorial, Canberra

AIF Malaya. AA 1974/398.
Bennett, Gordon. Papers. PR 90/111.
War Diary of 9th Indian Division, G Branch. 553/5/22.

Imperial War Museum, London

Bell, Lieutenant S. E. "Hospital in No Man's Land: The Atrocity at Alexandra Hospital, Singapore." 88/63/1.
Flower, H. S. Diary of Lieutenant Colonel H. S. Flower, 9th Battalion Royal Northumberland Fusiliers. Compiled by R. C. Fenwick. 86/87/1.
Glanfield, Lieutenant D. J. 118th Royal Artillery Field Regiment. 90/15/1.
Hammond, Major R. 88/34/1.
Hannam, Captain S. 2nd/26th Battalion, P 470.
Heath, Lieutenant General Lewis. Papers. LMH 5, P 441, LMH 11, P 442.
Key, Major General B. W. Papers. 11th Indian Division, P 456.
Mackenzie, Lieutenant A. G. 1st Malay Regiment. 90/15/1.
Percival, Lieutenant General A. E. Papers.
Sawyer, Lieutenant Colonel E. L. Royal Artillery, 22nd Mountain Regiment attached to the 11th Indian Division. 88/33/1.
Sugita, Colonel Ichiji. 2839/03.
Webber, Lieutenant D. H. 1st Malay Regiment, 88/33/1.

Ministry of Defence Historical Section, New Delhi

Haffenden, Lieutenant Colonel E. L. Wilson, History of the 4th/19th Hyderabad Regiment, Operations in Malaya, MISC/707-A/H.
History of the 4/19th Hyderabad Regiment after the Slim Battle up to Capitulation, MISC/707/H.
War Diary GS Branch, HQ 9th Indian Division, 601/229/WD/Part 2.
War Diary of 9th Indian Division, 601/229/WD/Part 5.

National Army Museum, London

Ballentine, Brigadier G. C. Account of Brigadier G. C. Ballentine, Commander 44th Indian Infantry Brigade, 1973-09-2.
Deakin, Lieutenant Colonel C.C., and Major G. M. S. Webb. 5th/2nd Punjab Regiment, 6509-14.

Frith, Lieutenant Colonel J. History of the 2/10 Baluch in the Malayan Campaign, 1973-06-121.
Watt, Major S. A. 7th Rajputana Rifles in Malaya, 1977-09-62.

Nehru Memorial Museum and Library, New Delhi

Cabinet Papers
Memorandum by the Chiefs of Staff Committee. March 18, 1940, WP(40)102.
Memorandum by the Chiefs of Staff Committee. July 25, 1940, WP(40)291.
Memorandum by the Chiefs of Staff Committee. September 19, 1940, WP(40)380.
Memorandum by the Secy. of State for India. June 29, 1940, COS(40)504.
Memorandum by the Secy. of State for India. January 30, 1942, WP(42)54.
Oral History Interview with General J. N. Chauhduri. New Delhi, March 23, 1973, by B. R. Nanda, Acc No. 426.
Oral History Interview with Lord Mountbatten. London, July 26, 1967, by B. R. Nanda, Acc No. 351.
Oral History Interview with Dr. Lakshmi Sahgal. Kanpur, November 17, 1973, by S. L. Manchanda, Acc No. 277.
Protectorates and Mandated Territories, June 6, 1940, WP*(40), 164.
Reports for the Month of May 1940 for the Dominions, India, Burma, and the Colonies,
Reports for the Month of January 1941 for the Dominions, India, Burma, and the Colonies, Protectorates and Mandated Territories, 17 Feb. 1941, WP*(41)13.
Reports for the Month of July 1941 for the Dominions, India, Burma, and the Colonies and Mandated Territories, WP*(41)53.
Reports for the Month of December 1941 for the Dominions, India, Burma, and the Colonies and Mandated Territories, January 24, 1942, WP*(42)5.
Telegram from GoI, Defence Department to Secy. of State for India, August 9, 1940, 2177K.
Telegram from Viceroy to the Secy. of State for India, January 21, 1942, WP(42)43.

Oriental and India Office Collection (previously known as India Office Records and now known as Asia Pacific and Africa Collections), British Library, London

D1196/33.
L/MIL/17/5/284.
L/WS/1/136.
L/WS/1/456.
L/WS/1/645.
L/WS/1/952.
L/WS/2/71.

Public Record Office, Kew, London

CAB 44/203.
CAB 66/10/20.
CAB 66/28/33.

CAB 106/38.
CAB 106/57.
CAB 106/58.
WO 106/2592.
WO 172/136.
WP(40)222, CAB/66/9/2.
WP(42)145, CAB/66/23/25.
WP(42)177, CAB/66/24/7.
WP(42)314, CAB/66/26/44.

Articles, Books and Chapters in Edited Volumes

Allen, Louis. *Singapore: 1941–1942*. Oxon: Frank Cass, 2005. First published 1977.
Arthur, William. "The Martial Episteme: Re-Thinking Theories of Martial Race and the Modernisation of the British Indian Army during the Second World War." In *The British Indian Army: Virtue and Necessity*, edited by Rob Johnson, 153–65. Newcastle: Cambridge Scholars, 2014.
Barber, Noel. *A Sinister Twilight: The Fall of Singapore, 1942*. Boston: Houghton Mifflin, 1968.
Barkawi, Tarak. "Peoples, Homelands, and Wars? Ethnicity, the Military, and Battle among British Imperial Forces in the War against Japan." *Comparative Studies in Society and History* 46, no. 1 (2004): 134–63.
———. "Culture and Combat in the Colonies: The Indian Army in the Second World War." *Journal of Contemporary History* 41, no. 2 (2006): 325–55.
Bartov, Omer. "Daily Life and Motivation in War: The *Wehrmacht* in the Soviet Union." *Journal of Strategic Studies* 12, no. 2 (1989): 200–14.
Bayly, C., and Tim Harper. *Forgotten Armies: The Fall of British Asia, 1941–1945*. London: Allen Lane, 2004.
Bell, Christopher M. "'Our Most Exposed Outpost': Hong Kong and British Far Eastern Strategy, 1921–1941." *Journal of Military History* 60 (1996): 61–88.
———. "The 'Singapore Strategy' and the Deterrence of Japan: Winston Churchill, the Admiralty and the Dispatch of Force Z." *English Historical Review* 116, no. 467 (2001): 604–34.
Bennett, H. Gordon. "Review of The Conquest of Malaya, Singapore, the Japanese Version by Masanobu Tsuji." *Journal of Southeast Asian Studies* 2, no. 3 (1961): 91–100.
Bergerud, Eric. *Touched with Fire: The Land War in the South Pacific*. New York: Penguin, 1997. First published 1996.
Best, Antony. *British Intelligence and the Japanese Challenge in Asia, 1914–1941*. Basingstoke, UK: Palgrave Macmillan, 2002.
Bourke, Joanna. *An Intimate History of Killing: Face-to-Face Killing in Twentieth-Century Warfare*. London: Granta Books, 2000. First published 1999.
Bridge, Carl. "Crisis of Command: Major-General Gordon Bennett and British Military Effectiveness in the Malayan Campaign, 1941–42." In *British and Japanese Military Leadership in the Far Eastern War, 1941–1945*, edited by Brian Bond and Kyoichi Tachikawa, 64–74. London: Frank Cass, 2004.
Callahan, Raymond. *The Worst Disaster: The Fall of Singapore*. Singapore: Cultured Lotus, 2001. First published 1977.
———. "Churchill and Singapore." In *Sixty Years On: The Fall of Singapore Revisited*, edited by Brian Farrell and Sandy Hunter, 156–72. Singapore: Eastern Universities Press, 2003. First published 2002.

Carew, Tim. *The Longest Retreat: The Burma Campaign 1942*. Dehra Dun, India: Natraj, 1989. First published 1969.

Chaudhuri, Nirad C. "The Martial Races of India," Part 1. *Modern Review* 48, no. 1 (1930): 41–51.

———. "The Martial Races of India," Part 3. *Modern Review* 49, no. 1 (1931): 67–79.

———. "The Martial Races of India," Part 4. *Modern Review* 49, no.2 (1931): 215–28.

Chung, Ong Chit. "Major-General William Dobbie and the Defence of Malaya, 1935–38." *Journal of Southeast Asian Studies* 17, no. 2 (1986): 282–306.

———. *Operation Matador: World War II, Britain's Attempt to Foil the Japanese Invasion of Malaya and Singapore*. Singapore: Marshall Cavendish, 2003. First published 1997.

Churchill, Winston S. *The Second World War*. Vol. 3, *The Grand Alliance*. Middlesex: Penguin, 1985. First published 1950.

Coningham, Simon. "Air-Ground Cooperation between the RAF and the Indian Army in Waziristan, 1936–7." In *The British Indian Army: Virtue and Necessity*, edited by Rob Johnson, 127–35. Newcastle: Cambridge Scholars Publishing, 2014.

Coox, Alvin D. "The Effectiveness of the Japanese Military Establishment in the Second World War." In *Military Effectiveness*. Vol. 3, *The Second World War*, edited by Allan R. Millett and Williamson Murray, 1–44. Cambridge: Cambridge University Press, 2010. First published 1988.

Creveld, Martin Van. *The Art of War: War and Military Thought*. London: Cassell, 2000.

Cushman, Lieutenant General John H. "Challenge and Response at the Operational and Tactical levels, 1914–45." In *Military Effectiveness*. Vol. 3, *The Second World War*, edited by Allan R. Millett and Williamson Murray, 320–40. Cambridge: Cambridge University Press, 2010. First published 1988.

Dockrill, Saki. "Hirohito, the Emperor's Army and Pearl Harbor." *Review of International Studies* 18, no. 4 (1992): 319–33.

———. "Britain's Grand Strategy and Anglo-American Leadership in the War against Japan." In *British and Japanese Military Leadership in the Far Eastern War, 1941–1945*, edited by Brian Bond and Kyoichi Tachikawa, 6–24. London: Frank Cass, 2004.

Doud, Lieutenant Colonel Harold. "Peace-Time Preparation: Six Months with the Japanese Infantry." In *How the Jap Army Fights*, edited by Lieutenant Colonel Paul W. Thompson, Lieutenant Colonel Harold Doud, and Lieutenant John Scofield, 34–46. New York: Penguin, 1943. First published 1942.

Drea, Edward. "The Imperial Japanese Army (1868–1945): Origins, Evolution, Legacy," In *War in the Modern World since 1815*, edited by Jeremy Black, 75–115. London: Routledge, 2003.

———. *Japan's Imperial Army: Its Rise and Fall, 1853–1945*. Lawrence: University Press of Kansas, 2009.

Duby, Georges. *The Legend of Bouvines: War, Religion and Culture in the Middle Ages*. Translated by Catherine Tihanyi. Cambridge: Polity, 1990.

Englander, David. "Mutinies and Military Morale." In *The Oxford Illustrated History of the First World War*, edited by Hew Strachan, 191–203. Oxford: Oxford University Press, 1998.

English, John A. *On Infantry*. New York: Praeger, 1984. First published 1981.

Farrell, Brian P. "1941: An Overview." In *Sixty Years On: The Fall of Singapore Revisited*, edited by Brian Farrell and Sandy Hunter, 173–82. Singapore: Eastern Universities Press, 2003. First published 2002.

———. *The Defence and Fall of Singapore: 1940-1942*. Stroud, UK: Tempus, 2006. First published 2005.

Farrell, Brian P., and Sandy Hunter. *Sixty Years On: The Fall of Singapore Revisited*. Singapore: Eastern Universities Press, 2003. First published 2002.

Ferris, John. "'Worthy of Some Better Enemy?': The British Estimate of the Imperial Japanese Army, 1919-41, and the Fall of Singapore." *Canadian Journal of History* 28 (August 1993): 223-56.

———. "Student and Master: The United Kingdom, Japan, Airpower, and the Fall of Singapore, 1920-1941." In *Sixty Years On: The Fall of Singapore Revisited*, edited by Brian Farrell and Sandy Hunter, 94-121. Singapore: Eastern Universities Press, 2003. First published 2002.

Flower, Sibylla Jane. "Allied Prisoners of War: The Malayan Campaign, 1941-42." In *Sixty Years On: The Fall of Singapore Revisited*, edited by Brian Farrell and Sandy Hunter, 208-17. Singapore: Eastern Universities Press, 2003. First published 2002.

Forster, Jurgen. "From 'Blitzkrieg' to 'Total War.'" In *A World at Total War: Global Conflict and the Politics of Destruction, 1937-1945*, edited by Roger Chickering, Stig Forster, and Bernd Greiner, 89-107. Cambridge: Cambridge University Press and German Historical Institute, Washington DC, 2005.

French, David. "'Tommy is No Soldier': The Morale of the Second British Army in Normandy, June-August 1944." *Journal of Strategic Studies* 19, no. 4 (1996): 154-78.

———. "Big Wars and Small Wars between the Wars, 1919-39." In *Big Wars and Small Wars: The British Army and the Lessons of War in the 20th Century*, edited by Hew Strachan, 36-53. London: Routledge, 2008. First published 2006.

Gat, Azar. *The Origins of Military Thought from the Enlightenment to Clausewitz*. Oxford: Oxford University Press, 1989.

Gates, David. *The Napoleonic Wars: 1803-1815*. London: Arnold, 1997.

Ghosh, Amitav. *The Glass Palace*. New Delhi: Ravi Dayal, 2000.

Glantz, David M., and Jonathan M. House. *When Titans Clashed: How the Red Army Stopped Hitler*. Lawrence: University Press of Kansas, 1995.

Gordon, Andrew. "Ratcatchers and Regulators at the Battle of Jutland." In *The Challenges of High Command: The British Experience*, edited by Gary Sheffield and Geoffrey Till, 26-33. Hampshire, UK: Palgrave Macmillan, 2003.

Grey, Jeffrey. *A Military History of Australia*. Cambridge: Cambridge University Press, 1990.

Hack, Karl, and Blackburn, Kevin. *Did Singapore Have to Fall? Churchill and the Impregnable Fortress*. Oxon, UK: Routledge, 2008. First published 2004.

Hall, David. "Lessons Not Learned: The Struggle between the Royal Air Force and Army for the Tactical Control of Aircraft, and the Post-mortem on the Defeat of the British Expeditionary Force in France in 1940." In *The Challenges of High Command: The British Experience*, edited by Gary Sheffield and Geoffrey Till, 113-25. Hampshire, UK: Palgrave Macmillan, 2003.

Hall, Timothy. *The Fall of Singapore*. Oxon, UK: Routledge, 2015. First published 1983.

———. *New Guinea: 1942-44*. London: Routledge, 2015. First published 1981.

Haron, Nadzan. "Colonial Defence and British Approach to the Problems in Malaya: 1874-1918." *Modern Asian Studies* 24, no. 2 (1990): 275-95.

Harries, Meirion, and Susie Harries. *Soldiers of the Sun: The Rise and Fall of the Imperial Japanese Army*. New York: Random House, 1991.

Hart, Stephen. "Montgomery, Morale, Casualty Conservation and 'Colossal Cracks': 21st Army Group's Operational Technique in North-West Europe, 1944-45." *Journal of Strategic Studies* 19, no. 4 (1996): 132-53.

Harvey, A. D. "Army Air Force and Navy Air Force: Japanese Aviation and the Opening Phase of the War in the Far East." *War in History* 6, no. 2 (1999): 174–204.

Hauser, William L. "The Will to Fight." In *Combat Effectiveness: Cohesion, Stress, and the Volunteer Military*, edited by Sam C. Sarkesian, 186–211. Beverly Hills: SAGE, 1980.

Hill, Colonel Milton A. "Lessons of Bataan." In *How the Jap Army Fights*, Lieutenant Colonel Paul W. Thompson, Lieutenant Colonel Harold Doud, and Lieutenant John Scofield, 88–118. New York: Penguin, 1943. First published 1942.

Hills, Carol. "Nationalism and Feminism in Late Colonial India: The Rani of Jhansi Regiment, 1943–1945." *Modern Asian Studies* 27, no. 4 (1993): 741–60.

Hogg, Ian. *Tank Killing: Anti-Tank Warfare by Men and Machines*. London: Sidgwick and Jackson, 1996.

Hoiberg, Anne. "Military Staying Power." In *Combat Effectiveness: Cohesion, Stress, and the Volunteer Military*, edited by Sam C. Sarkesian, 212–43. Beverly Hills: SAGE, 1980.

Holmes, Richard. *Acts of War: The Behaviour of Men in Battle*. New York: Free Press, 1989. First published 1985.

Horner, David. "The ANZAC Contribution: Australia and New Zealand in the Pacific War." In *The Pacific War: From Pearl Harbor to Hiroshima*, edited by Daniel Marston, 143–57. Oxford: Osprey, 2010. First published 2005.

———. "Australia in 1942: A Pivotal Year." In *Australia 1942: In the Shadow of War*, edited by Peter J. Dean, 11–29. Melbourne: Cambridge University Press, 2013.

Howard, Michael. "Leadership in the British Army in the Second World War: Some Personal Observations." In *Leadership and Command: The Anglo-American Military Experience Since 1861*, edited by G. D. Sheffield, 117–40. London: Brassey's 1997.

Hughes Jr., Wayne P. "The Strategy-Tactics Relationship." In *Seapower and Strategy*, edited by Colin S. Gray and Roger W. Barnett, 47–73. London: Tri-Service, 1989.

Irwin, Alistair. "The Buffalo Thorn: The Nature of the Future Battlefield." *Journal of Strategic Studies* 19, no. 4 (1996): 227–51.

Ishizu, Tomoyuki, and Raymond Callahan. "The Rising Sun Strikes." In *The Pacific War: From Pearl Harbor to Hiroshima*, edited by Daniel Marston, 47–61. Oxford: Osprey, 2010. First published 2005.

Jackson, Ashley. "The Evolution and Use of British Imperial Military Formations." In *The Indian Army, 1939–47: Experience and Development*, edited by Alan Jeffreys and Patrick Rose, 9–29. Surrey, UK: Ashgate, 2012.

Jackson, General Mike. "The Realities of Multi-National Command: An Informal Commentary." In *The Challenges of High Command: The British Experience*, edited by Gary Sheffield and Geoffrey Till, 139–45. Hampshire, UK: Palgrave Macmillan, 2003.

Jeffreys, Alan. "Training the Indian Army, 1939–1945." In *The Indian Army, 1939–47: Experience and Development*, edited by Alan Jeffreys and Patrick Rose, 69–86. Surrey, UK: Ashgate, 2012.

———. "The Indian Army in the Malayan Campaign, 1941–42." In *The British Indian Army: Virtue and Necessity*, edited by Rob Johnson, 177–97. Newcastle: Cambridge Scholars Publishing, 2014.

———. *Approach to Battle: Training the Indian Army during the Second World War*. Solihull, UK: Helion, 2017.

Johnson, Robert. "Small Wars and Internal Security: The Army in India, 1936–1946." In *The Indian Army, 1939–47: Experience and Development*, edited by Alan Jeffreys and Patrick Rose, 215–39. Surrey, UK: Ashgate, 2012.

Johnston, Mark. *At the Frontline: Experiences of Australian Soldiers in World War II*. Melbourne: Cambridge University Press, 1996.

Keegan, John. *The Face of Battle: A Study of Agincourt, Waterloo and the Somme*. Harmondsworth, UK: Penguin, 1978. First published 1976.

———. *Six Armies in Normandy: From D-Day to the Liberation of Paris*. London: Pimlico, 1992. First published 1982.

———. *The Mask of Command*. London: Penguin, 1988. First published 1987.

Kennedy, Greg. "Symbol of Imperial Defence: The Role of Singapore in British and American Far Eastern Strategic Relations, 1933-1941." In *Sixty Years On: The Fall of Singapore Revisited*, edited by Brian Farrell and Sandy Hunter, 42-67. Singapore: Eastern Universities Press, 2003. First published 2002.

Khera, P. N. *Technical Services: Ordnance & IEME*. New Delhi: Government of India, 1962.

Kiszely, John. "The British Army and Approaches to Warfare since 1945." *Journal of Strategic Studies* 19, no. 4 (1996): 179-206.

Kotani, Ken. "Pearl Harbor: Japanese Planning and Command Structure." In *The Pacific War: From Pearl Harbor to Hiroshima*, edited by Daniel Marston, 31-45. Oxford: Osprey, 2010. First published 2005.

Leake, Elisabeth Mariko. "British India versus the British Empire: The Indian Army and an Impasse in Imperial Defence, circa 1919-39." *Modern Asian Studies* 48, no. 1 (2014): 301-29.

Lee, Nigel de. "'A Brigadier Is Only a Co-ordinator': British Command at Brigade Level in North-West Europe, 1944: A Case Study." In *Leadership and Command: The Anglo-American Military Experience since 1861*, edited by G. D. Sheffield, 129-40. London: Brassey's, 1997.

Lewy, Guenter. "The American Experience in Vietnam." In *Combat Effectiveness: Cohesion, Stress, and the Volunteer Military*, edited by Sam C. Sarkesian, 94-106. Beverly Hills, CA: SAGE, 1980.

Lyman, Robert. "The Art of Manoeuvre at the Operational Level of War: Lieutenant-General W. J. Slim and Fourteenth Army, 1944-45." In *The Challenges of High Command: The British Experience*, edited by Gary Sheffield and Geoffrey Till, 88-112. Hampshire, UK: Palgrave Macmillan, 2003.

———. *The Generals: From Defeat to Victory, Leadership in Asia 1941-45*. London: Constable, 2008.

Macri, Franco David. "Canadians under Fire: C Force and the Battle of Hong Kong, December 1941." *Journal of the Royal Asiatic Society Hong Kong Branch* 51 (2011): 237-56.

Man, Kwong Chi, and Tsoi Yiu Lun. *Eastern Fortress: A Military History of Hong Kong, 1840-1970*. Hong Kong: Hong Kong University Press, 2014.

Marston, Daniel P. "End of the Raj, 1945-1947." In *A Military History of India and South Asia: From the East India Company to the Nuclear Era*, edited by Daniel P. Marston and Chandar S. Sundaram, 131-38. Westport, CT: Praeger, 2007.

Melvin, Mungo, and Stuart Peach. "Reaching for the End of the Rainbow: Command and the Revolution in Military Affairs." In *The Challenges of High Command: The British Experience*, edited by Gary Sheffield and Geoffrey Till, 177-206. Hampshire, UK: Palgrave Macmillan, 2003.

Menezes, Lieutenant General S. L. *Fidelity and Honour: The Indian Army from the Seventeenth to the Twenty-First Century*. New Delhi: Viking, 1993.

Middlebrook, Martin, and Patrick Mahoney. *Battleship: The Loss of Prince of Wales and the Repulse*. Middlesex, UK: Penguin, 1979. First published 1977.

Miller, Jr., Jesse J. "Forest Fighting on the Eastern Front in World War II." *Geographical Review* 62, no. 2 (1972): 186–202.

Millett, Allan R. "The United States Armed Forces in the Second World War." In *Military Effectiveness*. Vol. 3, *The Second World War*, edited by Allan R. Millett and Williamson Murray, 45–89. Cambridge: Cambridge University Press, 2010. First published 1988.

Millett, Allan R., and Williamson Murray. *Military Effectiveness*, Vol. 3, *The Second World War*, Cambridge: Cambridge University Press, 2010. First published 1988.

Mitcham, Jr., Samuel W. *The Desert Fox in Normandy: Rommel's Defense of Fortress Europe*. Westport, CT: Praeger, 1997.

Moreman, T. R. "'Small Wars' and 'Imperial Policing': The British Army and the Theory and Practice of Colonial Warfare in the British Empire, 1919–1939." *Journal of Strategic Studies* 19, no. 4 (1996): 105–31.

———. *The Jungle, the Japanese and the British Commonwealth Armies at War, 1941–45: Fighting Methods, Doctrine and Training for Jungle Warfare*. London: Frank Cass, 2005.

Muller, Richard R. "Close Air Support: The German, British and American Experiences, 1918–41." In *Military Innovation in the Interwar Period*, edited by Williamson Murray and Alan R. Millett, 144–90. Cambridge: Cambridge University Press, 1996.

Murfett, Malcolm H. "Reflections on an Enduring Theme: The 'Singapore Strategy' at Sixty." In *Sixty Years On: The Fall of Singapore Revisited*, edited by Brian Farrell and Sandy Hunter, 3–28. Singapore: Eastern Universities Press, 2003. First published 2002.

Murfett, Malcolm H., John N. Miksic, Brian P. Farrell, and Chiang Ming Shun. *Between Two Oceans: A Military History of Singapore from 1275 to 1971*. Singapore: Marshall Cavendish, 2011. First published 1999.

Murray, Williamson. "Armored Warfare: The British, French and German Experiences." In *Military Innovation in the Interwar Period*, edited by Williamson Murray and Alan R. Millett, 6–49. Cambridge: Cambridge University Press, 1996.

———. "Innovation: Past and Future." In *Military Innovation in the Interwar Period*, edited by Williamson Murray and Alan R. Millett, 300–28. Cambridge: Cambridge University Press, 1996.

———. *Military Adaptation in War: With Fear of Change*. Cambridge: Cambridge University Press, 2011.

———. *War, Strategy, and Military Effectiveness*. Cambridge: Cambridge University Press, 2011.

Neidpath, James. *The Singapore Naval Base and the Defence of Britain's Eastern Empire, 1919–1941*. Oxford: Clarendon Press, 1981.

Okumiya, Masatake, and Jiro Horikoshi, with Martin Caidin. *Zero: The Story of Japan's Air War in the Pacific as Seen by the Enemy*. New York: ibooks, 2002. First published 1956.

Omissi, David. *The Sepoy and the Raj: The Indian Army, 1860–1940*. London: Macmillan, 1994.

———. "A Dismal Story? Britain, the Gurkhas and the Partition of India, 1945–1948." In *The Indian Army, 1939–47: Experience and Development*, edited by Alan Jeffreys and Patrick Rose, 195–214. Surrey, UK: Ashgate, 2012.

Owen, Frank. *The Fall of Singapore*. London: Penguin, 2001. First published 1960.

Pike, Francis. *Hirohito's War: The Pacific War, 1941–1945*. London: Bloomsbury, 2015.

Place, Timothy Harrison. *Military Training in the British Army, 1940–1944*. London: Frank Cass, 2000.
Preston-Hough, Peter. *Commanding Far Eastern Skies: A Critical Analysis of the Royal Air Force Air Superiority Campaign in India, Burma and Malaya 1941–1945*. Solihull: Helion, 2015.
Probert, Henry. *The Forgotten Air Force: The Royal Air Force in the War against Japan, 1941–45*. London: Brassey's, 1995.
Raghavan, Srinath. *India's War: The Making of Modern South Asia, 1939–1945*. New Delhi: Penguin, 2016.
Reid, Brian Holden. "Introduction." *Journal of Strategic Studies* 19, no. 4 (1996): 1–9.
Richardson, F. M. *Fighting Spirit: Psychological Factors in War*. Dehra Dun, India: Natraj, 1978.
Rose, Patrick. "Indian Army Command Culture and the North West Frontier, 1919–1939." In *The Indian Army, 1939–47: Experience and Development*, edited by Alan Jeffreys and Patrick Rose, 31–55. Surrey, UK: Ashgate, 2012.
Rosen, Stephen Peter. *Societies and Military Power: India and Its Armies*. New Delhi: Oxford University Press, 1996.
Roy, Kaushik. "Axis Satellite Armies of World War II: A Case Study of the *Azad Hind Fauj*, 1942–45." *Indian Historical Review* 35, no. 1 (2008): 144–72.
———. "Military Loyalty in the Colonial Context: A Case Study of the Indian Army during World War II." *Journal of Military History* 73, no. 2 (2009): 497–529.
———. *Sepoys against the Rising Sun: The Indian Army in Far East and South-East Asia, 1941–45*. Leiden: Brill, 2016.
Samuels, Martin. *Command or Control? Command, Training and Tactics in the British and German Armies, 1888–1918*. London: Frank Cass, 1995.
Schrijvers, Peter. *Bloody Pacific: American Soldiers at War with Japan*. Houndmills, UK: Palgrave Macmillan, 2010. First published 2002.
Scofield, Lieutenant John. "The Japanese Soldier's Arms and Weapons." In *How the Jap Army Fights*, edited by Lieutenant Colonel Paul W. Thompson, Lieutenant Colonel Harold Doud, and Lieutenant John Scofield, 23–34. New York: Penguin, 1943. First published 1942.
The Seven Military Classics of Ancient China. Translated and commentary by Ralph D. Sawyer with Mei-chun Sawyer. Boulder, CO: Westview, 1993.
Sharma, Lieutenant Colonel Gautam. *Nationalisation of the Indian Army: 1885–1947*. New Delhi: Allied, 1996.
Sheffield, Gary. "Introduction: Command, Leadership and the Anglo-American Experience." In *Leadership and Command: The Anglo-American Military Experience Since 1861*, edited by G. D. Sheffield, 1–16. London: Brassey's, 1997.
———. "The Challenges of High Command in the Twentieth Century." In *The Challenges of High Command: The British Experience*, edited by Gary Sheffield and Geoffrey Till, 1–12. Hampshire: Palgrave Macmillan, 2003.
Shils, Edward A., and Morris Janowitz. "Cohesion and Disintegration in the Wehrmacht in World War II." *Public Opinion Quarterly* 12, no. 2 (1948): 280–315.
Showalter, Dennis. "Global Yet not Total: The US War Effort and Its Consequences." In *A World at Total War: Global Conflict and the Politics of Destruction, 1937–1945*, edited by Roger Chickering, Stig Forster, and Bernd Greiner, 109–33. Cambridge: Cambridge University Press and German Historical Institute, Washington, DC, 2005.
Singh, Brigadier Jasbir. *Escape from Singapore*. New Delhi: Lancer, 2010.

Smith, Colin. *Singapore Burning: Heroism and Surrender in World War II*. London: Penguin, 2006. First published 2005.
Stephens, Alan. "Effects Based Operations and the Fighting Power of a Defence Force." In *On New Wars*, edited by John Andreas Olsen, 131–49. Oslo: Norwegian Institute for Defence Studies, 2007.
Strachan, Hew. "Training, Morale and Modern War." *Journal of Contemporary History* 41, no. 2 (2006): 211–27.
Sundaram, Chandar S. "Soldier Disaffection and the Creation of the Indian National Army." *Indo-British Review* 18, no. 1 (1990): 155–62.
———. "The Indian National Army, 1942–1946: A Circumstantial Force." In *A Military History of India and South Asia: From the East India Company to the Nuclear Era*, edited by Daniel P. Marston and Chandar S. Sundaram, 123–30. Westport, CT: Praeger, 2007.
Tachikawa, Kyoichi. "General Yamashita and his Style of Leadership: The Malaya/Singapore Campaign." In *British and Japanese Military Leadership in the Far Eastern War, 1941–1945*, edited by Brian Bond and Kyoichi Tachikawa, 75–87. London: Frank Cass, 2004.
Thomas, Martin. "Disaster Foreseen? France and the Fall of Singapore." In *Sixty Years On: The Fall of Singapore Revisited*, edited by Brian Farrell and Sandy Hunter, 68–93. Singapore: Eastern Universities Press, 2003. First published 2002.
Thompson, Lieutenant Colonel Paul W. "Behind the Fog of War: A Glance at the History and Organization of the Jap Army." In *How the Jap Army Fights*, edited by Lieutenant Colonel Paul W. Thompson, Lieutenant Colonel Harold Doud, and Lieutenant John Scofield, 7–23. New York: Penguin, 1943. First published 1942.
———. "The Jap Army in Action: Campaigns in the China Incident." In *How the Jap Army Fights*, edited by Lieutenant Colonel Paul W. Thompson, Lieutenant Colonel Harold Doud, and Lieutenant John Scofield, 46–62. New York: Penguin, 1943. First published 1942.
———. "The Jap Army in Action: The Fight for Malaya." In *How the Jap Army Fights*, edited by Lieutenant Colonel Paul W. Thompson, Lieutenant Colonel Harold Doud, and Lieutenant John Scofield, 63–88. New York: Penguin, 1943. First published 1942.
Thompson, Peter. *The Battle for Singapore: The True Story of the Greatest Catastrophe of World War II*. London: Piatkus, 2013. First published 2005.
Till, Geoffrey. "The Gallipoli Campaign: Command Performances." In *The Challenges of High Command: The British Experience*, edited by Gary Sheffield and Geoffrey Till, 34–56. Hampshire, UK: Palgrave Macmillan, 2003.
Van der Vat, Dan. *Standard of Power: The Royal Navy in the Twentieth Century*. London: Pimlico, 2001. First published 2000.
Wallace, J. J. A. "Manoeuvre Theory in Operations Other Than War." *Journal of Strategic Studies* 19, no. 4 (1996): 207–26.
Warren, Alan. "'Bullocks Treading Down Wasps'? The British Indian Army in Waziristan in the 1930s." *South Asia* 19, no. 2 (1996): 35–56.
———. "The Indian Army and the Fall of Singapore." In *Sixty Years On: The Fall of Singapore Revisited*, edited by Brian Farrell and Sandy Hunter, 270–89. Singapore: Eastern Universities Press, 2003. First published 2002.
———. *Britain's Greatest Defeat: Singapore 1942*. London: Hambledon Continuum, 2002. First published 2002.

Watts, Barry, and Williamson Murray. "Military Innovation in Peacetime." In *Military Innovation in the Interwar Period*, edited by Williamson Murray and Alan R. Millett, 369–415. Cambridge: Cambridge University Press, 1996.
Wavell, General Archibald. *Generals and Generalship*. London: Penguin, 1941.
Weist, Andrew M. "Haig, Gough and Passchendaele." in *Leadership and Command: The Anglo-American Military Experience Since 1861*, edited by G. D. Sheffield, 77–92. London: Brassey's 1997.
Wesbrook, Stephen D. "The Potential for Military Disintegration." In *Combat Effectiveness: Cohesion, Stress, and the Volunteer Military*, edited by Sam C. Sarkesian, 244–78. Beverly Hills: SAGE, 1980.
Yenne, Bill. *The Imperial Japanese Army: The Invincible Years 1941–42*. Oxford: Osprey, 2014.
Yoji, Akashi. "General Yamashita Tomoyuki: Commander of the Twenty-fifth Army." In *Sixty Years On: The Fall of Singapore Revisited*, edited by Brian Farrell and Sandy Hunter, 185–207. Singapore: Eastern Universities Press, 2003. First published 2002.
Yokoyama, Hisayuki. "Air Operational Leadership in the Southern Front: Imperial Army Aviation's Trial to Be an 'Air Force' in the Malaya Offensive Air Operation." In *British and Japanese Military Leadership in the Far Eastern War, 1941–1945*, edited by Brian Bond and Kyoichi Tachikawa, 134–49. London: Frank Cass, 2004.

Autobiographies/Diaries/Memoirs

Alanbrooke, Field Marshal Lord. *War Diaries 1939–1945*. Edited by Alex Danchev and Daniel Todman. London: Weidenfeld & Nicolson, 2001.
Bennett, H. Gordon. *The Fall of Singapore*. New Delhi: Natraj, 1990. First published 1944.
Crasta, John Baptist. *Eaten by the Japanese: The Memoir of an Unknown Indian Prisoner of War*. Bangalore: Invisible Man, 1999. First published 1998.
Gilchrist, Andrew. *Malaya 1941: The Fall of a Fighting Empire*. London: Robert Hale, 1992.
Masters, John. *Bugles and a Tiger: My Life in the Gurkhas*. London: Cassell, 2002. First published 1956.
McEwan, John. *Out of the Depths of Hell: A Soldier's Story of Life and Death in Japanese Hands*. Barnsley, UK: Pen & Sword, 2014. First published 1999.
Molesworth, Lieutenant General G. N. *Curfew on Olympus*. Bombay: Asia Publishing House, 1965.
Morrison, Ian. *Malayan Postscript*. London: Faber and Faber, 1942.
Percival, Lieutenant General A. E. *The War in Malaya*. Calcutta: Orient Longmans, 1957. First published 1949.
Sakai, Saburo, with Martin Caidin and Fred Saito. *Samurai!* Annapolis MD: Naval Institute Press, 1991. First published 1957.
Singh, Major General Gurkbakhsh. *Indelible Reminiscences: Memoirs of Major-General Gurbakhsh Singh*. New Delhi: Lancer, 2013.
Singh, Lieutenant General Harbakhsh. *In the Line of Duty: A Soldier Remembers*. New Delhi: Lancer, 2000.
Singh, Mohan. *Soldiers' Contribution to Indian Independence*. New Delhi: Army Educational Stores, 1974.
Tanner, R. E. S., and D. A. Tanner. *Burma 1942: Memories of a Retreat, The Diary of Ralph Tanner, 2nd Battalion the King's Own Yorkshire Light Infantry*. Gloucestershire, UK: History Press, 2009.

Tsuji, Colonel Masanobu. *Japan's Greatest Victory Britain's Worst Defeat from the Japanese Perspective: The Capture of Singapore, 1942*. Edited by H. V. Howe, translated by Margaret E. Lake. Gloucestershire, UK: Spellmount, 2007. First published 1952.

Ugaki, Matome. *Fading Victory: The Diary of Admiral Matome Ugaki 1941–1945*. Foreword by Gordon W. Prange, translated by Masataka Chihaya, with Donald M. Goldstein and Katherine V. Dillon. Annapolis, MD: Naval Institute Press, 2008. First published 1991.

Zaman, Mohammad. *India's Freedom Struggle and the Great INA, Memoirs of Major-General Mohammad Zaman Kiani*. New Delhi: Reliance, 1994.

Biographies

Connell, John. *Wavell: Supreme Commander*. Completed and edited by Michael Roberts London: Collins, 1969.

Kinvig, Clifford. *Scapegoat: General Percival of Singapore*. London: Brassey's, 1996.

Lewin, Ronald. *The Chief: Field Marshal Lord Wavell, Commander-in-Chief and Viceroy, 1939–47*. London: Hutchinson, 1980.

———. *Slim, the Standardbearer: A Biography of Field-Marshal the Viscount Slim*. London: Pan, 1978. First published 1976.

Lodge, A. B. *The Fall of General Gordon Bennett*. Sydney: Allen & Unwin, 1986.

Official Histories

Aggarwal, S. C. *History of the Supply Department: 1939–46*. New Delhi: Manager of Publications, 1947.

Bhargava, K. D., and K. N. V. Sastri. *Campaigns in South-East Asia 1941–42*. Edited by Bisheshwar Prasad. Official History of the Indian Armed Forces in the Second World War 1939–45 (Combined Inter-Services Historical Section India & Pakistan, Distributors Orient Longman, Delhi, 1960).

Crew, F. A., *The Army Medical Services: Campaigns*. Vol. 2. History of the Second World War, United Kingdom Medical Services. Uckfield, UK: Naval & Military Press, n.d. First published 1954.

Kirby, Major General S. Woodburn with Captain C. T. Addis, Colonel J. F. Meiklejohn (succeeded by Brigadier M. R. Roberts), Colonel G. T. Wards, and Air Vice Marshal N. L. Desoer. *The War against Japan*. Vol. 1, *The Loss of Singapore*. History of the Second World War. Dehra Dun: Natraj, 1989. First published 1957.

Prasad, Sri Nandan. *Expansion of the Armed Forces and Defence Organization 1939–45*. Edited by Bisheshwar Prasad. Official History of the Indian Armed Forces in the Second World War 1939–45. Calcutta: Saraswaty Press, 1956.

Wigmore, Lionel, *The Japanese Thrust*. Vol. 4 of *Australia in the War of 1939–45*, Series 1, Army. Canberra: Australian War Memorial, 1957.

Official Publications

Military Intelligence Division, *Notes on Japanese Warfare on the Malayan Front*, Information Bulletin No. 6. Washington, DC: War Department, 1942.

Military Intelligence Service, *Japanese Tanks and Tank Tactics*. Washington, DC: Military Intelligence Service, War Department, 1944.

———. *Soldier's Guide to the Japanese Army*. Washington, DC: Military Intelligence Service, War Department, 1944.
Office of the Chief of Military History. *South-East Area Air Operations Record, Phase I, Nov. 1941–Feb. 1942*, Japanese Monograph No. 55. Washington, DC: Department of the Army, Office of the Chief of Military History, 1962.
US Department of the Army. *History of the Southern Army*, Japanese Monograph No. 24. Office of the Chief of Military History.
US War Department. *Handbook on Japanese Military Forces*. With an introduction by David Isby and an afterword by Jeffrey Ethell. Baton Rouge: Louisiana State University Press, 1991. First published 1944.

Printed Primary Sources

Omissi, David, ed. *Indian Voices of the Great War: Soldiers' Letters, 1914–18*. Basingstoke, UK: Macmillan, 1999.
Sareen, T. R., ed. *Select Documents on Indian National Army*. Delhi: Agam Prakashan, 1988.

Published Despatches

Layton, Vice Admiral Geoffrey. "Loss of HM Ships Prince of Wales and Repulse." *Supplement to the London Gazette*. February 26, 1948. London: HMSO, 1948.
Maltby, Paul. "Report on the Air Operations during the Campaigns in Malaya and Netherland East Indies from 8 December 1941 to 12 March 1942." *Third Supplement to the London Gazette*. February 26, 1948. London: HMSO, 1948.
Percival, Lieutenant General A. E. "Operations of Malaya Command, from 8 December 1941 to 15 February 1942." *Second Supplement to London Gazette*. February 26, 1948. London: HMSO, 1948.

Regimental Histories

Bellers, Brigadier E.V.R. *The History of the 1st King George V's Own Gurkha Rifles (The Malaun Regiment)*. Vol. 2, *1920–1947*. Aldershot: Gale & Polden, 1956.
Betham, Lieutenant Colonel Geoffrey, and Major H. V. R. Geary. *The Golden Galley: The Story of the Second Punjab Regiment 1761–1947*. New Delhi: Allied, 1975. First published 1956.
Khanna, Major General Prem K., and Pushpindar Singh Chopra. *Portrait of Courage: Century of the 5th Battalion, The Sikh Regiment*. New Delhi: Military Studies Convention, 2001.
McEwan, Agnes, and Campbell Thomson. *Death Was Our Bedmate: 155th (Lanarkshire Yeomanry) Field Regiment and the Japanese 1941–1945*. Barnsley, UK: Pen & Sword, 2013.
Moffatt, Jonathan, and Audrey Holmes McCormick. *Moon over Malaya: The 2nd Argylls and Plymouth Argyll Royal Marines in Malaya and Singapore*. Gloucestershire, UK: History Press, 2014.
9 Gurkha Rifles: A Regimental History (1817–1947). New Delhi: Vision Books, 1984.
Praval, K. C., *Valour Triumphs: A History of the Kumaon Regiment*. Faridabad, India: Thomson Press, 1976.
Singh, Brigadier Jasbir. *Combat Diary: An Illustrated History of Operations Conducted by 4th Battalion the Kumaon Regiment 1788 to 1984*. New Delhi: Lancer, 2010.

INDEX

Page numbers in italics refer to maps.

1st Hyderabad State Infantry, 78, 86
1st/8th Punjab, 74, 96, 114, 196
1st/14th Punjab, 38, 57–59, 74, 95–99, 102, 114, 131, 171, 177, 195
1 and 8 Royal Australian Air Force (RAAF), 55, 82
2nd Argyll and Sutherland Highlanders, 86, 127, 128, 132, 200
2nd/19th Australian battalion, 164
2nd/29th Australian battalion, 164
2nd/1st Gurkha Rifles (GR), 46, 95
2nd/2nd Gurkhas, 209
2nd/8th Punjab, 98, 99
2nd/16th Punjab, 74, 95, 96, 99
2nd/18th Royal Garhwal Rifles (RGR), 78
2nd/72nd Punjabis, 32
3rd/16th Punjab, 94, 119, 164, 167, 169, 173, 174
3rd/17th Dogras, 77, 151, 152, 166
4th/9th Jats, 154, 156, 157, 159–163, 165, 167, 168, 179, 195
4th/19th Hyderabad Regiment, 86, 108n98, 108n100, 108n101, 108n110, 108n111, 109n114, 109n118, 127, 137, 140n53, 142n112, 142n115, 142n123, 143n155, 143n165, 143n166, 209, 227n18, 229n78, 229n80, 230n103, 230n113, 230n114, 230n124, 230n128, 1230nn131–133, 231n134, 231n147, 231n172, 232n185, 232n191, 232n196, 233n213, 233n220
5th Japanese Division, 17, 44, 79, 81, 82, 94, 99, 127, 152, 175, 180, 204
5th/2nd Punjab, 86, 114, 116, 118–120, 126–128, 130–133, 135–138, 205
5th/11th Sikhs, 39, 46, 57, 78, 154, 156, 172, 176, 180, 206
5th/14th Punjab, 94, 116, 135–138, 170, 195, 209, 211
5th/16th Punjabis, 173
6th Indian Brigade, 47, 74, 96, 103, 116, 152
6th/1st Punjab Regiment, 197, 199
6th/14th Punjab Regiment, 197, 199
7th Rajputana, 161
7th/8th Punjab Regiment, 197, 199, 205
8th Australian Imperial Force (AIF), 2, 38, 48, 73, 74, 160, 162, 190, 204, 207, 209, 211, 216–219, 221–223, 227, 229, 233, 248

9th Indian Division, 5, 49, 50, 135, 163, 164, 166
11th Indian Division, 5, 39, 49, 50, 52, 57, 73, 74, 83, 93, 94, 100, 101, 103, 113–120, 122, 124, 126, 128, 130, 131–133, 137, 138, 148, 151–153, 169, 170, 172, 175–177, 180, 191, 193, 194, 196, 203–205, 207, 208, 209, 211, 214–216, 219, 222
12th Indian Brigade, 26, 46–48, 50, 58, 75, 86, 104, 113, 114, 116–120, 126, 128, 131–135, 137, 147, 200, 201, 205–208, 213, 215
15th Indian Brigade, 74, 95–97, 99, 103, 116, 118, 119, 123, 129, 169–176, 191, 194, 196, 207, 208, 210, 211, 213, 215
18th Japanese Division, 44, 79, 81, 82, 84, 204, 218
22nd Indian Brigade, 45, 46, 78, 85, 120, 124–126, 150–152, 154, 163, 165, 166, 169, 171, 172, 177, 178, 181, 196
28th Indian Brigade, 39, 43, 46–48, 51, 74, 93–96, 103, 114–116, 118–120, 128–131, 133, 134, 137, 152, 169, 170, 177, 178, 191–193, 195, 196, 208, 209, 214, 216
44th Indian Brigade, 191, 197–200, 205, 206, 208–213, 215
45th Indian Brigade, 122, 123, 145, 146, 149, 150, 154, 161, 164–166, 168–170, 175, 182, 195, 196, 198

Admiralty, 11, 12, 15, 16;
Alanbrooke, Field Marshal, 37, 43, 54
All India Muslim League (AIML), 58, 224
Alor Star, 80, 81, 94–97, 99, 102, 103, *xix*
Anglo-Japanese Treaty of 1902, 11
Anglo-Japanese War, 10
anti-aircraft artillery/gun, 123
anti-tank, 54, 94, 114, 117; artillery, 53, 168, 240; batteries, 16, 152, 194; defense, 99, 133; gun(s), 50, 51, 53, 87, 88, 94, 98, 129, 137, 165, 192, 238, 240; mine(s), 51, 53, 78, 96, 133–136, 138; minefields, 77, 152; Regiment, 74, 96, 122, 191; rifles, 47, 51, 52, 99, 133; shooting, 53; troops, 135, 205; weapons, 97, 123, 138, 198
armored: brigade, 211; car, 15, 34, 48, 53, 87, 100, 134, 203; carrier, 52, 125; cruisers, 12; and German blitzkrieg, 239; Japanese columns, 146; landing craft, 204; miles, 119; *Repulse*, 90; superiority, 81; vehicles, 94, 122
Asia-Pacific War, 49
Asun, 96, 97, 99, *xxii*

Australia/Australian, 2, 4, 5, 11, 17, 19, 41–44, 46, 48, 60, 73, 75, 79, 123, 128, 145, 147, 149, 150, 152, 153, 159, 162, 168, 169, 171, 175, 177, 178, 180, 182, 190–192, 197, 199, 200, 203–212, 215–217, 225, 226, 237, 239, 240; Corps, 148; infantry, 6
Australian Imperial Force (AIF), 2, 38, 48, 73–76, 147, 149, 150, 152, 153, 161–163, 165–167, 171, 172, 174, 176, 177, 178, 180–182, 191, 194–199, 202–209, 211, 214–217, 220, 235, 238, 232n185
Australian Military Force, 49
Australian War Memorial (AWM), 3

Bakri, *xxiv, xxv*, 159, 161–163, 165
Balfour, Arthur James, 11
Barstow, Major General A. E., 54, 73, 85, 89, 90, 125, 151, 152, 154, 171, 172, 178
Bata River, 100
Batu Pahat, *xix, xxiv–xxvi*, 146, 158, 161–164, 167–172, 179, 204
Bennett, Major General Henry Gordon, 2, 5, 6, 38–42, 48–50, 54, 55, 66n144, 74, 75, 78, 100, 101, 120, 145, 147, 149, 150, 152–154, 168, 169, 172, 175, 179, 182, 192, 194, 205, 206, 208, 211, 212, 215, 219, 220, 226, 236–238
Benut, *xxvi*, 169–172, 174–179
Bernam River, 130
bicycle, 44, 51, 135, 136, 153, 159, 168, 239; and blitzkrieg, 5, 236; and Japanese troops, 97
Bidor, 128–131
Bond, Major General Lionel V., 15, 16, 20, 53
Bose, Rash Behari, 221, 222
Bose, Sarat, 58
Bose, Subhas Chnadra, 58, 102, 103, 132, 221–225
Boys anti-tank (A/T) rifle, 52, 53, 99
Bren carrier, 48, 52, 53, 79, 127
Bren Gun, 45, 46, 50–53, 77, 87, 159, 161, 198
Brewster Buffalo fighters, 54, 80
Bristol Blenheim bombers, 54
Britain, 3, 10–18, 20, 37, 51, 57, 126, 146, 193; Holland as commercial rival in Southeast Asia sea, 9; Indian Army, expansion dependent on, 25
British Army, 5, 7n12, 27, 34, 35, 42, 43, 47, 48, 53, 56, 117, 118, 181, 215
British Empire, 10, 58, 72, 77, 212, 239
British Library (BL), 3
Brooke, Alan Francis. *See* Alanbrooke, Field Marshall
Brooke-Popham, Robert, 1, 18, 19, 72, 76, 78–80, 83, 84, 90, 105n1, 122, 136, 194
Bukit Belah-Pelandok, 163, 164

Bukit Brown, 219
Bukit Cherman-Mount Washington and Henderson Road, 218
Bukit Muar, 162
Bukit Panjang, 205, 209–211, 213
Bukit Timah, 190, 194, 196, 207, 209–214, 216, 217, 219, 220
Burma, 2, 5, 17–19, 26, 27, 41, 44, 59, 80, 122, 123, 190, 211, 217, 221, 222, 239, 240

Canning, Fort, 18, 193, 216, 219
Carpendale, Brigadier W., 39, 43, 46–48, 51, 95–97, 99, 100, 103
centralized command, 36, 160, 167
Changi, 15, 75, 190, 191, 201, 218
Chiefs of Staff Committee (CoSC), 16–18, 26, 51, 121
China, 9, 12, 14, 15, 34, 40, 44, 50, 53, 54, 101; chemical warfare practice in, 49; success in, 39; Japanese atrocities in, 200; Tiger Tomoyuki Yamashita combat experience in, 79
China Station, 10, 15, 18, 20, 83
Chong Dong, 89
Churchill, Winston, 3, 10, 15, 16, 19, 83, 90, 93, 100, 121, 147, 148, 193, 212, 214, 235
close air support (CAS), 1, 34, 54, 76, 82, 236
Committee of Imperial Defence, 13
Cooper, Duff, 121, 122, 148

DALFORCE, 200
Deakin, Lieutenant Colonel C. C., 116
decentralized command, 36–38, 117, 161, 182, 204
Dobbie, Major General William, 14–16, 53
Doro Nawa Unit, 41

EASTFORCE, 169, 175
Emergency Commissioned Indian Officer (ECIO), 56, 57
Endau, 73, 74, *xxiv*, 175, 177

Far East/Eastern, *xvii*, 1, 3, 9, 13, 27, 53, 55, 60, 72, 74, 75, 90, 93, 121, 123, 124; Command, 80; defense, 122; markets, 11; waters, 10; War, 12, 14–20, 95, 147
Far Eastern War Council, 219
Farrar Park, 220, 221
First World War, 9, 11, 20, 31, 37, 38
fish hook tactics, 89
fluid tactics, 60, 97
Force Z, 84, 90–93, 146
Fujiwara *Kikan*, 59, 102, 132, 178

Gemas, 5, 73, *xxiv*, 145, 150–154, 217
General Headquarters India (GHQ India)/India Command, 4, 5, 20
Gong Kedah, 19, 78, 83, 87, *xx*, *xxii*
Government of India (GoI)/Raj, 5, 26, 31, 33, 56, 223
grenade, 33, 34, 48, 50, 51, 77, 86, 125, 136, 157, 161, 166, 174, 182, 210
Grik Road, 117, 119, 120
Gurkha Battalion, 27
Gurkha *kukris,* 99
Gurkha regiment, 198
Gurkha Rifles (GR), 32, 46
Gurkhas, *xxiii*, 5, 28, 29, 33, 46, 95, 99, 101, 102, 114, 130, 179, 218, 225
Gurun, 93–104, 114

Harrison, Colonel A. M. L., 170, 193, 208, 209, 213, 215
Heath, Lieutenant-General Lewis, 14, 19, 37, 43, 44, 73, 74, 89, 90, 114, 115, 117, 119, 121, 124, 125, 137, 145–152, 169–172, 175, 169, 213, 214, 216–219, 226, 235–238
Hindu/Hindustani, 29, 45, 223–225
Hong Kong, *xvii*, 5, 10–12, 15, 17–19, 59, 72, 205, 239
Hurricane fighter, 20, 54, 179
Hutton, Major General T. J., 26

Imperial Guards Division, 79, 82, 127, 154, 162, 163, 165, 168, 170, 175, 179, 180, 204
Imperial Japanese Army (IJA), 2, 4, 5, 25–27, 29, 31, 34, 37, 39, 40, 42, 43, 49, 52–55, 59, 61, 73, 75, 88, 91, 99, 113, 117, 128, 136, 138, 146, 147, 156, 182, 202, 206, 212, 220, 221, 236, 238
Imperial Japanese Navy (IJN), 10, 15
Imperial War Museum (IWM), 3
India, 4, 7n9, 9, 11, 16, 17, 25–27, 32, 39, 45, 46, 49, 57–60, 74, 101, 102, 122, 123, 126, 136, 147, 149, 157, 197, 200, 206, 222–225; Aryan conquest of, 28; imperial commitments, 42; social groups joining army for pay, 27
India Office Records (IOR), 3
Indian Army, 2–6, 21, 25–29, 31–34, 37, 38, 42, 44, 45, 49, 59, 60, 114, 117, 119, 151, 177, 181, 201, 212, 221–225, 240; combat motivation, 196; command culture of British, 161; deployment in Middle East, 237; non-Gurkha soldiers of, 102; personal performance, 120; position of corporals to VCOs and NCOs, 88; Sikh community, 58
Indian Independence League (IIL), 59, 60, 101–103, 132, 178, 179, 182, 222

Indian National Army, or *Azad Hind Fauj*, 6, 27, 57, 59, 101, 102, 131, 132, 179, 190; origin and consequences of, 221–225
Indian National Congress (INC), 7n9, 26, 58, 103, 221, 224
Indian officers, 3, 7n9, 28, 37, 38, 56–58, 102, 213, 220, 223, 224
Indochina, 12, 16, 17, 19, 20, 40, 80, 82, 83, 92
Infiltration as tactic, 35, 43, 44, 78, 80, 88, 93, 97, 98, 104, 124, 125, 132, 137, 154, 158, 159, 164, 171, 175, 182, 192, 193, 209, 211, 236, 239, 240

Japan/Japanese, *xxix*, 6, 11, 12, 15–18, 20, 25, 27, 28, 31, 33, 39–41, 49, 76, 81–104, 126–138, 145–183, 235–239; advance in Malayan Peninsula, *xx*; aerial tactic, 44; attack on Northern Malaya in 1941, *xxi*; attack on Singapore Island, 190–226; bicycle blitzkrieg, 5; infantry, 44, 48, 50; jungle warfare, 5; maneuver warfare, 35; paradigm of war in Malaya, 3; renounce Washington naval limitations in 1934, 13; riflemen, 53; rise of threat in Far East, 9; Singapore surrender to, 1; soldier famous for long marching, 43; sponsor INA, 57; training emphasizing outpost duty and patrol works, 43; war declaration on United States in 1941, 72, 73
Japanese Army Air Force (JAAF), 54, 82, 154, 179
Japanese Navy Air Force (JNAF), 54, 82, 84, 91, 154, 179, 203
Jats, *xxiii*, 5, 27–29, 31, 32, 58, 74, 95, 96, 99, 100, 102, 114, 127, 148, 154, 156, 157, 159–163, 165, 167, 168, 176, 177, 179, 194–196, 207, 210, 211, 213, 220, 225
jawans, 5, 6, 27, 28, 31–33, 38, 45–47, 57, 58, 64n71, 85, 86, 88, 98, 99, 101–103, 114, 118–120, 126, 128, 136, 148, 151, 156, 158, 162, 180, 181, 195–198, 201, 205, 213, 220–226, 237, 239
Jitra, *xx*, *xxiii*, 5, 57, 58, 74, 93–104, 114, 120, 131–134, 138, 155, 239
jitter attacks, 44
Johore, *xviii*, *xix*, *xxiv*, *xxvi*, *xxvii*, 5, 9, 10, 12–15, 74–76, 81, 115, 121, 138, 146–150, 152–154, 162, 169–183, 190, 193–195, 197, 203, 204, 209, 212, 236
Jorak, *xxv*, 157, 159
jungle, 2, 5, 6, 12, 15, 38, 42, 45, 48, 49, 51, 76, 78, 87–89, 96, 99, 103, 116, 118, 126, 127, 130, 132–134, 137, 138, 153, 155–164, 166–168, 171, 173, 182, 190, 200, 214, 236–239; and covered terrain, 119; fear, 46; fighters, 40; fighting, 42, 43, 52, 104; impenetrable, 150;

Index 259

jungle (*cont.*)
    Japanese regarded as supermen of, 197; and swampy terrain, 43; training, 40, 45; wildlife, 47
jungle warfare, 5, 38, 39, 41, 43–46, 50, 61, 162, 169, 177, 186, 211, 228, 250, 253
Jurong, *124*, 204, 206, 209, 211, 212, 214, 220, 221, 224, 226

Kampar, 113, 117, 119, 124, 126–137, 168, 180
Kawamura, Major General Saburo, 99
Kedah, 10, 19, 74, 78, 82, 83, 87, 95–97, 100, 103, 115, 118
Kelantan River, *xxii*, 10, 73, 76, 77, 83, 84, 87, 89, 90, 118, 120
Kiani, Captain I. J., 114
Kiani, Mohammad Zaman, 57, 58
Kluang, *xxi*, *xxiv*, *xxvi*, 74, 146, 147, 149, 150, 167, 169–172
Kota Bahru, *xvii*, *xxii*, 13, 54, 74, 76, 78–87, 89, 91, 119, 124, 181
Kranji River, 193, 196, 204
Krian River, 114–120
KROHCOL, 94, 104
Kuala Lumpur, *xvii*, *xix*, *xx*, 73, 78, 81, 120, 124, 125, 129, 132, 145, 146, 148–150, 152, 153, 178, 179, 195
Kuantan, *xix*, *xx*, 13, 73, 74, 76, 78–81, 92, 120, 124–126, 146, 150, 151

Layton, Vice Admiral Geoffrey, 20
Linlithgow, Viceroy Lord, 26, 58
London, 10, 14, 18, 41, 83, 115; Chiefs of Staff in, 147; and Japanese superiority in air and on land, 122; Naval Conference of 1930, 13, 15; War Cabinet, 123
London Naval Conference, 13, 15

Machang, 19, 85, 87–90
Malacca, *xix*, *xxi*, *xxiv*, *xxv*, 10, 47, 146, 149, 151, 157, 159, 179, 190
Malay Barrier, 11
Malaya, *xvii*, *xxi*, 5, 6, 12, 14, 15, 17, 19, 20, 101, 104, 113, 115, 117, 119, 120, 126, 129, 137, 146–149, 156, 159, 166, 168, 175, 177, 178–180, 190, 194, 198, 222, 225, 237; allied armies, structure and functions of, 25–34; allied casualties in, 181; battle for, 2; Britain acquisitions in, 10; campaign, 1, 202, 221, 235, 239; command and doctrine, 35–38; deployment of allied units in, 72–82; morale of soldiers in, 55–60; retreat from beaches of, 82–93; training of soldiers in, 38–50; use of weapons by soldiers, 50–55

Malaya Command, 14, 20, 39, 47, 49–51, 53, 61, 75, 83, 95, 115, 117, 119, 135, 155, 156, 160, 180, 191, 194, 202, 203, 215, 216
Malayan Peninsula, *xx*, 1, 4, 6, 9, 10, 12, 39, 41, 44, 72, 76, 81, 113, 119, 121, 145, 146, 178, 180–182, 191, 203, 205–207, 225, 226, 236, 240
Mandai Road, 196, 197, 207–209, 211, 214
martial race ideology/theory, 5, 28–30, 56, 138
MATADOR, 1, 74, 83, 95, 100
Matsui, Lieutenant General Takuro, 79, 204
Maxwell, Brigadier D. S., 75, 150, 196, 211
Mersing, *xix*, *xxiv*, 12, 73, 74–76, 78, 79, 81, 147, 149, 169–172, 175, 196
Middle East Command, 20
milking process, 5, 33, 50, 86, 88, 99, 136, 198; effect on Indian infantry battalions, 55; definition of, 64n71
Ministry of Defence Historical Section (MODHS), 3
Moir, Brigadier R. G., 130
Molesworth, Lieutenant General G. N., 30, 32
Molotov cocktail, 135
morale, 2, 5, 6, 25, 28, 29, 32, 44, 45, 54–61, 85, 86, 89, 95–104, 118, 145, 149, 155, 167, 171, 173, 177, 180, 192, 194, 197, 200, 202, 210, 212, 225, 236, 238, 239
mortar, 33, 44–46, 48, 50–52, 78, 79, 85, 86, 88, 94, 97, 99, 100, 114, 116, 117, 123, 133, 134, 159, 163, 166–168, 171–174, 176, 177, 182, 195, 200, 201, 214, 215
motor transport, 42, 43, 46, 48, 103, 123, 159
Muar Battle, 166, 168, 182
Muar River, *xix*, *xxiv*, *xxv*, 4, 5, 121, 124, 138, 145, 146, 149, 150, 153, 171, 175, 179, 196, 198, 199, 201; retreat from, 154–168
Muda River, 103, 113–121
Murray-Lyon, Major General D. M., 103, 120, 156, 160, 161, 235–237
Muslim, 28, 223–225; Deccani, 30; Punjabi, 29, 31, 32, 78, 116, 137, 138, 195
Mutaguchi, Lieutenant General Renya, 79, 204

Nambu Light Machine Gun (LMG), 50, 53, 159
National Archives (TNA), 3
National Archives of India (NAI), 3
National Army Museum (NAM), 3
nationalism, 2, 28, 58, 102, 201; Indian, rising in Thailand and Malaya, 59
Nee Soon village, 207, 212, 214, 215
Nishimura, Lieutenant General Takumo, 44, 79
noncombatants, 73

noncommissioned Officer (NCO), 30, 42
nonmartial; classes, 30; races, 30

Oil Tanks of Normanton, 217–218

Pacific Ocean, 11, 146
Pacific War, 9, 18, 81
Pahang River, 78, 151
Paris, Brigadier A. C. M., 26, 113, 114, 116, 119, 124, 126, 130, 135, 137, 148, 151, 192, 193, 200, 201, 209, 212
Patani, 47, 57, 74, 81, 83, 91, 93, 94, 96, 102, 103, 113, 114
Pathans, 28, 29, 31, 32, 171
Pekan, 78
Penang, *xix*, 10, 14, 78, 82, 94, 119, 129, 147, 202, 204
Perak, 4, 10, 57, 117, 120, 123, 180; coast, 130; river, 72, 81, 117–120, 127, 130, 217
Percival, Lieutenant General A. E., 1–3, 7n8, 14, 15, 20, 25, 47, 49, 51, 53, 55, 73–75, 79, 81–84, 89, 99, 101, 113, 115, 117, 118, 120–126, 129, 130, 132, 134, 136–138, 145–151, 153, 154, 159, 161–163, 168, 169, 172, 174, 175, 177, 179, 183, 191, 192, 194, 202, 204–207, 211–220, 225, 226, 235–238
Perlis, 10, 96
Phillips, Brigadier H. C., 202
Phillips, Admiral T. S. V., 16, 90–93
Pound, Admiral of the Fleet Alfred Dudley, 26
Pownall, Lieutenant General Henry, 122
Public Works Department (PWD), 180, 218
Pulford, Air Vice Marshal C. W., 19, 179
Punjab, 26–29, 38, 58, 59
Punjabi Muslims, 28, 29, 31, 32, 78, 116, 137, 138, 195

Rajputs, 5, 27–29, 31,
Rajputana Rifles (RR), 154
Rengam, *xxiv*, *xxvi*, 171, 172, 174, 175
Rengit, *xxiv*, *xxvi*, 171–176, 178
Rice, E. B., 20
Royal Air Force (RAF), 13, 14, 16–20, 34, 54, 55, 76, 78, 80, 83, 85, 87, 91, 97, 120, 126, 146, 177, 203
Royal Artillery (RA), 14, 50, 74, 165, 191, 193
Royal Engineers (RE), 14, 180
Royal Military Academy Sandhurst, 37
Royal Navy (RN), 1, 10, 13–16, 18–20, 90, 178
Russo-Japanese War (1904–5), 11

Saigon, 41, 82, 91, *xvii*
Second World War, 18, 25, 30, 33, 39, 42, 44

Segamat, *xxv*, 145, 147, 149–159, 154, 161–163, 165, 169, 195
Seletar, 11, 13, 18, 191–194, 196, 218
Senggarang, *xxiv*, *xxvi*, 183–189, 191
Serangoon Road, 195, 211, 216, 217
Sikhs, 5, 28, 29, 31, 32, 39, 46, 57, 58, 59, 78, 101, 126, 138, 148, 154, 156, 172, 176, 179, 180, 206, 215, 224
Simson, Brigadier Ivan, 207
Singapore, *xvii*, *xviii*, *xxiv*, *xxvi*–*xxix*, 1–3, 6, 26, 27, 34, 39, 45, 47, 53, 57, 58, 72, 74, 75, 78–84, 89, 91–93, 113, 121–125, 137, 146–149, 153, 154, 157, 162, 163, 165, 167, 169, 170–172, 174–177, 179–181, 183, 205–207, 210–221, 224–226, 235–240; defensive forces in, 203–216; evolution of defense in interwar era, 9–14; and strategic context before Far Eastern War, 14–20
Singapore Naval Base, 6, 9, 10, 12, 19
Singapore Sub-Committee Report of 1925, 12
Singh, Harbakhsh, 39, 46, 55, 57, 206
Singh, Captain Mohan, 38, 57–59, 98, 102, 131, 132, 202, 221, 222
Singh, Pritam, 59, 60, 102, 114, 132
Singora, 74, 81–83, 91, 93, 95, 96, *xx*, *xxi*, 127, 204
Skudai, *xxiv*, *xxvi*, 169, 170, 176–178, 195, 203, 204
Slim River, 104, 126, 124, 126–138, 145, 146, 148, 200, 239
South China Sea, 13, 19, 47, 90, 91
Southern Area, 216, 217
Southern Army/Southern Expeditionary Army Group, 79, 80
Spitfire, 20, 54
Spooner, Vice Admiral Ernest John, 20, 219
Stewart, Ian, 47, 126, 137, 148
Sugawara, Lieutenant General Michiyo, 80
Sungei Patani, 47, 57, 74, 94, 96, 102, 103, 114
Sungei Seput, 127
Swettenham, Port, 47, *xix*, *xx*, 125, 145, 146

Takumi, Major General Hiroshi, 84
Takumi Detached Force, 84, 87
Takumi Detachment, 124
tank, 5, 15, 25, 52, 53, 61, 94, 99, 114, 129, 137, 138, 153, 162, 165, 166, 200, 201, 203, 207, 210, 218, 236, 238, 239; fear, 115; infantry cooperation in British Army, 42; Japan use of, 98, 104, 134–136, 167, 168; light, 34, 81, 122, 214; mechanized, 34; medium, 81
Taylor, Brigadier H. B., 75, 175, 180, 196, 204
Tengah; airfield, 83, 204, 206, 207; airport, 205, 206, 208, 209
Terauchi, Hisaichi, 79

Index 261

Thailand, 1, 12, 14, 17, 59, 60, 72–74, 81, 83, 92, 94, 96, 97, *xx*, *xxi*, 203
III Indian Corps, 14, 37, 46, 48, 73, 74, 93, 117, 118, 130, 137, 146–149, 162–164, 167, 169, 170, 202, 216, 217, 236, 238
Thomas, Major H. P., 6, 39, 40, 89, 205
Thomas, Lieutenant Colonel L. C., 208
Thomas, Shenton, 84, 136, 219
Thompson submachine gun, 46, 50, 53, 122
Tojo, Hideki, 20
TOMFORCE, 208, 214
Tommy gun, 46, 97, 100, 122, 127, 159, 195, 203, 217
Treaty of London, 9
training, 5, 25, 26, 33–36, 38–51, 60, 76, 77, 80, 87, 101, 104, 116, 123, 133, 152, 154, 155, 158, 167–169, 176, 192, 195, 197, 198, 201, 210, 226, 239, 240; Allied forces, 237; collective, 55, 61, 78; combined, 73; harsh, 89; at IMA, 37; individual, 73; in Japanese armed forces, 31, 3; rigorous, 103, 117, 165; small-unit, 237; sparse, 6; subreserve, 27; tough, 31
Trolak, 130–133
Tsuji, Colonel Masanobu, 1, 40
Twenty-Fifth Japanese Army, 1, 2, 40, 79, 81, 82, 113

United States, 11–13, 72, 121, 124, 182

Viceroy's Commissioned Officer (VCO), 30, 32, 33, 38, 45, 46, 48, 57, 64n71, 86, 88, 93, 101, 114, 128, 136, 155, 162, 164, 181, 195, 197, 213, 220, 222, 237
Vildebeestes/Wildebeestes torpedo bomber, 54

War Office, 3, 5, 10, 11, 15, 18, 19, 49, 59, 66n117, 68n203, 68n204, 121–123, 140n74
Washington Naval Treaty of 1922, 12, 13
Watt, Major S. A., 155, 158, 159
Wavell, Archibald, 2, 7n8, 49, 50, 124, 147–150, 151–154, 169, 170, 172, 174, 177, 179, 183n6, 184n18, 190–192, 194, 198, 204, 211, 212, 214, 216–219, 226n7, 236, 241n20
Wehrmacht, 37, 63n36, 195, 239
WESTFORCE, 150, 167, 169, 171, 172, 174, 175–178, 180, 188n187, 188n189
World War I. *See* First World War
World War II. *See* Second World War

Yamashita, Tomoyuki, 1–2, 37, 40, 79–83, 88, 100, 102, 107n56, n59, 108n80, 121, 122, 129, 130, 132, 134, 153, 154, 191, 203, 204, 212–215, 219, 221, 227n16, 234n242, 235, 236, 238
Yong Peng, *xxiv–xxvi*, 162–168, 171

Zero fighter, 81, 87

KAUSHIK ROY is Guru Nanak Chair Professor in the Department of History, Jadavpur University, Kolkata, India, and Global Fellow at the Peace Research Institute, Oslo, Norway. Roy specializes in various aspects of medieval and modern Indian and Asian military history. He has published many books from various presses such as Ashgate, Bloomsbury, Brill, Cambridge University Press, Oxford University Press, Pickering & Chatto, and Routledge, as well as articles in many peer-reviewed journals, including *First World War Studies, International Area Studies Review, Journal of Global History, Journal of Military History, Journal of the Society for Army Historical Research, Modern Asian Studies*, and *War in History*.

www.ingramcontent.com/pod-product-compliance
Lightning Source LLC
Chambersburg PA
CBHW041311240426
43661CB00065B/2896